The American Academic Profession

The American Academic Profession

Transformation in Contemporary Higher Education

Edited by
Joseph C. Hermanowicz

The Johns Hopkins University Press
Baltimore

© 2011 The Johns Hopkins University Press
All rights reserved. Published 2011
Printed in the United States of America on acid-free paper
9 8 7 6 5 4 3 2 1

The Johns Hopkins University Press
2715 North Charles Street
Baltimore, Maryland 21218-4363
www.press.jhu.edu

Library of Congress Cataloging-in-Publication Data

The American academic profession : transformation in contemporary higher
education / edited by Joseph C. Hermanowicz.
        p. cm.
    Includes bibliographical references and index.
    ISBN-13: 978-0-8018-9977-5 (hardcover : alk. paper)
    ISBN-10: 0-8018-9977-X (hardcover : alk. paper)
    ISBN-13: 978-0-8018-9978-2 (pbk : alk. paper)
    ISBN-10: 0-8018-9978-8 (pbk : alk. paper)
1. Education, Higher—United States. 2. Educational change—United States.
3. Universities and colleges—United States. 4. Educational technology—
United States. I. Hermanowicz, Joseph C.
    LA227.4.A446 2011
    378.1'20973—dc22   2010042483

A catalog record for this book is available from the British Library.

*Special discounts are available for bulk purchases of this book. For more
information, please contact Special Sales at 410-516-6936 or specialsales@press
.jhu.edu.*

The Johns Hopkins University Press uses environmentally friendly book
materials, including recycled text paper that is composed of at least 30
percent post-consumer waste, whenever possible. All of our book papers are
acid-free, and our jackets and covers are printed on paper with recycled
content.

Contents

Preface

When sociologists speak of professions, they customarily refer to a type of occupation that possesses, in greater or lesser degrees, specific characteristics. Abstract, theoretic knowledge; restricted access; protracted training; certification; a license and mandate; trust and authority; a code of ethics; altruism; and autonomy—these are the hallmarks that socially differentiate types of work and workers along a professional continuum. The points of stress placed on these characteristics vary, to be sure, among sociologists and the approaches they adopt to study professions (see, e.g., Abbott 1991; Greenwood 1957; Johnson 1972; Larson 1977; Parsons 1949). But here our concern is not with competing approaches to professions or even with definitional conundrums, but instead with establishing a general idea of what they are and what is happening to one of them—the contemporary American academic profession.

We may begin with Eliot Freidson:

> It is useful to think of a profession as an occupation which has assumed a dominant position in a division of labor, so that it gains control over the determination of the substance of its own work. Unlike most occupations, it is autonomous and self-directing. The occupation sustains this special status by its persuasive profession of the extraordinary trustworthiness of its members. The trustworthiness it professes naturally includes ethicality and also knowledgeable skill. In fact, the profession claims to be the most reliable authority on the nature of the reality it deals with. (1970, xv)

For academe, as for other professions, we may question the amount of dominance that the occupation continues to command in the division of labor, since such dominance arises by a profession's capacity to preserve its distinguishing traits. Disregarding for the moment the various types of credentialing institutions that have arisen across the organizational landscape of American higher education (see, e.g., Ruch 2001), it remains true that only universities, colleges, institutes, and their faculty confer degrees; thus, in this most basic way they preserve a monopoly of practice. But here, as for Freidson writing about medicine, a central problem lies in how a profession maintains its autonomy, since we no longer have a profession when its practitioners lose control of the terms of their work.

For academe in particular and for society in general, the stakes are high. Following an institutionalist perspective, professions may be taken to be the chief organizing institutions of modern societies (Parsons and Platt 1973). The most full-fledged professions have customarily included law, medicine, ministry, and the military. Academe, however, may be taken to be the most central profession. It is uniquely situated in society as the profession that trains people for all other professions and numerous other lines of work requiring certified education. It is for this reason that Freidson, in other writing, understood academe as "the host occupation" (2001).

In principle, the academic profession may be understood to guard culture by upholding cognitive and behavioral standards to ensure the competent role performance of practitioners throughout the occupational spectrum. The profession may also be seen to functionally uphold generalized ideals: in their roles, professors seek precision and excellence and aim, ideally, to inculcate these humanistic characteristics in student clientele, so as to produce a higher learning by individuals and a more advanced collective civilization.

But the American professoriate is increasingly differentiated on many counts. To examine the condition of academe as a profession—what has happened to it and where it may be headed—we turn to several facets that illuminate academe's evolving structure:

- Socialization—the varying ways in which future faculty are prepared for the professoriate with different outcomes of success and with different demands and expectations for faculty to train them, as evident in a spectrum of institutions with differing priorities and missions.
- Tenure—the changing institutional expectations and organizational methods of evaluating faculty performance, including debates about

the future of tenure, its history, current problems, and intended goals.

- Reward structures—the allocation of positive and negative sanctions of faculty performance; how such structures vary by institutional type, among fields, and between departments; and with what consequences to institutions, to careers, and to the coherence of a profession broadly.
- Recruitment—the means and standards by which institutions supply their labor stock, and the accommodations that institutions are and are not prepared to make in order to satisfy various needs.
- Mass schooling—the significantly increased access to higher education by a markedly heterogeneous population of students; its consequences for teaching, the size and effectiveness of institutions, and relations between faculty and students; and its effects on academic achievement.
- Politics—the nature and extent of the role it should normatively play in academic work and its relationship, or lack thereof, to the historical understanding and motivation of academic freedom.
- Ethics—the normative yet contested and often poorly understood, weakly codified, and rarely taught principles that govern academic work, in teaching, scholarship, and citizenship in universities and in society at large.

The development and intensification of these and other conditions have produced, to a perversion of William J. Goode's (1957) original term, "communities within communities." One might also venture to argue that they have splintered, or even obliterated, the idea of academe as a coherent profession capable by a solidarity of its members.

Several of the chapters in this volume emerged from a three-day conference at the University of Georgia, in which participants addressed from a variety of topical vantage points the event's main organizing theme, "Wither the American Academic Profession? Its Changing Forms and Functions." Other authors unable to attend the conference were invited to contribute chapters to this book based on their current work and ongoing research interests connected to the study of the academic profession.

Posed as a question, the theme of the conference—and this book—asked contributors to examine the ways by which the status of American academe may be eroding *as a profession*. Further, contributors were asked to consider both how, in light of change, academe may be evolving in the attributes that structurally define it in occupational terms (the forms of academe) and what purposes such structural shifts satisfy and with what consequences (the functions of academe). "Wither" is the intransitive verb that denotes something that has lost force. But by examining change in the status of academe as a profession and the avenues along which it appears to be charting a different course, we are in turn led to consider "whither" the profession—the adverb meaning to what situation, position, or end. In the present case, the asking of one question invites the other.

Organization of the Book

The book begins with a sobering chapter by Jack Schuster, which establishes the context for large-scale change in the contemporary American academic profession. Schuster contends that a new era has emerged in American higher education, which amounts to more than merely an extension of ongoing trends. Rather, Schuster argues, the profession is in the midst of an unprecedented period of change marked, and perhaps interminably marred, by five concurrent, interactive developments: the ascendance of contingent faculty appointments; the changing mix of faculty work responsibilities, which now more heavily emphasize teaching; the transfiguration of the profession by technology, privatization, and globalization; an increasingly skewed senior age distribution of faculty who will not be replaced, on balance, by traditional hires; and, finally, an economic crisis that has riddled the academic profession with more than the usual financial uncertainties.

Starting with the premise that faculty constitute the very core of universities, Schuster outlines a new paradigm of the contemporary academic profession, which he describes as becoming "restratified." This new system of stratification is emerging; its principal characteristics are the preponderant use of off-track, full-time academic appointments; the gradual erosion of tenure (as a consequence of this redistribution rather than as a function of a frontal assault on tenure); and resultant market-driven compensation arrangements that are increasingly differentiated among types of faculty, within and among types of institutions, and among fields.

Put in other terms, consider that at many American universities it is now possible to complete an undergraduate degree without ever being taught by a regular faculty member holding a traditional appointment. Under what circumstances would a client in need of legal counsel seek someone other than a licensed attorney? Under what conditions would a patient in need of important medical care seek someone other than a bona fide physician? Thus, in Schuster's introductory chapter, nothing less than a pervasive reconfiguration of the faculty is posited. At stake, he argues, are the defining features of an academic career—just what it means to be a faculty member in the unfolding new era—and, in a larger sense, how postsecondary education likely will be practiced.

Following the introduction, the book is organized into five substantive parts. In part one, on structural and cognitive change in the profession, the first chapter, by Roger Geiger, examines the divide between teaching and research roles in research universities and interprets such divides through the institutional lens of seeking to maximize outputs of learning through both research and instruction. Geiger argues that an expansion of academic research since the 1990s has driven a restructuring of faculty work. Institutional aspirations for prestige through greater participation in sponsored research and academic publishing compel research universities to concentrate regular faculty effort in these areas while increasingly assigning instruction to full-time, non-tenure-track teachers. Geiger shows how patterns of bifurcation in faculty roles have varied among three clusters of fields—the sciences, liberal arts, and business—but in each instance the patterns prompt more general questions about the vitality of the traditional faculty role. Geiger provides many of the details about how the American professoriate has, and will increasingly, become restratified on the terms outlined by Jack Schuster in the introduction.

In chapter two, Steven Brint complements Geiger's consideration of faculty roles by focusing on the classroom and on movements to reform college teaching. Brint contends that two movements arose in the later part of the twentieth century to reorient the academic profession to teaching rather than research. One movement was sponsored by foundation advocacy organizations, such as the American Association of Colleges and Universities and the Carnegie Foundation for the Advancement of Teaching, and the other by the federal government and the states. Each movement was motivated by the notion that college professors can do a better job of producing and assessing student learning. Brint advances three key ideas: boundary-spanning organizations now work in consequential ways to shape the classroom environment; variation in favored forms of academic organization among competing actors has deeply influenced their ideals, practices, and successes; and the strongest force in the academic environment—students, faculty, and administrators—has existed as a system of mutually reinforcing interests whose net effects consist of low achievement standards across many colleges and universities. While the quality of instruction may have indeed risen, an ancillary effect of these teaching advocacy movements, according to Brint, was the crystallization of a teaching identity among college professors (committed to a host of behaviors—posting lecture notes online, study abroad, "active learning" styles of teaching, social service goals, and so on) that has come at the expense of the scholarly role rooted in disciplinary norms. For Brint, the result is a divided and weakened academic profession.

In a chapter concerned with professional control over the jurisdiction of college teaching, Gary Rhoades argues that teaching is increasingly controlled by new professions—emanating from instructional technology—that are laying claim to expertise about instruction. For Rhoades, if we are to understand the status of academe as a profession, we must turn to the classrooms on many campuses across the country to see what is actually going on inside them. Rhoades draws upon three sets of archival sources to identify patterns in how professional jurisdiction is being negotiated in the increasingly high-tech academy. One source consists of policy positions and publications from national faculty organizations, including the American Federation of Teachers, the American Association of University Professors, and the National Education Association. A second source consists of the publications and Web sites of two institutional associations, the League for Innovation and the Association of American Colleges and Universities, which reveal the position of academic managers in reconceptualizing education and the role of faculty. A final source consists of the Web sites of nonacademic, interstitial offices on two major campuses, which cast light on the types of claims that new institutional actors are making about the framing and control of pedagogy, expertise, and higher learning. If instruction is thought to be part of the academic profession's core, Rhoades's chapter leads the reader to question the profession's structural integrity.

Whereas the chapters by Geiger, Brint, and Rhoades each concern aspects of structural change in the academic profession, a chapter by Neil Gross on the role of politics in the production and dissemination of knowledge addresses cognitive change. Gross examines the ways in which faculty construe the place of their own politics in defining what comes to count as knowledge. This process is intertwined with cognitive change in academic areas of study that, in varying degrees, utilize and interact with political concerns. Drawing on interviews with professors across five fields, Gross finds variation in the degree to which notions such as objectivity and value-free knowledge are seen as unproblematic and desirable. He finds that professors observe norms against overt partisanship in the classroom but equivocate on their classroom roles when discussing politically volatile subjects. He also uncovers disagreement on how professors understand academic freedom, with just under half of his sample accounting for it in ways consistent with the concept's original meaning. Gross's chapter thus identifies an additional contributing source of uncertainty about the status of academe as a profession: faculty members themselves, the values they embrace, the attitudes they espouse, and the varied training and varied disciplinary cultures that have left them with equally heterogeneous views about the nature and substance of how to perform the professorial role.

In part two of the book, on socialization and deviance in the profession, Ann Austin considers the linkage between doctoral education and the vibrancy of academe. She argues that changes in academic work, in faculty appointment patterns, in student characteristics, and in doctoral students' expectations of careers prompt questions about the effectiveness of the academic profession in preparing future faculty. In light of changes that Austin considers, she poses the question, what should the socialization process emphasize and what possibilities might enrich the socialization of aspiring future faculty members? In the course of addressing this question, Austin considers important counterarguments. For example, strong new faculty members have arguably always managed to find their way in the academy. Why is it necessary now to give more attention to their socialization? Furthermore, why should socialization processes respond to conditions of the academy that many would assert are themselves undermining the status of academe as a profession? Austin's chapter demonstrates the power, and perhaps the dangers, inherent not only in observable changes in the profession but also in how to respond to them.

Shifting from a consideration of how to make things right to what goes wrong in graduate education, John Braxton, Eve Proper, and Alan Bayer, in chapter six, study professionalism in teaching and mentoring. Using an instrument called the "Graduate Teaching and Mentoring Behaviors Inventory" administered to eight hundred faculty members across the United States, the authors derive a normative structure for faculty behavior in graduate education. The structure consists of inviolable norms, those rules that academics view as warranting severe sanctions when breached, such as misappropriation of student work, harassment of students, and directed research malfeasance. In turn, the authors examine whether faculty espousal of inviolable norms varies among research institutions, across fields, and by gender and administrative experience. Using their results, Braxton, Proper, and Bayer argue that doctoral-granting programs should develop explicit codes of conduct that govern faculty behavior in teaching and mentoring in addition to clearer faculty processes of review and sanctioning capacity in determined cases of malfeasance. More effective self-regulation, the authors contend, endows a profession with greater coherence and stability.

A profession experiencing marked change brings about problems for the ways in which people experience professional careers. Anna Neumann and I contribute chapters to part three of the book, on experience of the academic career. Considering different objects of inquiry, Neumann and I share a concern for the meaning, value, and future promise of performing academic work. In chapter seven, Neumann is concerned about learning, not by students per se, but by the professors who teach them, mentor them, and, in turn, learn alongside them. For Neumann, the future of the academic profession is predicated on whether the social institution of higher education allows for their thinking and learning. As Neumann sees it, the production of knowledge and the advancement of civilized society cannot occur in the absence of supporting creative minds who work toward those ends. Institutional policies designed for efficiency but averse to scholarly learning do little more than make the academic profession penny wise but pound foolish.

"Anomie" is the concept developed by the French sociologist Emile Durkheim to refer to a condition of normlessness or lack of meaning that is produced by a divide between present realities and future desires. In chapter eight, I discuss anomie in terms of a divide between the achievement aspirations among members of the academic profession and the profession's capacity to recognize individuals for their contributions. In order to conduct its affairs, the academic profession relies on review, assessment, and critique. Competitive labor conditions have ascended to a point where the instances are many in which the conferral of recognition is more difficult: getting a job, getting a tenure-track job, publishing in top-tier journals and with top-tier academic presses, earning tenure, earning further promotion, moving among institutions, winning significant increases in salary, and so on. Under these conditions, it is reasonable to ask, who will want to enter the academic profession? I consider the ways in which anomie may vary in the contemporary era by career stages of academics, by organizational types of higher education institutions, by scholarly field, and by historical time. I conclude by suggesting that a means by which the profession will cope with its changing conditions is by attracting people of lesser talent, who will in turn bring lower and thus easier-to-realize expectations about what they can accomplish in an academic career.

Academic freedom may be viewed as the foundation for academic expertise, which, following Freidson from the outset of this discussion, is central to academics' control over the terms of their work and thus to the establishment and maintenance of professional authority. In part four of the book, on autonomy and regulation of the profession, Sheila Slaughter examines the complex relationship between academic freedom, politics, and the state in the early twenty-first century. She does so through an interwoven discussion of three key cases. One consists of the University of California, Berkeley–Novartis case, which, according to Slaughter, illustrates how legislation reshaped state agencies that permitted faculty to respond to new incentive structures in their work, some of which challenge traditional scholarly incentives of discovery and publication and thus arguably contradict tenets of academic freedom. A second instance consists of the *Urofsky v. Gilmore* case originating in the state of Virginia. Slaughter argues that this case illustrates how legislation enacted to enforce a socially conservative morality, stemming from a Virginia law that prohibits professors' use and representation of sexually explicit material in their research and teaching, restricts academic freedom. Finally, Slaughter examines the *Ward Churchill* case at the University of Colorado. By Slaughter's treatment, the *Churchill* case speaks to the ways in which security concerns play out in universities and governing boards during times of war, severely challenging academic freedom in the United States.

In chapter ten, Daniel Kleinman, Jacob Habinek, and Steven Vallas also examine connections between industry and academe and their implications for the profession. They do so, however, not by examining cases or by confining themselves to the practices of major research universities, but instead by examining how academic administrators have *talked* about the use of commercial practices in academic settings. Drawing on publications of national organizations for university administrators over a forty-year period of time beginning in the 1960s, the authors reveal "codes of commerce," or the manners by which university leaders have conceived of commercial practices and how these conceptions have changed over time. In one set of patterns, the authors find that commercial language was not prominent in discussion of academic leaders during the 1960s but ascended in prominence in the 1970s and underwent consolidation in the 1980s, such that by the 1990s business talk was increasingly institutionalized, but still not uniform or fully institutionalized across university types. The authors advise caution with regard to overlooked concerns. The virtues and vices of academic-industry partnerships constitute one realm of concern. Academic culture constitutes another. The authors warn that viewing students as consumers and adopting business management practices in higher education likely come with significant costs.

In chapter eleven, Erin Leahey and Kathleen Montgomery review the extent and nature of the rapid change to regulate academic research and its implications for professional autonomy and control. They draw on institutional theory to specify the organizational field of academic research and the relevant professional and organizational actors who participate in the regulation of academic research. They detect historical changes in the nature of professional autonomy and research regulation, including shifts from a strong dependence on self-regulation, to a heavy reliance on external regulation, to what they characterize as the current hybrid model. Leahey and Montgomery's outlook is more sanguine: they point out that pure self-regulation for individual academics has been more myth than reality, and that while today's academics operate in an environment of far greater regulation, these structures have arisen to ensure the quality and integrity of research practice.

In the final part of the book, Teresa Sullivan and John Thelin offer, respectively, contemporary and historical views of the profession as a summative means to identify the principal problems confronting the professoriate, as well as their sources. Writing from the perspective of a president of a major research university and as a sociologist of work and occupations, Teresa Sullivan examines the distinctive features of academe as a profession, focusing on academic freedom, peer review, and shared governance. The chapter explores the contemporary trends of these traits that are potentially deprofessionalizing. One such point, reminiscent of the discussion found in Gary Rhoades's chapter, consists in the rise of occupations found in universities and their jurisdictional claims. Drawing parallels with other professions, such as medicine, Sullivan makes the interesting point that all advanced professions delegate labor, which by this account helps to explain why a stock of non-tenure-track faculty are being hired by universities. The reasoning places faculty members as agents, rather than merely as victims, of how academic work is divided and controlled. An irony, reminiscent of the discussion found in Roger Geiger's chapter, is that faculty members of the contemporary era who are highly active and successful in research, and who in turn are excused from teaching through external monies, create an ongoing institutional demand for short-term teaching staff. Sullivan contends that threats to shared governance are at greatest risk of crippling the academic profession. The proliferation of occupations within universities, the deepening of tensions among faculty with varying allegiances themselves, and an inability to maintain professional solidarity amidst this diversity may come to severely impair academe as a profession.

Finally, in a historically astute overview, John Thelin makes readers aware that sounds of alarm in the academic profession constitute a recurrent theme since World War II. He remarks that if there is decline, then it must represent an erosion from some higher point. His chapter suggests that one plausible point is that period roughly between 1945 and 1970 often billed as American higher education's "Golden Age." Thelin credits a convergence of social trends through the 1960s and 1970s for a contemporary decline in the confidence of the academic profession. Why does the contemporary American professoriate see itself as underappreciated and at risk in the same period in which academic administrators are seen by faculty as having trumped them in power and prestige? For Thelin, the answer lies in "the great crossover:" a storied academic revolution of decades past, where professors ascended as respected experts in a variety of prestigious and valued fields, eclipsed most recently by a managerial revolution, a kind of entrepreneurial initiative in the administration of higher education, where a proliferation of management poses as an urgently needed solution to mounting crises. The changes can make faculty look like "whiners." But for Thelin, the concerns remain real, and the future depends on whether bona fide higher education leaders *accept* such stereotypical depictions of their faculty *or* are able to see, understand, and respond intelligently to the currents of change.

Numerous people made this work possible, including those who supported the academic conference, cosponsored by the Department of Sociology and the Institute of Higher Education at the University of Georgia, from which the book originates. At the University of Georgia, great thanks are given to Michael F. Adams, university president; William Finlay, head of the Department of Sociology; Jere W. Morehead, provost of the university; Arnett C. Mace Jr., former provost of the university; Libby V. Morris, director of the Institute of Higher Education; and Garnett S. Stokes, dean of the Franklin College of Arts and Sciences. Funding for this work was provided by the Office of the Senior Vice President for Academic Affairs and Provost, the President's Venture Fund through generous gifts of the University of Georgia Partners, the Franklin College of Arts and Sciences, the Department of Sociology, and the Institute of Higher Education at the University of Georgia. I additionally thank Libby Morris for assistance in navigating numerous logistical matters, as well as Susan Sheffield, Teresa Taylor, and Mariea Tountasakis, without whose steadfast involvement and heroic feats this work would not have come to fruition. Finally, for her structure and grace, I express great gratitude to Ashleigh Elliott McKown, with whom it has been a pleasure to work at the Johns Hopkins University Press.

REFERENCES

Abbott, Andrew. 1991. *The system of professions: An essay on the division of expert labor.* Chicago: University of Chicago Press.

Freidson, Eliot. 1970. *Profession of medicine: A study of the sociology of applied knowledge.* Chicago: University of Chicago Press.

———. 2001. Professional knowledge and skill. In *Professionalism: The third logic,* 17–35. Chicago: University of Chicago Press.

Goode, William J. 1957. Community within a community: The professions. *American Sociological Review* 22:194–200.

Greenwood, Ernest. 1957. Attributes of a profession. *Social Work* 2:45–55.

Johnson, Terence J. 1972. *Professions and power.* London: Macmillan.

Larson, Magali Sarfatti. 1977. *The rise of professionalism.* Berkeley: University of California Press.

Parsons, Talcott. 1949. The professions and social structure. In *Essays in sociological theory,* 34–49. Glencoe, IL: Free Press.

Parsons, Talcott, and Gerald M. Platt. 1973. *The American university.* Cambridge, MA: Harvard University Press.

Ruch, Richard S. 2001. *Higher Ed, Inc.: The rise of the for-profit university.* Baltimore: Johns Hopkins University Press.

The American Academic Profession

The Professoriate's Perilous Path

Jack H. Schuster

What shall become of the faculty? It is a question that has been posed, in one form or another, for close to a millennium and on North American shores for several centuries. The intent of this essay is to provide an overview of the condition of the American academic profession and to suggest implications for the faculty's proximate and longer-term future. Attention will be directed to the stakes that are involved—for the academic profession, for higher education in general, and for national interests—as well as strategies that might be useful to ameliorate commonly anticipated adverse outcomes.

Several questions guide the discussion of the chapter: Do the forces now reshaping the academy and its faculty portend a *withering* away of the traditional faculty—who they are and what they do as of the early twenty-first century? Correspondingly, does the purported new paradigm project dim prospects for reasonably reliable, relatively attractive academic careers? Put another way, can the adversities now pressing upon the academic profession be sufficiently offset to ensure a viable, vital career outlook for current and would-be academics?

This chapter argues that a new era has swiftly emerged for higher education and its faculty and that the new era is more than an evolutionary extension of well-established trends. It is a product of forces, introduced briefly below, that are reshaping a venerable institution and profession and that in the decades ahead likely will have profoundly changed what higher education institutions are and what their faculty members do. Although the faculty "makeover," so the argument goes, will have an attenuated impact on the small number of well-endowed, prestigious institutions, most of higher education will have been powerfully transformed. What is the evidence—and logic— upon which this proposition is based?

The future of the U.S. academic profession clearly has entered a new phase, arguably constituting a new paradigm for the faculty and their colleges and universities. Thus, the evolution is ongoing. Of course, change, more than stagnation, has always characterized the status of this complex, multifaceted profession, notwithstanding a reputation for resistance to new ways. And now the instructional staff, whose numbers are approaching one and a half million practitioners, has transitioned rapidly into a new phase—and perhaps has just recently been thrust by a harsh economy into yet another phase. This suggestion is predicated on several interrelated developments that powerfully affect the profession, from outside and from within the academy itself. Consider the following dynamic dimensions.

First, and perhaps most visibly, the composition of the faculty as measured by the proportion of them who do not hold traditional, full-time, tenure/tenure-track appointments has escalated dramatically in the past two decades. The numbers of both part-time faculty and especially full-time but nontenurable appointments have swelled to unprecedented levels (Knapp, Kelly-Reid, and Ginder 2008). Together these so-called *contingent* appointments now constitute approximately two-thirds of all faculty appointments. The "traditionals" still abound, but they now constitute a significantly smaller proportion of the entire faculty (Schuster and Finkelstein 2006).

Second, closely connected to the redistribution of faculty appointments is the changing mix of work responsibilities for many faculty. That is, the nature and mix of academic work have been, and by all indications will continue to be, in flux, gravitating toward more emphasis on teaching (among the numerous contingent faculty). Accordingly, the modal academic job itself is quite different from what it had been, say, twenty years ago. It appears that fewer and fewer faculty members' roles entail playing all "positions" of the "complete scholar": teaching, research, and service.

Third, powerful trends continue to sweep through the academy, seemingly still gathering momentum; they are extensively reshaping higher education and its faculty. Among them, three phenomena—the rapid growth of technology and online education, the rise of the privatized/for-profit sector of higher education, and the expanding globalization of higher education—are especially noteworthy.

Fourth, the age distribution of faculty features a graying professoriate. Whereas the academic labor market has been tight for many years, with the supply of academic aspirants routinely exceeding the demand for them in most (but not all) fields, that supply-demand ratio *was* apparently beginning to reverse as the number of retirees and prospective retirees among retirement-eligible faculty proliferated. This openness of faculty to retirement no doubt was reinforced by years of healthy pension fund performances and the anticipation of a comfortable retirement. Indeed, an abundance of new openings had recently become evident. It appears that the academic pipeline, so congested for so long by the persistent "old guard," was beginning to unclog. Although data are sparse, a common perception holds that, in the current economic environment, faculty contemplating retirement are likely to be more inclined to persist longer until a greater measure of personal economic security is assured.

Fifth, the economic status of the academic profession (and the financial condition of the employing colleges and universities) is now laced with more than the usual uncertainties. Some concerns are perennial; compensation, for example, is invariably a key issue. From the vantage point of the academicians, compensation always has been marginal to inadequate (and is perceived to be less attractive than that afforded some other highly trained professionals). The most recent data once more show some slippage, with the average annual increase in salary (3.8% for 2007–8) trailing the 4.1 percent inflation rate for the year (American Association of University Professors 2008). The enduring pattern of faculty discontent with compensation recently has encountered a relatively new phenomenon: the heightened influence of the marketplace has worked to favor, sometimes substantially, those faculty in some high-demand fields while many other fields—encompassing the preponderance of "traditional" academics—lag behind their well-positioned colleagues. Thus, the economic status of the profession has been increasingly characterized by a polarizing effect; the once-lofty ideal of "one faculty" (historically excepting law and medicine), although never realized, has by now long disappeared.[1] These conditions influence faculty morale and, relatedly, the attractiveness of academic careers, as discussed later.

Finally, given the prevailingly bleak state of the current U.S. economy, the economic outlook for the higher education sector, vis-à-vis the intensification of competing social needs, is ever more problematic. As the current national economy struggles to regain stability, the spillover adverse effects on public and private institutions of higher education alike are both deep and broad. Economic factors, along with the aforementioned trends, amplify the uncertainties that pervade the outlook for the academic profession.

In all, the academy has been undergoing an accelerating rate of change, almost surely at an unprecedented pace. The pace of change is sometimes breathtaking, reflecting society's galloping transformations, but perhaps especially notable for an "industry" long identified with measured, cautious change (Kerr 1991).[2]

Further, this rapid rate of change outruns our ability to measure it and to gauge the implications. That is to say, despite the advent of more sophisticated analytical tools and an outpouring of higher education data, there remains a significant, sobering data gulf. Here is the issue: indicators of change need to be monitored carefully, of course, but arguably even *more* attentively than perhaps ever before. This is because consequential changes seem often to have occurred before we have an adequate handle on the facts beyond anecdotal evidence, much less before we analysts and practitioners have had time to sort through the implications. Relatedly, it is striking that, despite the abundance of some measures, so much is *not* known about critical developments even by those scholars whose focused interest revolves around understanding the academic profession and how academic life is changing. This challenge to being able to chart what has been happening in order to project what is likely to happen is made all the more serious by the budgetary threats to the U.S. Department of Education's National Center for Education Statistics, which may undermine systematic, large-scale data collection. The result would be the diminished likelihood of periodic national surveys of sufficient scope and frequency to yield reasonably timely measures of key developments. In short, we know a lot less than we need to know about vital developments that are redefining the faculty experience.

The Centrality of the Faculty

The starting point for this discourse is a simple proposition. Whatever the venues and boundaries of postsecondary education, the faculty reside at the very core of the enterprise (Clark 1987). They constitute the intellectual capital. This observation is perhaps obvious, but it bears underscoring in an era in which higher learning is delivered in so many different ways—and increasingly so. That is, the role of the faculty may be perceived by some as less pivotal in the multifaceted "new era." Technology, obviously, plays a more prominent part in creating options for delivering educational content, including "outsourcing" to expert providers; the use of such providers—for packaged lectures and the like—is almost certain to expand, perhaps exponentially, for many campuses. Accordingly, familiar, traditional faculty work roles and careers become less dominant, displaced in part, or augmented—depending on one's view—by these external resources. Further, as ever-larger numbers of contingent faculty become more loosely linked to their respective institutions, many faculty members may be reckoned as less crucial, more interchangeable, more disposable temporary staff. Thus, the truism of the faculty's centrality is now being subjected to intensifying pressures. Notwithstanding these challenges, the extent to which higher education is effective (or not) in accomplishing its missions turns on the quality of the faculty. Whatever the new era brings that is creating "The New U," it follows that being able to field a qualified and dedicated faculty is the indispensible variable, as discussed subsequently.

The National Economic Downturn

As noted earlier, at this writing the economic outlook for the U.S. economy is bleak and, correspondingly, the consequences for American higher education (and, it follows, the faculty) are daunting. Every few days, it seems, the news media announce that this or that economic indicator—unnerving volatility in the equity markets and sliding real estate values, residential housing foreclosures and delinquent mortgages, stunning job loss figures and soaring numbers of unemployment insurance claimants, and on and on—is the worst since the Great Depression, or the past twenty-five or forty years, or since such-and-such metric was first measured. As of late 2008, the national economy has been deemed to be in "official" recession already for a year, and its duration is already among the longest-lasting recessions since World War II. Speculation about when the bottom will be reached and the projected pace of recovery spans many scenarios, some of which foresee a recession of historic duration. Uncertainties abound, hindering efforts to peer into a future murkier by far than usual.

As recently as mid-2008, the outlook for the academy was quite positive. The economy seemed to be relatively strong (and stock market indices were still high, albeit below the historic heights reached in fall 2007, and endowments and annual giving were robust). The indicators of serious economic duress had not yet coalesced in a plainly visible way. As for the faculty itself, as noted earlier, the age distribution promised many retirements and, consequently, a rejuvenated, younger faculty. Various trends, also as noted earlier, posed significant challenges to the accustomed way of "doing business." And colleges and universities of every kind were adding part-time and off-track full-time faculty at a rapid, some would say alarming, rate in order to both contain expenses and build in more flexible staffing. Notwithstanding the norms of perpetual underfunding, the academy and its faculty, on the whole, seemed to be reasonably well positioned.

But the rapid national economic implosion during the fall of 2008 has abruptly transformed many aspects of higher education. The checklist is extensive: tumbling endowment values, shrunken state appropriations, threatened enrollment-linked revenues (as family apprehension apparently becomes commonplace about being able to financially support their children's higher education aspirations, especially for attending away-from-home pricier institutions), deferred capital projects (as institutions are obliged to reprioritize), and advancement offices' challenges to collect pledges already made and to obtain new pledges. Further, and of great concern, intensifying federal budgetary pressures promise to squeeze numerous vital programs, ranging from federal student financial aid to research. The popular and "industry" press is replete with anecdotal illustrations, even if reliable industry-wide data are slow to surface. The particulars of this inventory of formidable challenges could go on.

Another factor may exacerbate this financial impact on colleges and universities anxious about maintaining enrollments. Over the years conventional wisdom has held, and the data have been supportive, that higher education enrollments benefit from economic downturns that constrict the larger labor market; under these not-so-uncommon circumstances, the choice of continuing one's higher education often becomes a relatively attractive, realistic option. In turn, applications to undergraduate and post-baccalaureate programs sometimes swell. Now, however, given the very gloomy economic outlook, diminished higher education revenues for the more costly colleges and universities may well offset, even overwhelm, whatever modest revenues that are generated by fresh (but aid-hungry) enrollees.

Prelude to a New Paradigm: Thinking Historically

Perhaps what we are witnessing is the emergence of a new paradigm to describe higher education's new permutation. In any event, the emerging realities will surely have implications, presumably profound, for the world of faculty work and the quality of academic life. So much has happened to transform American higher education in recent decades; that much is certain. Both sides of the ledger sheet are crowded with entries, both positive and threatening.

What is the backdrop for this purported new paradigm? Having taught for years seminars on the history of American higher education, I am keenly aware that in some sense there truly is "nothing new under the sun." Everything in contemporary higher education has its precedents, sometimes tracing back to medieval predecessors. There never was, of course, a "pure" university solely dedicated to learning and free from the compromising influences of an environment replete with stakeholders. As for the past half century or so, the post–World War II era is characterized by an evolution of models. Postwar model A was the "multiversity," to use Clark Kerr's evocative term of the early 1960s (Kerr 1963). This label captured the traditional university as it had been amplified—some would say compromised, others would argue enriched and made the more relevant—by having taken on multiple missions to serve an expanding array of "clients" with their multiple, sometimes conflicting, demands.

Perhaps it was not the first new postwar model; so much was already happening, starting with the university's partnership with government in developing the technology to prosecute the war effort and, then, the infusion of millions of veterans into college classrooms via the GI Bill. Nevertheless, Kerr's conceptualization made an indelible imprint on how we thought of the university's uses—its role (or, more accurately, *many* roles) in a swiftly evolving society.

Clearly that paradigm has been eclipsed. In the nearly half century since Kerr's landmark pronouncement, the literature has poured forth describing the twists and turns of higher education and its amazing achievements, its numerous shortcomings, and its many entanglements. Critiques of late twentieth-century higher education abound, issuing from astute and scholarly academics and from outside observers alike (Kirp 2003). But for me, perhaps none of the meta-interpretations have surveyed the landscape as convincingly as the book coauthored by Sheila Slaughter and Gary Rhoades in 2004, *Academic Capitalism and the New Economy*.[3]

The authors, longtime critics of the commercialization of higher education, describe in great detail, bolstered by numerous examples, the many ways in which the university has taken on, to its detriment, the values of those interested parties with whom it interacts, mostly out of perceived mutual benefit. The authors are not unaware of the often inadequately appreciative political actors that drive resource-hungry colleges and universities to go places they might not want to in order to remain competitive in an intensely challenging and competitive environment.

In portraying the Academic Capitalist University, or model B for present purposes, Slaughter and Rhoades do not claim this to be a new paradigm, for indeed theirs is a description of contemporary higher education long in the making. But they have, as I suggest, brought together the elements and evidence in such a way as to take the description of capitalism-on-campus to more robust and convincing levels, delving into the venues of patents, copyrights, big-time Division I athletics, interlocking directorates between governing boards and corporations, and so on.

The New Paradigm Emerges

The metamorphosis continues. Now I want to describe what I believe to be the emergence of a new paradigm, the restratified university. Perhaps it is merely a variation of the capitalist university model described by Slaughter and Rhoades. Model C, we shall call it for now, has several features that are particularly noteworthy and problematic. Most prominent of these features are (1) the groundswell of off-track, full-time academic appointments; (2) the partially obscured but very serious threat to tenure; and (3) the more sharply differentiated compensation packages for faculty, within institutions, by institutional type, and across institutions by discipline. Each of these developments is set within, and fueled by, the rampant economic uncertainties and fiscal constraints referenced earlier.

Foremost is the increasingly stratified academic status that characterizes this new look. It represents a kind of reversion to a more highly layered, even more castelike university of long ago—a regression, it would seem. The university has always and unavoidably been a stratified employment venue. The "community of scholars" has never been an enclave of coequal seekers and imparters of knowledge, although some modest experiments have consciously sought to minimize hierarchy. We recall readily the dons and masters and their surrounding concentric circles of "lessers" aspiring to higher status. And we are reminded of the model from which the American research university imported so much in the way of academic values, the nineteenth-century German university in which "Herr Doktor Professor" presided authoritatively, stereotypically autocratically, while relegating underlings to long apprenticeships with significantly diminished status.

American higher education arguably pointed the way to a more democratized, more egalitarian academic profession. The academic ranks on these shores took on a more balanced numerical distribution, moving away from a steep pyramid featuring a chair holder at the pinnacle and inferiors arrayed below. There developed, instead, a different, flatter configuration, a more balanced professoriate of more equally distributed ranks—professors, associate professors, assistant professors—and lecturers, graduate assistants, and so on: hardly a democratic commune of academic workers, but a move in the direction of a less accentuated hierarchy. The tenure hurdle poignantly defined a threshold difference in academic status; for those on-track faculty, it is a career-enhancing—or potentially career-destroying—portal. Nonetheless, an American model had emerged—if not exactly egalitarian then assuredly more democratic.

But in the evolving restratified university, more sharply differentiated statuses become more visible as the shrinking proportion of tenured faculty occupies a highly privileged position compared to off-track faculty (Finkelstein, Seal, and Schuster 1998). Then there are the part-time faculty whose numbers have skyrocketed—now approaching seven hundred thousand—and who now appear to exceed the number of full-time appointments (Knapp, Kelly-Reid, and Ginder 2008).[4] Their circumstance varies from exploited academic pieceworkers, paid minimally per course and bearing marginal status within their respective institutions, to those part-time faculty seeking only a part-time appointment and whose appointments often result in highly satisfying mutual advantage.

But the steady rise of the part-time phenomenon, of course, is old news. What is quite recent, however, is the rapid growth in full-time but non-tenure-track appointees; this is what defines the essence of the restratified university. The extraordinary fact is that since 1993, the clear *majority* of all new, that is, first-time, full-time appointments to faculty positions have been *off* the tenure track. The proportion has built steadily at every two-year interval, as measured by the U.S. Department of Education's Integrated Postsecondary

Education Data System (IPEDS) fall administrative staff survey. From just over 50 percent of new full-time appointments made off-track in 1993, the proportion built steadily to a peak of 58.6 percent in 2003—very nearly three in every five appointments. The fall 2005 data appear to show a slight reversal in the proportion of such appointments, but the fact remains that perhaps fifty-five of every hundred new full-time appointments for the past decade and a half have been off the tenure track.[5] By now, in the aggregate, nearly two of five (37.1%) of all full-time appointments are off-track—and that proportion is growing every year.[6]

What makes this development all the more remarkable is that not so many years ago such appointments were, if not rare, at least scarce. A full-time appointment *meant* tenure-track, at least at those institutions that had a tenure system. To be sure, there were off-track appointments, a scattering of clinical professorships, for example. But nothing existed even remotely like the deluge of such appointments in recent years. As noted, they have become the *modal* new full-time appointment, now for a decade and a half, with no sign of abating.

It is not that this phenomenon has escaped notice. However, I think it is safe to say that only much more recently has this trend been emblazoned on the consciousness of higher education and more serious attention devoted to the likely consequences of this "faculty makeover." Viewed another way, these full-time, nontenurable *contingent* appointments, coupled with the massive number of part-time appointments that are essentially *all* contingent appointments, mean that the American faculty has been massively transformed into a *predominantly* contingent faculty.

The reasons for this phenomenon are multiple; the attraction of cost savings (lesser salaries and often minimal benefits), combined with a built-in staffing flexibility that enables redeployments to correspond more nimbly to ever-shifting student interests, appears to be irresistible. It is a topic for another day to dwell on the positive as well as the negative side of this development, for it is clear that many faculty *prefer* the off-track full-time or part-time appointments because it means focusing on teaching, emphasizing relationships with students, and, in the mix, evading the Damoclean sword of "publish or perish." For some part-timers, likely many, the appointment, rather than a holding position awaiting "promotion" to full-time, is a satisfying complement to other academic or nonacademic work.

To summarize, the academy has witnessed the dramatic, radical transformation of the faculty, and only recently, it appears, have analyses begun to tease out the trade-offs, the far-reaching implications for the faculty and their work and for the academy more generally (Schuster and Finkelstein 2006).[7] This reconfiguration of faculty is the central hallmark of the restratified university.

A second characteristic of the restratified university has to do with what appears to be happening to tenure. As suggested earlier, tenure has long been a line of demarcation defining basic status within the faculty. That feature is not itself changing. But consider this aspect of what is happening. Tenure, in one sense, is alive and well and intact. It is remarkable that tenure has been challenged frontally so few times in recent years, despite oftentimes highly skeptical governing boards, as well as numerous critics of higher education (not least among them politicians) objecting to higher education's allegedly unique and outdated tenure system. Yet I believe that there are perhaps nearly as many instances of institutions of higher education that have adopted tenure in recent years as there are institutions that have jettisoned tenure (at least for their new hires). In any event, presumably the political cost of assaulting tenure directly from within the academy seems to have dissuaded even the fiercest critics from attempting to eliminate tenure.

But the critics, internal and external, may realize that they need not launch frontal attacks because, with patience, the "problem" may be taking care of itself. After all, as just noted, the clear majority of new full-time hires have for some time now, year after year, been made off-track, that is, *nontenurable*. Put in other terms, tenure is being slowly—or perhaps not so slowly—but surely *circumvented*, in a sense made less and less relevant. That is, the proportion of faculty who are tenure holders, and thereby more clearly afforded the protection of "free expression," is destined to shrink dramatically over the coming years, barring some unforeseen intervention that would reverse the powerful trends.

Thus, tenure is being undermined by this subtle but deadly assault from the flank. This process is very likely to accelerate even more as the number of faculty approaching retirement climbs sharply, meaning that in the proximate future more and more faculty are likely to be replaced by faculty appointed to non-tenure-bearing positions. The implications of this development are serious, but for immediate purposes, it suggests dwindling numbers of privileged tenure holders and large cohorts of vulnerable "others." This is, I submit, another prominent characteristic defining the restratified university.

Compensation trends and how they fit into the concept of the restratified university constitute a third feature. The evidence in recent years is very clear: compensation for the professoriate is becoming ever more dispersed—by rank and type of appointment, by institutional type, and by discipline—as the marketplace dictates. These trends are underscored by recent compensation data reported by the American Association of University Professors in its annual "Report on the Economic Status of the Profession" (2008). This analysis also emphasizes the growing polarization in the resources of individual institutions, in a sense mirroring the rapidly polarizing distribution of income in the larger society.

Thus, model C, the restratified university, is arguably a new paradigm, constituting something of a melding of the two robust postwar models that I have sketched: the first, the more-or-less traditional university, expanded in its mission and its engagement with its environment, as characterized by Clark Kerr as a multiversity, and the second, the contemporary freewheeling, consumer-driven, market-responsive, capitalist model that is ever more entrepreneurial and decreasingly constrained by traditional academic convention. But the newly surfacing model C is distinct because it is more compartmentalized, more stratified, than its predecessors and, at the same time, is subjected to ever more intense financial pressures. This emerging construct has numerous implications for faculty and their work. The new paradigm accentuates the faculty's role, to employ the label used by Slaughter and Rhoades (2004), as "managed professionals." It means a more tightly managed faculty workforce, a greater vulnerability for large and growing proportions of faculty holding contingent appointments, and, in all, a more sharply polarized, more layered, more stratified faculty.

Conclusion

There are two jousting scenarios for the future of the faculty, taking cognizance of the national economic crisis and the strictures that are beginning to be imposed on higher education. In this rapidly changing, highly volatile environment there are nevertheless some exciting opportunities for higher education and its faculty in the longer term. Recalling the lessons of the past, higher education and its faculty have been strikingly resilient over the centuries. The enterprise has always risen to the challenges of the times, adapting creatively and opportunistically, and, within limits, has prospered. Through every kind of upheaval over a near millennium of history—wars, depressions, plagues, revolutions—the universities have not only survived but, in the main, thrived. Accordingly, it might be foolish to posit eventual calamity in view of history's basic lesson that higher education always comes through, albeit modified to be sure, for the experience.

There is, then, the possibility that the faculty will manage as always to persist and even to prosper, albeit in a very different form. (Of course, it depends on where observers position themselves on the continuum of preference for an older traditional model of higher education as to the extent to which one is heartened, or dismayed, by the changing postsecondary education permutations.)

My own concerns run very deep. The threat is real. The faculty makeover is real. Adaptation may well mean large-scale compromise of principle. What can the faculty do? In the era of the restratified university, the path will continue to be perilous. The stakes are enormous—nothing less than the robust health of a postsecondary system to better assure a vibrant, vital society. The faculty and its advocates must ever redouble their efforts to demonstrate just what the stakes are, however challenging it may be to articulate those precious yet abstract values to a sometimes skeptical public.

Will there emerge sufficiently influential allies of higher education and its faculty to generate necessary support (albeit in the name of the national interest)? Perhaps higher education's most crucial potential allies in the struggles for resources are those who are convinced, or can be convinced, that the United States' ability to compete globally is enmeshed with the capabilities of present and future students and their teachers/mentors. This recognition becomes potentially even more salient when coupled with the observation that American higher education, while still the strongest in the world, is no longer the clear leader in terms of comparative national efforts—that is, the proportion of national resources that support "tertiary" education. Often this awareness is informed most starkly by the data that indicate that the United States is currently lagging other countries especially in the preparation of adequate numbers of students in the areas of science, mathematics, and engineering. The relevant data include many measures, such as research and development's share of gross domestic product, changes in tertiary education expenses per student, and public and private expenditures for tertiary education as a proportion of higher education income. While such metrics do not entirely settle the claim that the United States' comparative national effort is losing ground, the recently emerging data showing U.S. slippage among developed nations are eye-opening to many sophisticated observers. For a detailed examination of such data, the recent analysis by William K. Cummings of the multinational Changing Academic Profession Project is particularly revealing (Cummings 2008; Finkelstein and Cummings 2008).

Beyond those not so new arguments, what is at stake for the academic profession and, accordingly, for the higher education enterprise itself is something basic, yet quite intangible: it is the ability of higher education to attract *quality* faculty members in the future. There is no simple metric that can capture the ephemeral nature of quality, but that dimension is nevertheless pivotal to the professoriate's future effectiveness. History demonstrates that through thick and thin for higher education, classrooms have been, and undoubtedly will be, staffed by instructors, presumably with few exceptions. The numbers—the quantity—will be there. But that fundamental fact bypasses the elusive question of whether they will be faculty who are adequately qualified. What does this mean? As a first cut, I suggest that the core components are a relevant, strong educational/experiential background and personal commitment to the job's tasks, that is, a dimension of caring, of dedication. However loose these criteria may be and however many other formulations might better boil down the meaning of "adequate quality," the point remains that the criteria resist measurement. While candidate interviews, candidates' references, and the like may serve search committees well, and productivity indices (for number of publications and citations) have their uses, there is no real longer-term measure of "how well are we doing?" as a profession in attracting good candidates—including a significantly more diverse faculty (Smith 2009).

The answer is connected to the strength of application pools. In the future, as in the past, higher education's effectiveness turns on the ability of the profession to draw able and committed persons into academic careers. This is a simple, yet elusive, formulation. Put another way, unless the prospects of an academic career are sufficiently attractive to career choosers, the enterprise itself will be fated to ineffectiveness. There are at least some worrisome signs that the attractiveness of academic careers may be weakening for traditional research university work (June 2009; Mason and Goulden 2002; Mason, Goulden, and Frasch 2009). It is a proposition too intangible and too future-oriented to gain the attention of policy makers both inside and beyond the academy. Further, one must always take into account that sweeping generalizations about any aspect of higher education obscure the reality that "higher education" is an aggregate of numerous realities and that those conditions vary strikingly by institutional type, auspices, discipline, and so on. Thus, labor market conditions, as well as every other dimension of academic life, reveal great variation "on the ground." In Burton Clark's apt phrase, academic life is composed of "small worlds, different worlds" (Clark 1987). The stakes indisputably are immense.

The immediate outlook, given the economic woes pressing upon higher education, is replete with formidable challenges. In the longer term, sweeping changes from within and without will inevitably lead to substantial academic restructuring. Higher education is nothing if not resilient. But, in all, the effectiveness of higher education and the contributions that will accrue to the nation are inextricably linked to the future attractiveness of academic careers.

NOTES

1. Another significant dimension of trends in academic compensation is the growing divergence favoring private institution faculty over their public counterparts, especially at doctorate-granting institutions (see, for instance, Byrne 2008).

2. For an account of earlier postwar transformative changes, see, for example, Kerr 1963.

3. See also Slaughter and Leslie 1997 for an earlier description and commentary.

4. Knapp, Kelly-Reid, and Ginder 2008 at table 1, p. 4: "Staff whose primary responsibility is instruction, research, and/or public service" is shown as 667,562 part-time and 627,809 full-time staff. (These numbers exclude the subset of faculty at medical schools where full-time faculty predominate.)

5. At this writing, the IPEDS data for fall 2007, referenced earlier, do not include a breakout for *new* full-time appointments by tenure status.

6. According to the most recent data released by the IPEDS in late 2008 for fall 2007, among full-time staff with faculty status at degree-granting institutions, there are (in the thousands, rounded) 702.4 total faculty. Of these, 290.6 have tenure, 134.8 are on the tenure track, 171.1 are not on the tenure track, 80.2 are not part of a tenure system, and 25.7 are "staff without faculty status." Thus, among *full-time* faculty at institutions with tenure systems, most by far (ca. 425,000, or 71%) are still tenure/tenure-track, compared to 171,000 (29%) not on tenure track. If the 80,000 faculty at institutions with no tenure system are added to those on tenure track, then

the total of nontenurable faculty climbs to 37.1%. See Knapp, Kelly-Reid, and Ginder 2008 at table 4, p. 8.

7. See especially Schuster and Finkelstein 2006, table 10.3, pp. 340–41, for a list of trade-offs attributable at least in part to restructuring.

REFERENCES

American Association of University Professors. 2008. The annual report on the economic status of the profession, 2007–08. *Academe*, March-April, 94 (2).

Byrne, Richard. 2008. Gap persists between faculty salaries and public and private institutions. *Chronicle of Higher Education*, April 18.

Clark, Burton R. 1987. *The academic life: Small worlds, different worlds.* Princeton: Carnegie Foundation for the Advancement of Teaching.

Cummings, William K. 2008. The context for the changing academic profession: A survey of international indicators. In *The changing academic profession in international and quantitative perspectives*, 33–56. Hiroshima: Research Institute for Higher Education, Hiroshima University.

Finkelstein, Martin J., and William K. Cummings. 2008. The changing academic profession in the United States: 2007. In *The changing academic profession in international and quantitative perspectives*, 75–88. Hiroshima: Research Institute for Higher Education, Hiroshima University.

Finkelstein, Martin J., Robert K. Seal, and Jack H. Schuster. 1998. *The new academic generation: A profession in transformation.* Baltimore: Johns Hopkins University Press.

June, Audrey Williams. 2009. Grad students think twice about jobs in academe. *Chronicle of Higher Education*, January 23, 1, 10.

Kerr, Clark. 1963. *The uses of the university.* Cambridge, MA: Harvard University Press.

———. 1991. *The great transformation in higher education, 1960–1980.* Albany: State University of New York Press.

Kirp, David L. 2003. *Shakespeare, Einstein, and the bottom line: The marketing of higher education.* Cambridge, MA: Harvard University Press.

Knapp, Laura G., Janice E. Kelly-Reid, and Scott A. Ginder. 2008. *Employees in postsecondary institutions, fall 2007, and salaries of full-time instructional faculty, 2007–08: First look (NCES 2009-154).* Washington, DC: National Center for Education Statistics, Institute of Education Sciences, U.S. Department of Education.

Mason, Mary Ann, and Marc Goulden. 2002. Do babies matter? The effect of family formation on the lifetime careers of academic men and women. *Academe* 88 (6).

Mason, Mary Ann, Marc Goulden, and Karie Frasch. 2009. Why graduate students reject the fast track. www.aaup.org/AAUP/pubsres/academe/2009/JF/Feat/maso (accessed September 2010).

Schuster, Jack H., and Martin J. Finkelstein. 2006. *The American faculty: The restructuring of academic work and careers.* Baltimore: Johns Hopkins University Press.

Slaughter, Sheila, and Larry L. Leslie. 1997. *Academic capitalism: Politics, policies, and the entrepreneurial university.* Baltimore: Johns Hopkins University Press.

Slaughter, Sheila, and Gary Rhoades. 2004. *Academic capitalism and the new economy: Markets, state, and higher education.* Baltimore: Johns Hopkins University Press.

Smith, Daryl G. 2009. *Diversity's Promise for Higher Education: Making It Work.* Baltimore: Johns Hopkins University Press.

PART I

Structural and Cognitive Change

CHAPTER ONE

Optimizing Research and Teaching

The Bifurcation of Faculty Roles at Research Universities

Roger L. Geiger

Academic drift is the term that has long been employed to indicate institutional or departmental aspirations for greater participation in sponsored research and academic publishing (Clark 1983). This tendency has also long been interpreted as detrimental to undergraduate teaching. Thus, the expansion of academic research in the 1980s was countered in the years around 1990 with accusations of overemphasis on research and underemphasis on undergraduates. I have argued elsewhere that such a critique was simplistic and misleading. However, these oscillations in faculty effort, real or imagined, occurred with little change in faculty structure or roles. If data from the National Survey of Postsecondary Faculty can be believed, faculty reverted to previous form in the 1990s, devoting more time to teaching and less to research (Geiger 2004).

Conditions have changed—the expansion of academic research since the late 1990s has been accompanied by forces that are driving a restructuring of faculty work. The purpose of this chapter is to identify the changes now occurring and the forces behind them. The first section presents a conceptual scheme for analyzing the balance between research and instruction. The second examines factors in the research economy causing an intensification of research in faculty roles. The third examines changes in teaching roles and particularly the growth of the full-time, fixed-term faculty appointments. The final section documents the bifurcation of faculty roles and considers possible implications.

The Optimization Hypothesis

Universities are complex multipurpose organizations. Numerous models have been proposed to account for their behavior, and all seem to capture some important features (Garvin 1980). However, at the most fundamental level universities consistently seek to maximize learning—the learning of their faculty, the learning of students, and the sharing of learning with external actors, particularly in ways that contribute to internal learning. This view may not explain all university undertakings, but it is consistent with the thrust of most university behavior. Universities try to employ the most learned faculty possible; they prefer and seek the best learners for students. Universities are generally willing to assume other functions that contribute in some way to learning, like agricultural experiment stations, special library collections, or research for the Department of Defense. Conversely, they avoid providing services that offer no learning feedback; or, if need be, they seal them off as auxiliary enterprises that make no claims on general funds. Prestige maximization has often been posited as the driver of university behavior, but in this view learning is the most powerful underlying source of prestige. Similarly, resources are obviously essential for universities, but prestige based on learning is the surest means for securing the revenues and supplemental income that bolster university quality. The most learned American universities are ultimately the most admired institutions, domestically and globally.

For present purposes, the two central activities of universities are the advancement of learning through research, scholarship, and research-based graduate education and conveying learning through instruction for non-research degrees. Research and teaching: these are the principal outputs of universities and the principal components of the faculty role. Since both contribute to learning, how do universities determine how much of each to produce?

Several decades ago, economist Marc Nerlove (1972) posed this question in a different context. He proposed hypothetical amounts of "value-adjusted units" devoted to research and teaching to suggest several interesting relationships. In institutions devoted almost exclusively to research or teaching, limited amounts of the other activity can be offered on a complementary basis. For example, major medical schools, which resemble enormous research institutes, are able to offer education at small cost and in ways that support research. Conversely, colleges that offer no provision for research might add small amounts of faculty research that would contribute to upgrading educational services. However, for most universities research and teaching are substitutes for one another. But Nerlove (1972) did not imply a teaching-versus-research scenario. Rather, he posits that universities choose a combination that optimizes the outputs of both teaching and research. This *optimization hypothesis* makes good sense if one considers what universities are able to do with given resources, not what they might wish to do. A university might wish to perform more research but be unable to invest in the research capacity that this would require. Similarly, universities would no doubt like to improve the quality of educational services, but most lack the wherewithal to make those investments too. In the real world, universities satisfice, or optimize these outputs (Birnbaum 1988).

Further, Nerlove (1972) argued that an increased social provision of academic research "may well have the effect of making the provision of undergraduate education more expensive, but this increase in cost is desirable from society's point of view" (S204). By increased cost, Nerlove meant employing greater resources, so that the value of educational services would also increase. Additional resources do not come entirely from research funds, but from universities seeking to optimize their outputs.

How, we might ask, does this relate to the real world? The critical question is to what extent research and teaching are substituted for one another. Consider a simple example. If I were suddenly to receive a research grant that would buy out my two courses for next fall, the department would scramble to find replacement teachers. Most likely they would be part-time teachers or, for undergraduate courses, graduate teaching assistants. Although my replacements might be terrific teachers, they would be paid far less than a full professor. In Nerlove's (1972) value-adjusted units, this would represent a diminished input to teaching—a substitution of research for teaching.

Substitution clearly takes place in the short run, but does it also occur longer term? In *Knowledge and Money* (Geiger 2004) I examined two cases in which substitution occurred as institutional policy. In the first, a public university rose to distinction in the 1970s but found its budgets badly squeezed in the 1980s. With a captive clientele of in-state students, it was insulated from competition for undergraduate enrollments. To preserve its academic prestige, it deployed more valuable resources for research-related purposes and used less valuable inputs for undergraduate education. The university's optimal balance of outputs shifted toward research. However, this development soon caused a reaction—not in the student market but in the political arena.

Accused of neglecting undergraduate education, the university was compelled by its governing board to increase investments in that area substantially. This was done through addition, that is, in ways intended not to diminish (substitute for) research and endanger its reputation.

In the second case, a private university that was losing its competitiveness in the admissions market consciously determined to raise its profile for undergraduate teaching. Given limited resources, this was done by substitution—by cutting resources for research. The optimal balance in this case shifted toward greater teaching and less research. This strategy accomplished its purpose, raising tuition income and selectivity, but abandoning research in several areas. This movement also brought a reaction. Once the university had improved its position in undergraduate recruitment and bolstered its finances, it announced the need to direct increased investments toward research. Again, this was envisioned to occur through additions, not substitution.

Princeton supplies an additional example of enhancing the output of instruction. In 2000 it resolved to increase undergraduate enrollments by five hundred. This was justified as a correction to a long-term upward creep in graduate/research education. No cutbacks in research were envisioned, but clearly the university intended to increase the weight of undergraduate education in its optimal balance (Geiger 2004).

Both research and teaching are powerfully supported not only within universities but by markets and influential external constituencies. However, teaching and research represent different organizational processes. Universities control their output of teaching directly by adjusting the inputs of students, faculty, and organizational resources devoted to that end. Research, however, is a two-step model. Universities make internal investments with the expectation that they will attract external support for research. Although the research economy is relatively stable, there is still a degree of uncertainty. Hence, the optimal balance of teaching and research might fluctuate somewhat in the short run. However, in the long run both are stabilized by more powerful dynamics.

As universities seek to maximize their learning and prestige, they try to hire the highest-quality faculty members that are available. If successful, they should over time enhance research capacity—replacing less capable scholars and researchers with more capable ones or making net new additions. (This assumes that the supply of high-quality academic labor exceeds demand, discussed below.) Thus, competently run universities should be able to expand

Table 1.1   Increase in teaching, research, and spending at thirty-three private and sixty-six public universities, 1980–2000 (in percentages)

	Private	Public
Enrollments	16.5	11
Regular faculty	20	10
Research expenditures	105	141
Real spending / student	139	67

Source: Geiger 2004

their research capacity over time and, given an expanding research economy, their research expenditures as well.

At the same time, universities have a largely fixed amount of teaching output that cannot be easily reduced. Moreover, any public questioning of teaching quality would be severely punished in the student marketplace. Thus, the secular expansion of research does not take place by substitution, but rather by the expansion of value in both research and teaching, hence Nerlove's (1972) assertion that more research makes undergraduate education more expensive, and that this is socially desirable. That something like this has actually occurred is shown in table 1.1.

Over two decades, the increase in tenure-eligible faculty at both public and private research universities was roughly proportional to the increase in enrollments. At the same time, growth in the amount of research performed—and the amount of research per faculty member—was far greater. We can probably infer that more faculty were engaged in sponsored research, and that active researchers had become even more so. However, non-research spending of general funds increased as well—more than research at private universities and less than research at public ones. In value-adjusted units, therefore, teaching inputs increased too.

The dynamics behind these developments are evident for private research universities. These two decades brought extraordinary prosperity for these institutions, based largely on increasing tuition revenues and generous alumni support. In other words, the goose laying the golden eggs was the undergraduate college. Excellence in research burnished prestige, which helped to enhance the attractiveness of these institutions, but volume of research was less critical. Universities thus spent their growing revenues on both education and research quality, but research expenditures rose less than the national university research economy. These universities ceded 1 percent of their research share in nonmedical fields every five years from 1980 to 2000 (Geiger 2004).[1] Given their growing prosperity, one can only assume that they considered their research output to be optimal even though it was growing more slowly than national totals.

The Intensification of Research

Academic trends may be slow to develop and long to persist, but one can sometimes perceive a tipping point where certain ideas begin to dominate the thinking of universities and their actions. Such a point occurred around the turn of the twenty-first century when a consensus emerged inside and outside of higher education around the belief that the contribution of university research to economic development was crucial to the global competitiveness of the U.S. economy.[2] This particular movement coalesced with several other existing trends in ways that are barely separable: interdisciplinarity, the proliferation of research institutes, and what might be called "raising the bar" in faculty hiring.

These trends have been backed by forces that universities can scarcely resist. The science agencies of the federal government, led by the National Science Foundation (NSF), have tied major programs and center grants to collaboration with industry and translational research intended to yield inventions and innovations. Nearly every state government has created programs with multiple forms of support for technology-based economic development (TBED), and probably half of these provide explicit support for relevant forms of university research. Finally, in the knowledge base itself, science-based technologies, like the multiple strands of biotechnology and nanotechnology, not only promise fruitful inventions arising from basic research but also represent the cutting edge of scientific discovery. Together, this constellation of factors has been driving greater orientation toward research, at the margin, in faculty hiring and faculty work (Geiger and Sá 2008).[3]

Economic Development

Federal research policies aimed at stimulating economic development have the same impact on universities as federally sponsored research. That is, they exert a powerful influence indirectly by shaping university behavior. Many state policies affect universities directly by supporting additional faculty or funding units intended to collaborate with local industries, foster innovation, and generate spin-off companies. Faculty members hired under such programs are expected to concentrate primarily on their research roles.

One admired initiative is the Eminent Scholars Program of the Georgia Research Alliance. It provides matching funds to create and endow professorships in economically relevant fields at the state's principal universities. The matching funds are usually given by corporations, so that a working relationship with industry is assured from the outset. Similar state programs for hiring faculty in strategic fields now operate in South Carolina and New York.

Other state initiatives have provided support for the creation of large research institutes at universities in economically relevant areas. New York has several such programs, but its largest commitment has been to nanotechnology at the University of Albany. Arizona, in implementing its Biosciences Roadmap, has provided extra funds that were used for the huge new Biodesign Institute at Arizona State and additional institutes at the University of Arizona. Another economically inspired initiative is the Georgia Electronic Design Center at Georgia Tech. Originally intended to support new professors who would undergird the broadband industry in the state, it is now a large collaborative research unit with at least thirty participating faculty. California in 2000 launched the four large California Institutes for Science and Innovation spanning the UC system. Michigan's policies inspired the Life Sciences Institute at the University of Michigan, which hires faculty members in various departments with half-time research appointments in the Institute. All of these and similar units recruit regular faculty for substantial research commitments and usually provide partial support for salary and start-up costs. Teaching responsibilities no doubt vary, if they teach at all, but their primary responsibility is certainly research.

Interdisciplinarity

The mixing of disciplinary expertise has long been in fashion for both teaching and research. However, when curriculum committees recommend socioeconomic-ethical-ecological perspectives for undergraduate courses, they generally turn to campus idealists to staff these creations. For research, multidisciplinary approaches are mandated by NSF for certain types of grants or are inherently necessary for some investigations, especially in science-based technologies. Thus, when interdisciplinarity becomes an explicit factor in hiring faculty, the critical criterion becomes research.

For universities eager to become more interdisciplinary, superseding departmental control over faculty hiring has been a challenge. This generally requires that the central administration provide additional resources to support the kinds of positions it wishes to create. These positions are defined in terms of the research expected by the new hires. Two specific strategies for doing this have been described: cluster hiring and hiring mediated through institutes (Sá 2008).

The University of Wisconsin may have been the first to undertake a cluster hiring initiative in 1999. It asked the faculty to define interdisciplinary clusters, and those approved were then funded by the provost. This fairly crude approach allowed for little strategic direction and left open questions about subsequent administrative control. Florida State University initiated a similar program in 2005. At UC Berkeley, numerous rounds of negotiations eventually defined four interdisciplinary areas for additional appointments. This was a laborious process, however, with meager results. Rensselaer Polytechnic Institute has implemented an ambitious strategy for building faculty "constellations" in biotechnology and information technology.

Penn State began in the 1990s to coordinate interdisciplinary hiring through several overarching institutes. With the central administration promising half the support, departments were invited to define faculty positions that would engage in cross-disciplinary research through the institutes. After five years, if interdisciplinary research was no longer being pursued, the university would withdraw its support. More recently, the university has undertaken a major initiative in energy research. Using this basic approach, and with some state support, the Energy Institute has committed to fill twelve new positions in fuel sciences. Although new curriculum is proposed as well, these faculty members will be doing far more research than teaching.

Research Institutes

Much has already been said about the role of research institutes. They have existed since the Harvard Observatory was opened in 1847. When I last wrote about them almost two decades ago, they continued to suffer from two major problems: the inability to influence departmental hiring and thus to perpetuate their own special competencies as personnel changed, and the equivocal status of full-time researchers, sometimes called the "unfaculty." These conditions have changed. Contemporary universities for the most part do not wish to make nonfaculty research appointments, but prefer positions with full faculty status. And, as just seen, institutes now are sometimes given an active role in hiring. These procedural changes are only part of a larger structural transformation.

First, there has been a proliferation of university centers and institutes. Not only are they growing in number, but they are spreading to all academic fields. The humanities, always fearful of neglect, well illustrate this trend. In 1992, universities registered fifty-three centers or institutes devoted to the humanities. These units, moreover, were recipients of a steady stream of major gifts. In 2008, there were 121 such centers. By any reckoning, opportunities for faculty research and scholarship had expanded impressively (Consortium of Humanities Centers and Institutes 2008; D'Arms 1997).

The essential function of centers and institutes is to facilitate research in a defined area and to serve as conduit for external relationships. Often ongoing projects are conducted by a director and core faculty. But institutes also provide resources for a wider group of faculty (and often visiting faculty from other institutions). They offer services for the preparation and administration of grants, sometimes seed money for developing proposals, and opportunities to participate in large institute grants. Moreover, institutes play a crucial role in supporting graduate students. Faculty members having access to institutes are more readily able to buy out teaching time with sponsored research. Major research universities now possess centers and institutes that provide nearly all of their faculty members with access to research units.

Thus, the second change has been an evolution away from the dichotomy of core departments and peripheral institutes and toward greater integration in a matrix type of organization. Increasingly, faculty define themselves by full membership in one academic department, joint appointments to other departments, and affiliation with one or more research units. Large medical schools have long operated on this basis (Mallon and Bunton 2005). As universities evolve toward greater research outputs, they too have evolved toward a matrix organization. In addition, universities contain a variety of units that provide other types of services. These units represent another nonteaching dimension of the faculty role—one especially prominent in professional schools but not absent in the arts and sciences. In fact, it is somewhat misleading to classify these activities as teaching, research, or service, since these activities are often inherently intermingled. What they are not, however, is the traditional model of teaching college students in a classroom.

Raising the Bar

The difficulty of new PhDs obtaining academic appointments is widely recognized. The other side of this coin has been less noticed—the fact that those who are appointed to tenure-track positions today are likely to possess extensive research experience and accomplishments. This pattern is best documented in the natural sciences, where postdoctoral appointments have become standard. Existing data on postdocs tell little about their subsequent employment.[4] For a current snapshot, I performed a microinvestigation. At Pennsylvania State University, information was available for thirty assistant professors in biology, chemistry, and physics appointed in the College of Science from 2001 to 2006.[5] On average, they had spent four years and ten months as postdocs—about the same amount of time most of them spent earning a PhD. A generation ago, a new assistant professor fresh from graduate school would have this much time to prepare for the sixth-year tenure review. Teaching experience was virtually absent from the postgraduate experience of these scientists. Including their PhD research, they had been engaged in full-time research for the previous nine to ten years. Well prepared, to say the least, they were unlikely to be distracted from pursuing further research. In fact, newly hired assistant professors are given extensive support, including relief from teaching, to establish their research—and this is generally true for fields outside the sciences as well.

The clogged labor market for university faculty has had the effect of raising the bar for qualifications, and it also raised the bar for subsequent promotion to tenure (Burgan 2006). This upgrading of faculty research accomplishments was evident in the rise in departmental quality ratings from the 1982 to the 1995 *Assessments* (Geiger 2004). This is a positive development from the perspective of American science, although the negative side effects have been cause for complaints. Proposal pressure at federal science agencies has reached troubling levels. And the unattractiveness of careers in science may be one reason why fewer than half of the thirty scientists hired at Penn State were native-born citizens.

The four factors identified here as furthering the intensification of research are ultimately part of a larger transformation taking place. Universities are basically increasing their outputs of research, with strong encouragement from American society, and looking to their faculty for greater productivity. The optimal output level for research has clearly risen, but how has that affected the output of teaching?

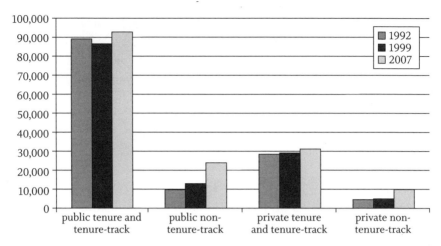

Figure 1.1. Number of full-time faculty, research universities

Restructuring Teaching Roles

A former provost once observed, "if you want to increase research, hire more regular faculty; if you want to increase teaching, hire fixed-term teachers." In fact, this is what universities have been doing—appointing full-time, non-tenure-track (FTNTT) faculty, whether to compensate for the teaching deficit as regular faculty devote greater effort to research, to preserve flexibility, or to limit faculty payrolls (fig. 1.1).

Figure 1.1 shows the proportion of FTNTT faculty rising to 24.4 percent at private universities and 20.5 percent at public ones.[6] In both sectors, what had been a minor trend in the 1990s accelerated after 2000. Since that date, twice as many additional full-time positions were off the tenure track as were on it (6,000 vs. 11,000 at public universities; 2,000 vs. 5,000 at private universities). Since FTNTT instructors have been hired solely to teach, they each account for two to three times as many credit hours on average as regular faculty members. Collectively, they teach a substantially higher proportion of student credit hours than numbers alone would indicate (see below). This bifurcation of the faculty raises numerous issues—on both sides of the divide.

The job of tenure-track university professor is unique in the amount of continual investment made by employers in the human capital, or intellectual growth, of the employee. These investments include a generous amount of time expected to be allocated for scholarship and research, about 40 percent of the year entirely free from assigned work, paid leaves for intellectual development, and the supporting infrastructure of libraries, laboratories, and information/communication technology. The quid pro quo, of course, is that these resources will be employed to develop a very high level of expertise in a specialized field, to utilize that expertise to advance the field through research and publications, and sometimes to share that knowledge through service—in addition to teaching. Individuals who meet these criteria are rewarded with tenure, and the university continues to invest in their knowledge growth until retirement.

As the faculty role becomes more research intensive, structural changes become increasingly evident. Two strategies are apparent: staffing redundancy and reliance on FTNTT instructors (sometimes called instructional or contingent faculty).

Departments heavily engaged in sponsored research have long resorted to staffing redundancy by employing many more faculty members than are strictly needed to teach their courses. Of the trends reported above, economic development and interdisciplinarity essentially reinforce this pattern, while research institutes and raising the bar tend to extend it to more departments. Without redundancy it would be difficult to accommodate buyouts, leaves, and other reductions in teaching loads.

Departments in which sponsored research creates fewer buyouts—humanities, social sciences, and business—have developed other coping strategies. They face a critical problem in the considerable cognitive distance that exists between faculty scholarship and undergraduate learning needs. Mathematics has long recruited adjunct teachers to staff multiple introductory sections, as have English and foreign language departments to handle first-year language/writing courses. Now the same kind of problem is faced by prestigious economics departments, for example, which prefer to have professors focus on economic theory; or business schools, where esoteric faculty research bears little relation to the basic courses needed by a multitude of undergraduate majors. In such situations, departments have increasingly resorted to full-time, fixed-term faculty to fill the gap. In this way, these departments are able to utilize tenure-track faculty to teach advanced seminars, conduct research, and publish in leading journals, while still meeting student demand for basic courses.

A good deal has been written in recent years about part-time or contingent faculty. Part-time teachers are employed for a variety of reasons, both good and bad (Gappa and Leslie 1993). Freshman math and language courses have already been mentioned. Sometimes, part-timers are used as short-term stop-gaps to cover necessary courses (my windfall grant). All too often, they are employed to reduce costs.[7] In many fields, they bring diverse perspectives and real-world experience. With a partial exception for this last situation, employing large numbers of part-timers generally is believed to have adverse consequences for student learning. Anyone familiar with running a department would no doubt agree that the variability in teaching effectiveness for part-timers is greater than for regular faculty.

FTNTT faculty present a different case. They too have received some scholarly attention. However, the picture depicted by these studies is complicated by the different types of and reasons for these appointments (Baldwin and Chronister 2001; Gappa 1996; Gappa, Austin, and Trice 2007). Six different situations have been identified:

- Senior lecturers: appointed for a limited duration to bring particular expertise to the curriculum.
- Clinical faculty: usually combine clinical teaching and service in applied settings.
- Professors of practice: appointed on the basis of their experience in the field.
- Under-credentialed faculty: appointed as instructors in fields like computer science where PhDs may be in short supply for tenure-track appointments.
- Short-term fully credentialed teachers: wealthy private universities appoint recent PhDs to temporary teaching positions when no additional tenure lines are available in distinguished, tenured-up departments.
- Fully credentialed fixed-term teachers: appointed with single- or multiyear contracts to provide flexibility and possibly cost savings by fulfilling demand for undergraduate or lower-division courses.

Good reasons can be offered for the first five of the six types of appointment, based on the special needs of professional programs, the experience such appointments can bring to the classroom, or necessity. However, the last type, labeled the "the marginalized model," raises concerns. The American Association of University Professors (1996) has been particularly critical: "Nontenure-track appointments do considerable damage both to principles of academic freedom and tenure and to the quality of our academic institutions—not to mention the adverse consequences for the individuals serving in such appointments" (as cited in Trower 2000, 116).

Nevertheless, in some cases these appointments can be justified as well. If they consolidate part-time positions, they should actually improve instruction. Where individuals understand that they will be expected to concentrate their efforts on instructing students, they may be fully devoted to the task, presumably enjoy undergraduate teaching, and might be more effective teachers. Perhaps the strongest argument is that lecturing to several hundred students takes special skills that these instructors master with time. At least, that is the hope. Still, the longer-term drawbacks to this type of appointment would seem to outweigh any short-term benefits.

Numerous studies have shown that student engagement with faculty members has positive effects on student learning and outcomes (Pascarella and Terenzini 2005). Adjunct and part-time faculty might be expected to be less engaged with students, and hence less effective in promoting student learning. Attempts to determine the effects of contingent faculty have largely focused on part-time teachers. Increased use of part-time teachers was associated with reduced rates of completing associate degrees in one study and reduced rates of subject continuation in another (Bettinger and Long 2004; Jacoby 2006). The only study to estimate the effects of FTNTT faculty found more negative effects on graduation rates than for part-time teachers (Ehrenberg and Zhang 2005). The reported effects are small, and confounding variables large, but existing studies all point in the same negative direction.

Traditional practice would seem to argue that on balance arts and sciences courses, even lower-division ones, are better taught by tenure-track faculty who are active in research and scholarship. In the nineteenth century, educational leaders such as Charles W. Eliot could speak with great confidence of the inherent differences between education in the practical and the liberal arts. This distinction can only be made with greater qualification in the twenty-first century. However, the practical arts require that students acquire a good deal of codified knowledge in introductory courses. Probably this type of knowledge can be conveyed adequately by teachers without research qualifications or, for that matter, online. While basic knowledge in the liberal arts disciplines has been codified to some extent, one could argue that these subjects ought to be taught with some degree of depth and nuance, which requires teachers who have a deep knowledge of their subject acquired through active scholarship.

These adverse effects on student learning should not be viewed in isolation. There could be offsetting effects that would have positive influences on learning, like additional teachers to provide smaller classes or a richer advanced curriculum offered by regular faculty. Furthermore, it can be argued that FTNTT teachers should improve student learning if they replace part-time faculty, as seems to be the case (see below). It is possible that FTNTT faculty are more dedicated teachers and thus preferable to scholars who may resent teaching basic subjects, perform lackadaisically, or rely excessively on teaching assistants. However, a different set of considerations pertains to the effects on the faculty and the institution.

Generally, universities do not invest in the intellectual growth of FTNTT faculty. Departments may assist them to attend professional conferences, but the substantial allocation of time for research and graduate research assistants is lacking. Faculty fresh from graduate school may still be familiar with the frontiers of disciplinary knowledge, but longer term the different slate of activities makes it increasingly difficult for them to stay abreast. In most cases, FTNTT teachers are hired to be generalists, to teach more general lower-division courses, precisely the role that specialized regular faculty disdain. Thus, those who are hopeful of eventually joining the tenure track face the attenuation of their skills over time.

The growing distance from the research frontiers is just one source of a pronounced status differential between a tenure-track and non-tenure-track faculty member. After all, the essential situation is that one has been hired to teach the least attractive courses so that the other can have more freedom for research and publication. Lack of involvement with graduate students is another status marker, one to which undergraduates have been found to be sensitive (Baldwin and Chronister 2001). Departments can and sometimes do take steps to mitigate this status differential, but it is fundamental to this situation and fundamentally unhealthy as well.

The positions given to FTNTT appointments are to some extent subtracted from the regular academic market, as implied in figure 1.1. The clogged academic job markets provide the excess manpower that makes nontenured appointments possible, but these appointments in turn reduce the number of tenure-track positions. This situation represents a profound change from the academic labor market of a generation ago, where new PhDs were hired in greater numbers and given the opportunity to compete for coveted tenured slots. Today, large numbers of aspiring academics in clogged fields never get that chance.

Why, then, is the trend toward FTNTT faculty growing? One study found the practice most prevalent at master's-level institutions, where it is probably driven by financial pressures (Ehrenberg and Zhang 2005). At research universities, a more complicated dynamic exists. The intensification of research at public universities, in particular, has been accompanied by persistent underfunding of the academic core (Geiger 2004). The result has often been a squeeze on the budgets of colleges and departments, where staffing decisions are made. Sometimes the extra funds allocated to cover teaching obligations are provided on a year-to-year basis and hence cannot be used for long-term, tenure-track commitments. Also, competitive pressures have been reducing the teaching loads of regular faculty. Under these conditions, colleges and departments have resorted to appointing FTNTT faculty in order to meet undergraduate teaching obligations. FTNTT hires appear to be the path of least resistance. However, the hiring rationale and the work of FTNTT teachers also vary across academic departments.

Restructuring the Faculty Role?

If growing staffing redundancy in some departments represents the intensification of research, the increasing hiring of FTNTT faculty represents a compensatory effort to maintain or strengthen the output of teaching. In terms of the optimization hypothesis, universities have sought to substantially increase their outputs of research, but not to detract from their instructional role. Indeed, they learned from the university and research bashing that took place, circa 1990, that they would pay a high price for any suspicion of neglect of their teaching mission. Moreover, economics (resource dependency) sends the same message, perhaps more forcefully. Public universities are now heavily dependent on tuition revenues, just like private ones (Geiger 2007). And after tuition, both public and private universities look to the goodwill and generosity of alumni. A visible substitution of research for teaching is not an option.

In the larger picture, the trends described here actually represent a substantial augmenting of instructional output (in "value-adjusted units"). The intensification of research has significant spillovers for instruction. The most important of these is the increase in the learning of the faculty through "raising the bar" and access to institutes. The appointment of "nonmarginalized" FTNTT faculty is intended—ignoring mixed motives—to enrich the curriculum with professors of practice or young academics who can profess trendy

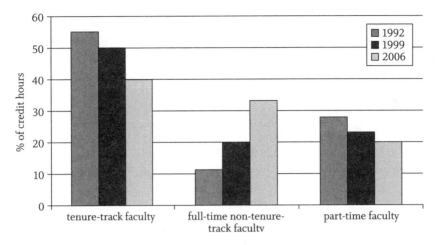

Figure 1.2. Public research university increase in instruction

topics with youthful energy. The most problematic use of FTNTT teachers—for high-enrollment, lower-division courses, or the "marginalized model"—is sometimes defended as improving instruction or shoring up areas of traditional weakness in the university curriculum. Evidence suggests that this type of FTNTT faculty is the chief cause of the current expansion.

The following data provide a closer view of this phenomenon at a representative public research university. FTNTT appointments constitute 25 percent of full-time faculty, slightly above the average for such institutions (fig. 1.1). However, this phenomenon is concentrated in a few colleges where the impact is large and growing.

Figure 1.2 shows the change in student credit hours—i.e., instruction consumed by students—by the three principal categories of instructors (some minor categories are ignored). In just fourteen years, credit hours taught by regular faculty declined from 55 percent to 40 percent. Credit hours taught by FTNTT faculty tripled from 11 percent to 33 percent. That gain reflected 15 percent of credit hours withdrawn from regular faculty and 8 percent transferred from part-time teachers. Moreover, the shift from regular to FTNTT faculty accelerated in the 1999–2006 time frame. Just three colleges accounted for two-thirds of the credit hours taught by FTNTT faculty—liberal arts, natural sciences, and business.

Liberal arts departments have long endured the brunt of responsibility for providing basic and general education courses for undergraduates. At the same time, these departments have sought to raise their academic stature by recruiting and retaining distinguished scholars. In the years covered in figure 1.2, these departments have shed about ten regular faculty positions and added 150 additional FTNTT positions, making the latter 39 percent of full-time faculty. Regular faculty have a teaching load of four courses per year, or less; FTNTT lecturers usually teach six courses, and possibly as many as eight. Since they mostly teach lecture courses, FTNTT instructors teach almost three times more students, on average. Regular faculty taught 27 percent fewer student credit hours than in 1992. Even part-time instructors (now mostly grad assistants) teach more credit hours than regular faculty (32% vs. 25%). Given the large number of sections to teach and limited budgets, liberal arts departments could not possibly cover all of their courses with regular faculty. Furthermore, a significant portion of the budget is an annual allocation that cannot be used for tenure-track commitments.

Natural science departments bear a burden of general education courses for non-science majors and also teach large introductory lecture courses. They increased the use of FTNTT instructors in the late 1990s, when 15 percent of teaching was shifted onto these teachers despite no increase in the total teaching load. Since 1999 there has been a drift in that direction (about 1% per year) but relatively little change. These departments have added almost as many regular faculty positions as those for FTNTT (twenty-four vs. thirty-two), which probably reflects staffing redundancy and the growth in external research support. FTNTT instructors are used primarily to teach lab sections and to coordinate large lectures. In at least one department, a deliberate decision was made to hire these faculty to strengthen undergraduate laboratory instruction. In other departments FTNTT instructors also teach general education courses. Scientists generally prefer to have regular faculty lecture to the introductory courses for science majors. Thus, science departments appear to have preserved a traditional faculty structure with only minor adaptations.

Business has undergone the most drastic shift to FTNTT teachers during this period. Regular faculty positions dropped by 21 and FTNTT instructors increased by 23, while total credit hours actually fell. For business departments, MBA programs are foremost for rankings and prestige, and they in turn are rated in part by the scholarly productivity (or notoriety) of the faculty. This appears to be rational behavior, as recent research has found academic publishing to be positively associated in MBA programs with increases in rankings, student selectivity, and the starting salaries of graduates (Mitra and Golden 2008). However, these conditions have induced an intense competition for productive scholars that has driven salaries sky high and workloads to rock bottom. At the same time, undergraduate majors and minors produce very large enrollments in required courses like accounting, management, and finance. These are now taught by FTNTT instructors, who teach three times as many credit hours as tenure-track colleagues.

There are similarities and significant differences in the ways these three fields have structured their full-time faculty. All have to deal with budgetary limitations, high undergraduate teaching responsibilities, and a highly competitive market for academic status. In this sense, these patterns stem from a university policy that favors focusing limited resources to achieve academic distinction. This policy, however, reflects a paradox: greater resources for teaching might trigger a loss of academic reputation that would be injurious to all concerned, including undergraduates. Students may derive greater benefit from the prestige of the institution than from the qualifications of their instructors. This would seem to be the assumption of liberal arts and business.

The decisions taken by liberal arts departments reflect the necessity of coping with a huge teaching burden while defending scholarly reputations. They have chosen a bifurcated faculty even while recognizing that the large number of FTNTT instructors will not contribute to their national stature. This is the path of least resistance, perhaps, but any other course might have diluted the faculty with little gain for undergraduate teaching.

Business departments have pursued this path more ruthlessly and under somewhat less pressure. Their goal has clearly been to build the reputation of the regular faculty, the MBA program, and the business school. They have sought to choke off the demand for undergraduate courses (declining credit hours) and to consign necessary courses to FTNTT instructors. In both business and liberal arts it would appear that research is being substituted for teaching *in value-adjusted units*. Still, the partial substitution for part-time instructors represents a compensatory enhancement of value.

Substitution has not occurred in science departments. Scientists in general have a greater concern for the quality of undergraduate education. They are natural proselytizers and elitists who naturally want to see strong students "go into science." They originally resorted to FTNTT appointments to counteract a perceived deterioration of undergraduate instruction related to the expansion of research. They regard their instructional faculty as specialists in undergraduate education and, in that respect, partners with the regular faculty. Since the scientific departments have more staffing redundancy and less budgetary pressure, their more limited use of FTNTT faculty seems to be a reasoned choice that has expanded the value-adjusted units devoted to teaching.

In one respect the use of FTNTT faculty is a grassroots phenomenon that needs to be understood at the departmental level. However, it is also a national trend. Thus, the data from this public university exemplify both aspects of this phenomenon. Most disturbing are the magnitude and speed of these developments. At bottom, the more the use of FTNTT faculty is practiced and legitimized, the more the traditional role of tenured and tenure-track faculty is likely to be undermined. Already, tenure-track faculty are a minority of the professoriate when part-time faculty are counted. But the trend is more worrisome than the sheer numbers. The intensification of research, highlighted in this chapter, is only one of the forces pushing colleges and departments to turn to FTNTT faculty.

From this perspective, the erosion of the traditional faculty role is most problematic in the humanities and social sciences. There, the persistent oversupply of PhDs has been a prerequisite for these developments. Since the collapse of liberal arts majors in the 1970s, the vitality of those subjects has been buoyed principally by the selective sectors of higher education—private research universities, liberal arts colleges, and public research universities (Geiger 2006). In fact, the strong support for the traditional faculty role by these highly regarded institutions is probably its greatest strength. Nonetheless, the dynamics may be somewhat different in the two sectors. Private institutions tend to concentrate on sustaining a prestigious core faculty in their departments, but they are also quite conservative about the number of tenured slots. They may resort to a variety of nontenured appointments to provide variety and enrichment, but safeguarding flexibility and controlling costs are also primary considerations. Low student-teacher ratios provide additional flexibility for their privileged tenure-line faculty to expand their research. Public universities have relatively high student-teacher ratios combined with greater incentives to conduct research (Brint 2007). They consequently resort out of necessity to instructional faculty to cover basic instruction in lower-division courses, with no pretense of curricular enrichment. Both these dynamics serve to erode the base of tenured faculty and increase the separation, in tasks and status, of tenured and nontenured faculty. The question for the future, given the stagnant base of tenure-track faculty, is, how close are we to a tipping point that would radically undermine the traditional faculty role? How long can the center hold?

NOTES

1. Medical research has little connection with instruction and volume counts. For many private universities, most funded research is in biomedical fields.
2. This subject is analyzed in Geiger and Sá 2008.
3. For TBED, see *SSTI Weekly Digest*.
4. For 2005, NSF reported 48,000 postdocs, five-eighths of them in biology and medicine. A National Academy of Sciences study in the 1990s found that the average length of time as a postdoc was 3.8 years for biological scientists, but that figure would undoubtedly be higher in 2008. See Richard B. Freeman et al., "Careers and Rewards in the Bio Sciences: The Disconnect between Scientific Progress and Career Advancement," MS (August 2001).
5. Profiles of new faculty are published in *Science Journal* of the Eberly College of Science. Information was available for thirty of thirty-one junior appointments in biochemistry, biology, chemistry, and physics. Mathematicians tended to have both research and nontenure teaching positions between PhD and PSU appointment; only statisticians (not included) tended to receive faculty appointments directly after receiving a PhD.
6. The values in fig. 1.1 are derived from IPEDS data. These data can be accessed in different ways, which in some cases indicate higher percentages of FTNTT faculty. The values in fig. 1.1 were derived in ways to ensure comparability from 1992 to 2007.
7. Zhang and Ehrenberg 2006 have estimated an average salary differential of over $14,000 between tenure-track and non-tenure-track faculty in 2006.

REFERENCES

American Association of University Professors. 1996. *Policy documents and reports.* 8th ed. Washington, DC: AAUP.
Baldwin, Roger G., and Jay L. Chronister. 2001. *Teaching without tenure: Policies and practices for a new era.* Baltimore: Johns Hopkins University Press.
Bettinger, Eric, and Bridget Terry Long. 2004. Do college instructors matter? The effects of adjuncts and graduate assistants on students' interests and success. NBER Working Paper 10370.
Birnbaum, Robert. 1988. *How colleges work.* San Francisco: Jossey-Bass.
Brint, Steven. 2007. Can public universities compete? In *Future of American public research university*, ed. R. L. Geiger et al., 91–118. Rotterdam: Sense Publishers.

Burgan, Mary. 2006. *What ever happened to the faculty? Drift and decision in higher education.* Baltimore: Johns Hopkins University Press.

Clark, Burton R. 1983. *The higher education system: Academic organization in cross-national perspective.* Berkeley: University of California Press.

Consortium of Humanities Centers and Institutes. 2008. CHCI Member Directory: www.chcinetwork.org/chcisearch-home.html (accessed April 29, 2008).

D'Arms, John H. 1997. Funding trends in the academic humanities: Reflections on the stability of the system. In *What's happened to the humanities?* ed. Alvin Kernan, 32–60. Princeton: Princeton University Press.

Ehrenberg, Ronald G., and Liang Zhang. 2005. Do tenured and tenure-track faculty matter? *Journal of Human Resources* 40:647–59.

Gappa, Judith M. 1996. Off the tenure track. AAHE Working Paper Inquiry #10. Washington, DC: AAHE.

Gappa, Judith M., Ann E. Austin, and Andrea G. Trice. 2007. *Rethinking faculty work.* San Francisco: Jossey-Bass.

Gappa, Judith M., and David W. Leslie. 1993. *Improving the status of part-timers in higher education.* San Francisco: Jossey-Bass.

Garvin, David A. 1980. *The economics of university behavior.* New York: Academic Press.

Geiger, Roger L. 2004. *Knowledge and money: Research universities and the paradox of the marketplace.* Stanford: Stanford University Press.

———. 2006. Demography and curriculum: The humanities in American higher education from the1950s through the 1980s. In *The humanities and the dynamics of inclusion since World War II*, ed. David A. Hollinger, 50–72. Baltimore: Johns Hopkins University Press.

———. 2007. Expert and elite: The incongruous mission of public research universities. In *Future of the American public research universities*, ed. R. L. Geiger et al., 15–34. Rotterdam: Sense Publishers.

Geiger, Roger L., and Creso Sá. 2008. *Tapping the riches of science: American universities and the promise of economic growth.* Cambridge, MA: Harvard University Press.

Jacoby, Daniel. 2006. Effects of part-time faculty employment on community college graduation rates. *Journal of Higher Education* 77 (6): 1081–1103.

Mallon, William, and Sarah Bunton. 2005. Research centers and institutes in U.S. medical schools: A descriptive analysis. *Academic Medicine* 80 (11): 1005–11.

Mitra, Debanjan, and Peter N. Golden. 2008. Does academic research help or hurt MBA programs? *Journal of Marketing* 72 (September): 31–49.

Nerlove, Marc. 1972. On tuition and the costs of higher education: Prolegomena to a conceptual framework. *Journal of Political Economy* 80 (May-June): S178–S218.

Pascarella, Ernest T., and Patrick T. Terenzini. 2005. *How college affects students.* San Francisco: Jossey-Bass.

Sá, Creso. 2008. Strategic faculty hiring in two public research universities: Pursuing interdisciplinary connections. *Tertiary Education and Management* 14 (4): 285–301.

Trower, Cathy A., ed. 2000. *Policies on faculty appointment.* Bolton, MA: Anker.

Zhang, Liang, and Ronald G. Ehrenberg. 2006. Faculty employment and R&D expenditures at research universities. MS, November 12. CHERI.

CHAPTER TWO

Focus on the Classroom

*Movements to Reform College Teaching
and Learning, 1980–2008*

Steven Brint

O ver the last quarter century, two movements have arisen to encourage a reorientation of the academic profession in the direction of a focus on teaching, rather than research. One has been promoted most actively by foundation-sponsored advocacy organizations, and the other by the federal government and the states. Both of these movements have questioned the priorities of institutions and the preparation and effectiveness of college teachers. They have promoted the idea that college teachers can do a much better job of producing and assessing student learning. The causes of this renewed focus on the classroom are quite similar to those that provoked rethinking of classroom teaching in secondary schools at the turn of the twentieth century: the construction of a mass system, fueled by the incorporation of working-class and immigrant students, in which a majority of students have limited intrinsic interest in learning and in which chronically underfunded schools have limited resources to create powerful learning communities. Expansion, combined with continuing fiscal pressures in the public sector, encouraged concerns about the effectiveness of college teaching, while diversification led to concerns about the possibility of unequal results for women, minorities, and immigrants. While sharing a critical stance toward the current condition of teaching and learning in the academy, the two movements otherwise shared little in common: the one led by liberal philanthropies worked on the improvement of teaching skills, while the state-based movement focused on constructing hard evidence of student learning outcomes.

Higher education policy analyst Peter T. Ewell described the character of the two movements as they emerged in the mid-1980s:

Two antithetical "ideologies" . . . arose almost simultaneously in higher education discourse. The first came from inside the academy. . . . Its tenets were most clearly stated in an influential national report, *Involvement in Learning* [1984] . . . which argued that breakthrough improvements in undergraduate education could be achieved by establishing high expectations, deploying active and engaging pedagogies, and providing feedback about performance. . . . The second ideology had roots outside the academy based on strong state interest in pursuing [testing-based] educational reform. . . . Its tenets were embodied in a high visibility report by the National Governors Association, *A Time for Results* [1986]. . . . The report argued that colleges and universities should be held accountable for establishing clear standards for performance with respect to student learning and that the results of student assessments should be publicly reported and coupled with consequential actions. (2005, 107)

This chapter shows how the two movements grew out of structural weaknesses in the organization of the academic profession following a period of massive demographic expansion and increased demand on scarce public resources. In the chapter I trace the ideas and projects of the two movements. I also describe the tensions between the major actors in the two worlds of reform—and the commitment of some foundations to work in both worlds. I will emphasize three primary analytical points. The first is simply that large boundary-spanning organizations, always important influences on the research topics of professors, are now working in a serious way to shape the classroom environment. Conventional views about the autonomy of teaching professionals in the organization of classroom life therefore require revision. The second is that variations in favored forms of organization among the competing actors have deeply influenced their ideals, their practices, and their relative levels of success. On one hand, the network-organized, discipline-based, and voluntaristic character of academe has shaped the preferences of the main actors in the teaching reform movement. On the other, the social control interests and metric-driven character of state government have shaped the preferences of the main actors in the outcomes assessment movement. The third is that the strongest force in the environment—stronger thus far than either wealthy philanthropies or powerful state educational bureaucracies—has been the system of mutually reinforcing interests among students, faculty, and administrators that reproduces low achievement standards in many college classrooms. This system of interests has limited the successes of both movements.

Although the final outcome of the clashes between the two philosophies of reform is as yet unknown, it is clear that one strand of the teaching reform movement gained considerable ground during the period under study. Networks of teaching practitioners have succeeded in disseminating selected principles of what I will call the "new progressivism"—specifically, those principles promoting active learning, civic engagement, and sensitivity to the interests of diverse learners. By contrast, and perhaps surprisingly, the outcomes assessment movement has failed to transform practice, as a result of frequent changes in policy, linked to partisan upheavals, and the capacity of higher education associations and regional accrediting bodies to effectively blunt state preferences for the implementation of standardized performance metrics. Particular disciplines—notably, engineering—have, however, been more completely transformed, as a result of the adoption by professional accrediting agencies of the goals and means of the outcomes assessment movement. The policies adopted by engineering educators could plausibly serve as models for the future.

The primary conclusion of the chapter is that, in spite of tremendous effort over a generation by philanthropies and states, the effectiveness of teaching in American colleges and universities has not changed greatly. What has changed is the rise of progressive education practices. These practices have encouraged greater student engagement, but have shown no strong effects on learning. Indeed, progressive education practices align well with the priorities of student culture, which has been interested in enjoyable activities, but not as interested in demanding requirements and high standards that would help to increase skill development and learning. Another important consequence has been the increased legitimacy attached to the teaching function. This outcome, I will argue, has helped to diminish the status and perhaps also the net social contribution of the profession.

The Contradictions of Postwar Academe

In 1895, William Rainey Harper, of the University of Chicago, was the first American university president to tell newly hired professors that they would be evaluated primarily on the basis of their research contribution. Thus began, in fits and starts, the era of the research-based academic profession. The emphasis on research intensified in the years following World War II and spread beyond the science and technology fields. By the mid-1960s, the trend toward populating academe with professional researchers was so noticeable that David Riesman and Christopher Jencks coined the term "the academic revolution" to mark what they assumed would be a permanent turning point in the shift of the profession from teaching to research (1968).[1] For research university professors, the requirement to meet the exacting standards of colleagues evaluating articles and books warranted careful training; half-awake, half-interested undergraduates sitting in the back rows of large lecture halls were another matter. In graduate training programs of the period, students were not required to demonstrate skills in pedagogy during their studies for the PhD, nor understanding of the relation between types of pedagogy and subject matter content, nor understanding of the aims or purposes of education. Rather, those who were not fortunate or promising enough to obtain research assistantships were thrown into graduate student-run discussion sections to sink or swim. For most would-be professors, teaching was an amateur activity, performed with limited regard to effectiveness, by people whose real training was for something else entirely.

Many observers within the university welcomed this era of the research-centered professoriate. For Clark Kerr, the new multiversity served the nation by providing greater access, technological progress, and expert advice to every constituency in its state and region. But, Kerr acknowledged, undergraduate teaching suffered: "There seems to be a 'point of no return' after which research, consulting, [and] graduate instruction become so absorbing that faculty efforts can no longer be concentrated on undergraduate instruction as they once were" (1963, 65). Kerr provided no solution to the "cruel paradox that a superior faculty results in an inferior concern for undergraduate teaching," although he hoped that an escape from the paradox could eventually be found (ibid.). More astringent critics, like Jacques Barzun, pointed out the injustice of shortchanging undergraduate students:

> (T)he student . . . is conscious . . . (that his teachers) subject him to cavalier treatment . . . unpunctual, slipshod in marking papers, ill-prepared in lecture, careless about assignments. . . . To put it another way, the student sees and resents the fact that teaching is no longer the central concern of the university. . . . After making all due exceptions (for there are still thousands of devoted teachers and vigilant college heads), the students' complaint is justified.

> The great shift to research after 1945 would alone modify the university atmosphere sufficiently to warrant the impression of neglect, supported as it is by the reality of "publish or perish." (1968, 69)

Although Barzun and others (see, e.g., Schaar and Wolin 1965) expected a student uprising against desultory and negligent undergraduate teaching, these hopes were quickly disappointed. Instead, an ethic of consumerism emerged. In part, this ethic reflected the growth of mass higher education, which brought many more ill-prepared and nonacademically oriented students to campus. The average number of hours spent in class and studying per week dropped from about forty to about twenty-seven in the years between 1961 and 2004. Declines were evident in all institutions, all disciplines, and among all demographic groups (Babcock and Marks, 2010). Moreover, students now had the power, in the form of student evaluations, to register their desires effectively. First introduced in the 1920s, the use of student evaluations of teaching became widespread in the 1970s (Riesman 1980). At large state universities, these forms became the primary method for evaluating performance in the classroom, and they eventually served to encourage faculty to pay attention to the preferences of student consumers for a more entertaining delivery, greater clarity in the structure of lectures, and faculty expressions of kindness and respect. These were improvements over the teaching norms of earlier eras, but student evaluations also encouraged many professors to lower their expectations of student work in the hope of retaining high scores or in response to a declining academic ethos among students (Johnson 2003; Riesman 1980, 249–55).

The contradictions of academic careers were also encouraging renewed attention to teaching among those left out of the "academic revolution."[2] In *The Academic Marketplace*, Theodore Caplow and Reece McGee noted, "For most members of the profession, the real strain in the academic role arises from the fact that they are, in essence, paid to do one job, whereas the worth of their services is evaluated on the basis of how well they do another" (1958, 82). This theme gradually became standard among social scientists writing about higher education (see, e.g., Clark 1987; Ladd, 1979).

In a 1989 national survey of faculty, more than 40 percent of professors strongly agreed that it was difficult to achieve tenure without publishing, up from one-fifth in 1969—and many were not happy about it (Miller et al. 1990). Large majorities at master's- and baccalaureate-granting institutions said that teaching effectiveness should be the primary criterion in promotion. Nearly as high a proportion of faculty members teaching at smaller doctorate-granting institutions expressed similar sentiments. Only a minority of faculty—those teaching at research universities—could be expected to be rewarded in the labor market for their publications. Others were being required to publish, but with course loads that limited their capacity to do so. Moreover, research funds were not expanding at the same rate as institutional demands for publication. The upshot was that many professors were oriented to teaching and thought they should be granted as much respect as researchers.[3] The academic procession led by the Harvards and Berkeleys was breaking up along institutionally defined lines—dividing those institutions emphasizing research from those emphasizing teaching.

The national context of higher education policy also brought issues concerning the quality of college teaching to the forefront. During the 1980s, the sense that colleges were connected to great national purposes wavered. Policy makers, influenced by the "free market" conservative wing of the Republican Party, began to see higher education as a private consumption good. As demand for credentials grew, some also began to express concerns about educational quality. Some policy makers saw the universities as responding to ill-prepared students with less challenging courses. In many states, political differences between conservative politicians and liberal academics fueled suspicion about the aims and purposes of higher education (Geiger 2004, chap. 2; McLendon, Hearn, and Deaton 2006). In this cauldron of professorial discontent, student consumerism, and Republican Party skepticism, educational quality emerged as a cutting-edge issue.

Teaching Reform Movements

The principal agents of *teaching reform movements* have been foundations and foundation-sponsored advocacy organizations, such as the Association of American Colleges and Universities (AAC&U) and Carnegie Foundation for the Advancement of Teaching (CFAT). These institutions picked up and advanced pedagogical principles in the work of leading educational thinkers of the period. The approach developed by these thinkers, which I will call the "new progressivism," advocated active learning experiences, commitments to diversity and civic engagement, *and* challenging academic standards. However, educators' calls for heightened academic standards proved to be no match for the consumerist ethos and utilitarianism of college student life. The trajectory of the new progressivism consequently mirrored the pattern of K–12 progressive education in the early twentieth century, when followers of John Dewey, such as William Heard Kilpatrick, de-emphasized Dewey's insistence on rigor and frequent assessment and highlighted the student-centered, active learning, community engagement themes in his work (Cremin 1961).

Teaching Guides

The popularity of guides to good teaching can be seen as one early indicator of change. The National Institute of Education's influential *Involvement in Learning* (1984) signaled both the growing importance of effective teaching and the challenges facing faculty in a system of mass higher education. This document, heavily influenced by the thinking of UCLA higher education professor Alexander W. Astin, advocated movement away from the standard lecture format, so that students could become inquirers—producers, as well as consumers, of knowledge. Following the lead of progressive educators, the report recommended the introduction of "active modes of learning," such as group research projects and classes held in the field, internships and other forms of carefully monitored experiential learning, small discussion groups, in-class presentations and debates, and individual learning projects and supervised independent study. It also advocated timely feedback and more rigorous standards for evaluating student performance (National Institute of Education 1984, 27–28).

Arthur W. Chickering and Zelda Gamson's "Seven Principles for Good Practice in Undergraduate Teaching" represented a similar cast of mind. Their easy-to-remember principles became a touchstone for reformers and formed a basis for subsequent national surveys of student engagement. In a pithy opening sentence, Chickering and Gamson defined the maladies of colleges and universities in an age of mass higher education: "Apathetic students, illiterate graduates, incompetent teaching, impersonal campuses—so rolls the drumfire of criticism" (1987). The seven principles offered something for both progressives (frequent faculty-student contact, collaborative and active learning experiences, and respect for the variety of students' talents and ways of learning) and traditionalists (focus on time spent on task, prompt feedback, and high expectations for performance).

A New Ideology Emerges

Ideologies provide blueprints for action, and by the end of the 1980s organizational changes had created the conditions for an ideological shift—from the research-centered hierarchy of the "academic revolution" to something new reflecting the variety of institutional missions found in U.S. higher education. That new ideology was formulated in Ernest L. Boyer's *Scholarship Reconsidered* (1990). As president of the Carnegie Foundation, Boyer was well positioned to affect the changes in institutional practices he proposed.

Boyer's explicit aim was to install a confederation of interests in the place of academic hierarchy. To do so, he identified four legitimate forms of academic life: the scholarships of discovery, integration, application, and teaching. The use of the venerable term "scholarship" united academe under the idea of studiousness and learning, rather than research and teaching. Indeed, Boyer explicitly hoped to end debates about the relative value of research and teaching. "The most important obligation now confronting the nation's colleges and universities," he wrote, "is to break out of the tired old teaching versus research debate and define, in more creative ways, what it means to be a scholar. It's time [for the profession] to recognize the full range of faculty talent and the great diversity of functions higher education must perform" (1990, xii).[4]

The critical innovation in Boyer's work was the integration of teachers as equal partners in the confederation of scholars. Before Boyer, one rarely thought of teaching as scholarship, only as reflecting knowledge of scholarship. Although the term "scholarship" suggests the possibility of professionalizing the teaching function, for Boyer it remained the province of the inspired amateur, albeit one who thinks deeply about subject matter and reflects often on the effectiveness of his or her practice. Yet the very naming of teaching as a form of scholarship encouraged steps in the direction Boyer himself initially failed to anticipate. More than that, Boyer's essay was a "game-changing" document—the point at which the teaching plebs rose up to challenge the aristocracy of researchers in the name of pluralistic academic democracy. Boyer's book was an academic best seller—the Carnegie Foundation had trouble keeping the book in stock—and Boyer and his colleagues were invited to dozens of campuses and high-profile conferences to discuss the new paradigm he proposed (Glassick, Huber, and Maeroff 1997).

The Rise of Teaching and Learning Centers

Some of the organizational groundwork for teaching reform had already been laid during the period of postwar expansion. The first center for teaching and learning opened at the University of Michigan in 1962, inspired by the work of English and linguistics professors who offered instruction to graduate students on teaching. The faculty senate committee that recommended the establishment of the center observed that opportunities for improving instruction were more important on research university campuses than elsewhere in academe, because most professors were oriented to graduate training and publication.[5]

The form taken by the Michigan center shows many of the characteristics of subsequent faculty-sponsored approaches to improving instruction. It remained voluntary, discipline-based, modular in organization, and reliant on networks of motivated professors to transmit interest and ideas. Michigan resisted "the idea that [faculty and graduate students] are going to be under surveillance" and considered the teaching and learning center's main purpose to be "engendering conversation" (M. Kaplan, personal communication). In 1978, the center began offering orientations to new teaching assistants, and the great majority of teaching assistants at Michigan now receive some common experiences, including discussion of the first days of class; discussion of classroom communication, including teaching in multicultural classrooms; and feedback from analysis of short bits of videotaping. The activities of the center, like those on other campuses, reflected the organization and ethos of academe: the disciplines were preeminent; professors decided how to allocate their time outside of class; and personal interest, rather than university prescription, fueled the enterprise. These strengths of academe, which provide maximum freedom and flexibility for professors to choose their own intellectual and professional paths, were consistent with improved basic training for graduate teaching assistants but arguably led to only a relatively shallow penetration of good practices in the classroom.

By the late 1970s, dozens of universities had opened teaching centers. The Professional and Organizational Development (POD) Network formed in 1975 to provide a professional association for "instructional developers." The largest of the teaching centers, such as those at Ann Arbor, Berkeley, and Austin, provided training to seven to eight hundred new teaching assistants every year. Berkeley required a day-long teaching conference, including five modular online courses related to pedagogical strategies, ethics, and the educational opportunities and challenges presented by diverse classrooms. In addition, every department offered a seminar on "teaching in the discipline" open to interested graduate students. UT Austin offered minicourses every semester, on a strictly voluntary basis, on topics such as leading discussions and effective lecturing, combined with departmental courses on teaching in the disciplines.

The quality and staffing of teaching centers varied enormously, however. At universities like UC Berkeley with strong demonstrated commitments and relatively stable budgets, well-trained professionals led workshops and provided feedback from videotapes. At budget-strapped campuses, training programs were sometimes led by mentor teaching assistants who were themselves just learning their craft. Nor did all campuses mandate teacher training orientations. In 2001, one-third of research universities said they required no mandatory orientations for teaching assistants (Reinvention Center 2002). Moreover, seminars on teaching in the disciplines were rarely required, according to respondents; only 10 percent of responding research universities in 2001 said they required such seminars (ibid.).[6]

Institutionalizing the New Progressivism: AAC&U and NSSE

The Association of American Colleges and Universities (AAC&U), which defined itself as the only major national organization focusing on liberal and general education, added the theme of diversity to the new progressivism and became one of the most important agents of change in the undergraduate curriculum. During the 1980s and 1990s, the vision of AAC&U focused on reshaping the liberal arts to bring diversity within the compass of the fundamental commitments of liberal education.[7] In the early 1990s, AAC&U effectively advocated the addition of courses on gender, diversity, and non-Western cultures to the general education curriculum (see, e.g., Cornwell and Stoddard 1999; Musil 1992). The organization saw itself as a "leading edge of change" whose goal was to "amplify what [it] sees in the field" (D. Humphreys, personal communication).

This work culminated in the American Commitments initiative (1993–2001), funded by the Ford Foundation, the Hewlett Foundation, and the National Endowment for the Humanities. The connection between diversity and democracy provided a signal theme for this work. AAC&U drew on familiar images of pluralism, but with a new twist: "Higher education," it wrote, "can nurture Americans' commitment and capacity to create a society in which democratic aspirations become democratic justice. Diversity proves a means of forging deeper civic unity" (Beckham 2000, 2). This conceptual link between diversity and democracy brought diversity thoroughly into the mainstream of liberal education, while updating the Dewey tradition to incorporate the race- and gender-conscious movements on campus.

The AAC&U developed powerful organizational tools to realize its vision. These included the formation of a national panel, composed of prestigious figures in academe, modeled on the blue-ribbon commissions that had long been used by the federal government as a means for focusing support for pol- icy initiatives. They also included Diversity Leadership Institutes, held dur- ing the year and, more intensely, during summers for teams from twenty to thirty member institutions. These institutes disseminated best practices for reforming general education as a vehicle for teaching about diversity and for promoting "global social awareness." They also included community seminars to "discuss and re-imagine what it means to be a citizen in a multiracial soci- ety" (www.aacu.org). AAC&U was one of the first to find effective use of the Web for creating compendia of campus practices and resources to promote diversity and for highlighting successful efforts to implement changes in or- ganizational practices. Its flagship magazine, *Liberal Education*, highlighted diversity initiatives on member campuses and the connection between diver- sity and democracy at the heart of the American Commitments initiative. The association claimed that 160 campuses were involved in at least one of the face-to-face programs and that 100 institutions undertook efforts to rethink curriculum and to provide opportunities for students to consider "critical questions about American pluralism." The association itself grew from six hundred to eight hundred members during the period of the diversity and democracy initiative.

AAC&U's efforts to update progressive education ideals for the twenty-first century took a new turn in the late 1990s as it confronted the challenges of the state-based accountability movement. Its new initiative took up the fun- damental issue, what should be the characteristics of a liberally educated per- son in the twenty-first century? In its projects, AAC&U promoted a new vision of liberal education combining traditional aims with progressive ideals and a new conception of twenty-first-century skills. The program built clev- erly on the dynamic new force of perceived employer dissatisfaction with the qualifications of college-educated labor,[8] and it mobilized support for alternatives to standardized testing of student learning outcomes.

Funded by four foundations (the Carnegie Corporation of New York, the Charles Engelhard Foundation, the Pew Foundation, and the John Templeton Foundation), together with the federal Fund for the Improvement of Postsecondary Education, AAC&U offered what amounted to a tripartite solution to the re-creation of liberal education, blending exposure to the traditional core fields of knowledge (natural and social science, humanities, and arts), cross-curricular work on cognitive and expressive skills (analytical and critical reasoning, written and oral communications, quantitative and information skills), and commitment to the values of educational progressivism (intercultural understanding, personal development, civic and social engagement, and integrative and collaborative learning).

Like the American Commitments initiative before it, the Liberal Education and America's Progress (LEAP) initiative drew on a familiar set of opinion formation mechanisms mastered by powerful Washington lobbies: reports of national panels of distinguished academics and business leaders, Web site resources extolling the values of the new policy agenda, community forums to discuss the new vision, and magazine articles focusing on the implementation of campus reforms reflecting the new vision. Both AAC&U magazines, *Liberal Education* and *Peer Review*, took up the cause. These magazines were sent to five administrators on member campuses, broadening exposure within the communities of change agents on the campuses. By 2009, organizational membership had grown to 1,200 institutions, each one sponsoring five campus representatives; these 6,000 campus representatives connected to AAC&U through member institutions and periodical subscriptions constituted a core of reform-minded activists spread through academe.

The new vision had much to do with countering the growing threat of state regulation of the college classroom through standardized testing. Together with its new vision of the essential skills and values for the twenty-first century, the initiative brought a new approach to assessment to the fore. This new approach focused not on standardized testing, along the lines of K–12 accountability, but instead on electronic portfolios and senior capstone courses. As the association's main report on accountability and assessment stated, "Capstone courses and portfolios provide promising anchors for a meaningful approach to educational accountability" (AAC&U 2004, 8). This work left out the details about how students' course work could be fairly sampled or assessed for improvement over the college career or examined for evidence of proficiency in specified outcome areas. These matters were to be left to the colleges, to develop in ways that fit local conditions, rather than by independent third parties.

The National Survey of Student Engagement (NSSE) represented another powerful force in the institutionalization of the new progressivism. Led by George D. Kuh, a professor of higher education at Indiana University, NSSE was launched with Pew Foundation funding in 2000. NSSE built on decades of research by Kuh and his colleague Robert Pace on the College Survey of Educational Quality (CSEQ) (Kuh 2009). This work closely paralleled the precepts of *Involvement in Learning*. Conceived in part as an alternative to the resources- and reputation-based college rankings of *U.S. News and World Report*, NSSE intended to measure more accurately the actual quality of undergraduate students' educational experiences. The five NSSE benchmarks, each addressed through scaling related questions, probed levels of student-faculty contact, active and collaborative learning, academic challenges, educational enrichment activities, and institutional climates conducive to learning.

In its inaugural year, NSSE was administered at more than 270 institutions; this number grew to more than 600 annually by the end of the decade (www.nsse.iub.edu). Institutions were soon comparing their engagement scores on the five key dimensions to national norms and norms for institutions of their type. NSSE generated an impressive number of reports detailing the distribution and consequences of engagement experiences, and it also championed case analyses of institutions that showed exceptional effectiveness in the production of engaged learning environments (Kuh et al. 2005). However, NSSE measured engagement, not learning,[9] and although many college educators assumed that higher levels of engagement should register more or less directly in improved learning outcomes, empirical efforts to demonstrate this proposition were disappointing. Student scores on NSSE scales were, for example, only weakly associated with scores on the Collegiate Learning Assessment (CLA), and most factors failed to reach statistical significance once students' prior academic records (grade point average and SAT scores) were controlled (Carini, Kuh, and Klein 2006).[10] Other studies showed that high grades were more common in humanities and social science courses, in which the culture of engagement emphasized participation, interaction, and active learning experiences, and were less common in the natural sciences and engineering, where engagement typically meant long hours of study, with groups of peers, to master demanding quantitative material (Brint, Cantwell, and Hanneman 2008).

Promoting Teaching for Understanding: CFAT

The forces of the new progressivism had impressive organizational tools under their command and a relatively easy-to-implement checklist of reforms to attach to existing curricula. The same could not be said of the more ambitious and less completely realized project of the Carnegie Foundation for the Advancement of Teaching under Ernest Boyer's successor, Lee S. Shulman. Under Shulman's leadership, the Carnegie Foundation embarked on a program to redefine and realize Boyer's vision of a scholarship of teaching. These efforts eventually steered the foundation away from the tenets of the new progressivism to a deeper inquiry into aims and methods of undergraduate teaching. Shulman's approach came to share only part of the faith of the new progressivism in the power of student engagement. Engagement, he wrote, "is not enough." "Understanding is not independent [of engagement] but is an additional standard" (Shulman 1989).

For Shulman, all good teaching was built, in the first instance, on subject matter mastery. Shulman emphasized, in addition, "pedagogical content knowledge"—the special materials and methods tied to knowledge making in the disciplines, such as work with primary textual materials in history, surveys and ethnography in sociology, and diagnostic clinical rounds in medicine. Based on this knowledge and these disciplinary resources, teaching and learning could be conceived as an interactive process of bringing "something inside" of the teacher out in a methodical and powerful way, as well as bringing "something outside" of the student, the lesson, into strong relief in students' consciousness. In all good teaching, methods of expression and bases of apprehension and understanding were consequently closely linked (Hutchings and Shulman 1999).

Shulman and his colleagues emphasized that the first obligation of the teacher is to determine what students know and can do, as well as their interests and passions. Working from these bases, Shulman and his associates (Huber and Hutchings 2005) advocated that teachers create "cognitive apprenticeships" in which students are asked to make their mental processes accessible to their fellow students and teachers and to work toward more expert understandings of course materials. Through a process of "uncoverage," teachers were encouraged to focus their first lessons on ideas and concepts that were both difficult to grasp and fundamental to subsequent learning in the class. Teachers made their own thinking accessible to students by explicating the "intermediate processes" of understanding—the understandings that are employed habitually by expert learners but are often hidden in the process of instruction. These could include, for example, explicit discussions of the flow of an argument or text, the translation of terms no longer in wide use, or a detailed, step-by-step interpretation of the architecture of a statistical table. Other techniques for making knowledge accessible included slowing down students' reading to elicit students' descriptions of their thinking about passages in text; administering oral rather than written midterms; employing structured online discussions to create learning communities oriented to key issues and ideas in a course; and posting examples of beginning, intermediate, and advanced understandings of texts with detailed explications of the major differences between these levels of mastery. Similar pedagogies were developed for mathematics—for example, in James Sandefur's "think alouds," in which math students were asked to describe, step by step, how they were thinking about a problem as they worked through its solution.

Shulman argued that students should demonstrate competence by performing skills in front of their teachers and classmates, rather than by passively absorbing information. For Shulman, the pathologies of learning—amnesia (forgetting what was just learned), fantasia (misperceiving the lesson to reinforce existing knowledge), and inertia (inability to use knowledge in new contexts)—were ultimately issues of ownership. Understanding implied ownership and ownership typically required performance (see also Shulman 1997).

The institution of the Carnegie Academy for the Scholarship of Teaching and Learning (CASTL) was the first of Shulman's organizational vehicles. CASTL was based on the idea that reform began in small groups, rather than as a broad ideology. It sought not to transform but to create strong emotional loyalties among those who self-selected as reformers. The Pew Foundation provided a $5 million grant to Carnegie to inaugurate CASTL.[11] Pew funds provided support for a summer academy located at the foundation where successful applicants, approximately fifteen a summer, met together to discuss and develop the ideas from their proposals for improvements in teaching and learning. The projects ranged widely, but most sought to understand the learning process or to develop conditions under which broader and deeper learning could occur in classroom settings. They included, for example, a project by the English teacher Mariolina Salvatori to develop the idea of "difficulty papers," in which students identify and begin to hypothesize the reasons for a possible difficulty they experience reading a poem, play, or essay. Another project, by the psychologist Jose Feito, mapped the conditions for more broadly distributed learning in seminar settings, including ways of helping students take responsibility for "owning" the learning process, building appreciation of multiple perspectives, creating expectations for the contributions of all members, and creating a space in which students could safely acknowledge their lack of understanding.

Growing out of the Carnegie program, Scholarship of Teaching and Learning (SoTL) colloquia sprouted up on hundreds of college and university campuses during this period. These colloquia took up visually effective presentation of lessons, new ways to assess student learning, uses of technology to improve pedagogy, the impact of learning communities, and many other topics consistent with the Carnegie agenda. On most campuses, SoTL sought to foster discussion and incremental change based on emulation of appealing approaches to the challenges of teaching. Rooted in the precepts of the constructivist pedagogy, the philosophy was not an industrial search for better systems, but rather an apprenticeship system for craftsmen, based on sharing the distinctive visions of master teachers.

Other Shulman-inspired projects led to the creation of Web sites intended to spread pedagogical practices consistent with the "teaching for understanding" approach. Georgetown professor Randy Bass's *Visible Knowledge Project* Web site (1999) was the most important for advancing and codifying ideas about pedagogies of understanding. Bass obtained a five-year, $2.6 million grant from Atlantic Philanthropies "to improve the quality of college and university teaching through a focus on student learning and faculty development in technology-enhanced environments." His Web site spotlighted techniques for slowing down and deepening knowledge transmission, for building on core ideas and concepts, and for making teachers' intermediate processes and performance standards visible to students, while revealing students' prior understandings and making their difficulties in understanding course materials visible to teachers.

Shulman's interest in updating the shop talk of teachers included advocacy of electronic "teaching commons" where proven ideas could be "documented, shared and built upon" and thereby gain wider currency (Shulman 1993). In 1995, University of Nebraska professor Dan Bernstein launched the Web site *Peer Review of Teaching* to realize Shulman's goal of making teaching "community property." Peer review of teaching, as developed by Bernstein, began with the exchange of three memoranda between colleagues. These memoranda discussed the objectives of the courses, the instructional design for the course, and the quality and breadth of student understanding demonstrated in the course. Based on these memoranda, Bernstein's Web site allowed college teachers to document what they did in their classes through electronic course portfolios. The portfolios included graded examples of student work, representing a range of how well students had achieved course goals. They also included a section identifying the next steps in the development of the course. As in other Carnegie-inspired efforts, the Web site touched the work lives of only relatively small numbers of devoted practitioners. They did, however, help to launch the leading alternative that emerged during the period to standardized testing of student learning outcomes—electronic teaching portfolios, which included detailed analysis of course-level assessment data.

The organizational apparatus Carnegie used to spread these ideas showed neither the panache of the AAC&U campaigns nor the reach of NSSE. Instead, an artisanal model, built on networks of sympathetic practitioners, prevailed. This approach generated fresh insights about teaching and learning—insights with the potential to create more effective college teachers. But its insistence on "scaling down" through small-scale actions of unusually committed practitioners was destined to create islands of improved practice in a sea of relative indifference. According to Huber and Hutchings, "the key is not the scale and scope but the care and thoughtfulness of the work, its capacity to change thought and practices, its generosity, even, perhaps, its power to surprise and delight" (2005, 30).[12]

Carnegie itself changed dramatically with the selection of Anthony Bryk in 2007 to replace the retiring Shulman. Bryk launched an effort to "scale up" R&D in education through well-supported industrial-style prototyping and mass diffusion, beginning with a project to turn around the low success rates of community college students in remedial mathematics. This represented a sharp departure for a foundation modeled under Shulman as a think tank for teaching craftsmen. Russell Edgerton, who did so much as a program officer at the Pew Foundation to promote Shulman's agenda, concluded ruefully that more than two decades of reform activity sponsored by liberal philanthropies like Pew had resulted in "neither professional nor institutional transformation" (R. Edgerton, personal communication).

Outcomes Assessment Movements

I now turn to the other movement to reform college teaching and learning, that led by the states. Outcomes assessment can be defined as a response of state governments and regional accrediting bodies to the perception that colleges and universities have not done enough to ensure that students are learning course materials and essential academic competencies. Where the teaching reform movement took root in foundation-supported advocacy organizations, the *outcomes assessment movement* was promoted primarily by the states and the federal government.[13] Following the K–12 reform model, state officials have sought to investigate these issues using relatively low-cost, quantitative measures. Policy think tanks, such as the National Center for Public Policy and Higher Education and the National Center for Higher Education Management Systems (NCHEMS), played important roles articulating and promoting the objectives of the assessment movement. Interinstitutional higher education associations, such as the National Association of State Universities and Land Grant Colleges (NASULGC), later renamed the Association of Public and Landgrant Universities (APLU), and the American Association of State Colleges and Universities (AASCU), have attempted to mediate between universities and the states, as have the regional and disciplinary accrediting bodies. Both the higher education associations and the regional accrediting agencies followed the goals of the assessment movement by insisting on evidence of student learning outcomes. The regional accrediting agencies allowed institutions and disciplines to define their own measures of student learning outcomes, while the higher education associations developed a voluntary system of accountability that allows participating institutions to choose from three authorized assessment instruments to test "core academic skills."

Fledgling efforts to encourage institutional assessment of learning outcomes began in the 1970s. The Educational Testing Service (ETS) fielded the first open-response test of core skills, Academic Competencies in General Education, tested at 140 institutions, but later abandoned as a result of the tendency of institutions to magnify small pretest/posttest differences and the test's unreliability in the midranges of scoring (Adelman 2007). By the mid-1970s, twenty states had introduced minimal competency testing for graduating seniors, mirroring popular high school exit exams (Gilman 1978). Calls for action continued in the early 1980s. *A Nation at Risk* (1981) documented the shortcomings of U.S. primary and secondary education in the face of increasing competition from East Asia. Only four years later, *A Time for Results* (1985) stressed the same fears about the competency of U.S. college graduates and the same looming threat of Asian competition. It noted that U.S. higher education had set a new standard for access, but observed that "access without quality is a cruel deception." In the document, a subcommittee of governors, led by John Ashcroft of Missouri and including future president Bill Clinton of Arkansas, questioned common assumptions about higher education: "Learning is assumed to take place as long as students take courses, accumulate [credit] hours and progress satisfactorily toward a degree." But, the subcommittee observed, "tests of elementary and high school teachers show that the BA is not a guarantee of even basic literacy, let alone competence." The report also cited, with little documentation, "substantial levels of dissatisfaction" among employers about the skills of college graduates. The report advocated systematic programs using multiple measures to assess undergraduate student learning, and it cited with approval institutions like Alverno College that had pioneered systematic assessment in the 1970s. It also applauded the Southern Accreditation Commission for being the first of the regional accrediting bodies to require an assessment component for reaccreditation.

Performance Funding: The First Wave

Beginning in the 1980s, states began to demand that universities account in detail for the ways they were spending their money, the amount professors were teaching, and, to a lesser degree, how much students were learning. A study team led by political scientist Michael McLendon reported in the 1980s that state financial resources became conditioned upon institutional performance in specified areas. These often included student retention and graduation rates, student scores on licensing examinations, job placement rates, faculty research productivity, and measures of undergraduate access and campus diversity (McLendon, Hearn, and Deaton 2006). Between 1979 and 2007, twenty-five states enacted performance funding, but ten of those states dropped it during the period (Burke and Minassians 2003; Dougherty and Reid 2007). Performance funding proved costly to implement, susceptible to institutional manipulation of performance measures, and subject to reversal under new administrations, or when unstable state finances caused deep cuts in regular higher education funding (Burke and Serban 1998; Dougherty and Natow 2009; Shulock and Moore 2002; Zumeta 2001).

Nevertheless, new demands for accountability, including direct assessment of student learning, slowly gained ground during this period. A 1983 report of the Education Commission of the States showed that two-thirds of states had initiated some form of required student assessment. However, many states used minimal competency measures at graduation, or even more indirect measures, such as graduation rates and pass rates on professional licensing examinations. Although assessment of student learning was in the air, few knew how to test directly for student learning outcomes in a cost-effective, relatively unobtrusive way. Regional accrediting agencies, like the North Central Association, began requiring institutions to plan for ways to directly assess evidence of student academic achievement, and state higher education policy think tanks, such as ECS and NCHEMS, issued statements of support for the endeavor. The large testing companies, ACT and ETS, also geared up for the new era by introducing or revamping multiple-choice tests, the Collegiate Assessment of Academic Proficiency (CAAP) and the Measure of Academic Proficiency and Progress (MAPP), respectively, that institutions could administer to their freshmen and seniors to determine the institution's "value added" to student academic competencies.

Pressure on state budgets contributed to this sharper focus on the college classroom. In the 1990s, state appropriations for higher education declined for the first time in real terms. Although funding recovered in the later 1990s, the recovery was slow and shallow, and state appropriations fell steeply in real terms with every new recession. In the context of limited and unstable revenue bases and stiff competition for public dollars, some state governments began to demand performance assessments in return for funding commitments (Alexander 2000). These state actors wanted to know whether they were receiving value from their investments in higher education.

As critics of government waste continued to score points, Democratic Party centrists argued that government could become much more efficient by monitoring the performance of its functional units closely, with an eye for creative ways to meet consumer service goals. David Osborne and Ted Gaebler's *Reinventing Government* (1992) became a popular guidebook for state reformers; its animating ideas were endorsed by Vice President Al Gore and others who were interested in defusing long-standing concerns about the wastefulness of government spending. Broader trends in the appropriation of powers to regulate professional work were also at play. State officials emphasized the tendency of unregulated professionals to feather their own nests and to prescribe overly expensive treatments. In many cases, doubts about the effectiveness of professional practices, combined with the increasing cost of providing services, led to third-party regulation, greatly reducing the autonomy of professionals.[14] State dissatisfaction with control of work by the occupational community was, in this respect, another central context out of which higher education accountability movements grew.

A Bandwagon Forms

To the extent that an analogue exists in the outcomes assessment movement to Ernest Boyer's *Scholarship Reconsidered*, it was produced by two state college professors in California, Robert Barr and John Tagg, in a widely cited 1995 article from *Change* magazine. In this article, Barr and Tagg sought to shift thinking in academe from an "instruction paradigm" to a "learning paradigm": "In the briefest form, the paradigm that has governed our colleges is this: A college is an institution that exists to provide instruction. Subtly but profoundly we are shifting to a new paradigm: A college is an institution that exists to produce learning. This shift changes everything" (1995, 1). The new paradigm fostered a change in focus from a pedagogy based on instructors' expectations about what students should learn to one emphasizing what students actually do learn. The article advocated sophisticated assessments grounded in "minds-on" problem solving, while it explicitly supported external evaluations of learning. Barr and Tagg looked forward optimistically: few external evaluations of learning had, to this point, focused on sophisticated assessments of learning; instead, nearly all sought inexpensive ways to assess student learning through multiple-choice instruments.

The idea of a shift to a "learning paradigm" resonated strongly among state educational bureaucrats and in the world of higher education policy analysts. By 2001, ten states, concentrated in the South and Midwest, had experimented with or adopted standardized testing of student learning outcomes (Ewell 2001b). The idea of demonstrating how much institutions added to learning was gaining widespread appeal. Advocates of this "value-added" approach argued that this could be done by controlling for predicted gains based on student "input" characteristics at college entry, such as their social backgrounds and SAT scores, and then attributing residual gains to institutions. However, few in the policy community agreed on what types of learning should be measured or how it should be demonstrated. Some argued for discipline-specific knowledge, others more general cognitive skills (such as analytical thinking and writing), and still others wanted to focus on work-related skills. Some advocated multiple-choice tests for their cost-effectiveness, but others concluded that higher-level cognitive skills could not be demonstrated in this context and required the completion of more complex, "real-world" tasks.

In spite of disagreements about what should be tested, the learning outcomes movement gained traction as higher education leaders in the national associations and regional accrediting bodies concluded that they could no longer ignore state pressures to "show results." The list of supporters for increased accountability included many of the foundations that were simultaneously supporting projects to reform teaching. Already active in promoting "assessment forums" at the annual meetings of the American Association for Higher Education, the Pew and Danforth Foundations provided grants to regional accrediting agencies in 1999 to work on criteria for collection of data on student learning outcomes.

Over the next five years, a chorus of influential voices called for measurement of student learning outcomes and created demonstration projects to show how this measurement could be done. In 2000, the National Center for Public Policy and Higher Education, funded by several major foundations and led by the former governor of North Carolina and educational reformer James B. Hunt, began to publish report cards about state higher education performance, including "incomplete" grades for all states on student learning. In the same year, the Accreditation Board for Engineering and Technology (ABET), the accrediting agency for engineering schools, began its *Engineering Criteria 2000* policy, requiring outcomes measures and plans for continuous improvement based on results of outcomes assessments. In 2002, the Pew Trusts provided funding to two leaders of the assessment movement, Margaret Miller and Peter Ewell, to demonstrate the possibility of measuring college learning in six states for future incorporation into the National Center for Public Policy and Higher Education's "Measuring Up" reports. In 2003, the Carnegie Corporation of New York and the Teagle Foundation sponsored the development of a new type of test of core academic skills, the Collegiate Learning Assessment, based on the use of document libraries to solve "real-world" problems. In the same year, the national council of regional and disciplinary accrediting agencies, the Council for Higher Education Accreditation (CHEA), announced a policy of "mutual responsibility" between institutions and regional accrediting agencies for demonstrating student learning outcomes.

An opinion survey published by ETS, also in 2003, discovered evidence of public concerns about educational quality, stronger among political conservatives and high school–educated people. Primed by questions linking costs to quality assurance, a majority surveyed by ETS agreed that colleges should provide evidence that they were producing the learning results they promised, if they were going to continue to raise costs (ETS 2003). In 2004, the Business–Higher Education Forum argued for the first time in favor of assessments of student learning outcomes. Also in 2004, the State Higher Education Executive Officers launched a National Commission on Accountability in Higher Education, chaired by former secretary of education Richard Riley and former Oklahoma governor Frank Keating, both Republicans. The report they produced in 2005 concluded that most state systems "do not meet their intended purpose to improve and to provide evidence of student learning" and endorsed collection of data on student learning outcomes (National Commission on Accountability in Higher Education 2005). In the same year Miller and Ewell published their six-state report showing that states could demonstrate student learning outcomes through a variety of measures, such as proficiency benchmarks modeled on the K–12 National Assessment of Educational Progress (Ewell and Miller 2005).

The Spellings Commission and the VSA

Buoyed by this swelling interest in higher education accountability, the Bush administration turned its attention from K–12 reform to higher education. Secretary of Education Margaret Spellings appointed a Commission on the Future of Higher Education, chaired by Texas businessman Charles Miller, to recommend reforms in higher education accountability. In 2004 and 2005, the commission issued a number of preliminary reports critical of higher education's commitment to transparency, cost containment, and, most important, demonstration of results for student learning. In 2006, the commission issued its final report, *A Test of Leadership*, which was highly critical of the performance of America's colleges and universities. The report dismissed previous efforts to bring accountability for student learning outcomes. "Despite increased attention to student learning results by colleges and universities and accreditation agencies, parents and students have no solid evidence, comparable across institutions, of how much students learn in colleges or whether they learn more at one college than another. Similarly, policymakers need more comprehensive data to help them decide whether the national investment in higher education is paying off and how tax payer dollars could be used more effectively" (Commission on the Future of Higher Education 2006, 14). The commission advocated measuring student achievement on a value-added basis that took into account students' previous achievements when assessing outcomes. It stated that this evidence should be made available to consumers and policy makers in an accessible, understandable way, and it encouraged the implementation of "meaningful" interstate comparison of student learning in all states (ibid., 4).[15]

The specter of high-stakes testing haunted many in academe, who argued that such tests would yield little of value for students studying such a wide variety of disciplines (see, e.g., Chatman 2007; Hawthorne 2008). The only way to test learning would be discipline by discipline, these educators argued, and this seemed an impossible task given the limited resources of colleges and universities and the limited capacity of state educational bureaucrats to grade such a wide variety of tests. An article by the assessment expert Trudy Banta summarized the experience of educators who had attempted to implement standardized tests of general intellectual skills, such as interpretation, critical analysis, and writing. Banta argued that such instruments primarily test entering ability, are not content neutral and therefore privilege students specializing in some disciplines more than others, contain questions and problems that do not match the learning experiences of all students at any given institution, and measure at best 30 percent of the knowledge and skills that faculty want students to develop. She also raised doubts, based on her own research, about the reliability of gain scores at the individual level, the extent to which students take such tests seriously, and the dangers posed by high-stakes testing for narrowing the higher education curriculum to focus on the skills and content emphasized in the tests (Banta 2007).

Leaders of the testing movement countered that tests of general skills were an important, if not the only important, measure of student achievement in college. Instead of relying on one test, they argued, multiple forms of assessment would be necessary—some to assess general skills, others to assess disciplinary knowledge, and still others to assess the "soft skills" required in leadership positions (see, e.g., Ewell 2004; Shulenburger 2008). Institutions could be responsible for these assessments, provided that they took their responsibilities seriously.

Following publication of the Spellings Commission report, attention in Washington shifted to the struggle over the reauthorization of the Higher Education Act of 1966, which had been languishing in Congress since 2003. The Bush administration, which had already placed several accountability-minded trustees on the national Council for Higher Education Accreditation, proposed that the federal government take a larger role in quality assurance. Some influential senators, including a leading Democrat, Edward M. Kennedy, argued for bringing higher education into an accountability structure parallel to that of No Child Left Behind (NCLB). As in the case of NCLB, Kennedy wanted to focus on the education of minority and first-generation students by tying increased federal spending to increased federal responsibility for quality assurance. Following extensive lobbying by the higher education associations, Senator Lamar Alexander, a former secretary of education, was convinced to allow the existing system of voluntary accreditation to continue and to bar the federal government from prescribing standards that these agencies were required to use in assessing institutional effectiveness. But, in exchange for his support, Alexander insisted that higher education institutions themselves take on the responsibility to measure student learning outcomes in a serious way.

The reauthorization passed without an enhanced federal role. Alexander's intervention led to the creation of the Voluntary System of Accountability (VSA), organized, with support from the Lumina Foundation, by two of the leading higher education associations, APLU and AASCU. The creators of VSA were very clear about wanting to avoid an NCLB-type system in which important subjects might be driven out of the curriculum. They were also very clear about the need for a voluntary system until such time as the construct validity of existing assessments could be definitively established. Finally, they were aware of the pressure they were under from state and federal education officials, who believed that the time had long passed for higher education institutions to take accountability seriously. As David Shulenburger, the vice president for academic affairs of APLU, put it: "Our detractors allege that we are unproductive, wasteful, and that our students benefit less than we have claimed. . . . If it accomplishes nothing else, generating and publishing transparent, comparable, and meaningful data will serve to diminish the volume of those who believe we are hiding something" (Shulenburger 2008, 21–22). VSA set as an explicit goal the development of a system of accountability that would "facilitate comparisons of learning outcomes among institutions of higher education."

Testing companies were quick to sense the opportunity to expand their higher education markets. ETS sponsored a national advisory panel to discuss the virtues and defects of existing instruments. ETS issued two reports on "creating a culture of evidence" (Dwyer, Millet, and Payne 2006; Millett et al. 2007). The first of the reports was influenced by the debate surrounding the Spellings Commission and the reauthorization of the Higher Education Act, the second by the triumph of the VSA approach. On the basis of the second report, the creators of VSA chose three tests as acceptable measures of institutional "value-added" to core academic skills: ETS's own Measurement of Academic Proficiency and Progress, ACT's Collegiate Assessment of Academic Proficiency, and the Council for Aid to Education's Collegiate Learning Assessment.

Of these three, the CLA elicited the most interest among policy makers and others who wanted to compare institutions. Like MAPP and CAAP, the CLA tested capacities for analysis and synthesis, not simple recall, but it tested these capacities using document libraries and real-life scenarios, rather than the true/false and multiple-choice format of more conventional instruments. Specifically, the CLA asked students to complete a performance task and two analytical writing tasks. Each performance task had its own document library that included a range of sources, such as letters, memoranda, research reports, newspaper articles, maps, and photographs. The performance task required students to answer open-ended questions about "a hypothetical but realistic situation." One sample question asked students to evaluate whether available data tend to support or refute claims about weaknesses in the construction of the wing of an airplane that a fictitious company was planning to purchase for its sales force. The analytical writing tasks required students to make and critique arguments. One sample question asked students to make an argument that responded to the following claim: "There is no such thing as 'truth' in the media. The one true thing about the information media is that it exists only to entertain." Another asked students to evaluate whether fast-food restaurants contribute to childhood obesity based on a report about a research study.

As a measure of higher-level general skills learning outcomes, the CLA had clear strengths in comparison to multiple-choice tests, but it was also not without some weaknesses when used as a measure of institutional "value added." The creators of the CLA claimed that value-added information could be obtained with samples as small as one hundred. Given the small sample sizes permitted by VSA, it was impossible to know whether differences among institutions were due to the composition of student samples by major fields of study or other student characteristics, differences in motivating incentives, or true institutional differences in educational effectiveness. Although the creators of CLA controlled for incoming SAT scores, they did not require controls for the disciplinary composition of samples. Samples composed mainly of communications majors, for example, would likely perform rather differently from samples composed mainly of engineering majors. The test therefore attributed "value-added" to institutions in some cases in which changes might be more accurately attributed to disciplinary or other more specific educational experiences.[16] Moreover, the CLA did not regularly report total error or confidence intervals (see Braun 2009). In state systems, less prestigious institutions tended to show greater gains than more prestigious institutions. The creators of CLA denied that ceiling effects could be a factor in these results, but the fact remained that most entering freshmen at state flagship universities scored high on the test before any institutional effects came into play. Students at less prestigious branches of the university scored low and had more ground to gain.[17] Many institutions put off implementation of tests of core academic skills prescribed by the VSA. Of the more than three hundred institutions participating in VSA as of fall 2009, less than one-third had reported results of "core academic skills" using one of the three authorized testing instruments. Of those institutions reporting results, the expected two-thirds reported results within a standard deviation for institutions with similar student academic ability profiles, but, oddly, among the remaining institutions three times as many reported results "above" (one standard deviation above the predicted mean) or "well above" (two standard deviations above the predicted mean) as reported results "below" or "well below" expected. Only 5 of 104 reporting institutions said that they were performing below expected levels.

An Incremental Approach: CHEA and the Regional Accrediting Bodies

The six regional accrediting agencies are organized and directed by academics (or former academics) as quality assurance agencies. The system was developed as an explicit alternative to state regulation of higher education. Although regional accrediting agencies are independent of the states, they are nevertheless subject to state recognition, which has proven to be an important lever. In 1989, federal regulations first required accrediting organizations to examine student learning outcomes as a condition of recognition. The efforts of the regional accrediting agencies to implement review rubrics and to train peer reviewers were aided by funds from the Pew Foundation. By the mid-1990s all six of the regional accrediting agencies had policies in place requiring institutions to demonstrate not only that they were tracking conventional measures of student success, such as four- and six-year graduation rates, but also that they had mechanisms in place to achieve established goals for student learning. In 1998, Congress formalized this commitment by making student achievement the first of nine areas in which the regional accrediting agencies were required to have standards.

Even as they followed federal directives, regional accrediting bodies buffered colleges and universities from state pressures to introduce standardized testing. Some of the "regionals" have allowed institutions to take responsibility for assessing and achieving a unique set of learning outcomes that institutions have established for themselves. Others have named a core set of learning outcomes that ought to be examined by all institutions. These typically encompassed, at a minimum, critical and analytical thinking, written expression, and quantitative reasoning. Institutions and departments have been granted considerable autonomy so long as they provide evidence that they are establishing learning objectives and developing ways to assess and report the achievement of these objectives. This permitted a variety of assessment approaches, ranging from the presentation of portfolios of student work to requirements for integrative research papers in senior capstone courses. Others built in learning objectives to required courses and required samples of work from these courses or adopted exit examinations as a way of determining whether learning objectives had been met. Although the regional accrediting bodies developed elaborate procedures to ensure that institutions did more than pay lip service to their demands for evidence of student learning, their requirements were nevertheless often treated as an encumbrance requiring the appearance of compliance without deeper commitments to the goals of evaluating student learning in a broader way than class grades allowed. The limited resources and experience of accrediting agencies also encouraged institutional autonomy; most, if not all, lacked experience in evaluating evidence of student learning or the qualifications to establish clear standards by which to do so (Ewell 2001a).

Even so, the regionals created much more attention to student learning outcomes than had existed before. In 2009, the National Institute for Learning

Outcomes Assessment (NILOA), housed at the University of Illinois, fielded a study of the incorporation of assessment instruments. The study was funded by the Carnegie Corporation, the Lumina Foundation, and the Teagle Foundation. Officials at half of U.S. two- and four-year institutions responded to the survey, and the vast majority (92%) said that they were engaged in institution-level assessments of student learning. Most said they were using survey instruments like NSSE, but 39 percent said they were also using standardized tests of general knowledge and skill like the CLA. At the program level, four of five respondents said they were assessing student learning outcomes in at least one program, and here portfolios dominated. Most said that accreditation was the primary driver of their interest in assessment (Kuh and Ikenberry 2009).

Engineering, with its competency-based outlook and favorable attitude toward operational planning and evaluation, provided the most ambitious mechanism for transforming undergraduate education through reforms developed by its disciplinary accrediting board, ABET. ABET's *Engineering Critieria 2000 (EC 2000)* offered both a more prescriptive orientation to expected outcomes of the undergraduate curriculum and stronger mechanisms for planning and demonstrating achievement of these outcomes. Specifically, *EC 2000* required detailed published educational objectives, a process in which objectives were determined and evaluated, a curriculum that ensured achievement of these objectives, and a system for using results of assessments for continuous improvement of the effectiveness of the program. In addition, it established specific outcome criteria that all engineering graduates were, in theory, required to demonstrate. These included the ability to apply knowledge of mathematics, science, and engineering; the ability to design and conduct experiments, as well as to analyze and interpret data; the ability to design a system, component, or process to meet desired goals; and the ability to identify, formulate, and solve engineering problems. The criteria also included social and communication skills, such as the ability to function on multidisciplinary teams, to understand professional and ethical responsibility, to communicate effectively, and to demonstrate knowledge of contemporary issues (ABET 2000).

ABET's focus on learning led to changes in instruction. In an evaluation of *EC 2000,* between one-half and two-thirds of faculty surveyed reported that they had increased their use of active learning methods, such as group work, design projects, case studies, and application exercises, to meet learning objectives. In this study, a comparison of 1994 and 2004 engineering graduates showed small but significant self-reported gains in technical abilities, such as the application of mathematics and science to engineering problems. Students also self-reported more sizable increases in social areas specified by *EC 2000*: ability to work in teams, understanding of professional ethics, understanding of contemporary issues, and global cultural awareness (Lattuca, Terenzini, and Volkwein 2006). Outside of engineering, the controls imposed by accrediting agencies were still relatively weak by the end of the decade, but they were slowly changing the way institutions thought about the outcomes of higher education. Most institutions were engaged in assessing their contributions to student learning. Undergraduate program reviews had been institutionalized across the country, and although these varied dramatically in quality, they provided regular feedback to departments based on external, third-party review. Departments have been required to think, sometimes seriously, about what they expect students to gain from their programs and to provide at least skeletal evidence that these objectives were being met. The "audit culture" (Tuchman 2009) spread with each new reaccreditation.

Consequences of the Two Reform Movements

What in the end have the two movements for reform of college teaching and learning produced? The answer to this question depends on whether we look at their practical consequences or their consequences for the legitimacy of teaching work as the central identity and activity of academic professionals.

Practical Consequences of the Reform Movements

It is safe to say that preparation for classroom teaching improved during the period, thanks to the diffusion of basic training for graduate teaching assistants through the auspices of teaching centers. When William Cummings and Martin Finkelstein surveyed U.S. faculty in 1992, they found that only 30 percent of respondents said they had any training for teaching before they took their first jobs (Cummings and Finkelstein 2007). The proportion of graduate students receiving basic training for teaching has now more than doubled in recent cohorts (Boice 1992; Golde and Dore 2001; Reinvention Center 2002).[18]

Classroom practices also changed dramatically in the direction advocated by the new progressives, even as part of their message was lost. Here the best data come from the Higher Education Research Institute's (HERI) triannual studies of the American faculty. From the late 1980s through the mid-2000s, extensive lecturing showed a marked decline as a teaching method, even in public research universities, and cooperative (small group) learning opportunities showed a corresponding increase. Full-time college faculty increasingly said they were bringing their students into field settings, asking them to demonstrate their knowledge in front of class through oral presentations, relying on reflective writing and journaling, using real-life problems to illustrate lessons, and putting student-centered inquiry, rather than recitation of facts and concepts, at the center of their teaching work (Astin, Dey, and Korn 1991; DeAngelo et al. 2007; Dey et al. 1993; Lindholm et al. 2002, 2005; Sax et al. 1996, 1999). These changes have gone together with an expanded conception of the goals of undergraduate education. Consistent with principles of the new progressivism, the *American College Faculty* studies also show sharp increases in the centrality of social goals: reaching out to surrounding communities through community-based research, teaching appreciation of multicultural diversity, and interest in using undergraduate education as a vehicle for promoting social change. Just as the twentieth-century progressives socialized their ideals of citizenship through the schools, so too do college faculty now overwhelmingly endorse the goals of diversity and community engagement.

These preferences were evident in all segments of American four-year colleges and universities, as much in private colleges as in public universities. The main proponents of these changes have been younger and female faculty members (DeAngelo et al. 2007, 5, 9, 11), suggesting that the trends are likely to continue as older faculty retire and college teaching faculties become increasingly populated by women and those brought up in the norms of the new progressivism.

Active learning experiences reflect a time-honored way to engage the interests of students—particularly less academically oriented students—and are, in this sense, responsive to the changing demography of undergraduate student bodies. The changing demography of the professoriate provides complementary support. At the same time, the checklist character of progressive education has likely also mattered in its widespread adoption. Professors can ask themselves and mentally check off whether they have added hands-on learning experiences, collaborative learning projects, and readings that are responsive to diverse learners.

Active learning pedagogies have apparently not led to great change in student learning, however, at least insofar as this can be measured by students' performance on the CLA. Looking at a sample of 2,400 students who took the CLA at the beginning of their freshman and middle of their sophomore years, sociologists Richard Arum and Josipa Roksa (2011) found that students had improved their critical thinking, complex reasoning, and writings skills, as measured by the CLA performance task, by only .18 standard deviations, or an average 7 percent gain. Forty-five percent of students showed no statistically significant change in their CLA scores. Arum and Roksa concluded that students' completion of three semesters of college had made a "barely noticeable" impact on the higher-level cognitive skills tested by CLA. Follow-up work on the same sample found that, even after four years of college, 36 percent of students showed no statistically significant change in their CLA scores.

Trend data from NSSE provide clues about why this may be so. These data show that many active and collaborative learning activities have grown more popular over time, while challenging requirements, such as the amount of time students spend studying per week and the number of twenty-page papers they write, have remained static or fallen (NSSE 2000, 2008). In the 2008 NSSE report, nearly two-thirds of seniors in NSSE sample institutions said they studied fifteen or fewer hours per week, and half said they had never written a paper of twenty pages or longer (NSSE 2008). In both cases, challenging requirements were less common in 2008 than those found eight years earlier.

The acquiescence of faculty to the preferences of student consumers explains many of these trends. Students have effectively resisted professorial demands for higher levels of effort by simply refusing to engage their studies at a deep level. Ethnographic studies indicate that students have relied on posted lecture notes, the prevalence of relatively easy courses to fill out their schedules, and teachers' openness to negotiations concerning work demands and grades (see, e.g., Grigsby 2009; Moffatt 1989; Nathan 2005). Arum and Roksa report that more than 90 percent of students say they have talked to a professor about grades, but only one-quarter say they have talked to a professor about ideas presented in class. A majority of the 2,400 college students in the Arum and Roksa study said they had not taken a course during the previous term that required a total of twenty pages of written work, and 25 percent said they had not taken a course that required even forty pages of reading per week. Arum and Roksa conclude that students learn little because they do not study much and little is demanded of them. The college experience, they argue, is perceived by many students as at its core a social experience, rather than an academic experience.

The current low expectations system of undergraduate education does not accurately describe the practices common at some liberal arts colleges or in some of the more demanding disciplines, such as engineering, math, and physics. But it does accurately describe the system of undergraduate education in most institutions and in a majority of non-STEM fields. The system exists because it serves the interests of all major actors who are in daily contact with the classroom. The majority of students see college as a period of fun, friendship, and personal development before they begin adult life. They hope their investments in college-level training will pay off in the labor market, but many assume that credentials will add value, not what they have learned in college. While faculty members are interested in making their classes lively and interesting, they also want to preserve time for research, correspondence, committee work, and other socio-professional activities. Often the livelihoods of adjunct faculty depend on high student evaluations. Administrators at nonselective institutions have been more interested in reaching enrollment targets and raising retention and graduation rates than in encouraging challenging course work or requiring students to demonstrate cognitive growth (Arum and Roksa, 2011; Bok 2006; Brint 2009).

The states have proven to be strong advocates of assessing student learning outcomes, but weak implementers. Early efforts to assess student learning outcomes focused not on direct evidence, but rather on such indirect measures as retention and graduation rates, pass rates on state licensing examinations, and student satisfaction surveys. Today, the states have been persuaded to defer to the regional and professional accrediting associations to provide quality assurance and to the VSA to experiment with the construct validity of several tests of general intellectual skills and to use these tests to monitor the "value-added" of institutions.

Neither the regional accrediting bodies nor the VSA have as yet transformed the college classroom by demanding evidence of student learning outcomes. Richer discussions are underway now about learning objectives, but the regional accrediting agencies have, for the most part, allowed institutions and departments to formulate their own objectives and to choose their own methods for demonstrating results. These choices reflect the cross pressures of regional accreditation, dependent on the state but responsive to the voluntarism, decentralization, and discipline-centered character of academic life. Similarly, the learning outcomes component of VSA has been slow to get off the ground. Its champions have wanted to allow for debate and discussion, and they have purposefully insisted on voluntary participation. But institutions have also dragged their heels when asked to provide evidence that could jeopardize their claims to excellence. VSA has also been plagued by doubts about the validity of value-added tests as compared to criterion-referenced tests of competence. Thus, while national and trans-institutional actors have succeeded in shaping the environment of discussion, their efforts have met both passive and active resistance whenever they have attempted to prescribe tough standards for the assessment of student learning outcomes.

Political considerations appear to have had an important influence on the preservation of teaching autonomy in higher education. These political considerations include the ability of higher education advocates to exploit doubts about the effectiveness of K–12 reform, partisan turnover in the governing coalitions of the states, and, in particular, the capacity so far of higher education associations and regional accrediting bodies to assure key legislators that they would implement accountability measures responsive to public interest in quality assurance. Finally, most states do not currently have the resources to fund third-party implementation and scoring of tests like the CLA.

Thus, the most obvious consequences of two decades of reform have been the diffusion of active learning pedagogies and surface-level adoption of relatively weak accountability measures. These will clearly not be enough to change the social relations of learning currently prevailing in most college classrooms. Instead, improvement will require the establishment of higher expectations and more challenging course requirements. They will also require wider penetration of the practices of teaching for understanding developed by Lee Shulman and others. A taste for confrontation with student culture will be essential for college teachers to make progress in improving students' academic skills and stimulating their interests in the life of the mind, as will rigorous assessment of the success of their efforts.

Consequences of the Legitimation of Teaching Identities

Even as course requirements leveled off or fell, the academic profession's self-concept was effectively altered by ideologies that placed teachers, rather than researchers, in the spotlight. The teaching reform and accountability movements have had perhaps their greatest success in raising the legitimacy of teaching as an object of concern and as a central identity for academics. In the most recent national survey of postsecondary faculty, more than three-quarters identified teaching as the most important activity in their professional lives (Schuster and Finkelstein 2008, 87). The faculty as a whole reported that 60 percent of its work time was spent on average in teaching-related activities, as compared to 15 percent on research (ibid., 88). Only the natural and social sciences and engineering showed any reapportionment of effort in the direction of research (ibid., 91). In addition, institutions more often required evidence of "teaching excellence" in applications for positions; such evidence was required in 60 percent of advertisements placed in the *Chronicle of Higher Education* (Meizlish and Kaplan 2008). These requirements grew at all types of institutions, including research universities, and particularly in the arts and humanities.

The establishment of teaching as an accepted core identity for professors solved the problem of status inconsistency (prestige for research, but requirements mainly for teaching) first identified by the sociologists Theodore Caplow and Reece McGee. But it also augured an era in which the academic profession devolved both in its aspirations and in its accomplishments. Ernest Boyer wished to maintain scholarship at the center of the profession. Yet the *American College Faculty* surveys suggest that the centrality of scholarly contributions has itself slowly eroded in the face of the participatory practices and eleemosynary goals of professors. Among full-time faculty in public doctoral-granting universities, interest in becoming an authority in one's field declined by 10 percent between 1989 and 2004, before increasing a bit in 2007. Interest in obtaining recognition from colleagues for scholarly achievements showed a similar rate of decline. American college faculty outside of private universities were more likely to say in 2007 that helping others was a more important goal than becoming an authority in one's field or obtaining recognition from colleagues for scholarly contributions (DeAngelo et al. 2007).

These data suggest that support for teaching did not preserve scholarship as the unifying feature of the academic profession, as promised in *Scholarship Reconsidered*, but rather that college teaching was transformed from more of a scholarly profession into more of a helping profession. This transformation was aided not only by the decoupling of the teaching-centered academy from the research-centered academy but by the success of a modern version of educational progressivism that catered to the interests of students in undemanding classes while reducing requirements for student performance.

At the same time that they begin to confront the consumerist and utilitarian norms of student culture, American academics may soon find it necessary to recreate the research-centered hierarchy of the post–World War II era. After decades of U.S. dominance, in recent years European scholars have taken over the lead in scientific publication. During the 1990s, the EU15 overcame the United States as the world's most productive region of scientific work. Where U.S. scientists produced nearly 40 percent of papers in the early 1970s, their share was down to one-quarter by the mid-2000s (National Science Foundation 2007; see also Galvez et al. 2000). Although the United States remains far ahead in articles with the highest citation rates, this gap is also closing (Horta and Veloso 2007). Other countries have improved their infrastructures for scientific production and the quality of their graduate programs. According to a 2007 survey, U.S. professors reported less time spent on research than professors in a number of countries, including Canada, Japan, Korea, Hong Kong, and China (Cummings and Finkelstein, cited in Jaschik 2009).[19] Moreover, three out of five U.S. professors characterized themselves as leaning toward teaching, rather than research, as their primary involvement, as compared to 30 to 40 percent of professors surveyed in five other developed countries (Canada, Hong Kong, Japan, Korea, and the United Kingdom). When weighing their involvement in teaching against research, the profile of U.S. professors resembled that of Brazilian and Mexican academics more than that of professors in developed countries (W. Cummings, personal communication).

These data are disturbing if one believes that the transmittal of the skills and practices of research and scholarship are at the center of the social contribution that university professors can make. Of course, the top research universities and liberal arts colleges will maintain a primary focus on the values of scholarship and the powers of mind that scholarship develops. But this is a narrow circle of institutions, and many faculty members at less prestigious institutions, empowered by Ernest Boyer and his followers, have been led to challenge its influence as elitist and remote from the everyday problems of students. As the academic profession has divided, the more numerous teaching group has begun to develop its own nonscholarly norms of practice. In non-STEM fields, faculty members have gravitated to active learning experiences and social service goals. Boyer expected pluralism to strengthen the usefulness and unity of the profession. But one might well ask, in the wake of the unintended consequences produced by *Scholarship Reconsidered*, whether a strong academic profession can be one whose sense of itself is focused more on progressive pedagogies than the scholarly disciplines. College professors can and should continue to improve their teaching practices. But one can only hope that professors will resist calls for reform that undermine the ultimate source of their profession's strength, its commitment to the standards of scholarly research.

NOTES

I would like to thank Scott Patrick Murphy for research assistance on this project. I would like to thank Richard Arum, William Cummings, Kevin J. Dougherty, Russell Edgerton, Martin Finkelstein, Mary Taylor Huber, Matthew Kaplan, Wendy Katkin, George Kuh, Mindy Marks, and Ernest Pascarella for bibliographic suggestions and access to unpublished data that helped to improve the quality of this chapter. I would like to thank Philip Babcock, Trudy Banta, Henry Braun, Steve Chatman, Kevin J. Dougherty, Judith Eaton, Russell Edgerton, Peter T. Ewell, David Fairris, Joseph Hermanowicz, Mary Huber, Jal Mehta, Margaret Miller, Gary Rhoades, Josipa Roksa, Carol Schneider, Jack Schuster, David Shulenberger, and Lee S. Shulman for conversations and correspondence that helped to challenge and advance my thinking about issues of teaching and learning in U.S. higher education.

1. Christopher Jencks and David Riesman described "the machinery" for producing researchers in *The Academic Revolution*: "[The top universities] have long been remarkably similar in what they encourage and value. They turn out Ph.D.s who . . . mostly have quite similar ideas about what their discipline covers, how it should be taught, and how its frontier should be advanced. . . . These men were not only like-minded at the outset, but they have established machinery for remaining like-minded. National and regional meetings for each academic discipline and subdiscipline are now annual affairs, national journals publish work in every specialized subject, and an informal national system of job placement and replacement has come into existence. The result is that large numbers of Ph.D.s now regard themselves almost as independent professionals like doctors or lawyers, responsible primarily to themselves and their colleagues rather than their employers, and committed to the advancement of knowledge" (1968, 13–14).

In the postwar era, Jencks and Riesman contended, college and university presidents ceded control to these professional men: "The typical president's greatest ambition for the future is usually to 'strengthen' his institution, and operationally this . . . turns out to mean assembling scholars of even greater competence and reputation than are now present" (1968, 17).

2. Market conditions also contributed to the renewed interest in the craft of teaching. The market for full-time faculty appointments turned markedly more com-

petitive in the tighter years following the great enrollment expansion of the 1960s and early 1970s. While the number of positions for new faculty remained roughly constant as a result of retirements and separations, new entrants faced markedly different circumstances for two reasons: the number of newly minted doctorates was growing much faster than positions for them—with larger cohorts of nearly 15,000 a year by 1997 (Schuster and Finkelstein 2008, 164)—and many more college teaching positions were being created off tenure track (ibid., 194). Between the 1970s and 1997, cohorts of new PhDs grew from fewer than 30,000 a year to more than 42,000 a year. Whereas most hiring had been on tenure track in the 1970s and 1980s, most new faculty members were being hired off the tenure track by the early 1990s (ibid.). The competition led graduate students to consider how best to give themselves an edge in the competition for faculty jobs. For students seeking jobs in research universities, this meant increased efforts to expand professional networks and to publish during graduate school. But some graduate students realized that evidence of teaching ability could constitute a plus factor that might tip appointment committees in their favor.

3. By the mid-1980s, clear signs were emerging of erosion in the "academic revolution" ideal of a research-centered profession. A study of department chairs by Burke (1988) revealed that research qualifications and research potential remained the most significant criteria used in hiring assistant professors, but that teaching ability had become an important part of the equation everywhere. Baccalaureate- and master's-granting institutions, in particular, were looking more and more at teaching as the primary criterion for hiring, even as research universities remained focused on publication and research potential.

4. The scholarship of discovery—or basic research—was, in Boyer's framework, the distinctive activity of professors in the arts and sciences of leading research universities, and particularly those working in the natural science disciplines. The scholarship of application—or applied research—was the distinctive activity of professors in professional schools at research and doctoral-granting institutions. It is the effort to apply knowledge to the solution of problems—"whether in medical diagnosis, serving clients in psychotherapy, shaping public policy, creating an architectural design, or working with the public schools" (23). The scholarship of integration—or synthetic interpretation—was the distinctive activity of humanistic scholars working in liberal arts colleges and research universities. Such scholars "give meaning to isolated facts, putting them in perspective." This was not, he cautioned, the work of the gentleman scholar or dilettante, but rather "serious, disciplined work that seeks to interpret, draw together, and bring new insight to bear on original research" (19).

5. Another initiative began at Harvard and a few other leading universities during the same period based on elective courses in teaching problems and methods offered to graduate students. At its peak, the Harvard course enrolled one in eighteen graduate students (Barzun 1968, 35).

6. The proportion of both universities requiring teaching assistant orientations and those requiring seminars on teaching in the disciplines dropped by the end of the decade (W. Katkin, personal communication).

7. As early as 1969, it had issued a statement crediting minorities for "giving a fresh and compelling impetus to the movement for restoring relevance to academic programs" (AAC 1969). Its studies on the "chilly climate" for women in college classrooms (Hall and Sandler 1982) received national attention in the 1980s.

8. Previous polls had shown employers to be relatively happy with higher education (see Lusterman 1977; Zemsky and Iannozzi 1998) and more interested in the development of social presentation skills and conformity than in the development of cognitive skills (see, e.g., Lesgold, Feuer, and Black 1997; Lusterman 1977; Squires 1979). AAC&U embraced the cognitive skills agenda and publicized its own poll of business executives, conducted by the Democratic pollster Peter D. Hart, showing that CEOs whose businesses employed high proportions of college graduates were in accord with the AAC&U agenda (Peter D. Hart and Associates 2006). If the poll results were unbiased—far from a certainty—businessmen and educators were, perhaps for the first time, developing a community of interest in the outcomes of higher education. Undoubtedly, workplace concerns helped to facilitate such rapport as existed, including a concordance of interest in collaborative and small group learning and intercultural understanding in increasingly diverse workplaces.

9. NSSE included student self-reports of learning gains in several skills areas. Self-reports show modest correlations with objective tests of learning gains and cannot be taken at face value as evidence of student learning (see, e.g., Bowman, forthcoming).

10. A similar study with more elaborate controls on students' prior achievements also yielded modest or insignificant relationships between NSSE benchmarks and cognitive growth on the Collegiate Assessment of Academic Performance (Pascarella, Seifert, and Blaich 2009).

11. Russell Edgerton, who moved from AAHE to the Pew Foundation in 1997, played an instrumental role in the institutionalization of the Carnegie reforms. Edgerton had "discovered" Shulman in national conference presentations in the 1980s and had become a devotee of Shulman's ideas for improving teaching and learning in academe. At Pew, Edgerton worked closely with colleagues at Carnegie throughout the decade of Shulman's presidency.

12. The total number of CASTL scholars topped out at fewer than one hundred. SoTL colloquia emerged on campuses throughout the country, but they attracted only a minority of motivated teachers to their events. Even at such a highly engaged campus as Indiana University, only about one-quarter of tenured and tenure-track faculty had participated in a SoTL event by 2002, and fewer than sixty people attended these events, on average, on a campus of more than two thousand faculty members. The Visible Knowledge Project ran out of funds in 2005, after a decade of pioneering work. Peer Review of Teaching remained operational, but attracted a dwindling

number of new portfolios after Pew funding ended. Carnegie's Knowledge Media Lab closed its electronic doors in September 2009, although its course portfolio software remained retrievable.

13. Outcomes assessment should be distinguished from the broader movement to increase accountability in higher education. Accountability has been linked to such performance indicators as graduation and job placement rates, as well as learning outcomes. Performance funding, a popular approach to provide incentives for improved institutional performance, is an outgrowth of the broader accountability movement (see, e.g., Burke 2005; Dougherty and Natow 2009).

14. In response to the breakdown of the ideal type of professional autonomy, understood as occupational control of work, sociologists have proposed a variety of alternatives to preserve professionalism or to reconfigure it for the contemporary world. These include blueprints for bolstering the ideological and ethical underpinnings of the professions (Freidson 2005), suggestions that professionals be able to demonstrate empirically that occupational control of work leads to better results for their clients than market or state-bureaucratic control (Brint 2006), and more comprehensive reworking of the professional model as part of a cooperating joint enterprise involving contributions from a variety of related occupations (Adler, Kwon, and Hechscher 2008).

15. Disappointing results from the National Assessment of Adult Literacy (NAAL) were one cornerstone of the commission's case for improved measurement and monitoring of student learning outcomes. NAAL data seemed to show that only 30% of college graduates could accurately interpret two competing editorials or make accurate inferences from a graph relating age, exercise, and blood pressure. Later administrations of the test to samples made up exclusively of recent college graduates showed no declines in literacy. The National Research Council concluded that the test as constructed could not detect who was proficient in literacy skills (National Research Council 2005).

16. The CLA and similar assessment instruments focus on important cognitive abilities related to analysis, synthesis, and evaluation. This strength of the CLA was not well aligned with two of the most important traditional aims of higher education: to provide general education in basic fields of knowledge and advanced training in a specialized discipline. In the past, every "high-stakes" test has brought a focus on the skills and content it privileges and only on those skills and contents. Indeed, the designers of the CLA acknowledged that they would be happy if colleges and universities taught to their test (see, e.g., Shavelson 2007). Some observers consequently argued that widespread adoption of the CLA or similar instruments would lead to the reconstitution of college classrooms around document-based performance tasks and tasks that involve making or breaking an argument (see, e.g., Brint 2008), at best an incomplete approach to undergraduate education.

17. It is perhaps not surprising under the circumstances that results for students at the El Paso and Permian Basin branches of the University of Texas showed higher

than expected gains on the CLA, while those at UT Austin did not, or those at the University of North Carolina–Wilmington showed higher than expected gains while those at the University of North Carolina–Chapel Hill did not (see www.collegepor trait.org/#).

18. The adequacy of preparation and, especially, pedagogical mentoring during graduate school remained open to doubt. Most PhD-granting institutions provided very limited incentives to improve teaching practice, beyond one-day orientation workshops. Semester courses on teaching in the disciplines remained uncommon. They were mandated at no more than 10% of universities (Reinvention Center 2002), and few teaching assistants were closely monitored for their work in the classroom. In an online survey, Golde and Dore (2001) found that fewer than 40% of 32,600 responding doctoral students reported that teaching assistants in their programs were adequately supervised to improve their teaching skills. Department chairs continued to indicate that incoming faculty would benefit from additional training in teaching (Benassi, O'Brien, and Seidel 1998; Meizlish and Kaplan 2008).

19. The triumph of the new progressivism may reflect a broader change in social values. In 1999, nearly half (47%) of Americans saw science and technology as the country's greatest achievement. That proportion slipped to just over one-quarter (27%) in 2009. By contrast, civil rights and equal rights were seen as America's greatest achievement by 17% of the population in 2009, up from 5% a decade before (Pew Center for People and the Press 2009). While the election of Barack Obama as president may help to explain these polling results, the results also suggest that the eroding prestige of science—and, with science, the research base of the university—could become a real concern. Increased public concern for equal opportunity has gone hand in hand with an increased emphasis on pedagogies of engagement and social goals in the university. These changes may or may not be compatible with the continuing centrality of cognitive rigor as the core value of the university.

REFERENCES

Accreditation Board for Engineering and Technology (ABET). 2000. *Criteria for accrediting engineering programs.* Baltimore: ABET, Inc.

Adelman, Clifford. 2007. Death to value-added. www.insidehighered.com/views/2007/01/26/banta (accessed October 30, 2007).

Adler, Paul S., Seok-Woo Kwon, and Charles Heckscher. 2008. Professional work: The emergence of collaborative community. *Oganizational Science* 19:359–76.

Alexander, F. King. 2000. The changing face of accountability. *Journal of Higher Education* 71:411–31.

Arum, Richard, and Josipa Roksa. 2011. *Academically adrift: Limited learning on college campuses.* Chicago: University of Chicago Press.

Association of American Colleges (AAC). 1969. *Racial problems and academic programs*. Washington, DC: AAC.

Association of American Colleges and Universities (AAC&U). 2004. *Our students' best work: A framework for accountability worthy of our mission*. Washington, DC: AAC&U.

Astin, Alexander W., Eric L. Dey, and William S. Korn. 1991. *The American college teacher: National norms for 1989–90 HERI Faculty Survey*. Los Angeles: Higher Education Research Institute, Graduate School of Education, UCLA.

Babcock, Philip S., and Mindy Marks. 2010. The falling time cost of college: Evidence from a half century of time use data. *NBER Working Paper No. 15954*. Cambridge, MA: National Bureau of Economic Research.

Banta, Trudy. 2007. A warning on measuring learning outcomes. *Inside Higher Education* (January 26). www.insidehighered.com/views/2007/01/26/banta (accessed October 12, 2008).

Barr, Robert B., and John Tagg. 1995. From teaching to learning: A new paradigm for undergraduate education. *Change* 27 (November/December): 12–25.

Barzun, Jacques. 1968. *The American university: How it runs, where it is going*. Chicago: University of Chicago Press.

Bass, Randall. 1999. The scholarship of teaching: What's the problem? www.doit.gmu.edu/Archives/Feb98/randybass.htm (accessed July 3, 2009).

Beckham, Edgar F. 2000. *Diversity, democracy, and higher education*. Washington, DC: Association of American Colleges and Universities.

Benassi, Victor A., E. J. O'Brien, and Lee F. Seidel. 1998. *The 1998 national survey of new faculty hiring practices*. Paper presented at the Lilly Conference on College University Teaching. Boston.

Boice, Robert. 1992. *The new faculty member: Supporting and fostering professional development*. San Francisco: Jossey-Bass.

Bok, Derek. 2006. *Our underachieving colleges*. Princeton: Princeton University Press.

Bowman, Nicholas A. Forthcoming. Can first-year college students provide accurate self-reports about their learning and development? *American Educational Research Journal*.

Boyer, Ernest L. 1990. *Scholarship reconsidered: Priorities of the professoriate*. Princeton: Carnegie Foundation for the Advancement of Teaching.

Braun, Henry. 2009. Finding the value in value-added. Paper presented at the 3rd SERU Research Symposium. University of California–Berkeley (May).

Brint, Steven. 2006. Saving the soul of professionalism: Eliot Freidson's institutional ethics and the defense of professional autonomy. *Knowledge, Work, and Society* 4:99–123.

———. 2008. The Spellings Commission and the case for professionalizing college teaching. *Academe* 94 (May-June): 21–24.

———. 2009. Student culture in an age of mass consumerist higher education. Unpublished lecture given at Teachers College, Columbia University (March).

Brint, Steven, Allison M. Cantwell, and Robert A. Hanneman. 2008. The two cultures of undergraduate academic engagement. *Research in Higher Education* 49:383–402.

Burke, Dolores L. 1988. *A new academic marketplace.* Westport, CT: Greenwood Press.

Burke, Joseph C., ed. 2005. *Achieving accountability in higher education: Balancing public, academic and market demands.* San Francisco: Jossey-Bass.

Burke, Joseph C., and Henrik Minassians. 2003. *Performance reporting: "Real" accountability or accountability lite. Seventh annual survey.* Albany: Rockefeller Institute of Government.

Burke, Joseph C., and Andreea M. Serban, eds. 1998. *Performance funding for public higher education: Fad or trend?* New Directions for Institutional Research #97. San Francisco: Jossey-Bass.

Business–Higher Education Forum. 2004. *Public accountability for student learning in higher education.* Washington, DC: American Council on Education.

Caplow, Theodore, and Reece J. McGee. 1958. *The academic marketplace.* New York: Basic Books.

Carini, Robert M., George D. Kuh, and Stephen P. Klein. 2006. Student engagement and student learning: Testing the linkages. *Research in Higher Education* 47:1–32.

Chatman, Steve. 2007. *Institutional versus academic discipline measures of student experience: A matter of relative validity.* Berkeley: Center for Studies in Higher Education. CSHE 8.07 (May).

Chickering, Arthur W., and Zelda Gamson. 1987. Seven principles for good practice in undergraduate education. *AAHE Bulletin* 39:3–7.

Clark, Burton R. 1987. *The academic profession: National, disciplinary, and institutional settings.* Berkeley and Los Angeles: University of California Press.

Commission on the Future of Higher Education. 2006. *A test of leadership: Charting the future of U.S. higher education.* Washington, DC: Commission on the Future of Higher Education. A Report of the Commission Appointed by Secretary of Education Margaret Spellings.

Cornwell, Grant, and Eve Walsh Stoddard. 1999. *Globalizing knowledge: Connecting international and intercultural studies.* Washington, DC: Association of American Colleges and Universities.

Cremin, Lawrence. 1961. *The transformation of the school, 1876–1957.* New York: Random House.

Cummings, William S., and Martin J. Finkelstein. 2007. The changing academic profession in the United States. Unpublished paper presented at the Hiroshima Conference on the Changing Academic Profession.

DeAngelo, Linda, Sylvia Hurtado, John H. Prior, Kimberly R. Nelly, Jose Luis Santos, and William S. Korn. 2007. *American college teacher: National norms for the 2007–2008 HERI Faculty Survey.* Los Angeles: Higher Education Research Institute.

Dey, Eric L., Claudia E. Ramirez, William S. Korn, and Alexander W. Astin. 1993. *The American college teacher: National norms for the 1992–93 HERI Faculty Survey.* Los Angeles: Higher Education Research Institute, Graduate School of Education, UCLA.

Dougherty, Kevin J., and Rebecca S. Natow. 2009. The political origins of state-level performance funding for higher education. Unpublished paper, Teacher's College, Columbia University.

Dougherty, Kevin J., and Monica Reid. 2007. *Fifty states of achieving the dream: State policies to enhance access to and success in community colleges across the United States.* New York: Teacher's College, Columbia University.

Dwyer, Carol A., Catherine M. Millet, and David G. Payne. 2006. *A culture of evidence: Post-secondary assessment and learning outcomes.* www.ets.org (accessed November 16, 2008).

Education Commission of the States. 1983. *Report of the task force on education and economic growth.* Denver: Education Commission of the States.

Educational Testing Service. 2003. *Quality, affordability and access: Americans speak of higher education.* Princeton: ETS. www.ets.org/media/2003/report.pdf (accessed January 4, 2007).

Ewell, Peter T. 2001a. *Accreditation and student learning outcomes: A proposed point of departure.* Washington, DC: Council on Higher Education Accreditation.

———. 2001b. Statewide testing in higher education. *Change* 33 (March-April): 50–70.

———. 2004. *Accreditation and the provision of additional information to the public about institutional and program performance.* Washington, DC: Council for Higher Education Accreditation.

———. 2005. Can assessment serve accountability: It depends on the question. In *Achieving accountability in higher education: Balancing public, academic, and market demands,* ed. Joseph C. Burke and Associates. San Francisco: Jossey-Bass.

Ewell, Peter T., and Margaret A. Miller. 2005. *Measuring up on college-level learning.* San Jose, CA: National Center for Public Policy in Higher Education.

Freidson, Eliot. 2005. *Professionalism: The third logic.* Chicago: University of Chicago Press.

Galvez, Antonio, Mercedes Maqueda, Manuel Martinez-Bueno, and Eva Valdivia. 2000. Scientific publication trends in the developing world—what can the volume and authorship of scientific articles tell us about scientific progress in various regions? *American Scientist* 88:526–33.

Geiger, Roger L. 2004. *Knowledge and money: Research universities and the paradox of the marketplace.* Stanford: Stanford University Press.

Gilman, David A. 1978. The logic of minimal competency testing. *NASSP Bulletin* 62:56–63.

Glassick, Charles M., Mary Taylor Huber, and Gene I. Maeroff. 1997. *Scholarship assessed: A special report on faculty evaluation.* San Francisco: Jossey-Bass.

Golde, Chris M., and Timothy M. Dore. 2001. *At cross purposes: What the experiences of doctoral students reveal about doctoral education.* www.phd-survey.org (accessed August 4, 2006). Report prepared for the Pew Charitable Trusts.

Grigsby, Mary. 2009. *Life through the eyes of students.* Albany: State University of New York Press.

Hall, Roberta M., and Bernice R. Sandler. 1982. *The classroom climate: A chilly one for women?* Washington, DC: Association of American Colleges.

Hart, Peter D., and Associates. 2006. *How should colleges prepare students in today's global economy?* Washington, DC: Peter D. Hart Research Associates.

Hawthorne, Joan. 2008. Accountability and comparability: What's wrong with the VSA approach? *Liberal Education* 94 (2): 24.

Horta, Hugo, and Francisco Veloso. 2007. Opening the box: Comparing EU and US scientific output by scientific field. *Technological Forecasting and Social Change* 74:1334–56.

Huber, Mary Taylor, and Patricia Hutchings. 2005. *The advancement of learning: Building the teaching commons.* San Francisco: Jossey-Bass.

Hutchings, Patricia, and Lee S. Shulman. 1999. The scholarship of teaching: New elaborations, new developments. *Change* 31 (September/October): 10–15.

Jaschik, Scott. 2009. Out of the loop. www.insidehighered.com/news/2009/06/12/survey (accessed August 31, 2009).

Jencks, Christopher, and David Riesman. 1968. *The academic revolution.* New York: Doubleday Anchor.

Johnson, Valen E. 2003. *Grade inflation: A crisis in college education.* New York: Springer.

Kerr, Clark. 1963. *The uses of the university.* Cambridge, MA: Harvard University Press.

Kuh, George D. 2009. The National Survey of Student Engagement: Conceptual and empirical foundations. In *Using student engagement data in institutional research, new directions for institutional research,* no. 141, ed. Robert Gonyea and George D. Kuh. San Francisco: Jossey-Bass.

Kuh, George D., and Stanley Ikenberry. 2009. *More than you think, less than we need: Learning outcomes assessment in American higher education.* Champaign, IL: National Institute for Learning Outcomes Assessment.

Kuh, George D., Jillian Kinzie, John H. Schuh, and Elizabeth J. Whitt. 2005. *Assessing conditions to enhance educational effectiveness: The inventory for student engagement and successes.* San Francisco: Jossey-Bass.

Ladd, Everett C., Jr. 1979. The work experience of American college professors: Some data and an argument. In *Current issues in higher education.* San Francisco: Jossey-Bass.

Lattuca, Lisa R., Patrick T. Terenzini, and J. Fredericks Volkwein. 2006. *Engineering change: A study of the impact of EC 2000.* Baltimore: ABET, Inc.

Lesgold, Alan, Michael J. Feuer, and Allison M. Black, eds. 1997. *Transitions in work and learning.* Washington, DC: National Academy Press. U.S. Department of Education, Office of Educational Research and Improvement.

Lindholm, Jennifer A., Alexander W. Astin, Linda J. Sax, and William S. Korn. 2002. *The American college teacher: National norms for the 2001–02 HERI Faculty Survey.* Los Angeles: Higher Education Research Institute, Graduate School of Education, UCLA.

Lindholm, Jennifer A., Katalin Szelenyi, Sylvia Hurtado, and William S. Korn. 2005. *The American college teacher: National norms for the 2004–2005 HERI Faculty Survey.* Los Angeles: Higher Education Research Institute, Graduate School of Education, UCLA.

Lusterman, Seymour. 1977. Education and industry. Report No. 719. New York: Conference Board.

McLendon, Michael K., James C. Hearn, and Russell Deaton. 2006. Called to account: Analyzing the origins and spread of state peformance-accountability policies for higher education. *Educational Evaluation and Policy Analysis* 28:1–24.

Meizlish, Deborah, and Matthew Kaplan. 2008. Valuing and evaluating teaching in academic hiring: A multi-disciplinary, cross-institutional study. *Journal of Higher Education* 79:489–512.

Miller, Richard I., Hongyu Chen, Jerome B. Hart, and Clyde B. Killian. 1990. New approaches to faculty evaluation—a survey, initial report. Athens, OH: Ohio University. Report submitted to the Carnegie Foundation for the Advancement of Teaching.

Millett, Catherine M., Leslie M. Stickler, David G. Payne, and Carol A. Dwyer. 2007. *A culture of evidence: Critical features of assessments for postsecondary student learning.* Princeton: Educational Testing Service.

Moffatt, Michael. 1989. *Coming of age in New Jersey: College and American culture.* New Brunswick: Rutgers University Press.

Musil, Carol M., ed. 1992. *The courage to question: Women's studies and student learning.* Washington, DC: Association of American Colleges and Universities.

Nathan, Rebekah. 2005. *My freshman year: What a professor learned by becoming a student.* Ithaca: Cornell University Press.

National Commission on Accountability in Higher Education. 2005. *Accountability for better results: A national imperative for higher education.* Washington, DC: State Higher Education Executive Officers.

National Governors Association. 1986. *A time for results: The governors' 1991 report on education.* Washington, DC: National Governors Association.

National Institute of Education Study Group on the Conditions of Excellence in American Higher Education 1984. *Involvement in learning: Realizing the potential of American higher education.* Washington, DC: National Institute of Education.

National Research Council (NRC). 2005. *Measuring literacy: Performance levels for adults.* Washington, DC: National Academies Press.

National Science Foundation, Division of Science Resources Statistics. 2007. *Changing U.S. output of scientific articles 1988–2003,* Derek Hill, Alan I. Rapaport, Rolf F. Lehming, and Robert K. Bell. Arlington, VA: National Science Foundation.

National Survey of Student Engagement (NSSE). 2000. *The NSSE 2000 Report: National benchmarks of effective educational practice.* Bloomington, IN: Indiana University, Center for Postsecondary Research.

———. 2008. *Promoting engagement for all students: The imperative to look within. 2008 results.* Bloomington, IN: Indiana University, Center for Postsecondary Research.

Osborne, David, and Ted Gaebler. 1992. *Reinventing government: How the entrepreneurial spirit is transforming the public sector.* New York: Penguin Books.

Pascarella, Ernest T., Tricia A. Seifert, and Charles Blaich. 2009. Validation of the NSSE benchmarks and deep approaches to learning against liberal arts outcomes. Paper presented at the annual meeting of the Association for the Study of Higher Education. Jacksonville, FL (November).

Reinvention Center. 2002. *Reinventing undergraduate education: Three years after the Boyer Report.* Stony Brook: Reinvention Center.

Riesman, David. 1980. *On higher education: The academic enterprise in an era of rising student consumerism.* San Francisco: Jossey-Bass.

Sax, Linda J., Alexander W. Astin, Marisol Arrendondo, and William S. Korn. 1996. *The American college teacher: National norms for the 1995–96 HERI Faculty Survey.* Los Angeles: Higher Education Research Institute, Graduate School of Education, UCLA.

Sax, Linda J., Alexander W. Astin, William S. Korn, and Shannon K. Gilmartin. 1999. *The American college teacher: National norms for the 1998–99 HERI Faculty Survey.* Los Angeles: Higher Education Research Institute, Graduate School of Education, UCLA.

Schaar, Jack, and Sheldon Wolin. 1965. A special supplement: Berkeley and the fate of the multiversity. *New York Review of Books* (March 11). www.nybooks.com/articles/13005 (accessed August 30, 2009).

Schuster, Jack H., and Martin Finkelstein. 2008. *The American faculty: The restructuring of academic work and careers.* Baltimore: Johns Hopkins University Press.

Shavelson, Richard J. 2007. *A brief history of student learning assessment: How we got where we are and a proposal for where to go next.* Washington, DC: Association of American Colleges and Universities.

Shulenburger, David. 2008. *Measuring core educational outcomes at research universities for improvement and accountability.* Washington, DC: National Association of State Colleges and Land-Grant Universities. Paper prepared for the October 2008 seminar on Measuring Undergraduate Learning Outcomes: A Working Agenda for Public Research Universities.

Shulman, Lee S. 1989. Toward a pedagogy of substance. *AAHE Bulletin* (June).

———. 1993. Teaching as community property: Putting an end to pedagogical isolation. *Change* (November/December): 6–7.

———. 1997. Professing the liberal arts. In *Education and democracy: Re-imagining liberal learning in America,* ed. Robert Orrill. New York: College Board Publications.

Shulock, Nancy, and Colleen Moore. 2002. *An accountability framework for California higher education: Informing public policy and improving outcomes.* Sacramento: Center for California Studies.

Squires, Gregory D. 1979. *Education and jobs: The imbalancing of the social machinery.* New Brunswick, NJ: Transaction Books.

Tuchman, Gaye. 2009. *Wannabe U: Inside the corporate university.* Chicago: University of Chicago Press.

Zemsky, Robert, and Maria Iannozzi. 1998. *A reality check: First findings from the EQW National Employer Survey.* ERIC #ED382811. EQW Issues No. 10.

Zumeta, William. 2001. Public policy and accountability in higher education: Lessons from the past and present for the new millennium. In *The States and public higher education policy: Affordability, access, and accountability,* ed. Donald E. Heller, 155–97. Baltimore: Johns Hopkins University Press.

CHAPTER THREE

Whose Educational Space?

Negotiating Professional Jurisdiction in the High-Tech Academy

Gary Rhoades

Contributions of leading scholars of the academic profession frame my analysis of professional jurisdiction in academe, as it relates to educational space in a high-tech academy. In saying that "teaching and learning are joined at the hip," Jack Schuster (2008) articulated the classic view of the academic profession, portraying professors as the fulcrum of the instructional enterprise, as the linchpin in teaching and learning. In saying that "typically, when we think about learning, we don't think about professors, we think about students," Anna Neumann (Neumann and Conway 2008) articulated (and then challenged) the prevailing perspective in public discourse about learning, which separates professors from learning. In saying that "we need to professionalize the college teaching function," Steven Brint (2008a) proposed a response by the academic profession to external demands for accountability, suggesting that the professoriate devote more systematic attention to "professionalizing" college teaching (see also Brint 2008b).

The above comments lie at the heart of a significant renegotiation of educational space in the academy and of faculty's position within that space. Once at the center of the teaching and learning equation, professors are no longer as central in our discussions and production of learning. To the extent that college teaching (and learning) is being professionalized, it is increasingly taking the form of new professions that are laying claim to expertise about teaching, learning, and the use of instructional technologies.

To understand the status of academe as a profession, we would do well to consider the position of academe relative to academic managers and to other professionals in the academy. We would also do well to consider the claims of professors, academic managers, and other professionals with regard to the faculty's core function of instruction and with regard to the educational spaces in which that function is performed. And we would do well to explore the ways in which those claims are advanced and negotiated by these groups at the national and campus levels. Historically, the academic profession has been seen and has seen itself as the core and indeed only profession on campus. That perception persists even as academe has become increasingly differentiated by field, institutional sector, and employment status (e.g., tenure-track vs. contingent faculty). Thus, I explore the extent and nature of academe's centrality in relation to a core function of most academics: instruction.

In this chapter I utilize three archival data sources to speak about the negotiation of professional jurisdiction in the high-tech academy. The introduction of new instructional technologies is a key dimension of the negotiation (Rhoades 1999, 2007; Smith and Rhoades 2006). Each of the data sources speaks to a different arena and type of negotiation, among different parties. Therein lies part of the complexity of competition over professional domain. One data source consists of the policy positions and publications of the three major national faculty organizations (American Federation of Teachers, American Association of University Professors, and National Education Association) that address the negotiation by faculty with management over the terms of labor surrounding the use of instructional technology in particular and the nature of education more generally. A second data source consists of the publications and Web sites of two institutional associations (the League for Innovation and the Association of American Colleges and Universities) that foreground the position of academic managers in advancing and framing certain conceptualizations of education that have implications for the place and role of faculty. A third data source consists of the Web sites of nonacademic, interstitial offices on two campuses, which feature the claims of emerging occupations and professions, in particular about pedagogy, expertise, and information technologies in education, and more generally about the nature and location of educational processes.

Conceptual Background

To frame my study of the negotiation of professional domain over educational space in the academy, I utilize concepts of professional jurisdiction (Abbott 1988), managed professionals (Rhoades 1998a), and emergent managerial professionals in new organizational structures that are part of academic

capitalism and the new economy (Slaughter and Rhoades 2004). What is revealed in my content analysis of the archival sources is not only a negotiation
between faculty and management over classroom and educational control,
but also a competition between existing and emergent professionals over
the definition and jurisdiction of different forms of expertise. These negotiations have profound implications for the place of professors in the educational
spaces of colleges and universities. They also have implications for what
counts as educational space, and for how universities invest in filling that
space. As I will suggest, the discourse of other groups is moving professors off
center stage, moving them from playing the leading role in a part that includes long soliloquies to the margins of the educational enterprise, with
smaller, more limited parts in the production of instruction and learning.
Moreover, the discourse of other groups is redefining where the educational
stages are and suggesting that institutions should invest in personnel and
places other than professors and classrooms, as well as in high-tech props for
these spaces.

In articulating a systems model of professions, Abbott (1988) examines
disputes among occupations over jurisdictional boundaries. Although his
framework eschews a focus on politically strategic practices by which professions negotiate control, Abbott does address the negotiation of task control.
He focuses on the qualities of work and tasks that are often negotiated publicly, in claims that are advanced in the public media as well as in discourse
and policy in the workplace. That is at the center of my analysis: how various
groups publicly claim expertise and define educational space.

In examining the negotiation between faculty and management in collective bargaining agreements, Rhoades (1998a) suggested that professors are
increasingly "managed professionals." The content and trend line of various
terms and conditions of academic labor point to increased managerial discretion and reduced professional prerogatives. Worse, in the case of educational
space I have suggested that the negotiating stance of faculty in bargaining
units (focused on controlling the use of technology in distance education and
limiting its immediate effects on current faculty) is leading to "professional
peripheralization." In trying to hold the use of instructional technology at a
distance, rather than establishing direct control over choices and uses of technology in various settings (not just in distance education), faculty are posi-
tioning themselves at the periphery of the issue, which is problematic.

The concept of "managerial professionals" (Rhoades 1998b; Rhoades and Sporn 2002) focuses on the fastest growing sector of the professional workforce in the academy. That sector consists of professionals who are not professors, are more closely linked to management, and now constitute on many campuses almost half of the professional workforce. As Slaughter and Rhoades (2004) detailed, part of the process of academic capitalism and the new economy involves the emergence of "interstitial units" in the margins of existing academic units, to perform new functions (and intersect with external markets and entities) as well as to insert themselves into the production process of existing functions in the academy. Some of these units, often staffed by managerial professionals, are involved in instructional matters, with the goal of modernizing and improving instruction, partly through the use of high-tech instructional technologies, and partly through an expanded definition of what constitutes educational space.

Professional jurisdiction, managed professionals, and managerial professionals are concepts that can help frame our understanding of faculty's changing position in the academy and of the contested and changing nature of educational space. These concepts help us to see how the position of professors and our definitions of educational space are being challenged and reconstructed. They also help us understand how other professions and academic managers articulate this reconceptualization. Utilizing these concepts helps us better understand the extent to which the professional domain of academics is withering away, as well as the ways in which academics are casting withering looks and exclamations at current developments. In taking these considerations into account, we can explore whither the academic profession is headed.

In examining the terms of discourse and debate in different arenas of negotiation, I focus on the following issues: What educational spaces are identified in the discourse, and what is the priority among them? To what extent and in what ways are professors featured in these educational spaces? To what extent and in what contexts is learning discussed, how is it defined, and are professors identified as being central to learning? What expertise (e.g., pedagogical and technological) is discussed and validated in regard to instruction and learning, and who is identified as having that expertise? To what extent and how are new instructional technologies featured in educational spaces and in learning? In each of the above questions, I seek to track how much mention is made of educational spaces, professors, learning, expertise, and technology. I focus on the meanings assigned to them in universities.

Educational Space according to Three Key Faculty Organizations: Faculty, Classrooms, and Distance Education

One vehicle for understanding the position of faculty in negotiating educational space is analyzing policy pronouncements and positions of the American Federation of Teachers (AFT), the American Association of University Professors (AAUP), and the National Education Association (NEA). Of the three, the AAUP is perhaps seen as the one that speaks most for the faculty as whole, although the number of faculty, professionals, and graduate student employees it represents is relatively small—about 48,000. The AFT and the NEA represent much larger numbers of faculty, academic professionals, and graduate student employees (about 185,000 and over 200,000, respectively). All three organizations have issued statements about instructional technologies, instruction, and learning (their Web sites were accessed in April 2008).

In general, for all three faculty organizations, the educational space of classrooms and of the formal curriculum is central to addressing instructional technology in education. The premise is that this is where curriculum is delivered with technology. Moreover, that educational space is faculty space, in which academics exercise control through formal mechanisms of academic governance. Indeed, that is really the only educational space that the AFT and NEA address—classrooms; by contrast, the AAUP addresses academic freedom and governance issues that extend beyond the classroom.

What is more, on all three Web sites, the focus on high technology in education almost exclusively addresses distance education. Yet there are many classes utilizing new instructional technologies that are "hybrid," a combination of online, asynchronous environments with face-to-face settings. There are also courses utilizing technology in campus classrooms. But one would not know that from the faculty organizations' sites. Nor do these sites address other educational spaces in which academics utilize computer technologies, such as responding to student questions via e-mail, or working in labs or off-campus settings. Faculty organizations are not attuned to new, so-called educational spaces on and off campus, which, in the language of the day, are learning spaces.

Finally, it is interesting that none of the organizations address course management software systems such as BlackBoard. Such systems, with their boilerplate structures for organizing courses, identifying objectives, and the like, are redefining the delivery of courses. There is an argument to be made that these systems are themselves new educational spaces. In the eyes of the three major faculty organizations, these boards are invisible, in contrast to old-style blackboards and new whiteboards.

The AAUP

The AAUP's home page mentions faculty and the academic profession but does not speak of teaching and learning. The "About the AAUP" page has three references to faculty—one in relation to professional values, one to shared governance, and one to academic freedom. Each realm encompasses more than classrooms. I conceptualize the educational space in which faculty function in broad terms. The space ranges from committee meetings in the academic governance structure to open areas that involve but also extend beyond classrooms. In all such space, academic freedom is operative.

By contrast, in the section titled "Issues," there is a 1990 statement on teaching evaluations, which is the only reference to teaching. As might be expected, given the topic, this statement refers repeatedly to "faculty," "professor," and "teacher." There are nearly twice as many references to teaching/instruction, only one of which refers to out-of-class activities. The terminology includes, for example, "teaching effectiveness," "teaching performance," "teaching strategies," "teaching competence," "teaching ability," "superior teaching," "enhancement of instruction," and "teaching styles." In the five-page statement there is only one reference to "student learning."

A similar pattern holds for another statement on the site, on distance education. There is only one reference to learning: "abilities of students to learn." By contrast, there are thirty-three references to faculty/teachers, who are foregrounded throughout the document. Language such as "Faculty should have primary responsibility for determining the policies and practices of the institution in regard to distance education" (www.aaup.org/AAUP/issues/DE/sampleDE.htm) conveys the idea that faculty should be at the center of the process, as they are in traditional classrooms.

However, the AAUP does not address instructional technology beyond distance education. It is as if there are two distinct classroom spaces—one on campus and the other at a distance, mediated by technology. Yet, instructional technologies have been extensively incorporated into campus classes through course management systems and other online structures.

In one section of its Web site, a statement on "Mandated Assessment of Educational Outcomes," the AAUP speaks about learning outcomes. Yet here, too, the faculty are foregrounded, mentioned forty-five times, versus eighteen references to learning. Moreover, references are largely distinct from the accountability language of the day. For example, teaching and learning are linked (as in Jack Schuster's classic view, at the hip). Linguistically, this connects professors and their teaching to the learning of students, invoking the necessary importance of teachers to the learning process. Overall, there is also a tone of external mandates to evaluate learning as a threat and as problematic—evident in phrases such as "difficulties of evaluating student learning."

The AFT and the NEA

The positions of the AFT and NEA are fairly consistent, although different in some respects. For example, the home pages of the Higher Education programs of both the AFT and the NEA mention faculty but not learning. Similarly, on the "About" pages of each organization "faculty" are again mentioned but not "learning."

Yet the NEA pages are somewhat different in their focus on teaching. On its home page, the Higher Education program has a section of the site reporting the title of the publication, "Advocate Online," which is entitled "Digital Immigrants." This title invokes a concept articulated by Educause, an organization that promotes the use of instructional technologies. That concept undermines the faculty's position and expertise by underscoring how they are new to and uncomfortable with technologies. Thus, the NEA text asks, "Has the digital age left the nation's professoriate in the dust?" It then later states, "Most professors are trying to pick up this second language on the run." Technology is featured and is a fulcrum for challenging the faculty's classroom expertise.

Similarly, the "About" page of the NEA site has references to teaching and implicitly to learning. Thus, there is a statement about how the NEA "works to improve teacher quality and student achievement" and about publications that provide "tips and advice on pedagogical and professional issues." Consistent with its history as a professional association, the NEA positions itself as a source of professional development, and the key area of such development is faculty's instructional work.

For both the AFT and the NEA, there is a considerable focus on technology. Each of the sites has separate sections, reports, and materials regarding technology. As with the AAUP, technology is conflated with distance education classrooms.

Again, however, there is a difference between the organizations. For the AFT, the focus is on faculty (seven mentions) almost as much as on technology (nine mentions), and there is only one reference to student learning. By contrast, the NEA site mentions technology far more than it does faculty (fifteen vs. two mentions). There are many (eight) references to student learning, including "enhancing learning," "changing the way students learn," "learner," "advancement of learning," "learning resources," and three references to "learning strategies." All are related to teaching and learning in distance education.

In sum, the AFT and NEA sites address faculty. The educational space addressed is overwhelmingly the classroom. Technology is addressed only in the context of distance education. Neither organization engages or articulates expanded conceptions of educational space, or reconstructed conceptions of traditional and virtual classrooms, not to mention office, lab, or library space. There is a limited conception of how and where faculty engage students and produce learning.

Programs of Two Key Institutional Organizations

Another means to understand the position of faculty in negotiating educational space is to analyze policy pronouncements and positions of key institutional associations (Web sites of institutional associations were accessed in April 2008). The institutional associations I address, the League for Innovation (LfI) and the Association of American Colleges and Universities (AAC&U), represent the diversity of the institutional settings in which faculty work is conducted and education provided. The diversity is particularly evident in the areas of instruction and technology.

The LfI is focused on the two-year college sector and consists of more than eight hundred members in fourteen countries, including more than 160 private corporations. Established in 1968, its goal, in its own words, is "catalyzing the community college movement." The flavor and rhetoric of the organization speak to newness, innovation, and dynamism.

By contrast, the AAC&U can call upon the legitimacy and tradition of nearly one hundred years, dating to its establishment as the Association of American Colleges in 1915. It now has 1,150 institutional members, representing the full range of U.S. higher education in institutional types, large and small, public and private. Of its members, about 17 percent are doctoral-granting institutions, 28 percent masters-granting, 26 percent bachelors-granting, and 12 percent associate's degree–granting (17% are "other"—a range of specialized schools, state systems/organizations, and international/organizational affiliates). The AAC&U's identity, and indeed its tagline on its Web site, is "A Voice and a Force for Liberal Education in the 21st Century." Even as it moves into the twenty-first century, it invokes a tradition of liberal learning.

With such different histories and memberships, it is not surprising that the two institutional organizations articulate different views of educational space, and that they have different perspectives about faculty and education. Yet despite such differences, there is an important similarity. The centrality of professors in defining twenty-first-century educational space and in operating within it is fundamentally challenged.

The League for Innovation

The site of the LfI provides a virtual lexicon of learning. Included in the twenty-three references on the "Home" and "About" pages are the following phrases: "distance learning," "teaching and learning," "learning community," "asynchronous learning community," "learning centered," "learner centered," "learning network," "learning initiative," "learning college," "learning outcomes," "learning evidence," "learning assessment," "adult learning," "student learning," "organizational learning," "learning environment," "learning revolution," and "culture of learning." That is a lot of learning.

Besides the number of references and the scale and number of programs focused on learning, it is remarkable to see an almost complete absence of reference made to teaching (there is just one reference). For example, in the hope of catalyzing more "learning-centered community colleges," the League has developed a Learning Initiative with the goal "to assist community colleges in developing policies, programs, and practices that place learning at the heart of the educational enterprise, while overhauling the traditional architecture of education." That is a fairly straightforward statement of the way in which the League's efforts are intended to displace faculty at the center of the educational enterprise and replace them with learning. The emphasis on learning communities outside the formal classroom points to the expansive notion of learning that the League adopts. As articulated in the title of a series of monthly articles published in *Community College Week* in 1998, it is a "learning revolution."

On these same pages, there are a total of three references to faculty (and two others to "educators"). One is a reference to an "assessment primer" that "helps faculty navigate assessment and shape curriculum, allowing students to stay on course." It is interesting that the expertise level of faculty in this regard is assumed to be at the "primer" level. Another of the references to faculty is to members of a leadership institute who in fact are not professors.

A key feature of the conception of educational space advanced by the League is that it places two key players and partners on stage. One of those is technology, which is partly a prop to facilitate learning and partly a mechanism that enables learning without any engagement with faculty. The other new player consists of large corporations. The home page, for example, identifies "Distinguished Corporate Partners," a group that consists of over 160 corporations. As the lead text on the page reads, "Corporations connect with us through partnerships." Later, there is reference to a "collaborative course exchange" in a "learning network" that targets "industry driven programs and certificates." The learning network appears to essentially consist of a business network.

Throughout the "About" page, there are repeated references to corporations in general and to particular companies, including references to awards received by the League from Compaq and from IBM "for influencing and advancing information technology use in higher education." For example, the League has a "Technology and Learning Community" (TLC), which sounds a lot like TCB (taking care of business). This asynchronous "learning" community is supported by Compaq, Microsoft, and Technomarketing, which later came to be supported for a time by the Department of Education, with the goal of promoting teachers' use of technology. Presumably, the members of these communities were largely "learning" about new products; it was a promotional/marketing network. Along similar lines, the League has created the Business and Industry Services Network (BISNET) "as a forum for leaders to share ideas and resources for serving business and industry."

In short, the League is working to restructure educational space by bringing onto center stage not only technology but also companies that promote and market information technologies. In this scheme there is not much place for faculty. The configuration of the academic workforce in the community colleges represented by the League provides an important context in which to understand implications for the academic profession. The proportion of community college faculty who are contingent runs at about two-thirds nationwide. That speaks to a particular conception of educational space, and of how learning takes place, delivered through information technology more than through the active engagement of students with full-time academics who are at the core of the educational space and the educational process.

Association of American Colleges and Universities

The site of the AAC&U offers a different lexicon. Reflecting its history and enduring purpose, the AAC&U provides a discourse of redefined liberal education and essential learning outcomes. Its strategic plan for 2008–12 features both ideas. Although faculty are identified as central, they are relegated to a very small bit in the document. Interestingly, technology goes virtually unmentioned. Surprisingly, business is introduced as an entity that defines liberal learning outcomes.

Given the history of the association, it is perhaps predictable that the AAC&U features liberal education. In the strategic plan, there are more references to this term (forty-seven) than to any other. But what is striking is how liberal education is redefined beyond the liberal arts, and especially beyond the humanities and fine arts. The AAC&U emphasizes the development of a twenty-first-century model of liberal education and even bemoans the continued power in people's minds of a traditional interpretation of the concept.

> The humanities play an essential part in AAC&U's vision for a 21st century liberal education. But, efforts to promote liberal education as "imperative" run directly into popular mental models that equate liberal education with the humanities and arts only. . . . These widespread public misunderstandings of liberal education remain a significant hurdle for AAC&U's efforts to establish liberal education as "essential" rather than "elective." (www.aacu.org/about/ strategic_plan.cfm#Priority)

Throughout the strategic plan, there is a language of "essential learning outcomes" that is nearly as prevalent as liberal education. There are forty-two mentions of learning. Most central of all to the plan is the concept of "essential learning outcomes," encompassing intellectual and practical skills, personal and social responsibility, and integrative and applied learning. The language clearly positions the organization in relation to assessment.

Yet technology is not presented as the key in promoting learning. Indeed, it is mentioned but once in the ten-page document. The focus instead is on terms such as engagement and active involvement in learning.

Faculty are cast at the core of the educational enterprise. However, that role is addressed in only one paragraph of the plan, called "The Central Role of Faculty in Achieving Inclusive Excellence and Authentic Assessment." The paragraph speaks to the value of featuring "faculty members' own curricular, pedagogical, technological, and assessment creativity."

There are hints in the document of other players coming on stage to help faculty in the work of facilitating essential learning outcomes. Thus, the title of the paragraph about faculty's central role is "Integrative and Applied Learning—In and Out of the Classroom." The AAC&U identifies the "larger educational institution as a crucial laboratory for liberal learning" and points to the importance of "academic and student-life partnerships" that target traditionally underserved students. The educational space is expanding considerably, with implications for who operates in that space and for the centrality of faculty in the educational enterprise.

Perhaps most striking in their conceptualization of essential learning outcomes is AAC&U's introduction of a new player on stage, one who plays a partnering role in defining those outcomes. The new, twenty-first-century liberal education focuses on learning outcomes identified by employers. Yet AAC&U sees these outcomes as consistent with those identified by faculty, indicating that "as AAC&U has documented over the past five years, there is a growing consensus on a set of educational goals that faculty and employers alike see as high priorities for a contemporary college education."

In sum, both the LfI and the AAC&U place learning front and center. Both organizations also center business in the definition of learning outcomes, although to differing degrees and through different mechanisms. Their stances are quite different, however, on technology and faculty. LfI emphasizes technology and leaves faculty virtually unmentioned. AAC&U mentions technology sparingly; although it refers to the significance of faculty, the organization suggests that faculty need to be led by "faculty developers."

Public Claims of Interstitial Teaching/Learning Units in Two
Universities: Asserting Jurisdiction, Decentering Faculty,
Relocating Space

A third means to understand the position of faculty in educational space is
to analyze the public claims of interstitial teaching/learning units (Web sites
were accessed in April and September 2008). I focus on units at two universities: Ohio University and the University of Arizona. Ohio University was selected because it was featured on the AAC&U Web site under "Member Innovations." The University of Arizona was selected because I have been studying
it as part of a larger NSF-funded study of instructional technology; moreover,
its teaching center is recognized as a national leader in the field.

Ohio University

The AAC&U featured innovation at Ohio University is faculty learning communities (FLCs). The goal of these communities is "nurturing pedagogical innovation." The idea is to "prepare faculty to help lead and support the transition" to
a "learning centric institution." The unwritten theme is to shift them from being
professor centric. Yet the strategy is for faculty development staff to "foster faculty
engagement" and for selected faculty to themselves lead the communities.

Three faculty development centers are at the core of Ohio University's
FLCs initiative. One, which previously was named the Center for Teaching
Excellence, is now titled the Center for Teaching and Learning, a telling linguistic shift given the prominence of the lexicon of learning. The center has a
director who has an appointment in sociology and an associate director who
is not a professor but has an MA degree. The center provides workshops, a
discussion series, individual consultations, and other resources for faculty,
graduate student teaching assistants, and other instructional staff. A second
interstitial unit, the Center for Writing Excellence, is staffed by one faculty
member and five other professionals; it provides various faculty resources. A
third unit, formerly the Center for Innovations in Technology and Learning
and now the Center for Academic Technology, is staffed by four professional
and technical staff, including a Web projects manager and a Web/multimedia
designer. It provides faculty with instructional resource materials and
technology-based tools and applications. The title is revealing in that on many
campuses two different sorts of interstitial units have been emerging: some
are focused on teaching and learning and others on technology.

Given the overall topic of educational space, it is interesting that these three centers have been relocated in a "faculty commons" in the library, moved from an old basement space to a newly renovated nine-thousand-square-foot facility. In some sense, the physical move signifies the increasing presence of faculty development activities and their connection to the ways libraries are being reconceptualized, often with technology as learning spaces. This relocation is part of the library's strategic plan. In short, Ohio University provides an example of emergent professions laying claim to authority on how to teach. It constructs new educational spaces to enable such emergent professions to teach professors how to teach.

University of Arizona

Two interstitial units at the University of Arizona (the University Teaching Center and the Learning Technologies Center) address a focal point of analysis. The difference in their titles speaks to the competing bases of their claims to jurisdiction in educational space and their conception of that space.

The University Teaching Center is staffed by six professionals, none of whom are faculty members, and a business manager. The center's mission is to support and enhance instruction: it offers new faculty orientation as well as an orientation for graduate teaching assistants; it also provides various workshops and consultations. In addition, the center manages two grants that are focused on learner-centered education.

The principal expertise claims of the center have to do with pedagogy. For instance, the center offers pedagogy workshops "for teachers interested in improving their classroom presentations, expanding the use of active learning strategies, and related methods for enhancing student learning." The extent of the center's claim to pedagogical expertise is evidenced in its "Certificate in College Teaching Program." The program offers structured courses that prepare graduate students to teach and thereby extends the center's jurisdiction to graduate education by providing the equivalent of an academic minor. Yet in making these claims the center remains largely focused on the traditional classroom.

The Learning Technologies Center has forty-two staff members (not including support staff), the equivalent of a large academic department. None of the staff are faculty members. Their titles convey the domain of expertise that characterizes the center: "Instructional Applications Support Liaison," "Instructional Applications Specialist," "Instructional Applications Support

Specialist," "ELearning Design Specialist," "Web Programmer," "Faculty Support Liaison," "Media Specialist," "Senior Consultant Learning Technologies," "Web Developer," "Graphic Designer."

Technology is the center's overriding focus. Thus, the assessment and evaluation section of the site is about assessing the productivity of new technological tools and also the use of technology to conduct assessments: "Although our primary focus is on computer-based instruction, we also support the use of computer-based technologies for assessment and evaluation in any course, including conventional face-to-face instruction." There are also services related to instructional design that focus largely on utilizing the course management system of the campus. The strategies are asserted to be "based on solid learning and instructional theory." Among the instructional tools offered are blogs, podcasts, iTunes, and "UA You Tube." Finally, perhaps because of its technological focus, the center extends its claims into distance education space.

In short, when it comes to professional jurisdiction over educational space, the centers at the University of Arizona offer two types of interstitial units. There is some overlap among the units; for instance, both invoke technology and bodies of knowledge about teaching and learning. But one grounds its principal claims to expertise in pedagogy, mostly in campus classrooms. The other does so in technology, through numerous types of classroom spaces, campus-based and virtual.

Conclusion

I return to the three quotes discussed in the introductory paragraph of the chapter. The classic view of teaching and learning being joined at the hip was evident in the stance of the three faculty organizations. Both the AFT and NEA constructed the educational space of teaching and learning in terms of the classroom. Their negotiating stance had largely to do with technology and the distance education classroom. By contrast, the AAUP addressed faculty's central role in larger educational spaces of the institution, invoking conceptions of academic freedom and shared governance. Yet the collective effect of the faculty organizations' positions is to distance themselves from key questions of educational space in the high-tech academy. They made no jurisdictional claims here, in Abbott's terms. Faculty organizations by their own actions marginalized faculty and opened the door for emergent professions in interstitial units to lay claim to new and old educational spaces.

The prevailing view of "learning having little to do with faculty and everything to do with students isolated from faculty" was evident in the stance of the two institutional associations. Although there were significant differences in the lexicons of the LfI and AAC&U, they both moved learning to center stage. In the process, faculty were moved to the margins. In place of faculty, the LfI moved technology and high-tech corporations into central roles in effective learning. Faculty were largely absent and without force, increasingly "managed," marginalized professionals in the high-tech academy. By contrast, the AAC&U accorded faculty an important yet minor role. However, the AAC&U introduced industry as a partner in defining learning outcomes and invoked the need for partners to assist faculty in enhancing learning outcomes. What is more, the AAC&U broadened the construction of educational space. The institutional associations created new spaces focused on technology and learning outcomes, which represented an opportunity for emergent professionals to take their place on the stage.

The positions adopted by faculty and institutional associations set the stage for a third party to enter the negotiations over educational space and for it to advance its claims. New categories of emergent professionals in interstitial units have stepped in to enhance teaching and learning. In contrast, then, to Brint's (2008b) call for faculty to professionalize teaching, this professionalization process is instead being driven by the efforts of new professionals on campus.

If one were to ask professors and students and people outside higher education to identify where education takes place, most would point primarily to classrooms. And by classrooms, most would be referring to on-campus, generally rectangular spaces filled with many students and one faculty member (with perhaps a teaching assistant or two as well). Classrooms are the conventional education spaces in the academy.

But in the high-tech academy the configuration of classrooms is changing. Moreover, there is a change in who claims this space as their professional jurisdiction. The configuration has changed in terms of what is in the classroom and what personnel figure in the production of the course. Whiteboards (and in a few places SMART Boards) have replaced blackboards. Laptops, projectors, and ELMOs are replacing overhead projectors. More and more classes are run on and structured by course management systems such as Blackboard or D2L. New categories of technical and professional personnel are involved in producing, supporting, and maintaining the course and literally unlocking and opening up the technology for use by faculty and students. The new, high-tech equipment in classrooms, which is expensive in initial costs, requires maintenance and regular updating. These developments change the costs of producing a course. Although the physical structure of classroom space has remained much the same, with a continued dominance of rectangles versus circles or other polygonal shapes, the construction and operation of the space itself have changed. Where faculty once ruled alone in this domain, they are increasingly being required to share the space in which education formally transpires.

Perhaps most important, in the high-tech academy the construction of educational spaces has expanded. Whether through the increased use of instructional technologies or through the increased emphasis on a broad range of learning outcomes, there is a rise of spaces in which professors are not central. These spaces are created, supported, and managed by professional personnel other than faculty.

In this chapter I have pursued the question of whither the academic profession is headed by exploring the negotiation of professors' jurisdiction in education and instruction. I have also addressed the issue of how the various parties are socially constructing educational spaces in the academy and their claims about what is required for these spaces. Drawing on various documentary and archival materials from online sources, I have examined the stance that (a) national faculty organizations are taking, largely in relation to academic managers; (b) institutional associations are taking, largely articulating the views of academic managers in relation to teaching and learning; and (c) interstitial units of emerging professionals are taking, largely in relation to faculty and students.

In negotiating their professional jurisdiction, faculty have for the most part taken a relatively narrow view of educational space, as if unaware of what is at stake. What is at stake is not simply the place of faculty, but also a conception of education that involves faculty actively engaging students and challenging their ideas in a relationship that broadens students' horizons and capacities.

By contrast, institutional associations and the academic managers they represent have taken a negotiating stance that stakes out broad claims about learning. Yet the conception of learning varies for the LfI and AAC&U. In the case of the former, it is about technology and business, suggesting a conception of education that is about efficiently, quickly, and conveniently delivering information. In the case of the latter, it is about faculty and business identifying learning outcomes, and about supporting faculty in the realization of such outcomes.

Finally, emerging professionals advance their claims. They offer conceptions of pedagogical and technical expertise that they assert are superior to those of faculty. What is more, these new professionals identify, construct, and lay claim over a range of educational spaces that extend into but also beyond traditional classrooms.

Whose educational space is it? In the high-tech academy, the answer to that question is still being negotiated among multiple parties. But the trend is of faculty having to share educational space, even in traditional classrooms. The trend is of faculty losing their authority of expertise in educational matters to other players and professionals who claim educational authority. In the process, we are seeing a renegotiation of what constitutes education and where it takes place. We are seeing a professionalizing of high-tech learning (and of teaching) that increasingly involves an investment in professional personnel and educational spaces other than tenure-track faculty. By the same token, we see classrooms reducing, in relative terms, the investment in and authority of the professoriate.

REFERENCES

Abbott, Andrew. 1988. The system of professions: An essay on the division of expert labor. Chicago: University of Chicago Press.

Brint, Steven. 2008a. No college student left behind? The case for professionalizing the college teaching function. Wither the American Academic Profession? Its Changing Forms and Functions. A Conference on the Future of the Academic Profession. Athens, GA.

———. 2008b. The Spellings Commission and the case for professionalizing teaching. Academe 9(3), 21–24.

Neumann, Anna, and Katie Mehan Conway. 2008. Learning profession: Transforming contexts of professors' scholarly learning. Wither the American Academic Profession? Its Changing Forms and Functions. A Conference on the Future of the Academic Profession. Athens, GA.

Rhoades, Gary. 1998a. Managed professionals: Unionized faculty and restructuring academic labor. Albany: State University of New York Press.

———. 1998b. Reviewing and rethinking administrative costs. In *Higher education handbook of theory and research*, vol. 13, ed. John C. Smart. New York: Agathon Press.

———. 1999. Technology and the changing campus workforce. Thought & Action 15 (Spring): 127–38.

———. 2007. Technology enhanced courses and a mode III organization of instructional work. Tertiary Education and Management 13 (1): 3–28.

Rhoades, Gary, and Barbara Sporn. 2002. New models of management and shifting modes and costs of production: Europe and the United States. Tertiary Education and Management 8 (1): 3–28.

Schuster, Jack H. 2008. The professoriate's perilous path: Does whither mean wither? Wither the American Academic Profession? Its Changing Forms and Functions. A Conference on the Future of the Academic Profession. Athens, GA.

Slaughter, Sheila, and Gary Rhoades. 2004. Academic capitalism and the new economy: Markets, state, and higher education. Baltimore: Johns Hopkins University Press.

Smith, Vernon, and Gary Rhoades. 2006. Community college faculty and web-based classes. Thought & Action 22 (Fall), 97–110.

CHAPTER FOUR

American Academe and the Knowledge-Politics Problem

Neil Gross

In recent decades social scientists have considered whether some long-established professions in American society, such as medicine and law, may be undergoing a process of deprofessionalization (Draper 2003; Ritzer and Walczak 1988; Rothman 1984; Van Hoy 1995). Deprofessionalization can be defined as a "decline in power which results in a decline in the degree to which professions possess . . . a constellation of characteristics denoting a profession" such as "altruism, autonomy, authority over clients, general systematic knowledge, and community and legal recognition" (Ritzer and Walczak 1988, 6). Although professionals in the United States continue to fare well in terms of life chances and occupational status, so much so that some analysts view the occupational closure that helps to characterize professions as a key driver of wage inequality in the labor market overall (Weeden 2002), various social changes are said to be working in tandem today to erode the professional standing of elite fields. For example, as Rothman (1984) notes, the dramatic growth of higher education and spread of new information technologies have made it harder for some professionals to claim the same kind of monopoly over esoteric knowledge as was key to most professionalization "projects" in the nineteenth and early twentieth centuries (Abbott 1988; Freidson 1986; Larson 1977). At the same time, changes in the organizational structures that house professionals, such as the rise of managed care organizations for doctors and large law firms for lawyers, threaten to undermine the workplace autonomy that has long been a hallmark of professions and to replace relatively autonomous principles of professional practice with principles of the market and bureaucratic rationality. Whether these and other changes are leading to deprofessionalization per se or simply a restructuring of the professions is subject to debate (Filc 2006; Freidson 1984; Haug 1975; Leicht and Fennell 1997), but they have certainly been consequential for professionals, the groups they serve, and competitor occupations for which structural shifts figure as openings allowing for the possibility of jurisdictional challenge.

Commentators on American academe have observed significant transformations in the higher education sector beginning in the 1980s that seem to entail parallel losses of power for the academic profession. These transformations include the expansion of for-profit higher education institutions, growth in the ranks of non-tenure-track faculty, increasing cooperation between universities and the corporate sector that allows the pursuit of profit to directly shape research agendas, growing pressures around institutional competitiveness that have empowered university administrators, and the emergence of a consumerist ethic among students (e.g., Bok 2004; Kleinman 2003; Readings 1996). Only occasionally considered in this context is another important development: a growing chorus of conservative critics who argue that segments of American academe have abandoned their traditional mission of impartial scholarship and become staging grounds for leftist thought and politics (e.g., D'Souza 1991; Horowitz 2006, 2007; Kimball 1998). These critics allege that for a significant minority of faculty today research amounts to little more than rehashing stale ideas of the left; that too often teaching is indistinguishable from political indoctrination; that academe as a whole is hostile to conservative viewpoints, thinkers, and students; and that the resulting lack of "intellectual diversity" on campus is detrimental to inquiry and student learning. Criticism of liberal professors has been a feature of American conservative discourse since the publication of William F. Buckley's *God and Man at Yale* in 1951, but such criticism reached a crescendo in 2002–8 as conservative advocacy organizations devoted to higher education carved out a stable niche for themselves in the landscape of the broader American conservative movement, gained routinized access to mainstream media outlets, and were able to capitalize on high-profile cases (for example, incendiary comments made by former University of Colorado ethnic studies professor Ward Churchill) that seemed to cast professors in a negative light. Because conservative critics call into question the legitimacy of such professional rights and prerogatives as tenure and the authority of academic departments to make decisions about hiring and promotion with little substantive input from external constituencies— and because they question whether professors, especially those on the far left, deserve the high levels of prestige they enjoy—such critics should be seen as mounting a significant extra-occupational challenge to the American academic profession, just as the feminist movement and a number of "health social movements" (Brown et al. 2004) were important challengers to the medical profession in the 1970s and beyond.

In this chapter I explore empirically an important set of issues directly related to this challenge: how in fact professors think about the proper relationship between their own politics and their research and teaching. To do so, I draw on interviews with fifty-seven American professors conducted in 2006–7. Five disciplines are represented in my sample: sociology, economics, literature, biology, and engineering. I selected these fields because they are large, central, and span a wide range of subject matters, and because survey research shows that there is variation in faculty political views across them (Gross and Simmons 2007). Here I present three main findings from the interview data. First, with regard to research, my data confirm what many observers of contemporary American academe have noted: there is significant variation across disciplines in the degree to which notions like objectivity and politically value-free knowledge are seen as unproblematic and desirable. The field of literature exhibits a high degree of epistemological skepticism and politicization, sociology a moderate degree, and the other three fields almost no skepticism whatsoever. Second, with regard to teaching, norms are in place in all five disciplines against overt partisanship in the classroom, and champions of "critical pedagogy," the view that education should alert students to instances of what the left sees as social injustice, are rare. The vast majority of professors think that the goal of teaching should be to instruct students in the subject matter of their fields or train them in various intellectual skills (although conservative critics are right to point out that the line between instruction and critical pedagogy becomes blurry in disciplines whose major problematics have a decidedly left valence). But there is disagreement on the question of whether, when discussing a politically controversial topic in class, professors should let their own political views be known. To some extent this variation crosscuts differences in disciplinary culture and is associated with the different institutional positions professors occupy, their political views, their gender, and ultimately their assumptions about students as learners.

Finally, I find disagreement within the academic profession about the meaning of academic freedom. This is not a topic to which most of the professors I interviewed appeared to have given much thought, but when queried, just under half described academic freedom in terms consistent with its original meaning, as a professional prerogative associated with their duties and obligations as pursuers and disseminators of truth (Dewey [1902] 1976; Hofstadter and Metzger 1955; Menand 1996; Post 2006). About a third described it as an extension of their speech rights, and the rest fell somewhere between these two extremes. My intention in presenting these findings is neither to validate nor debunk conservative complaints, but to shed light on the cultural terrain over which conservative critics of American higher education and the professoriate's defenders struggle, as a prelude to a more in-depth analysis of the campaign against the "liberal professoriate"—its origins, dynamics, and consequences.

A secondary goal of the chapter is to make a contribution to the sociology of knowledge. I aim to encourage more systematic attention to how academicians in various fields and at various points in time understand the relationship between their political views, values, and engagements and their activities of knowledge creation and dissemination, and to how such understandings inform and shape academic work and political practice. To be sure, considerable research has been undertaken on related topics. For example, a large body of scholarship in the field of science studies shows how scientists' political commitments, both conscious and tacit, may enter into and inflect their investigations (e.g., Barnes 1977; Haraway 1989; Shapin and Schaffer 1985), part of a larger process of "coproduction" by which states, economies, and social orders and science, knowledge, and technology become intertwined and help to reciprocally bring one another about (Jasanoff 2004). Likewise, among sociologists of science and academic life, there has been growing interest in phenomena that are even more clearly poised at the intersection of politics and scientific or academic work, such as fields of study with explicitly political agendas like African American studies (Rojas 2007) or efforts by social movement activists to steer science in new directions (Epstein 1996; Frickel 2004; Moore 2008). Research on the sociology of intellectuals, for its part, routinely explores their role as carriers of political values and agents of social change (Kurzman and Owens 2002). Finally, sociological and historical scholarship on the trajectories of disciplinary fields has considered how epistemological and methodological preferences—including views on objectivity and stances of political engagement or disengagement—may be a function of shifting political, cultural, and institutional circumstances (e.g., Gross 2008; Novick 1988; Steinmetz 2005).

These lines of investigation are important, but they could be usefully sup-plemented and made more commensurable by an explicit focus on the thick and often contested cultural understandings that knowledge producers have of how the boundaries should be drawn in general and in their own work between politics and intellectual inquiry. Such a focus need not be created *de novo* theoretically; it can be layered onto an existing conceptual apparatus, Knorr Cetina's (1999) notion of "epistemic cultures." Rejecting both philo-sophical and Mertonian norm-based conceptions of the unity of the sciences, Knorr Cetina (1999, 3) argues that fields may vary not just in what they study or their patterns of social organization, but also with respect to their "archi-tectures of empirical approaches, specific constructions of the referent, par-ticular ontologies of instruments," and in terms of the nature of the "social machines" they employ to bring knowledge about. In other words, fields vary in their members' common understanding of what it means to know, and in their sense for what is required of those who would advance credible, war-rantable claims to truth. The cultural schemas and practices that provide the basis for such variation, and thus help make possible the production of knowl-edge in a given field, constitute its epistemic culture.

I argue that an additional and neglected dimension of epistemic culture concerns the way in which fields deal with what I call the "knowledge-politics problem." This is the need faced by all communities of knowledge producers and disseminators, particularly those in a highly reflexive, politi-cized era, to formulate for their members more or less coherent stances that may be taken on the question of how if at all one's political views should factor into knowledge work. Answers to this question hinge to some extent on how those communities define concepts such as "politics" and "science" and are also closely tied but not reducible to understandings of the nature and desirability of objectivity (see Daston and Galison 2007). Mapping through empirical investigation how different epistemic cultures come down on the knowledge-politics problem—that is, how they conceive of the proper relationship between the personal politics of knowledge producers and their research and teaching activities—should yield additional insight into the mechanisms and dynamics of coproduction insofar as these are mediated by cultural understandings.

Data and Methods

The interviews I analyze here are follow-up interviews to a nationally representative survey of the American professoriate I conducted with Solon Simmons in 2006. The survey focused on professors' social and political attitudes. It covered professors with full-time appointments teaching in most fields and types of institutions, including community colleges, and achieved a 51 percent response rate with 1,471 valid cases. The final question on the questionnaire asked respondents whether they would agree to participate in an interview in which the issues raised in the survey could be fleshed out in more detail. To select respondents for the follow-up interviews, three research assistants and I first grouped professors who so agreed according to discipline, pooling those who gave more specialized designations into the focal disciplinary categories of sociologist, economist, biologist, engineer, and professor of literature. We then contacted potential interviewees by e-mail, employing quota sampling procedures in which our aim was to interview ten professors in each discipline, obtain a sufficiently large number of interviewees in each of three institutional strata (community colleges, four-year BA-granting schools, and PhD-granting schools) to allow for meaningful comparisons, and have a sample that was more or less reflective of the gender composition of the five fields. Only about half of the professors thus contacted responded to our query, and in the end we conducted fifty-seven interviews. Interviews were conducted by phone by my research assistants and me over the course of several months. A semistructured interview schedule was employed, and questions covered topics ranging from political self-identity to views of politics, research, and teaching. Pedagogical issues were given special attention because these were not extensively covered in the initial survey. The average length of the interviews was forty-eight minutes. Interviews were recorded and transcribed.

Two different research assistants then coded the transcripts according to an inductively derived standardized coding scheme. The coders began by coding the same five transcripts. They coded identically 85 percent of the time. Discrepant codings were discussed and corrected, and then three additional transcripts were processed by both coders. This time there was 90 percent intercoder agreement. The remaining transcripts were subsequently divided up between the two coders. Later, quantitative data were compiled about the distribution of codes.

Table 4.1 Select sample characteristics from follow-up
interviews with American professors, 2006–7

Field	Men	Women	Assistant professor (%)	Median age	Liberal* (%)
Sociology	8	6	57	48	86
Biology	6	4	10	53	50
Literature	9	5	21	50	86
Engineering	10	1	27	48	18
Economics	6	2	0	53	38

Institution type (%)	Region (%)
Community college (18)	West (26)
Four-year (65)	Midwest (29)
PhD-granting (18)	Northeast (26)
	South (20)

Note: Percentages may not add to 100 because of rounding.

* Self-identification, as opposed to moderate or conservative.

Table 4.1 shows the breakdown of the sample on key disciplinary, institutional, and sociodemographic characteristics. The interview data do not reflect the results of a random sampling procedure, and the composition of the sample is somewhat different than might have been expected had it been feasible to conduct such a procedure. Specifically, a comparison to the survey sample suggests that in the follow-up sample untenured assistant professors are overrepresented among sociologists and underrepresented among biologists and economists, and women are somewhat underrepresented among professors of literature.

The Possibility of Objective, Value-Free Knowledge

Nathan (here and elsewhere I have changed names and identifying characteristics to preserve anonymity) is a 37-year-old assistant professor of English at a public BA-granting university in the South. His doctorate is in communications, not literature, but he has been part of an English department for four years and is steeped in the epistemic culture of that field. When we asked how important the notion of objectivity was to him, he replied, "I'm not a big fan of the notion. . . . The idea of [a] separation from interest or situation is . . . suspicious to me." In lieu of claims to objective knowledge, Nathan would "much rather see . . . disclosed interest and disclosed situatedness and . . . being able to . . . work with that . . . in a constructive way." Nathan's epistemic views extend beyond his own field to color how he evaluates knowledge in general. "In everything from journalism to the sciences," he insisted, "claims and appeals to objectivity tend to do more to mask interest and situatedness than they do [to] actually assist in knowledge in any way."

At the opposite extreme from Nathan is Mark, an associate professor of electrical engineering at another state institution in the South. When we asked what role if any politics plays in his research, he replied by telling a joke we heard numerous times, always in slightly different form, from other respondents. "One of the beauties of engineering," he said, "is there is no such thing . . . as a Jewish volt, there is no such thing as a Republican ampere. . . . There's no such thing as a conservative kilogram. Or an atheist heater. . . . You know, the atheist looks at the volt meter and it reads 1.26 volts, the ardent Christian conservative reads 1.26 volts, the Muslim reads 1.26 volts. . . . There is some measure of objectivity in this profession."

The differences between Nathan and Mark are not idiosyncratic; they reflect assumptions about objectivity and the knowledge-politics problem that are built into the epistemic cultures of their respective disciplinary fields. Nathan's field, literature, is characterized by deep skepticism about the possibility of objective knowledge; by the sense that at every point in the knowledge production process, and no matter the nature of one's object of investigation, political and other value commitments enter in to inform one's theoretical and methodological approach as well as the substance of one's claims; and by a valuation in this context of intellectual practices of reflexivity whereby one endeavors not to hide one's political interests, but to bring them to the fore and frame one's knowledge claims in terms of them. By contrast, Mark's field, engineering, is characterized by a rampant and taken-for-granted objectivism, by a sense that the nature of the objects studied is such that political or other values can be kept at bay, and moreover that they should be kept at bay because the goal of inquiry is to produce knowledge that mirrors the world as it actually is, independent of the standpoint from which one views it. In neither of these two fields is subscription to these epistemic ideals unanimous, but it is the rare literature professor who thinks of objectivity as unproblematic, and the rare engineer who would prefer that engineering knowledge be properly "situated." Objectivism was also widespread in two of the other fields I studied: biology and economics. Sociology

I found to be an epistemological hybrid, combining elements of objectivism and skepticism.

In one sense it is unsurprising to find professors of literature embracing a culture of skepticism. Literature was one of the most affected of the traditional disciplines by a variety of intellectual movements that appeared on the scene in the late 1960s and 1970s and that by the 1980s had become institutionalized—movements such as deconstructionism, poststructuralism, postmodernism, neopragmatism, Lacanian literary theory, feminist theory, and postcolonial theory. These movements were theoretically and epistemologically diverse, but one thing they shared was skepticism toward naïve realism and empiricism as applied to literature or other arenas of knowledge. It is impossible, intellectual leaders of these movements claimed, for epistemic subjects to ever step fully outside the bounds of their own worldviews and assumptions—or, following Nietzsche, to remove themselves in their capacity as agents of knowing from their own practical purposes, designs, and wills to power. Knowledge is never a view from nowhere, and one of the main aims of literary criticism in light of this insight should be the interpretation of texts and cultural objects with a view to the hidden vantage points they express and the power relations they go to support. Many of my literary studies interviewees were explicit in linking their doubts about objectivity to these theoretical currents. For example, a 49-year-old associate professor of literature at a four-year school in New York State recalled that she "was in college in the late 70s, and it was still a period of what's called in literature 'new criticism.' You analyze a text as an autonomous work of art, and you don't contextualize it. And that never felt right to me. Even as an undergraduate, I . . . always vowed that if I ever did go on [in academe] something I would do is work on contextualization." "Art doesn't just arise without being influenced by political events and its cultural context," she insisted, noting that the theoretical "pendulum" in her field swung back toward a recognition of this when she was in graduate school. Her sense of the importance of context led her to specialize in a particular strain of eighteenth-century literature that "was very clearly at the intersection of political, legal, and economic theories, and the aestheticization of those things." At the same time it undermined her own belief in the possibility of objective knowledge. As far as objectivity goes, she told us, "there isn't any in my field. . . . [O]ne of the things we are now teaching is that there is no objectivity. . . . [T]here are fancy words for it, but you bring your personal baggage to a text when you analyze it."

This was not an unusual sentiment among the literary scholars to whom we spoke. Less than a third described objectivity in research as unproblematic or desirable. This did not mean that for them fidelity to textual or historical materials or adherence to high scholarly standards were concepts without meaning. As one scholar put it, "I certainly believe that every text . . . is the product of a person positioned . . . but I also believe that my approach to scholarship does try to be fair and judicious to what others have written and to take that into account." But professors of literature do tend to doubt that their own experiences and worldviews—and as part of this their political or other value commitments—can ever be bracketed when they undertake research and writing, and some suspect that such a bracketing cannot be successfully accomplished in other fields either. Importantly, nearly all professors of literature—12 out of 14 in my interview sample—consider themselves liberals or progressives and hold liberal views on a wide variety of social and political issues. When we asked another literature professor whether his own politics factor into his research, he replied simply, "They do." His politics, he told us, which he characterized as "very, very liberal," could not help but affect "the way I choose topics. The way I treat topics. The way I write." As noted above, in light of the success of movements like postmodernism, this sort of response to the knowledge-politics problem is not altogether surprising. But I was surprised to see how widely shared skepticism toward objectivity was within a discipline known more for disputatiousness than for consensus; by the extent to which it is so taken for granted that it was normatively acceptable for my interviewees to offer only schematic and halting justifications for it; and by the fact that nearly all seemed to regard a "hermenuetics of suspicion" as normal intellectual practice, with notions like objectivity, objective representation, and value-free knowledge seen as expressing a philosophical and theoretical naivety that is at once dangerous and somehow déclassé.

Things could not be more different in engineering and biology. Although some of the most trenchant critics of postmodernism have come from the ranks of the physical and natural sciences—think of physicist Alan Sokal, perpetrator of the so-called "Sokal hoax," or biologist Paul Gross, one of the authors of *Higher Superstition: The Academic Left and Its Quarrels with Science* (Gross and Levitt 1994)—almost none of the engineers or biologists we interviewed gave any hint that they were familiar with the kinds of intellectual and philosophical work that led literary scholars to be so skeptical of objectivity and the possibility of separating knowledge from politics. Only one of the ten biologists we interviewed expressed any real doubts about the possibility of objective knowledge, none of the engineers did, and the vast majority of professors in both fields insisted that their personal politics simply do not enter into their research.

Engineers and biologists ground their claims to this effect in three assumptions. First, they assume that the nature of the objects they study is inherently apolitical. For example, a tenured molecular biologist at a four-year school in California said, "I'm . . . interested in a topic called abiogenesis, and how a cell can come to function. . . . I don't think that has much of a political take on it." Earlier in the interview, in the context of a question about teaching, he noted that "molecules react the exact same way, whether you're . . . liberal [or conservative]." This view, that the objects of interest to science and the causal processes surrounding them are apolitical, and hence that there is no space for politics to intrude in legitimate scientific research, is what underlies the joke on which we heard so many variations. For Mark, the engineer mentioned earlier, the realm of science and the realm of political values are so distinct that it is literally ridiculous to mention them in the same breath, as in the phrase "conservative kilogram." A mechanical engineer born in 1979 expressed the same assumption when he joked that "a chunk of metal doesn't have politics," as did a 49-year-old developmental neurobiologist who studies bees and proclaimed, "honeybees do not have politics." Engineers and biologists obviously do recognize that the enterprise of science unfolds in a political context that may bear on its capacity to yield new findings. In this regard, a young software engineer at a PhD-granting school in the Pacific Northwest told the story of how "I got a grant . . . from NASA . . . a while back. . . . Got the award letter in October. . . . Two weeks to the day before it was supposed to turn on . . . NASA froze all funding that was not active and eventually killed the program." The story was meant to be an example of how politics and scientific research can collide, with the nature of that collision being that "politics affects the money that's put into research funding." But this kind of recognition, in which politics establish an external context for research, facilitating or impeding it, is worlds away from the notion that science itself, in the propositional claims that compose its theories, methods, and findings, could have an inherently political dimension.

A second assumption that grounds the culture of objectivism inhabited by engineers and biologists is less ontological than methodological: not only the nature of the objects studied, but as importantly the scientific method leaves no room for the intrusion of political values or views. When we asked the neuroscientist who studies bees his views of objectivity, he replied, "Being a scientist, we have to be objective. That's the whole thing! . . . I approach everything objectively, and I present the facts. I don't mind if people have a different opinion, but they'd better be able to convince me of that opinion by bringing in scientific facts." For engineers and biologists, the scientific method is not just a matter of following certain procedural conventions, like formalizing and testing hypotheses, but is also about a certain spirit one brings to research. A wildlife ecologist teaching in a biology department told us that for him objectivity means "designing a study that's well designed, looking at all the possibilities where there could be mistakes, figuring out what assumptions you're making ahead of time, knowing what those assumptions are and clearly stating 'em. And then with your results . . . trying to think of all the possibilities of what [they] really do mean." Someone conscientiously embracing such a spirit and aiming thereby to give a maximally accurate representation of the world could not perforce allow political values to intrude, even if they were somehow relevant. So "in science," the ecologist concluded, "I don't think . . . politics really can mesh in there."

Third, a number of engineers and biologists linked their exclusion of political considerations from research to the trust they see as being placed in them by the users of their findings. When we asked a composite materials engineer what role if any politics play in his research, he replied sharply, "None." His work involves "break[ing] things for research and report[ing] on how strong they are." Some of his research has military applications, and while Defense Department "program managers" who make decisions about the use of materials may have biases in favor of this or that "platform," his job as a scientist is to put aside any biases he may have, look the program manager in the eye, and say "Material A is stronger than material B. I have data to prove it." Only by doing so can he preserve his scientific credibility and fulfill his ethical responsibilities. "In my field," he said solemnly, "objectivity . . . is all we have."

But engineers and biologists were not the only ones in my sample to inhabit a culture of objectivity. Nearly all of the economists we interviewed also characterized objectivity in their research as unproblematic and desirable. Like engineers and biologists, economists view objectivity as grounded in the nature of the object they study, the methods they use, and their responsibilities to decision makers and the wider public. For economists, however, these are not discrete assumptions, but are bound together in a coherent paradigm and research program for their discipline. This paradigm, of course, revolves around the notion that markets are sites where prices are determined by laws of supply and demand playing themselves out via the preferences and choices of rational economic actors. For economists, it is the fundamental truth of this paradigm, and the requirements it makes of those working under its rubric, that ultimately ensures that economic research, properly carried out, will not be tainted by political values. Such a claim may sound strange to noneconomists. From the vantage point of other social sciences such as sociology or anthropology, the assumptions at the heart of contemporary economics are nothing if not political, for at least two reasons. First, these assumptions revolve around an image of human beings—as rational utility maximizers—that is so at odds with prevailing views in other disciplines that noneconomists will naturally suspect an ideological bias. Second, such assumptions seem to carry with them normative implications about how economies should be run—namely, more or less in line with the principles of free-market economics, putting more emphasis on market efficiency than on equitable resource distribution—in which political and economic actors have major investments. But economists don't see things this way. For most, it is simply a fact, an axiom of their science, that economic actors are utility maximizers and that therefore markets tend to work in certain predictable ways. Because this is so, proper economic research does not admit of political influence.

The clash between these two ways of thinking about economics is nicely captured in an exchange between one of the interviewers, a PhD candidate in sociology, and a 36-year-old male macroeconomist teaching at a community college in Maryland.

INTERVIEWER: How if at all do your politics factor into your research, such as selection of topics, methodology, theory, et cetera?

INTERVIEWEE: Not much at all.

INTERVIEWER: Any role in selection of topics, for example?

INTERVIEWEE: No.

INTERVIEWER: How about theory? I mean, for example, you don't take a Marxian economics [approach]?

INTERVIEWEE: No, I'm a free market capitalist economist, like 98 percent of the other economists out there.

INTERVIEWER: So do you think your politics factors into that?

INTERVIEWEE: No.

INTERVIEWER: Can you explain? If one were to make an argument that political bias is everywhere, they'd say, well, if you're a leftist, you're going to be
a Marxist economist regardless of what the facts tell you, and if you're on
the right, you're going to be a microeconomic Milton Friedman economist,
regardless of what the facts tell you.

INTERVIEWEE: Where politics enter into research agendas in my field is . . . in
terms of policy analysis and policy prescriptions, and that is not an aspect
of my professional activity.

This economist was not alone in believing that economic research in the
strict sense is objective and apolitical. Thus, it was in response to our question
about how politics might influence research that one economist responded,
"Not at all. My research tends to be more on the technical side." Another said,
"virtually none at all," and a third replied, "No, no. It wasn't the kind of research I was doing." Still another scholar, a 53-year-old labor economist, told
us, "one of my favorite titles in the economics literature is 'Let's Take the Con
Out of Econometrics' [the title of a 1983 paper by Edward Leamer in the *American Economic Review*]. And that to me is the objectivity part of it. In the process of doing research you state your assumptions clearly, you build your
model clearly, you share data, and you look for replication of results." In fact,
the only economist we interviewed who seriously doubted whether economic
research is objective is a 1960s-era radical, profiled in more detail below, who
barely completed his degree because he saw free-market assumptions to be
"bullshit." He now teaches at a community college in California and does no
research.

As several of these quotations suggest, however, economists do recognize
that when they move from analysis of the workings of the economy into the
formulation of policy prescriptions, they may then be entering the realm of
politics and political values. It is here, at the distinction between pure and
applied economics, that economists mark the boundary between science and
politics. A 40-year-old professor of economics was engaged in this kind of
boundary work when she said, "my research is completely away from politics.
So far it has looked at marital transactions in India. So the only place where
it would even remotely come close to politics would be where I formulate policies or I suggest ways to decrease marital transactions." In a similar vein,
another economist told us that because his policy work in the area of sports
economics is motivated by his personal political view that "government is in-

volved in too many different things, too many different areas" (as he sees it, municipalities should not be subsidizing the building of sports arenas), this was one area where his politics and academic work did intersect. Economists do not appear to believe that policy work is *necessarily* political—if it is strictly informed by economic theory and research it need not be—but at the very least there is potential for political considerations to enter in.

American sociologists, for their part, are positioned somewhere between literature and economics in terms of the knowledge-politics problem. As many observers have noted, sociology is a multiparadigmatic and fractious discipline composed of researchers focused on a wide array of problems and employing diverse theoretical approaches and methods. One important dividing line in the field is between sociologists who identify more with the humanities and those who view the discipline as a social science; another is between sociologists committed to an activist agenda and those who have more of a "professional" orientation. In tabulating the responses of sociologists to questions about objectivity and political neutrality, I found that nearly two-thirds do think critically about these notions, but that only one-third believe that objectivity is a chimera. The roughly one-third of sociologists who believe that objectivity is impossible tend to be in either the humanistic or activist camp or both and are remarkably similar in their epistemological views to professors of literature—with the difference being that their perspectives seem informed more by pedestrian "standpoint theories" than by more philosophically sophisticated intellectual approaches. In this regard, when we asked an assistant professor of sociology whether her research is influenced by her politics, she said, "the personal is political. When I teach research methods I tell my students, 'if we were all honest we would admit to the fact that what we all study is based on that which affects us.' I study fringe groups and issues of power. . . . I was born in the projects. We were the only whites and the only Jews in an all-Hispanic, black area. We were regularly beaten. So for me issues of fringe groups and power are important, plus I'm gay. What other ways could I be more powerless? . . . So absolutely, my political, social, personal experiences literally shape my research." Another female sociologist, a 37-year-old assistant professor, similarly told us, "I think that knowledge is inherently political and subjective, and so the idea that there's . . . knowledge out there that's not positioned somehow is really . . . difficult for me to think about. I think that all theories come from a place of politics and a particular kind of subjectivity." For these interviewees, research and politics are intertwined not simply in the sense famously outlined by Max Weber—that one's choice of research topic is inevitably influenced by one's values and interests—but also in the deeper sense that one's personal experiences and value commitments give one a worldview through which research problems are framed and in which different theoretical approaches and empirical claims gain varying degrees of plausibility.

But this was not the dominant epistemological position among the sociologists we interviewed. Ben Agger (2007, 4), a sociologist who has criticized the discipline from the perspective of deconstructionist theory, has argued that the epistemic culture of the field "attempt[s] to imitate the natural sciences in a 'hard' objectivity and indubitability." It may be the case, as Agger argues to substantiate this claim, that the literary conventions of sociological writing in the major academic journals are wrapped up with the performance of a certain kind of objectivity, but I found in my interviews that the majority of sociologists are aware of the many problems and difficulties associated with objectivity. Unwilling, however, to descend into subjectivism, they have forged and now inhabit a hybrid epistemological culture in which objectivity as a view from nowhere is seen as impossible to achieve in practice but is still held up as a kind of goal, and in which research is understood as being more objective the more researchers acknowledge and come to terms with their own biases and motivations. For most American sociologists, in other words, objectivity—and as part of this knowledge that is politically value-free in its factual, although not motivational, aspect—remains an ideal toward which they strive, even as they recognize the impossibility of ever fully achieving it. Typical in this regard was a 57-year-old African American sociologist teaching in the South. When we asked how his politics affect his research, he replied, "Well, just in terms of orienting me towards certain topics. Racial identity, racial reparations, health disparities, HIV/AIDS are all problems that . . . affect people in urban centers and African-Americans and other groups of color, so my politics orient me towards certain topics." He was quick to add, nevertheless, "I try to be balanced in my . . . analyses." Does "balance" mean that he considers the results of his research, what he finds after his political and other values have steered him toward a given topic, to be objective? Although this sociologist considers objectivity to be "very important," he also insisted that "it's an ideal type—you know, it's really impossible for humans to be totally objective, but it's a goal. . . . [W]e should strive for objectivity." A 41-year-old assistant professor of sociology who also teaches in the South said much the same. His own politics, he told us, which he characterized as moderate, do not factor into his research in the sense that "I definitely never go into research looking for certain outcomes. I think there's a tendency in social science for people to do the kind of work that is going to substantiate their political beliefs. I never do that." For him, "objectivity is critical to social science. I think it's critical to sociology." "What it means to me," he continued, "is that researchers follow a rigorous scientific method to carry out their research." But he too added the crucial caveat that distinguishes sociological views of objectivity from those found in more purely objectivist epistemological cultures: "Don't get me wrong, it's never going to be perfect. But we can at least try."

My interview data do not allow me to determine the extent to which these nods to the problems of achieving objective knowledge in the social sciences are linked to any *meaningful* reflexive practices on the part of sociologists—or whether, if pressed on the point, biologists, engineers, and economists might not also acknowledge that objectivity is difficult to achieve, if perhaps for different reasons than concern sociologists. But they do permit the preliminary conclusion that the epistemic culture of sociology is a hybrid one both in the sense that some champions of skepticism and subjectivism can be found in its ranks (although they do not tend to occupy positions of greatest power in the field) and in that among the rest acknowledgment of the difficulty of being objective—coupled with a commitment to grasp for it nevertheless—is regarded as important.

Political Neutrality versus Transparency in Teaching

In light of these differences in how fields respond to the knowledge-politics problem when it comes to research, I expected to find parallel differences by field in terms of teaching. I expected that professors of literature would readily admit to the role that their personal politics play in their own pedagogy and would express no great concern about this, that sociologists would acknowledge the influence of politics but that most would endeavor to minimize it, and that professors inhabiting more objectivistic disciplinary cultures would deny that politics affect their teaching at all. This is not what I found. There were differences among my interviewees in how they conceived of the politics-teaching nexus, but these differences could not be easily mapped onto views of research and did not follow automatically from disciplinary location.

Nearly all interviewees distanced themselves from professors who would impose their political views on students by grandstanding in the classroom or forcing students in their assignments to express political agreement with them. Beyond that, however, interviewees divided into two main camps. The first consisted of professors who either think their politics do not factor into their teaching because the subject matter of their courses does not allow for it or endeavor to conceal their political views from students even when controversial issues do arise on the grounds that doing so leads to better learning outcomes, like more meaningful student engagement. The teaching style of these professors can be described as one of "political neutrality." The second camp consists of professors who recognize the many ways in which their teaching is bound up with their politics, and who think it is fine and good for professors to share their personal political views with students—as long as they are clear about defining them as such and not as "truth," and as long as they are open to dissenting student opinion. The teaching style of professors in this second camp is one of "political transparency." Biologists and engineers were somewhat more likely than sociologists or professors of literature to say that the subject matter of their courses did not touch on the political, but disciplinary location is not a strong predictor of political neutrality versus transparency because many biologists and engineers teach courses that go beyond basic principles and research findings to intersect at least at the margins with questions of public policy or matters of political controversy, forcing them to stake out positions on one side or the other on these sticky pedagogical matters.

Although none of my interviewees mentioned critical pedagogy per se, there were a couple who fit the stereotype held by some conservative critics of a radical professor bent on converting students to his political point of view. Dave, the 68-year-old economist mentioned above who described free-market economics as "bullshit," is an example. Dave grew up in Beverly Hills. His father, who dropped out of school in the fourth grade, worked his way up and eventually came to run a successful defense contracting business. Raised in a conservative household by what he characterizes as "nouveau riche" parents— his father, he told us, "voted for Roosevelt first, and then after he got some money decided that Roosevelt wasn't the way to go"—Dave "went to college carrying all those conservative views and . . . racial prejudices . . . and I started learning. . . . I got to be more and more liberal and . . . involved with the possibilities that society could change and be better. . . . I was like everybody else in the 60s. I'm the same age as The Beatles and we rejected a whole bunch of things." He retained these political views over the years. Dave now describes his political identity as "left-wing liberal," and when we asked him to elaborate on the meaning of this he laughed and said, "well, I'm a 60s guy. I was in the streets with the long hair!" Although he went to graduate school for economics, he told us that he thinks of himself as "more of a sociologist"—presumably because of what he takes to be sociology's suspicion toward *homo-economicus*, the sociological insistence that economic exchange is always embedded in social and institutional relationships, and the sense that sociologists do not equate a free market with a good society. Dave's goal in teaching is to expose his students to his liberal, political-economy-centered point of view in the hope that they will come to see the world differently than they did before and become more aware of social injustice. When he was in college, an influential professor had asked him, speaking of the conservative views on which he had been reared, "Why do you believe all that stuff?" and Dave aims to play the same role for his students. "I think there is a place for getting out the liberal, radical type message," he told us. "I think the place of the university is to expose people to different things—not what they're used to." When we asked him to describe for us the ways in which he's involved in politics these days, he said, "I start in the classroom . . . and do what I can." One of his main teaching techniques is to bring to class magazine and newspaper articles that he can discuss. "I bring in articles all the time," he says, articles that are "pro-environmental, pro-egalitarian, pro-human rights, anti-war . . . and I do that with no excuses because they [his students] get plenty of the other stuff. . . . Just listen to the radio sometime on these right-wing talk shows. Whoa. Drives ya nuts." Beyond that, Dave helps to organize a "political economy" week at the college during which classes are cancelled and students come to hear speakers debate the merits of various political agendas and proposals. For his highly politicized approach to teaching Dave has gotten into trouble with students and parents over the years. "They call me 'pinko fag' and all that shit. . . . Parents would come and say, 'You're brainwashing my child . . .' And I just come back and say, 'Well, what can I say? I don't have to check with you before I say anything.'" Dave opposes forcing his students to agree with his politics on tests and says he encourages debate with conservative students, but he is unapologetic for his belief that college is a place where students raised in conservative families can be led to see the error of their ways.

Dave's pedagogical views were uncommon among my interviewees. The vast majority held more conventional beliefs about the aim of undergraduate instruction, seeing it as concerned with transmitting to students knowledge of a field, giving them familiarity with some of the major issues and debates confronting humankind today, exposing them to classic texts and ideas and works of art, or inculcating skills such as writing and reading well and thinking analytically and critically. On the basis of informal conversations I have had with many professors over the years, I suspect that some of my interviewees harbored secret hopes that the achievement of these conventional pedagogical aims would result indirectly in political movement to the left on the part of students, but few spoke of this explicitly. Instead, nearly all approached politics and teaching through stances of political neutrality or transparency.

The professors we interviewed who could be placed on the political neutrality side of the divide can in fact be divided once again. Some taught classes that they understood to be politically neutral in the sense that the subject matter of their courses did not bring them into a political orbit. Such professors can be seen as practicing "accidental political neutrality." As they talk about it, it is an accident of fate, a function of their particular specialization and the classes they have been assigned, that politics play no role in their teaching, as in the case of a 48-year-old professor of mechanical engineering who thought it a sufficient explanation of why politics do not intersect with his teaching to point out, with no further elaboration, that his classes are "in the area of what's called 'mechtronics'—it's a combin[ation] of mechanical engineering and electronics . . . computer science for designing smarter, more reliable, adaptable products." A recent survey by Smith, Mayer, and Fritschler (2008, 84) found that about 60 percent of American professors agree with the statement "politics seldom comes up in my classroom, because of the nature of the subjects I teach," suggesting that, in the university overall, accidental political neutrality may be the modal pedagogical category when it comes to knowledge-politics.

The second category consists of professors who practice what I call "cultivated political neutrality." It is not that such professors endeavor to keep politics from being discussed in their classes; some teach on highly politicized topics and encourage political debate. Rather, what distinguishes this pedagogical style is the effort to ensure that no matter the nature of the classroom conversation, the instructors' own political views will remain hidden or at least elusive.

Two assumptions seemed to be at work for professors in this category. The first is that college students are impressionable and that professors yield considerable authority in the classroom. To the extent that this is so, if a professor is outspoken about her own views, it may poison classroom discussion or otherwise interfere with the process by which students consider all sides in a debate and come to rationally form their own beliefs. Second, it is unethical for professors to reveal and argue for their own political views in class because in doing so they are, in effect, using their authority not for the purposes for which it was granted—to instruct—but for political ends. A professor of literature with "generally liberal" views who teaches in a Catholic college in the Midwest was typical of those interviewees who claimed to practice cultivated political neutrality, although the language he used in describing his rationale for doing so was unusually lighthearted. "How if at all do your politics factor into your teaching?" we asked him. "I try to keep it out of my teaching," he replied. "For example, I teach Conrad. And there is a political argument about imperialism that it is possible to make and I try to make it from all sides . . . and be as objective as I can be. But as far as bringing my politics—contemporary politics—into the classroom, I try to leave it out. I've always felt that was obnoxious. . . . I do make an effort to be receptive to all kinds of ideas. . . . But I think it's important that [students] get the education they paid for . . . and not some sort of radicalization camp." More vehement was the Virginia-trained economist quoted earlier who did not view economics as political. We asked him later in the interview whether he felt it was acceptable for professors to argue on behalf of their own political views in class. His response was, "Absolutely not. . . . I have some ethical problems with that [because it] . . . doesn't translate well into imparting critical thinking skills for students. I very strongly believe that 18- to 22-year-old college students have a very strong incentive to do whatever they need to do to make the professor happy, and there are certainly perceptions out there that Professor X wants to hear this on an exam or wants you to read this into an essay. . . . Now, I think that most of my students, if they would bother stopping by my office or talking to me . . . they could have a pretty good guess at my political beliefs, but in terms of bringing any of that into the classroom, I try very, very hard to avoid that."

In contrast, many professors we spoke to practice "political transparency" with their students. If the topic of the class on a given day calls for discussion of political issues—which it may or may not, as those who practice political transparency are distinguished from practitioners of critical pedagogy in part by the fact that they do *not* feel the need to bring every discussion around to contemporary politics—they may, if they deem it pedagogically helpful, reveal to students their own views while also working to ensure that this does not foreclose discussion. For example, a 47-year-old sociological social psychologist who teaches at a community college in California told us that her liberal views do affect the way she teaches. As she sees it, her politics "factor . . . in [to her teaching] by the topics that I might address." Viewing sociology as synonymous with the study of unequal distributions of power and resources in society, she elaborated by saying, "I'm a sociologist. I'm going to talk about race and racism. I'm going to talk about sex and sexism. I'm going to talk about social inequality and class in the United States." When she raises such matters, however, she attempts neither to directly divest students of their conservative views nor to conceal from them her own position. "I really try to be inclusive," she told us. "I don't . . . try to push a particular agenda or a candidate or anything like that. If I find that I have said [something to this effect], I will quickly . . . say, 'You know, this is just my personal opinion and I respect anybody else's opinion and you don't have to agree with me in order to understand the material that I'm trying to convey to you.'" By issuing such a disclaimer, she hopes to communicate to students that her political statements are not to be construed as reflecting the authoritative knowledge she has as a sociologist, but are simply the views she has as a fellow citizen. This move, she hopes, goes some way toward removing whatever power asymmetries might otherwise be present in the classroom situation, and she takes it as evidence that her strategy works that over the years she has had no real conflicts with students over politics: "I remember having discussions with students whose politics were different than my own," she says. These discussions might have become "heated" on occasion, but they ended up being "illuminating" for all concerned because her approach is ultimately "one of allowing and dignifying the other person's perspective." The operative assumption about students for practitioners of political transparency is that they are not delicate young things prone to indoctrination, but critical consumers of information and opinion who can understand where professorial authority ends and personal political views begin, and who are capable of taking part as equals with their professors and fellow students in wide-ranging and probing discussion of political matters. Thus it was that an English professor who teaches at a public four-year school in Pennsylvania justified his assertion that it was fine for him to present and argue for his own political views by claiming

Table 4.2 Percent of respondents in pedagogical category by field

Field	Critical pedagogy	Accidental neutrality	Cultivated neutrality	Political transparency
Sociology	7	7	7	79
Biology	0	30	10	60
Literature	0	7	14	79
Engineering	0	36	36	27
Economics	13	0	38	50

Note: Percentages may not add to 100 because of rounding.

that students are not going to accept them as gospel: "The students are not stupid, you know? They're . . . human just like the rest of us!" In the same vein, another literature professor told us that he doesn't have conflicts with students over politics because his goal in classroom discussions isn't to "win . . . them over" politically, but simply to get them to "argue and think about what their position is."

Examining how my interviewees break down in terms of these profiles reveals, again, that two of the fifty-seven professors in the sample were practitioners of critical pedagogy, ten said they teach in fields or on topics where political issues never arise, eleven said that professors should not divulge their political views in the classroom, and the rest practiced political transparency to a greater or lesser degree.

Multivariate statistical analysis is unhelpful on a sample of this size, but the bivariate distributions are intriguing. Some differences by discipline are apparent, as I have already suggested and as table 4.2 shows. Biologists and engineers were more likely than sociologists, literature professors, or economists to claim to teach classes that never touch on political issues, although only a third of professors in these two fields could be classified as claiming "accidental neutrality." Cultivated neutrality was practiced by a third of engineers and economists, but by only 7 percent of sociologists, 10 percent of biologists, and 14 percent of literature professors. Political transparency was equally common among sociologists and literature professors—79 percent in both fields—but was also relatively common among biologists (60%) and economists (50%). There was also variation by institutional location: half of professors teaching in doctoral-granting universities practiced cultivated neutrality, as compared to around 10 percent of professors teaching in community colleges or four-year schools. This may reflect the greater authority that professors at elite institutions understand themselves to have, the lesser intimacy that typically obtains in such institutions between students and instructors, or greater commitment to a certain understanding of academic professionalism. Professors' own political views also appear to affect the likelihood of their adopting one stance or another. Self-identified moderates were somewhat more likely to practice cultivated neutrality (25%) than conservatives (20%) but were much more likely to do so than liberals (12%), perhaps because liberals are more likely to view college students as adults and not worry as much about indoctrination. Finally, these pedagogical practices appear gendered: whereas 26 percent of male professors practice cultivated neutrality, this was true for only 6 percent of women. While possibly reflective of the differential distribution of men and women in different fields and types of institutions, this may also reflect larger differences between male and female academics in terms of their experiences with and orientations toward teaching, and in particular the fact that women tend to have less hierarchical relationships with students than do their male colleagues.

Conceptions of Academic Freedom

In light of these differences in how the knowledge-politics problem gets resolved with regard to research and teaching, a third empirical issue is worth considering: how American professors today understand the concept of academic freedom, a concept whose institutionalization is what allows professors any space to deviate in scientific, intellectual, political, or religious terms from the expectations of their employers. Many of the answers we received to the question we posed about the meaning of academic freedom were short, halting, and unelaborated. This could signify a problem with the wording of the question, the fact that it was asked relatively late in the interview, or a sense among interviewees that the meaning of the term is so obvious that describing it in shorthand should suffice. Alternatively, it could reflect what I suspect to be the case: that most professors simply have not given all that much thought to the concept. Although about 20 percent of American professors reported in the survey Simmons and I conducted that their academic freedom had somehow been threatened in the last few years, discussion of academic freedom is rare in the academic community. Academic freedom is a marginal subject in legal scholarship and political philosophy and is infrequently covered as part of graduate student training or in the context of continuing education efforts sponsored by national disciplinary societies. Recently, as conservative critics of the university have stepped up their efforts, a number of conferences on academic freedom have been staged and a few edited volumes have appeared (e.g., Doumani 2006; Gerstmann and Streb 2006). But it is an indication that interest in academic freedom has waned in recent decades that membership levels in the American Association of University Professors, the main organization concerned with the preservation of academic freedom, dropped off dramatically in the mid-1980s and never recovered.

This point aside, I found that my interviewees clustered into two broad groups when it came to understandings of academic freedom. The first consisted of those who thought that academic freedom granted them the right to work on any topic of their choosing, to say about it anything they might like, or to otherwise express themselves freely in print, in lecture, or in other settings—a view often linked to politicized understandings of academic inquiry. An associate professor of literature who teaches at a four-year college in the Northeast exemplified this view. When we asked what academic freedom meant to her, she responded, "It is the ability to do the research that we think is significant, and be free to follow that research or follow the findings wherever they take you, and not be afraid to publish what you find . . . Really being able to go out on a limb and take something on, take on an intellectual question, without fears of reprisal, either from your department or your university, or the economy at large. And that seems to be happening more lately, that there are more reprisals for positionings." When we asked her to give an example of how this had played out in her own life, she told us, "when I was on the job market, because I wrote on a set of what were called radical novels . . . I took a lot of heat for working on what I did, some of my interviews were very confrontational." The interviewer asked her to elaborate. Was this confrontation over the political nature of the subject matter? "Yeah," she said. "Why these particular novels should even be worked on, because they were somewhat marginal—a lot of criticism of my methodology being too ideologically driven. And a lot of questions about the value of interdisciplinary work, and whether it was possible to do it in a thorough way." Although she acknowledges that questions about interdisciplinarity might have some merit, she considers it a violation of her academic freedom, and not simply reasoned judgment by a scholarly community, that she was passed over for a job because of the topic on which she chose to write her dissertation. As she sees it, academic freedom gives her the right to "position" herself however she chooses on political-intellectual matters and should protect her from the charge of doing work that is too "ideological."

In a recent essay, legal scholar Robert Post (2006) charges that American academics today, immersed in a culture of rights, have forgotten the original meaning of academic freedom—as the freedom to pursue truth in one's area of research unimpeded by nonscholarly considerations—and have reimagined it as a kind of First Amendment protection to say in their classrooms and on the printed page anything they like, no matter how overtly political or disconnected from serious scholarship it may be. I did not find any interviewees who explicitly linked notions of academic freedom with the First Amendment, but I did find many who believed that academic freedom granted them the right not simply to work on any topic of their choosing, but more generally to have largely unrestricted speech rights in their capacity as professors. For example, an 81-year-old biologist (my oldest interviewee) who teaches at a Catholic college in the Northeast defined academic freedom as follows: "you should be free to say whatever you want to say, within reason, and you don't lose your job as a result of it." Interviewees who thought of academic freedom as the right to work on whatever topic they choose or say whatever they like varied as to whether they emphasized academic freedom in teaching or research or broader public engagement, but were united in viewing it as a right that carries with it few limitations.

Another larger group of interviewees, however, saw academic freedom in terms consistent with its original definition: as a professional prerogative intimately bound up with responsibilities. A typical comment in this vein came from a 55-year-old sociologist who teaches at a doctoral-granting university in the Northeast. As he sees it, academic freedom means that "I have a responsibility to act ethically and principled [sic] in my approach to my work. And, provided that I'm acting according to the ethical codes of my discipline, and my department, and my institution, I should be able to conduct my work as I see fit. And no one should be able to tell me that I can't do that research project or I can't teach from that book." A 47-year-old electrical engineer who studies nanotechnology expressed a similar view while tying academic freedom to notions of objectivity: "Academic freedom means . . . as far as research goes that I pursue a research direction that I think is important and . . . valid without someone else telling me what I should and shouldn't do. . . . That I try to be as objective as possible in my research, and I publish those results no matter how controversial they are. Now, in engineering, there's not a lot of controversial things, but sometimes . . . there are. But whatever it would be . . . if the results are controversial and cause some people to be uncomfortable, well, so be it." Whereas professors with a rights-oriented view of academic freedom tended not to contextualize the concept in terms of the social function of the academic profession or acknowledge any substantive limitations or correlative duties, professors with a prerogative-oriented view spontaneously did all of these things. Several also expressed concern about their colleagues who had a more rights-oriented view, who consequently had politicized academic discourse, and who had, paradoxically, helped to create a climate on campus that seemed to them decidedly unfree. This view was taken by a 46-year-old literature professor. Defining academic freedom as "the ability to pursue scholarly interests, regardless of where they may lead; to do so rigorously and fairly and objectively," this interviewee said that the only threat to his academic freedom had come "from the Fascist Left inside the faculty, not where we traditionally assume it comes from, from outside forces wanting to squelch unpopular views."

Classifying respondents into three categories depending on whether they described academic freedom primarily in terms of rights, primarily in terms of prerogatives and duties, or somewhere between the two, I found that about 32 percent fell into the first category, 47 percent into the second, and about 21 percent into the third. Looking at the bivariate distributions, the only evident disciplinary differences are that those with a rights-oriented view are overrepresented among literature professors (50%) whereas those with a prerogative-oriented view are overrepresented among economists (62.5%). In terms of institutional status, professors at doctoral-granting universities were more likely to hold a prerogative view of academic freedom. There were few other obvious sociodemographic or institutional correlates, but I did find a strong association with views on politics and teaching: none of the professors who claimed to practice "cultivated neutrality" in their classrooms had a rights-oriented perspective on academic freedom.

Conclusion

My aim in this chapter was to paint a portrait of how American professors in five disciplinary fields think about the knowledge-politics problem—about whether and how their own political values and views should enter into their

research and teaching practices, and, as a corollary, the nature of their understandings of academic freedom. This is not the first study to address such issues. As indicated previously, historical studies in a number of disciplinary
fields, research on science activism, case studies of intellectuals, and other
scholarship have explored professors' views on the question of whether objective, value-free knowledge is possible and/or desirable. Similarly, research on
teaching practices in American colleges and universities, although dominated
by the concerns of higher education scholars around issues of student engagement, has sometimes considered the connection between professors' politics
and their pedagogy (e.g., Colby et al. 2007). Yet most of these strands of investigation stop short of systematic cross-disciplinary comparison and fail to
problematize explicitly the dimension of epistemic culture that is their common object of inquiry. An interview-based study of five disciplines at one
point in time obviously cannot answer the question of how all American professors think about the relationship between knowledge and politics. Nevertheless, the chapter opens a window onto an important aspect of the complex
cultural worlds that contemporary American academics inhabit—an aspect
that has become an object of vigorous contestation in the public sphere. Future research could profitably extend this analysis by expanding its scope to
cover other fields and other temporal, institutional, or national contexts; by
identifying the cultural, structural, institutional, and historical factors responsible for variation in views of knowledge-politics; and by considering how
such views intersect and shape intellectual and political practice.

Although I cannot substantiate the claim here, my view is that the epistemological skepticism I found among professors of literature—a skepticism
that, on some accounts, appeared on the scene in the 1970s and 1980s and
quickly spread, becoming institutionalized in a number of humanities and
humanistic social science fields (Cusset 2008; Lamont 1987)—was one among
a number of factors that helped to stimulate the most recent round of conservative critique of American higher education. This was so not because conservative critics were worried about postmodernism and allied intellectual
movements per se (although some were) but because the widespread rejection
of notions of objectivity and value neutrality that such movements sanctioned,
and the explicit politicization of research they made possible, further undermined the legitimacy of the academic enterprise in the view of key constituencies of the conservative movement. If this is correct, then understanding

how such fields became positioned as they were and are on matters of knowledge-politics while other fields retained their objectivistic orientation will be important not just from the standpoint of intellectual history and the sociology of knowledge, but also for those who are interested in understanding the full range of institutional challenges currently faced by the American academic profession.

REFERENCES

Abbott, Andrew. 1988. *The system of professions: An essay on the division of expert labor.* Chicago: University of Chicago Press.

Agger, Ben. 2007. *Public sociology: From social facts to literary acts.* Lanham: Rowman and Littlefield.

Barnes, Barry. 1977. *Interests and the growth of knowledge.* London: Routledge and K. Paul.

Bok, Derek. 2004. *Universities in the marketplace: The commercialization of higher education.* Princeton: Princeton University Press.

Brown, Phil, et al. 2004. Embodied health movements: New approaches to social movements in health. *Sociology of Health and Illness* 26:50–80.

Colby, Anne, et al. 2007. *Educating for democracy: Preparing undergraduates for responsible political engagement.* San Francisco: Jossey-Bass.

Cusset, François. 2008. *French theory: How Foucault, Derrida, Deleuze, & Co. transformed the intellectual life of the United States.* Trans. Jeff Fort. Minneapolis: University of Minnesota Press.

Daston, Lorraine, and Peter Galison. 2007. *Objectivity.* New York: Zone Books.

Dewey, John. [1902] 1976. Academic freedom. In *John Dewey: The middle works, 1899–1924,* vol. 2, ed. Jo Ann Boydston, 53–66. Carbondale: Southern Illinois University Press.

Doumani, Beshara, ed. 2006. *Academic freedom after September 11.* New York: Zone Books.

Draper, Elaine. 2003. *The company doctor: Risk, responsibility, and corporate professionalism.* New York: Russell Sage Foundation.

D'Souza, Dinesh. 1991. *Illiberal education: The politics of race and sex on campus.* New York: Free Press.

Epstein, Steven. 1996. *Impure science: AIDS, activism, and the politics of knowledge.* Berkeley: University of California Press.

Filc, Dani. 2006. Physicians as "organic intellectuals": A contribution to the stratification versus deprofessionalization debate. *Acta Sociologica* 49:273–85.

Freidson, Eliot. 1984. The changing nature of professional control. *Annual Review of Sociology* 10:1–20.

———. 1986. *Professional powers: A study of the institutionalization of formal knowledge.* Chicago: University of Chicago Press.

Frickel, Scott. 2004. *Chemical consequences: Environmental mutagens, scientist activism, and the rise of genetic toxicology.* New Brunswick: Rutgers University Press.

Gerstmann, Evan, and Matthew J. Streb, eds. 2006. *Academic freedom at the dawn of a new century: How terrorism, governments, and culture wars impact free speech.* Stanford: Stanford University Press.

Gross, Neil. 2008. *Richard Rorty: The making of an American philosopher.* Chicago: University of Chicago Press.

Gross, Neil, and Solon Simmons. 2007. The social and political views of American professors. Working paper, Department of Sociology, Harvard University.

Gross, Paul, and Norman Levitt. 1994. *Higher superstition: The academic left and its quarrels with science.* Baltimore: Johns Hopkins University Press.

Haraway, Donna. 1989. *Primate visions: Gender, race, and nature in the world of modern science.* New York: Routledge.

Haug, Marie. 1975. The deprofessionalization of everyone. *Sociological Focus* 8:197–213.

Hofstadter, Richard, and Walter P. Metzger. 1955. *The development of academic freedom in the United States.* New York: Columbia University Press.

Horowitz, David. 2006. *The professors: The 101 most dangerous academics in America.* Washington, DC: Regnery.

———. 2007. *Indoctrination U.: The left's war against academic freedom.* New York: Encounter Books.

Jasanoff, Sheila, ed. 2004. *States of knowledge: The co-production of science and social order.* New York: Routledge.

Kimball, Roger. 1998. *Tenured radicals: How politics has corrupted our higher education.* Chicago: Elephant Paperbacks.

Kleinman, Daniel Lee. 2003. *Impure cultures: University biology and the world of commerce.* Madison: University of Wisconsin Press.

Knorr Cetina, Karin. 1999. *Epistemic cultures: How the sciences make knowledge.* Cambridge, MA: Harvard University Press.

Kurzman, Charles, and Lynn Owens. 2002. The sociology of intellectuals. *Annual Review of Sociology* 28:63–90.

Lamont, Michèle. 1987. How to become a dominant French philosopher: The case of Jacques Derrida. *American Journal of Sociology* 93:584–622.

Larson, Magali Sarfatti. 1977. *The rise of professionalism: A sociological analysis.* Berkeley: University of California Press.

Leicht, Kevin T., and Mary L. Fennell. 1997. The changing organizational context of professional work. *Annual Review of Sociology* 23:215–31.

Menand, Louis, ed. 1996. *The future of academic freedom.* Chicago: University of Chicago Press.

Moore, Kelly. 2008. *Disrupting science: Social movements, American scientists, and the politics of the military, 1945–1975.* Princeton: Princeton University Press.

Novick, Peter. 1988. *That noble dream: The "objectivity question" and the American historical profession.* New York: Cambridge University Press.

Post, Robert. 2006. The structure of academic freedom. In *Academic freedom after September 11,* ed. Beshara Doumani, 61–106. Cambridge, MA: MIT Press.

Readings, Bill. 1996. *The university in ruins.* Cambridge, MA: Harvard University Press.

Ritzer, George, and David Walczak. 1988. Rationalization and the deprofessionalization of physicians. *Social Forces* 67:1–22.

Rojas, Fabio. 2007. *From black power to black studies: How a radical social movement became an academic discipline.* Baltimore: Johns Hopkins University Press.

Rothman, Robert. 1984. Deprofessionalization: The case of law in America. *Work & Occupations* 11:183–206.

Shapin, Steven, and Simon Schaffer. 1985. *Leviathan and the air-pump: Hobbes, Boyle, and the experimental life.* Princeton: Princeton University Press.

Smith, Bruce L. R., Jeremy D. Mayer, and A. Lee Fritschler. 2008. *Closed minds? Politics and ideology in American universities.* Washington, DC: Brookings Institution Press.

Steinmetz, George, ed. 2005. *The politics of method in the human sciences: Positivism and its epistemological others.* Durham: Duke University Press.

Van Hoy, Jerry. 1995. Selling and processing law: Legal work at franchise law firms. *Law & Society Review* 29:703–29.

Weeden, Kim A. 2002. Why do some occupations pay more than others? Social closure and earnings inequality in the United States. *American Journal of Sociology* 108:55–101.

PART II

Socialization and Deviance

CHAPTER FIVE

The Socialization of Future Faculty in a Changing Context

Traditions, Challenges, and Possibilities

Ann E. Austin

D octoral education serves as a period of socialization during which those who are considering entering the professoriate learn the beliefs, norms, values, and behaviors that are valued within the academic profession. While disciplines vary in the specifics of their approaches, efforts to socialize future faculty have been embedded within long-standing understandings of what it means to be part of the academic profession. However, changes occurring in academic work and faculty appointment patterns raise questions about the nature of the academic profession. Faculty members are facing new roles and responsibilities, and the nature of faculty appointments is changing. Furthermore, doctoral students' expectations about the kinds of careers and life situations they seek sometimes differ in noteworthy ways from the expectations and assumptions of established faculty.

This chapter explores the implications of these changes in faculty work, faculty appointment patterns, and doctoral student expectations in regard to how doctoral education is preparing the faculty of the future. How can doctoral education effectively prepare aspiring faculty members to enter a profession that is experiencing considerable change? What is the role of doctoral education in preparing individuals ready to contribute to the vibrancy, relevance, and effectiveness of academe as a profession? What might characterize effective approaches to doctoral student socialization in the context of a changing academic workplace, changing academic careers, and changes in student characteristics? The chapter begins with a short discussion of socialization theory to highlight the functions of doctoral education as a period of socialization for academic careers. The next section discusses the significant changes underway in academic work as well as issues identified in research on doctoral education that lead to questions about how best to prepare the future faculty. The chapter concludes by addressing the central guiding question, What should the socialization process emphasize, and what possibilities might enrich the socialization of aspiring faculty members in light of the changing context for the academic profession?

The chapter builds on a wide array of research studies on faculty work, academic careers, and doctoral education. Thus, the paper draws on quantitative and qualitative studies, including policy analyses and sociological studies, concerning the experiences and perspectives of doctoral students and early-career faculty, the changing nature of faculty appointment patterns, and the societal context in which academic work occurs. I recognize that some institutions employ faculty members who do not hold doctoral degrees. In this chapter, however, I focus only on issues concerning doctoral education as a socializing experience, leaving a discussion of how to socialize those who enter the professoriate without a doctorate for another discussion. I also recognize that many doctoral students do not choose to pursue faculty careers. In recent decades, just over half of recent doctoral recipients (52.8% in 1980 and 51.8% in 2000) indicated that their career choice was academe (Nettles and Millett 2006, citing Hoffer et al. 2001). Furthermore, interest in a faculty career varies by discipline. Based on their research, involving more than nine thousand doctoral student respondents, Nettles and Millett (2006) reported that about three-quarters of the humanities doctoral students planned to enter a postdoctoral post or a faculty position, compared with somewhat more than half of the students in social sciences, sciences, and mathematics and only 28 percent of students in engineering and 28 percent of students in education. Given these disciplinary variations, faculty in different departments would be wise to assess the extent of interest in academic work among their students and to ensure that preparation is provided for the array of careers of interest to their students. However, while recognizing the importance of preparation for various careers, in this chapter I focus on preparation for faculty work.

Doctoral Education as Socialization for the Faculty Career

Building on the work on socialization of Merton and his colleagues (Merton 1957; Merton, Reader, and Kendall 1957), various authors have considered the meaning, processes, and implications of this concept. Bragg provided a useful definition, explaining that "the socialization process is the learning process through which the individual acquires the knowledge and skills, the values and attitudes, and the habits and modes of thought of the society to which he belongs" (1976, 3). The socialization process involves learning and adopting the norms, standards, and expectations of the group one is joining (Austin and McDaniels 2006a). Based on this definition, doctoral education constitutes the primary period during which future faculty members are socialized to the work and life of a professor.

Theorists in recent years have cautioned against taking a linear, one-way, overly rational approach to socialization. Rather, taking a postmodern stance, theorists such as Tierney and Rhoads (1994) framed socialization as a "cultural process" that involves bidirectional, dialectical influences. That is, newcomers certainly need to learn about the organization they are joining, including its values, norms, and practices. At the same time, however, those coming into an organization bring their own values, expectations, and viewpoints, which have an impact on and can change the organization. Thus, socialization experiences should not involve efforts to make all newcomers the same or to "homogenize" them (Tierney and Rhoads 1994, 70). Instead, socialization consists of dynamic processes that influence and affect both the individual and the organization. This perspective is especially useful when considering the graduate school period as a time of socialization. Just as doctoral students are learning about the nature of academic work and careers, they are also bringing their own hopes, dreams, plans, and practices into the academy. A changing academic environment and aspiring faculty with new characteristics and perspectives on work invite creative approaches to the socialization process so that the new faculty and the institutions they enter simultaneously benefit.

Weidman, Twale, and Stein (2001) developed a theoretical framework that specifically addresses aspects of graduate and professional student socialization. Acknowledging that socialization involves a two-way process, they explained that "[t]he outcome of socialization is not the transfer of a social role, but identification with and commitment to a role that has been normatively and individually defined" (36). The socialization process involves graduate students learning knowledge and skills, interacting with faculty and student peers, and becoming integrated into their fields. While students bring their own values, expectations, and behaviors to the process, they also are influenced by their professional and personal communities, including their families and peers, their faculty, and leaders in the professional associations.

While change is always occurring in any field, higher education institutions are arguably in a period of greater change than usual (Duderstadt 2000; Gappa, Austin, and Trice 2007). A discussion of some of the most significant changes and their impact on faculty work appears below. Given these changes, a key question deserves attention: How can today's faculty best prepare tomorrow's faculty when there are significant changes occurring in the work itself, the patterns of academic appointments, and the characteristics and expectations of the aspiring faculty?

The Changing Context and the Implications for Faculty Work

Doctoral students preparing to be faculty members are entering a career and work context that is increasingly different in important ways from the career paths and work contexts that their faculty advisors entered. The changes, which my colleagues and I have discussed extensively in a recently published book, *Rethinking Faculty Work* (Gappa, Austin, and Trice 2007), fall in three categories. First, the nature of faculty work itself is changing, so that professors must assume new roles and responsibilities. Second, the nature of the faculty career is changing, as appointment patterns shift, work becomes "unbundled," and career trajectories become more variable. Third, aspiring faculty—doctoral students—are bringing unique expectations to their career planning, shaped by changes in perspectives about work across the broader society. They also are expressing concerns about both the doctoral experience and the faculty career. Taken as a whole, these changes mean that today's faculty members are preparing their graduate students for careers and work experiences likely to be distinctively different from their own experiences. A legitimate question is whether the approach to doctoral education that has traditionally been followed in many fields may need to be supplemented, revised, or adapted to help aspiring faculty be ready for the work world they will enter.

Changes in the Nature of Faculty Work

While a number of changes could be listed in regard to faculty work, four significant developments stand out. Each of these has explicit implications for the work of the faculty. Many of today's professors who are currently advising doctoral students are themselves striving to adjust to the implications of these changes for faculty work.

The opportunities and challenges of ever-present technology. One of the major societal changes affecting academic work concerns the continuous development and expansion of new technologies. These changes affect how work is done and how faculty members interact with colleagues and students (Gappa, Austin, and Trice 2007; Gumport and Chun 2005). For example, the ubiquity of e-mail and other communication options imposes demands on faculty members for extensive availability. (A colleague recently commented to me that a student sent her a question at 2 a.m., at 3 a.m., and again at 5 a.m., when he bluntly asked her why she was so unresponsive. She found it necessary to remind him that the instantaneous nature and availability of e-mail does not mean that faculty members no longer sleep.) Electronic communication options open up new options for interactions and collaboration. At the same time, electronic communication enables constant interruptions that can interfere with sustained, creative thought. Faculty members must learn how to organize their time in an environment without traditionally defined time boundaries and how to help others learn appropriate ways for interacting with them within such an environment.

Technological advances also have opened up exciting possibilities for new kinds of research and teaching. Researchers can find colleagues all around the world, with whom they can easily exchange information and ideas. While large research teams are common in "big science," technological advances, including new databases, are also helping scholars in the humanities and social sciences pursue more complex studies and engage in collaborative work. Similarly, in teaching, technological developments enable faculty members to facilitate learning in new ways and to interact with students who may be geographically distant. The changes bring both opportunity and challenge. For example, faculty members have the freedom of doing much of their work at home or from a distance. Yet spending time away from campus may undermine a sense of community and institutional commitment. The possibilities for enhancing learning are promising, yet faculty members engaged in online teaching must find effective ways to create human connections with students they may never see in person, to help students interact across cyberspace, to organize course work in ways that make sense in the electronic medium, and to perceive students' dilemmas and questions without benefit of interacting with them in a face-to-face setting.

The move toward interdisciplinarity and the expansion of knowledge. At the same time that technology is developing and expanding, a move toward increased interdisciplinarity is also underway. The intersections of disciplines and fields create spaces for new questions—even new fields—to be defined. The expansion of knowledge, occurring at a faster pace than ever, is aided by the opportunities afforded by new technologies (e.g., databases can be linked and data can be analyzed in new ways). Faculty members certainly must have deep knowledge in their fields. Yet exciting paths are open to those willing to pursue interdisciplinary possibilities. Those engaged in interdisciplinary work must be comfortable and have the skills to work with colleagues from other fields—including an understanding of a range of epistemologies, ability to communicate perspectives in ways that are understandable to colleagues in other fields, and teamwork skills. Additionally, they must understand not only the structure of knowledge and the kinds of questions important in their own disciplines, but also how to enter newly created knowledge domains and frame questions informed by interdisciplinary interests. Furthermore, faculty members must have strategies to stay abreast of the rapid expansion of knowledge.

The changing characteristics of students. As the demand for higher education continues to grow, the diversity of students—in age, background, race and ethnicity, aspirations and goals—also expands (Keller 2001; Levine 2000). While this diversity is a feature to applaud within American higher education, it also requires faculty members to know how to work effectively with many different people who have a great range of needs. Specifically, faculty members must know how to motivate, counsel and guide, and communicate effectively with very diverse people. The ability to teach in a student-centered way is not a matter of simply having a "tool kit" of strategies; it involves deeper understanding of how learning occurs, what factors affect the learning process, and how learner characteristics play a role in the educational process. Furthermore, today's students are expecting relevance, convenience, economy, and attentiveness from faculty members (Levine 2000) in ways that established faculty members assess to be very different from the needs expressed by previous generations of students. Those aspiring to the professoriate face expectations and demands for the quality and nature of their work with students that differ from those encountered by faculty in previous decades.

Fiscal constraints, accountability, and increased competition. Across the country, higher education institutions face rising costs, volatility in state budgets, and stagnant federal support for higher education (Boyd 2005; Gappa, Austin, and Trice 2007; Newman, Courturier, and Scurry 2004). Budget reductions are common in recent years at both public and private institutions. Increased competition for resources and students also is another challenge facing most higher education institutions. Among the results of fiscal constraint and competition are a shift in power and control toward administrators and heightened pressure on faculty members to be entrepreneurial (Rhoades 1998). Finding ways to translate scholarly work into products and forms of interest to those outside the academy—which includes communicating with diverse audiences, leading teams, and managing budgets—is new for many faculty members. For tomorrow's faculty, one speculates that it is likely to be commonly expected work.

Coupled with fiscal constraint is increased competition for students and resources, as well as heightened demands for accountability. The public at large expects greater transparency in the work of the academy, as well as contributions to the public good in the form of effective teaching that results in graduates well prepared for the work world, excellent research that leads to important practical applications, and effective translation of knowledge into practical outcomes, including productive economic development. Faculty members are called on to engage in a wide range of activities, often involving interactions with audiences new to many professors.

Each of these changes—technological innovations, more interdisciplinarity, the changing characteristics of students, increased fiscal constraints, calls for accountability, and heightened competition—has an impact on the academic profession. Certainly academic work continues to include the key elements that have been central for years. Academics teach students; some engage in research and writing; most are expected to engage in service to their institution, the profession, and the broader society. Yet the changes underway affect what constitutes valued academic work within the academy and in the broader society, how members of the academic profession organize and carry out their work, and how they interact with key constituencies, including students, parents, employers, community members, institutional leaders, and even other colleagues. Those involved in doctoral education face the challenge of preparing aspiring faculty for this changing context in which academic work occurs.

Changes in the Pattern of Faculty Appointments

Not only is the nature of faculty work changing, but the pattern of faculty appointments—the relative percentages of various appointment types across academe—is also changing in dramatic ways (Rice 2004; Schuster and Fin-kelstein 2006). As explained by Jack Schuster (this volume), the primary change involves a shift away from tenure-track positions to alternative ap-pointment types. Structural changes in the pattern of faculty appointments have led to a tripartite arrangement with tenure track, renewable contract positions, and temporary or fixed-term appointments (Gappa, Austin, and Trice 2007). As Schuster and Finkelstein's analyses reveal (2006), there has been a decline in the percentage of faculty in tenure-track FTE (full-time-equivalent) positions. Several statistics punctuate this point. By 2003, 35 percent of all full-time faculty members did not hold tenured or tenure-track positions. Fur-thermore, 56 percent of new full-time hires were not in tenure-track positions (Gappa, Austin, & Trice 2007). Contract-renewable positions (those in which the position is based on a contract that is renewed periodically, such as annu-ally, or every three or five years) and fixed-term appointments (held for a spe-cific period of time) are also an increasing part of the higher education sector. Part-time positions also are increasing, with 44 percent of all faculty members in 2004 holding part-time positions (U.S. Department of Education, National Center for Education Statistics 2004).

The term "unbundling" refers to the division of faculty work among differ-ent people. For example, many part-time faculty members teach, while others are assigned to research activities. Even within the teaching domain, some specialists handle course design, while others focus on the "delivery" aspect of education. Those entering the academic profession today cannot assume that they will hold a full-time position or a tenure-track position, or that their institutional environment will value the connections between teaching, re-search, and service. How can doctoral programs best socialize aspiring fac-ulty members to value the norms, traditions, and values that have long char-acterized the academic profession, while also preparing them to understand the employment context in which the academic profession is currently situated?

The Changing Characteristics of Doctoral Students

While the nature of academic work and the pattern of academic appoint-ments are changing, some shifts are also apparent in how new scholars are thinking about the academic profession. Research on doctoral students and new faculty shows that they hold many perspectives that have motivated aca-demics for decades. They are excited about introducing new students to their fields. They look forward to advancing disciplinary knowledge in their areas of expertise. They often speak of seeking meaning in and bringing passion to their work, and using their education and experience to make a difference. They value the autonomy, flexibility, and intellectual excitement offered by an academic life (Rice, Sorcinelli, and Austin 2000; Trower 2005).

At the same time, aspiring and early-career faculty today articulate some perspectives that vary considerably from the single-minded commitment to work that typically has characterized those in the academic profession (Rice 1986). Many are quite clear about their interest in living a "balanced life" in which both work and other interests and responsibilities figure into the mix of daily activities (Austin, Sorcinelli, and McDaniels 2007; Trower 2005). In fact, finding sufficient time both to do excellent academic work and to pursue personal interests and commitments is a major factor contributing to the stress that many early-career faculty members report (Boice 1992; Sorcinelli 1988). Research studies show that some doctoral students, observing the hectic lives led by their faculty advisors, express uncertainty about whether they want to pursue academic careers (Austin 2002; Austin, Sorcinelli, and McDaniels 2007; Rice, Sorcinelli, and Austin 2000).

Changes in societal expectations about work are likely to be a factor influencing young academics. The notion of an "ideal worker" who constantly holds work as the first priority to which he or she devotes long, uninterrupted hours, a notion that emerged in the post–World War II period, is being challenged by employees across work sectors (Gappa, Austin, and Trice 2007). Gender roles have been changing, with both men and women today often holding significant domestic as well as professional responsibilities. Some evidence indicates that early-career professionals in academe and in other workplaces are more concerned with interesting work and working environments that enable them to enjoy a sense of balance between professional and personal roles than they are in job security (Gappa, Austin, and Trice 2007; Trower 2005). Within the broader society, there are also examples of corporate workplaces that are developing policies and practices that provide employees with flexibility and support for managing work/life balance.

In short, many doctoral students considering academic careers, along with faculty members in the early years of the profession, bring new expectations to the academic workplace. They seek opportunities for pursuing both their professional and personal passions as well as environments where they can work hard while also maintaining a sense of balance. While tenure (in situations where it is an option) remains attractive to many early-career faculty, some newcomers to faculty work claim that career flexibility and opportunities to choose interesting work may be more important than the security of tenure and long employment at one institution (Gappa, Austin, and Trice 2007; Trower 2005). How can doctoral programs best socialize and prepare prospective faculty as the characteristics of the doctoral students themselves change?

Concerns about the Doctoral Experience

The previous sections have discussed changes in academic work, academic appointment patterns, and perspectives of new scholars concerning the academic career, all of which have implications for how doctoral programs socialize those preparing to enter the academic profession. The literature that has emerged over the past fifteen years concerning the nature of doctoral education and its role in socializing those preparing to enter the professoriate adds further perspectives relevant to this discussion of the preparation of the next generation of faculty. Based on both qualitative and quantitative studies, the findings on the process of doctoral student socialization tend to be consistent in highlighting some key themes (Austin 2002; Golde and Dore 2001; Lovitts 2001, 2004; Wulff and Austin 2004).

First, the research indicates that the doctoral experience typically is not organized so that prospective faculty members engage in systematic learning about the faculty career (Austin 2002; Golde and Dore 2001; Nerad, Aanerud, and Cerny 2004; Nyquist et al. 1999; Wulff et al. 2004). Students may have opportunities to teach (as teaching assistants) or conduct research (as members of a research team or as they pursue their own dissertations), but they often are not guided in systematic ways as they explore and become proficient in these aspects of academic work. For example, a student may help grade papers in a large lecture class but not be involved in the early process of curriculum design for the course. A student on a research team may work on data analysis but have little opportunity to engage in grant writing. Golde and Dore have commented that "the training doctoral students receive is not what they want, nor does it prepare them for the jobs they take" (2001, 3).

Second, doctoral students often do not receive explicit guidance about expectations or specific feedback about the work that they do. Lovitts (2001) explained that one factor in attrition is the lack of information that students receive and their sense of inadequacy about being successful. Students often report what they call "mixed messages" about the priorities they should address, particularly in relation to how they should incorporate attention to teaching and research in their development (Austin 2002; Nyquist et al. 1999; Wulff et al. 2004). Doctoral students also report that there are few occasions in which they are guided by faculty members to engage in thoughtful reflection about their doctoral experience, the sense they are making of academic work, and the career options that they might consider. When provided with opportunities to think through their experiences and reflect with an experienced colleague about the challenges they are facing and growth they are experiencing, students are enthusiastic about the usefulness of the experience (Austin 2002; Nyquist et al. 1999; Wulff et al. 2004).

Third, doctoral students want to experience a sense of community. Not surprisingly, students report that they benefit from opportunities to learn from each other. When students feel isolated and a sense that they do not belong, as particularly occurs for some women and students of color, the lack of attention to integration and community can contribute to attrition (Antony and Taylor 2001, 2004; Lovitts 2001, 2004; Taylor and Antony 2001). Developing departmental cultures where students feel a sense of belonging does much to help retain students (Lovitts 2001, 2004).

Fourth, doctoral students report that they have little awareness of the range of career options that they might consider. In their study of degree recipients ten years out, Nerad, Aanerud, and Cerny (2004) reported that doctoral graduates would have valued more extensive information about job options and the labor market, how to assess their own potential for various career directions, and employers' expectations.

As professors in doctoral programs assess their work socializing students for the academic profession, they might consider these concerns that appear with consistency across a number of studies on the doctoral experience. Ensuring that newcomers are prepared to enter and succeed in the academic profession requires consideration of the shortcomings of the preparation experience in recent decades as well as of changes in academic work, academic appointments, and the expectations of aspiring and new faculty members concerning the nature of professorial life.

Implications for the Socialization of Future Faculty

Given the changing nature of faculty work, the changing patterns of faculty appointments, shifts in the perspectives of graduate students regarding academic work, and concerns about doctoral education, what are the implications for the preparation and socialization of future faculty? Doctoral students study in research universities. However, the majority of those who continue into faculty roles will not hold tenure-track, full-time appointments in such universities; rather, most will take appointments at other institutional types, and some will take non-tenure-track positions or part-time positions. If the academic profession is to retain its values, norms, and integrity, it must find ways to socialize aspiring entrants to understand and prize its long-established traditions, values, and norms, even as they also prepare for the array of institutional types and contexts in which they may work. The continuing strength of academic work as a profession partly depends on the extent to which those who take nontraditional appointments—non-tenure-track appointments or part-time appointments—understand and commit themselves to the central values and norms of the academic profession, including such values as commitment to excellence, autonomy, academic freedom, collegiality, self-regulation and peer review, and the place of research, teaching, and service within the profession (even if not equally addressed within a single individual academic's career) (Gappa, Austin, and Trice 2007; Rice 1986). The result of inadequately socializing future faculty, especially those who take less traditional positions, is likely to be the further weakening of faculty control over academic decisions and a greater bifurcation of the professoriate (which arguably is occurring as a result of a number of factors) into an elite, autonomous group that holds tenure-track positions and a less highly respected, less autonomous group that holds the non-tenure-track positions, renewable appointments, and part-time positions.

This section first takes up the issue of what future faculty need to know in order to ensure the viability of the academic profession in a changing context. I then turn to consideration of how graduate education can address these competencies, and who has responsibility for ensuring that it does. Finally, we consider several questions that might be raised in response to this call for more systematic attention to the socialization of future faculty.

Competencies for Future Faculty

What should all prospective faculty members learn during the doctoral socialization process? In another publication (Austin and McDaniels 2006a), a colleague and I proposed a set of competencies, based on assessment of the literature about the academic profession and how it is changing, that doctoral education should help future faculty members develop. Specifically, we proposed that socialization to the professoriate should be designed to help future faculty members develop competencies in four areas: (1) conceptual understandings, (2) knowledge and skills in key areas of faculty work, (3) interpersonal skills, and (4) professional attitudes and habits. Various studies are underway to test the extent to which faculty members and doctoral students agree about the importance of these competencies, and the extent to which different constituencies think these competencies should be addressed in doctoral education versus through professional development in the early career. In this section I briefly highlight the four areas, arguing that the values, behaviors, and understandings that they emphasize will help future faculty prepare for the changing context in which the academic profession is situated and the various institutional settings in which they will enact their understandings of the profession.

In terms of conceptual understandings, knowledge of one's discipline and its distinctive culture is a central requirement of membership in the academic profession (Austin and McDaniels, 2006a). New scholars need to understand the history of their disciplines, questions valued by the discipline, the theories and philosophical perspectives that guide work in the field, the methods considered appropriate to address those questions, the criteria used to assess excellence, and the forms in which work is typically presented (e.g., books vs. articles). With the expansion of interdisciplinary work, appropriate socialization experiences in graduate study would also introduce new scholars to the opportunities and challenges involved in interdisciplinary scholarship. Specifically, new scholars need to learn how to establish an intellectual home while also connecting to the margins of their field where interesting cutting-edge questions are likely to be emerging. They also need to understand the epistemological and pedagogical traditions in their own fields and how those traditions are challenged and enriched as they intersect with such traditions in other fields. They need to learn how to communicate with colleagues whose fields intersect with their own, how to critique work in other fields, and what norms guide interdisciplinary teaching, research, and curriculum planning (Austin and McDaniels 2006a).

The socialization process also should introduce aspiring faculty to the history of higher education and its responsibilities to American society. They particularly need to understand the role of American higher education institutions in contributing to the public good, through knowledge production, preparing citizens for their responsibilities as citizens and employees, and knowledge application to societal problems (Austin and Barnes 2005; Austin and McDaniels 2006a, 2006b). Future faculty members also need to be familiar with the types of higher education institutions, including liberal arts colleges, community colleges, comprehensive institutions, and research-oriented universities, and what distinguishes the culture of each type. Research has shown that only a small percentage of doctoral students indicate a preference for work in liberal arts or community colleges, although almost all doctoral students who seek faculty positions will need to find them in places other than the research university (Golde and Dore 2001).

Central to the socialization process is the opportunity for those who aspire to the faculty role to consider what it means to be a scholar and professor (Austin and McDaniels 2006a). This aspect of graduate school socialization is perhaps of more importance than ever, in the face of the changes in the nature of faculty work and the patterns of faculty appointment types. What does it mean to be part of the academic profession? How does academic identity relate to one's disciplinary affiliation or the kind of institution or appointment that one holds? To what extent is one's academic identity static or fluid? What are one's responsibilities as a member of the academic profession, in regard to such issues as contributing to the knowledge base, participating in scholarly associations, and reviewing others' work—and what are various ways in which a member of the profession can carry out these responsibilities? Bess has argued that graduate students should "understand fully the symbolic meaning of the activities in which a 'professor' engages" (1978, 293). As pressures challenge the coherence, strength, and integrity of the academic profession, these are questions that become especially important to weave through the doctoral experience.

In addition to conceptual understandings of the meaning of academic work, prospective faculty members need to be prepared to do the teaching, research, and other activities expected by those who work in the academic profession (Austin and McDaniels 2006a). Doctoral education in most disciplines has typically not emphasized explicit preparation for teaching; yet, most faculty members work not in research universities of the sort where they were prepared, but in institutions where teaching is heavily emphasized. Furthermore, across institutional types, faculty members are facing increasing expectations to demonstrate teaching excellence. Thus, new faculty members are likely to be more effective and more efficient with their time not only if they have deep knowledge of their disciplines but also if they have some basic knowledge and expertise in teaching. For example, they should know key findings concerning how learning occurs, the variety of teaching strategies that they might use and the advantages of each, approaches to designing learning contexts, specific pedagogical issues relevant to their specific disciplines (Hutchings and Shulman 1999), and uses of technology to encourage learning within their fields.

In regard to research, the socialization process usually occurs through apprenticeship relationships with faculty members, as doctoral students participate in research projects and conduct their own research, culminating in the dissertation. By the end of the doctoral socialization period, prospective faculty members should know how to frame important questions, design scholarly projects, collect and analyze data, present the results of their research, and give and receive feedback. Another component of academic work, engaging in service to the institution, profession, and wider community, is often not explicitly addressed in graduate education; studies have shown that prospective faculty members often have little familiarity with the concept of service (Austin 2002). Since membership in a profession involves participating in self-regulation and, in the case of professorial work, assuming responsibility for institutional governance, explicit attention to preparing aspiring faculty members for the role of service in their work would strengthen the academic profession.

Preparation around two other sets of competencies would also help those entering the professoriate handle their work and assume the responsibilities of being members of the academic profession. Faculty members need strong interpersonal skills, including verbal and written communication skills to explain their work to a wide range of audiences, and listening skills that enhance productive dialogue with diverse individuals. Competencies in functioning in groups, including collaboration and conflict resolution skills and appreciation of diversity, also help them conduct their work.

Finally, membership in the academic profession requires the cultivation of important professional attitudes and habits (Austin and McDaniels 2006a; Braxton and Baird 2001; Pelikan 1992; Stark, Lowther, and Hagerty 1986). Prospective faculty members must learn how to self-regulate, the standards and ethical issues involved in research in their fields, and how to handle such issues, among others, as conflicts of interest, confidentiality, and intellectual ownership. The strength and coherence of the academic profession—especially in the context of the contextual factors in which faculty members work today—depend on the proper socialization of new members to these values. In addition to cultivating values, new faculty members need to learn habits of lifelong learning (important in a context where their fields and institutions are engaged in ongoing change), strategies for nurturing professional networks (important strategies to help faculty stay connected with disciplinary as well as institutional colleagues), and strategies for nurturing passion about one's work along with balance in the dimensions of one's life (issues of concern often expressed by the diverse individuals entering the academic profession today).

Strategies for Socializing Prospective Faculty

Those who help socialize prospective faculty members need not abandon the processes that have been typical for years, including research apprenticeship under the guidance of faculty members, doctoral student participation in scholarly meetings, and peer relationships in which students provide important support to each other. Rather, I argue for building on well-established traditions, but making the socialization experience more purposeful, less serendipitous, more inclusive of the array of diverse doctoral students aspiring to academic work, and more explicitly attentive to preparing future faculty for the challenges confronting the academic profession and the changing contextual factors affecting academic work. More explicit attention to socializing and preparing new faculty should be shared by graduate deans, faculty advisors, scholarly associations, foundations and agencies, and doctoral students themselves.

Many strategies can be integrated into activities already occurring. For example, faculty advisors can be explicitly attentive to opportunities to integrate into their normal interactions with their advisees and research and teaching assistants conversations about ethical issues, the range of tasks they incorporate into their days, and their own choices about ways to construct a scholarly career and a satisfying life. Recognizing the importance of "social integration" (Lovitts 2001, 2004) to the satisfaction, learning, and retention of doctoral students, department chairs and graduate deans might help students establish disciplinary-based or cross-disciplinary discussion groups that explore changes underway in the academy, invite speakers from a range of institutional types, or provide space for conversations about strategies for managing work/life balance. Students themselves already rely heavily on peer interaction for support (Austin 2002). Building on this tradition, prospective faculty members can be proactive in creating their own conversations and inviting experienced faculty to talk with them about academic life and the career choices they face.

A number of scholarly associations have been quite active in the past decade in providing conference space for doctoral students to learn more about the academic profession. Conference programs in such disciplines and fields as sociology, biology, and the study of higher education include sessions to help aspiring faculty learn more about their roles as teachers, the professional networks to support them in their work, and the range of institutional types in which they might seek to live out their professional commitments. Foundations and national organizations also have a role in preparing the next generation of faculty. Some have helped develop opportunities through which prospective faculty can experience and explore academic work within different settings. The goal of the Preparing Future Faculty (PFF) program, for example, has been to facilitate opportunities for advanced doctoral students to explore the academic profession through mentored internships at institutions near their research universities (Pruitt-Logan and Gaff 2004).

With support from the National Science Foundation, the Center for the Integration of Research, Teaching, and Learning (CIRTL) (www.cirtl.net) is committed to preparing future faculty in science, technology, engineering, and mathematics (STEM fields) to be excellent teachers as well as excellent researchers. CIRTL provides resources and publications, as well as courses and workshops, open to STEM doctoral students and postdoctoral scholars at participating institutions, that prepare participants for college-level teaching. CIRTL emphasizes "teaching-as-research," an approach to teaching in which the same research skills that are used in research are applied to teaching; that is, participants ask questions, gather and analyze data, develop conclusions about their teaching and their students' learning, and apply the findings to the improvement of their practice. CIRTL students and faculty also participate in learning communities organized to foster discussions, interaction, and mentoring that support future scholars in becoming members of the academic profession.

The Carnegie Foundation for the Advancement of Teaching has offered their Initiative on the Doctorate, focused on supporting academic departments committed to "creating stewards of the discipline" (Walker 2004). The Initiative has aimed at preparing new faculty who understand the values of the profession as well as the contexts within which they may work. According to George Walker, who directed the program, "Disciplinary stewards are those responsible for preserving the essence of their fields while simultaneously directing a critical eye to the future, those to whom we entrust the vigor, quality, and integrity of the individual disciplines" (2004, 239). When faculty members, chairs and deans, and foundation and association leaders all are committed to taking a role in the socialization of the future professoriate, the responsibility will not be a burden to individual faculty members.

Considerations about Enhancing the Socialization of Future Faculty

This essay has argued that the changes occurring within the academic profession make the socialization process of new faculty more important than ever. Some readers may raise questions about the call for more thoughtful attention to the socialization process or the practicalities of how this enhanced attention might occur. Here I briefly address some of these questions.

Question 1: New faculty members, at least those who have the potential to be successful, have always managed to find their own way in the academy. Why is it necessary now to give more attention to their socialization? Several reasons lead me to argue that systematic and thoughtful attention to preparing new faculty is warranted. First, when they recruit and hire a new faculty member, universities and colleges invest heavily in terms of time, collegial energy, and financial outlays for such items as travel, equipment, and laboratories. It is in the interests of the institution, as well as of the new professor, for the newcomer to succeed. Second, new faculty members want to succeed, but can find their energy diverted as they try to make sense of a new institution and new responsibilities. If newcomers are more fully prepared for the expectations they must fulfill as new members of the academic profession, they are more likely to succeed in the various dimensions of academic work. More preparation for teaching, for example, does not mean that a faculty member is going to neglect research. Rather, being prepared for the demands of teaching can lead to efficiencies in time allocation that can result in more research productivity. Third, the demands on faculty members are arguably greater than in past decades. Given the factors discussed in this chapter, the context for working within the academic profession has become more turbulent. New entrants to the profession are facing more extensive expectations and more uncertain environmental conditions than senior faculty who entered the academy in the post–World War II expansion period.

Question 2: Perhaps the academy should not change. Why should the socialization process respond to the pressures on the academy that many would argue are leading to changes that undermine the professional autonomy long associated with the academic profession? Much of my argument for more explicit attention to the socialization process for aspiring faculty is built on a great respect for the values and norms that have long characterized the academic profession. Yet, I am also persuaded that significant changes are underway in regard to the nature of academic work, the patterns in academic appointments, and the perspectives of those considering entering the academic profession. I believe that new faculty members must experience deep exposure to and cultivation of the values and norms that inform the academic profession. At the same time, they must understand the context currently affecting the profession and the institutions in which academics works. I argue that new faculty members who have been carefully socialized to the profession and explicitly prepared to understand and handle the expectations and challenges of the current context will be best positioned to honor, respect, and maintain the integrity of the profession they are entering.

Question 3: Faculty members already find that their time is stretched thin. How can they possibly devote more time to preparing the next generation of faculty members? As discussed, efforts to ensure that those preparing for the professoriate understand the values of the profession as well as the expectations and challenges in the higher education contexts in which they will work need not become just one more additional task competing for time in the already full schedule of faculty advisors, nor need this responsibility fall solely on faculty members. The literature on socialization for academic careers emphasizes the important role played by various interested and influential parties, including institutional leaders, scholarly associations, and peers, as well as doctoral students themselves.

I also assert that faculty members need not spend more time, but rather more purposeful time, on guiding their doctoral students' socialization. Faculty members teach their students through the examples of their daily lives and work and through the informal, as well as formal, conversations they have with their students. Furthermore, today's faculty members are themselves adjusting to and learning how to manage a changing environment. They need not—and cannot—prepare tomorrow's faculty for all that the academic world will involve. However, they can share their understandings and engage with their students in reflecting on what it means to be a member of the academic profession. These conversations should enrich the academic profession today and ensure that tomorrow's professors are prepared for the challenges they will face.

REFERENCES

Antony, James S., and Edward Taylor. 2001. Graduate student socialization and its implications for the recruitment of African American education faculty. In *Faculty work in schools of education: Rethinking roles and rewards for the twenty-first century*, ed. William G. Tierney, 189–202. Albany: State University of New York Press.

———. 2004. Theories and strategies of academic career socialization: Improving paths to the professoriate for black graduate students. In *Paths to the professoriate: Strategies for enriching the preparation of future faculty*, ed. Donald H. Wulff and Ann E. Austin, 92–114. San Francisco: Jossey-Bass.

Austin, Ann E. 2002. Preparing the next generation of faculty: Graduate education as socialization to the academic career. *The Journal of Higher Education* 73 (2): 94–122.

Austin, Ann E., and Benita J. Barnes. 2005. Preparing doctoral students for faculty careers that contribute to the public good. In *Higher education for the public good: Emerging voices from a national movement*, ed. Tony C. Chambers, Adrianna J. Kezar, and John C. Burkhardt, 272–92. San Francisco: Jossey-Bass.

Austin, Ann E., and Melissa McDaniels. 2006a. Preparing the professoriate of the future: Graduate student socialization for faculty roles. In *Higher education: Handbook of theory and research*, vol. 21, ed. John C. Smart, 397–456. Dordrecht: Springer.

———. 2006b. Using doctoral education to prepare faculty to work within Boyer's four domains of scholarship. In *Analyzing faculty work and rewards: Using Boyer's four domains of scholarship*, ed. John M. Braxton, New Directions for Institutional Research No. 129, 51–65. San Francisco: Jossey-Bass.

Austin, Ann E., Mary Deane Sorcinelli, and Melissa McDaniels. 2007. Understanding new faculty: Background, aspirations, challenges, and growth. In *The scholarship of teaching and learning in higher education: An evidence-based perspective*, ed. Ray Perry and John Smart, 39–89. Dordrecht: Springer.

Bess, James. 1978. Anticipatory socialization of graduate students. *Research in Higher Education* 8:289–317.

Boice, Robert. 1992. *The new faculty member: Supporting and fostering professional development*. San Francisco: Jossey-Bass.

Boyd, Don. 2005. *State fiscal outlook from 2005 to 2013: Implications for higher education*. NCHEMS Web site: www.higheredinfo.org/analyses/.

Bragg, Ann K. 1976. *The socialization process in higher education*. Washington, DC: American Association of Higher Education.

Braxton, John M., and Leonard Baird. 2001. Preparation for professional self-regulation. *Science and Engineering Ethics* 7:593–610.

Duderstadt, James J. 2000. *A university for the 21st century*. Ann Arbor: University of Michigan Press.

Gappa, Judith M., Ann E. Austin, and Andrea G. Trice. 2007. *Rethinking faculty work: Higher education's strategic imperative*. San Francisco: Jossey-Bass.

Golde, Chris M., and Tim M. Dore. 2001. *At cross purposes: What the experiences of today's doctoral students reveal about doctoral education*. Philadelphia: Pew Charitable Trusts.

Gumport, Patricia J., and Marc Chun. 2005. Technology and higher education: Opportunities and challenges for the new era. In *American higher education in the twenty-first century: Social, political, and economic challenges*, 2nd ed., ed. Philip G. Altbach, Robert O. Berdahl, and Patricia J. Gumport, 393–424. Baltimore: Johns Hopkins University Press.

Hoffer, Thomas B., Bernard L. Dugoni, Allen S. Sanderson, Scott Sederstrom, Rashna Ghadialy, and Peter Roches. 2001. *Doctorate recipients from United States universities: Summary report 2000*. Chicago: National Opinion Research Center.

Hutchings, Patricia, and Lee S. Shulman. 1999. The scholarship of teaching: New elaborations, new developments. *Change* 31 (5): 10–15.

Keller, George. 2001. The new demographics of higher education. *Review of Higher Education* 24 (3): 219–35.

Levine, Arthur. 2000. Higher education at a crossroads. Earl Pullias Lecture in Higher Education. Los Angeles: Center for Higher Education Policy Analysis, Rossier School of Education, University of Southern California.

Lovitts, Barbara E. 2001. *Leaving the ivory tower: The causes and consequences of departure from doctoral study*. Lanham, MD: Rowan & Littlefield.

———. 2004. Research on the structure and process of graduate education: Retaining students. In *Paths to the professoriate: Strategies for enriching the preparation of future faculty*, ed. Donald H. Wulff and Ann E. Austin, 115–36. San Francisco: Jossey-Bass.

Merton, Robert K. 1957. *Social theory and social structure*. Glencoe, IL: Free Press.

Merton, Robert K., George C. Reader, and Patricia L. Kendall. 1957. *The student-physician*. Cambridge, MA: Harvard University Press.

Nerad, Maresi, Rebecca Aanerud, and Joseph Cerny. 2004. "So you want to become a professor!": Lessons from the "PhDs—Ten Years Later Study." In *Paths to the professoriate: Strategies for enriching the preparation of future faculty*, ed. Donald H. Wulff and Ann E. Austin, 137–58. San Francisco: Jossey-Bass.

Nettles, Michael T., and Catherine M. Millett. 2006. *Three magic letters: Getting to Ph.D.* Baltimore: Johns Hopkins University Press.

Newman, Frank, Lara Courturier, and Jamie Scurry. 2004. *The future of higher education: Rhetoric, reality, and the risks of the market*. San Francisco: Jossey-Bass.

Nyquist, Jody D., Laura Manning, Donald H. Wulff, Ann E. Austin, Jo Sprague, Patricia Kenney Fraser, Claire Calcagno, and Bettina Woodford. 1999. On the road to becoming a professor: The graduate student experience. *Change* 31 (3): 18–27.

Pelikan, Jaroslav. 1992. *The idea of the university: A reexamination.* New Haven: Yale University Press.

Pruitt-Logan, Anne S., and Jerry G. Gaff. 2004. Preparing future faculty: Changing the culture of doctoral education. In *Paths to the professoriate: Strategies for enriching the preparation of future faculty,* ed. Donald H. Wulff and Ann E. Austin, 177–93. San Francisco: Jossey-Bass.

Rhoades, Gary. 1998. *Managed professionals: Unionizing faculty and restructuring academic labor.* Albany: State University of New York Press.

Rice, R. Eugene. 1986. The academic profession in transition: Toward a new social fiction. *Teaching Sociology* 14:12–23.

———. 2004. The future of the American faculty. *Change* 36 (2): 26–36.

Rice, R. Eugene, Mary Deane Sorcinelli, and Ann E. Austin. 2000. *Heeding new voices: Academic careers for a new generation.* New Pathways Inquiry No. 7. Washington, DC: American Association for Higher Education.

Schuster, Jack H., and Martin J. Finkelstein. 2006. *The American faculty: The restructuring of academic work and careers.* Baltimore: Johns Hopkins University Press.

Sorcinelli, Mary Deane. 1988. Satisfactions and concerns of new university teachers. *To Improve the Academy* 7:121–33.

Stark, Joan S., Malcolm A. Lowther, and Bonnie M. K. Hagerty. 1986. *Responsive professional education: Balancing outcomes and opportunities.* ASHE-ERIC Higher Education Report No. 3. Washington, DC: Association for the Study of Higher Education.

Taylor, Edward, and James S. Antony. 2001. Stereotype threat reduction and wise schooling: Towards successful socialization of African American doctoral students in education. *Journal of Negro Education* 69 (3): 184–98.

Tierney, William G., and Robert A. Rhoads. 1994. *Enhancing promotion, tenure and beyond: Faculty socialization as a cultural process.* ASHE-ERIC Higher Education Report No. 6. Washington, DC: George Washington University, School of Education and Human Development.

Trower, Cathy. 2005. How do junior faculty feel about your campus as a work place? *Harvard Institutes for Higher Education: Alumni Bulletin.* Cambridge, MA: Harvard University.

U.S. Department of Education, National Center for Education Statistics. 2004. *National study of postsecondary faculty (NSOPF:04).* Washington, DC: Author. http://nces.ed.gov/das.

Walker, George E. 2004. The Carnegie Initiative on the Doctorate: Creating stewards of the discipline. In *Paths to the professoriate: Strategies for enhancing the preparation of future faculty,* ed. Donald H. Wulff and Ann E. Austin, 236–49. San Francisco: Jossey-Bass.

Weidman, John, Darla J. Twale, and Elizabeth L. Stein. 2001. *Socialization of graduate and professional students in higher education—a perilous passage?* ASHE-ERIC Higher Education Report No. 28 (3). Washington, DC: George Washington University, School of Education and Human Development.

Wulff, Donald H., and Ann E. Austin, eds. 2004. *Paths to the professoriate: Strategies for enriching the preparation of future faculty.* San Francisco: Jossey-Bass.

Wulff, Donald H., Ann E. Austin, Jody D. Nyquist, and Jo Sprague. 2004. The development of graduate students as teaching scholars: A four-year longitudinal study. In *Paths to the professoriate: Strategies for enriching the preparation of future faculty*, ed. Donald H. Wulff and Ann E. Austin, 46–73. San Francisco: Jossey-Bass.

CHAPTER SIX

Professionalism in Graduate Teaching and Mentoring

John M. Braxton, Eve Proper, and Alan E. Bayer

G raduate study is a powerful socialization process in the academic profession. Through this socialization process, graduate students acquire the attitudes, values, and disciplinary knowledge and skill required for faculty research and teaching role performance (Austin and Wulff 2004; Merton, Reader, and Kendall 1957). The professional choices and preferences of those faculty members who teach or serve as mentors to graduate students wield considerable influence over important dimensions of this socialization process: course requirements, qualifying examinations, the dissertation, research and teaching assistantships, and both formal and informal faculty-student relationships such as mentoring. Fox (2000) depicts such influences as highly decentralized and privatized. Accordingly, graduate faculty members possess maximum professional autonomy in graduate teaching and mentoring role performance. Because of such autonomy, graduate students may fail to adequately master disciplinary knowledge and skill and to acquire the requisite attitudes and values needed for competent professorial role performance.

Consequently, behavioral norms are needed to assure that graduate faculty members adhere to the ideal of service to graduate students as clients of graduate study. The ideal of service is the responsibility of professionals to base their professional actions on the needs and welfare of their clients (Goode 1969). Norms promote adherence to the ideal of service as they are shared beliefs about expected or prohibited behavior in a given situation that are espoused by a particular social or professional group (Gibbs 1981; Rossi and Berk 1985). Without graduate faculty adherence to the ideal of service to doctoral students as clients, inadequate professional socialization may obtain.

In *Faculty Misconduct in Collegiate Teaching* (1999), Braxton and Bayer describe an empirically derived normative structure for undergraduate college teaching. However, we have little or no empirical studies that describe a normative structure for graduate teaching and mentoring. This chapter strives to address this significant gap by describing an empirically derived structure composed of inviolable normative patterns. Norms differ in the degree of indignation that their violation elicits (Durkheim [1912] 1995). Inviolable norms are those norms that academics view as warranting severe sanctions when violated (Braxton and Bayer 1999).

Knowledge of such a normative structure looms important given recent attention to doctoral education. Such attention focuses on such pertinent issues as viewing the role of doctoral education as preparation for stewardship of the disciplines (Golde 2006). Stewardship entails disciplinary competence in the generation, conservation, and transformation of knowledge and serving as a moral compass for the disciplines by embracing a set of principles of integrity (Golde 2006). As norms function as a moral compass, a normative structure composed of inviolable norms plays an indispensable part in preparing graduate students for their role as stewards of their academic disciplines.

Conceptual Framework

Norms develop from a variety of situations or events that university faculty members experience either directly or indirectly from their day-to-day interactions with the university environment and their professional associations. When people engage in a particular pattern of behavior, typical behavior becomes expected and thus normative (Opp 1982). Norms also emerge from the consequences of the behavior of others (Demsetz 1967). Some behaviors might evoke approval because of benefits derived from the behavior. Other behaviors may result in harm and elicit disapproval (Horne 2001). These two generative conditions apply to circumstances, situations, and events associated with graduate teaching and mentoring. Thus, these formulations indicate that a normative structure for graduate teaching and mentoring exists. Moreover, this conceptual framework gives rise to the following four research questions:

1. *What inviolable patterns of behavior constitute the normative structure of graduate teaching and mentoring?*

2. *Does faculty espousal of the empirically identified inviolable normative patterns vary between faculty holding academic appointments in universities of high and of very high research intensity?* Kenneth Ruscio (1987) asserts that the mission of a college or university greatly influences institutional structures. Institutional structures, in turn, influence faculty work (Blackburn and Lawrence 1995). Accordingly, we might expect that faculty in high and very high research intensity university settings may differ in their espousal of the inviolable norms identified.

3. *Does faculty espousal of the empirically identified inviolable normative patterns vary across different academic disciplines?* From their review of research on disciplinary differences, Braxton and Hargens (1996) concluded that the differences among academic disciplines are "profound and extensive." More specifically, the level of paradigmatic development of an academic discipline affects teaching and research activities. Moreover, Braxton and Bayer (1999) found disciplinary differences on five of the seven inviolable norms of undergraduate college teaching that they empirically identified. Thus, it is possible that faculty espousal of inviolable normative patterns of graduate teaching and mentoring may also vary by their academic discipline.

    This study includes the academic disciplines of biology, chemistry, history, and psychology. Using Biglan's (1973) classification schema, biology and chemistry are high in their level of paradigmatic development, whereas history and psychology are low in theirs. However, as defined by Biglan (1973), all four disciplines are pure in their orientation.

4. *Does faculty espousal of the empirically identified inviolable norms vary by gender and administrative experience?* Women faculty members espouse a greater commitment to teaching than male academics (Bayer and Astin 1975; Finkelstein 1984; Tierney and Rhoads 1993). Moreover, perceptions of the characteristics of good teaching also differ between men and women faculty members (Goodwin and Stevens 1993). To elaborate, women faculty perceive that a concern for student self-esteem constitutes a characteristic of good teaching more than do male academics (Goodwin and Stevens 1993). To further reinforce the need to test for gender differences on faculty espousal of empirically identified inviolable norms, Braxton and Bayer (1999) found that gender exerts some influence on faculty espousal of inviolable norms of undergraduate

college teaching. Thus, gender may also affect faculty level of espousal for inviolable normative patterns of graduate teaching and mentoring.

Administrative experience may also influence the level of faculty norm espousal. Administrative experience includes present and past experience as either a dean or a department chairperson. Since deans and department chairpersons occupy positions within the administrative structure of a university, they hold some degree of formal authority (Leslie 1973; Tucker 1981). Dealing with inadequate performance and unethical behaviors constitute some of the responsibilities of these positions (Tucker 1981). Because of such responsibilities, faculty members with administrative experience are more likely to have observed or received reports of improprieties in graduate teaching and mentoring than faculty without such administrative experience (Braxton and Bayer 1999). Experience with such improprieties may, in turn, lead to the formation of opinions about acceptable decorum as well as the type of actions befitting malfeasances in graduate teaching and mentoring by faculty members with such administrative experience (Braxton and Bayer 1999).

Sampling

The population of inference for this study is full-time, tenured or tenure-track assistant professors, associate professors, and full professors in academic departments offering the PhD in U.S. research universities. A stratified cluster sampling design was used to develop a sample drawn from this population. The sample strata were academic discipline (biology, chemistry, history, and psychology) and the institution's research category of the Carnegie Foundation for the Advancement of Teaching (very high and high). For each discipline and institutional research category, only universities offering the PhD in the four academic disciplines were eligible for random selection. Rather than sampling faculty members within institutions, the entire departmental populations were used. The total sample size was 3,512 faculty members who met our selection criteria and had valid e-mail addresses.

Instrumentation

The Graduate Teaching and Mentoring Behaviors Inventory (GTMBI) was designed by first selecting or adapting proscribed behaviors relevant to graduate education as well as to undergraduate education, as earlier developed for our study of undergraduate teaching norms (Braxton and Bayer 1999). Second, behavioral standards which explicitly address relations between faculty and graduate students were derived from American Association of University Professors (AAUP) documents and professional associations' codes of conduct and adapted for inclusion in the GTMBI. Next, we added behavioral statements regarding graduate education from faculty colleagues at our home institutions and from sixteen other colleagues from other academic institutions who had published articles and books relevant to graduation education, the professoriate, and ethics in academe.

The resulting instrument consists of 124 behaviors that fall into one of the following categories: supervising graduate research assistants, mentoring and advising, planning for a graduate course or seminar, in-class practices and behaviors, class/seminar grading and examination practices, directing the thesis/dissertation, and other behaviors regarding graduate students and the graduate program. The 124 behaviors were negatively worded to follow Durkheim's ([1912] 1995) sociological premise that norms are best recognized when violated. Respondents used a five-point scale (1 = "appropriate behavior, should be encouraged," to 5 = "very inappropriate behavior, requiring formal administrative intervention") to register their perceptions of each behavior. The five-point scale was used to identify those behaviors that meet normative criteria.

The GTMBI was administered in the 2006–7 academic year as a Web-based instrument to the sample of 3,512 faculty members described above. A total of 793 individuals completed the GTMBI. This represents a response rate of 22.6 percent. Comparisons of respondents to the initial and subsequent mailing waves suggest that the obtained sample is representative of the population of inference for four of the five inviolable normative patterns described below. For the norm of *whistle-blowing suppression*, respondents to the initial mailing voice a somewhat greater level of disdain than do respondents to subsequent mailing waves.

In conclusion, to answer the four research questions, we used responses to items on the GTMBI survey. The sample consists of 793 faculty members who are full-time, either tenured or tenure-track, and hold the academic rank of assistant, associate, or full professor.

Statistical Procedures

To address this first research question, means were computed for each of the 124 behaviors of the GTMBI. Following Braxton and Bayer (1999), we used means of 4.00 ("inappropriate behavior, to be handled informally by colleagues or administrators suggesting change or improvement") to 5.00 ("very inappropriate behavior, requiring formal administrative intervention") on the five-point scale to identify those behaviors meeting the criterion for designation as an inviolable norm. Those specific behaviors meeting this criterion were submitted to a principle components factor analysis with varimax rotation to identify inviolable normative orientations.

Research questions 2 and 3 were addressed using 4×2 analyses of variance that were conducted for each of the five inviolable normative patterns. Academic discipline and university research intensity constitute the two factors of these analyses of variance. The four categories of academic discipline include biology, chemistry, history, and psychology, whereas the two levels of university research intensity consist of high and very high intensity. Following statistically significant main effects, the Scheffe method of post hoc mean comparisons was used. Independent *t*-tests were used to address research question 4. Separate *t*-tests were executed for gender (male, female) and administrative experiences (yes, am or have been a dean or a department chair vs. no such experience).

The .025 level of statistical significance was used to identify statistically reliable differences. This level of statistical significance was applied because cluster sampling increases the probability of committing Type I errors. This increased probability of committing Type I errors occurs because variances of variables of interest in the population may be underestimated as a result of the homogeneity of the elements of the clusters sampled (Kish 1957). Thus, a more conservative level of statistical significance was used rather than the customary .05 level.

Findings

Research Question 1: What inviolable patterns of behavior constitute the normative structure of graduate teaching and mentoring?

GMTBI items with means of 4.00 ("inappropriate behavior, to be handled informally by colleagues or administrators suggesting change or improvement") to 5.00 ("very inappropriate behavior, requiring formal administrative intervention") were labeled inviolable. The application of this criterion resulted in the identification of forty specific behaviors of the GTMBI that meet normative criteria. These forty behaviors were submitted to a principle components factor analysis with varimax rotation to identify inviolable normative orientations.

Using a screen plot, we choose a five-factor solution. Although submitted to the factor analysis with a five-factor solution, four of the forty GTMBI behaviors scoring above 4.00 failed to load on any of the five factors. The five resulting inviolable normative patterns of graduate teaching and mentoring are as follows: *disrespect toward student efforts, misappropriation of student work, harassment of students, whistle-blowing suppression,* and *directed research malfeasance.* Table 6.1 displays the specific GTMBI items that constitute each of these five normative orientations.

Disrespect toward student efforts. This normative pattern proscribes disrespecting the efforts students make in various aspects of their graduate studies. The fourteen specific proscribed behaviors that make up this normative pattern, which are displayed in table 6.1, disrespect the efforts of students in the classroom, graded assignments, thesis/dissertation work, and the research apprenticeship.

Misappropriation of student work. The failure to give graduate students the credit they deserve for their scholarly efforts typifies this inviolable normative configuration. This particular proscriptive norm demarcates inappropriate behavior of graduate faculty members in their role as "master" in the research apprenticeship for doctoral students. Table 6.1 presents the eleven specific censured behaviors that make up this normative orientation.

Harassment of students. This normative pattern pertains to graduate faculty behaviors that constitute the harassment of students. These proscribed behaviors occur within and outside of the classroom. This norm consists of six specific censured behaviors, displayed in table 6.1.

Whistle-blowing suppression. Whistle-blowing involves the reporting of suspected misconduct by the employer or one of its employees. The inviolable norm of whistle-blowing suppression applies to personally known incidents of scientific misconduct. Table 6.1 exhibits the three reproached behaviors that delineate this particular inviolable norm.

Directed research malfeasance. This inviolable norm also pertains to incidents of research wrongdoing. In this case, a graduate professor instructs his/

Specific behavior	Factor loading
Disrespect toward student efforts	
Students are not permitted to express viewpoints different from those of the professor.	.649
A student consistently cannot get an appointment with the thesis/ dissertation advisor within three or four weeks to discuss issues concerning the thesis/dissertation.	.649
A professor routinely awards A's to all graduate students enrolled in his/her seminar regardless of whether the students do any assignments or attend class.	.646
The professor routinely ignores comments or questions from international graduate students.	.643
The student's advisor often misses deadlines that affect the student's work or career.	.622
Individual student course evaluations, where students can be identified, are read prior to the determination of final seminar grades.	.603
The professor allows personal friendships with a graduate student to intrude on the objective grading of their work.	.597
A faculty member intentionally misrepresents graduate program requirements in order to recruit a graduate student.	.574
A professor makes condescending remarks to a student in class.	.562
No term papers, tests, lab reports, or other criteria are used by the professor for assigning final grades.	.561
Social, personal, or other nonacademic characteristics of graduate students are taken into account in the assigning of grades.	.504
The professor frequently makes negative comments in class about a student's dress, speech, or manner.	.486
Individual graduate students are offered extra-credit work in order to improve their final course grade after the term is completed.	.483
The professor delays the graduation of his/her best graduate students, in order to keep them around longer.	.475

Percent of variance explained = 29.83%
Cronbach alpha = 0.91

(continued)

Specific behavior	Factor loading
Misappropriation of student work	
A professor asks a graduate student to prepare a review of a manuscript or grant proposal that the professor then represents as his/her own review.	.638
A professor routinely removes graduate students from research projects when they begin to show innovative results.	.627
A faculty member publishes an article without offering coauthorship to a graduate assistant who has made a substantial conceptual or methodological contribution to the article.	.540
A professor routinely blames their graduate students when his/her own research work is called into question.	.530
A professor routinely borrows money from advisees.	.528
The mentor fails to write a letter of recommendation that he/she had agreed to send for a graduate student.	.524
A professor fails to provide or ensure safe research conditions or safe laboratory environments for their graduate assistants.	.490
A faculty member publishes an article using innovative ideas derived from a graduate student's term paper without acknowledging the student's contribution.	.472
A faculty member sometimes asks their graduate research assistant to perform personal chores such as babysitting or running household errands as a part of their assistantship duties.	.467
A professor accepts costly gifts from graduate students.	.432
A graduate student's mentor puts the student's name as coauthor of a publication even though the student made no contribution to the work.	.413

Percent of variance explained = 5.24%
Cronbach alpha = 0.83

Table 6.1 Factor loading of specific behaviors of the five inviolable norms
(continued)

Specific behavior	Factor loading
Harassment of students	
The professor makes suggestive sexual comments to a graduate student enrolled in their seminar.	.739
The professor sometimes makes racist or sexist remarks in class.	.625
While able to conduct the graduate class, the faculty member attends class while obviously intoxicated.	.623
A professor has a sexual relationship with a graduate student in their program.	.526
A male professor tells a female graduate student to avoid his specialty because only men can excel in it.	.474
A faculty member criticizes the academic performance of a graduate student in front of other graduate students.	.465
Percent of variance explained = 4.38% Cronbach alpha = 0.70	
Whistle-blowing suppression	
A professor advises his/her graduate research assistant who has personally witnessed an incident of research misconduct by another graduate assistant to ignore the incident.	.846
A professor advises his/her graduate assistant who has personally witnessed an incident of research misconduct by a faculty member to ignore the incident.	.792
A faculty member fails to report a graduate research assistant who has engaged in an act of research or scholarly misconduct.	.695
Percent of variance explained = 3.98% Cronbach alpha = 0.83	

(continued)

Table 6.1   Factor loading of specific behaviors of the five inviolable norms
(*continued*)

Specific behavior	Factor loading
Directed research malfeasance	
A professor instructs his/her graduate research assistant to alter data books or lab notes to support a study's hypotheses.	.735
The professor instructs the research assistant to fabricate citations for a publication.	.708
Percent of variance explained = 3.32% Cronbach alpha = 0.37	

her graduate research assistant to engage in wrongdoing. Table 6.1 displays the two specific rebuked behaviors that constitute this normative pattern.

Composite scales for the five normative patterns were developed to address the remaining three research questions. These five composite scales were calculated as the average of the specific behaviors composing each normative orientation.

Research Question 2: Does faculty espousal of the empirically identified inviolable normative patterns vary between faculty holding academic appointments in universities of high and of very high research intensity?

Invariant best characterizes the espousal of the five inviolable normative orientations between individual faculty members holding academic appointments in universities of high and very high research intensity. Thus, the normative patterns of *disrespect toward student efforts, misappropriation of student work, harassment of students, whistle-blowing suppression,* and *directed research malfeasance* function as core norms for these types of research universities. The findings of the analyses of variance exhibited in table 6.2 support these assertions.

Research Question 3: Does faculty espousal of the empirically identified inviolable normative patterns vary across different academic disciplines?

For the normative patterns of *disrespect toward student efforts, harassment of students, whistle-blowing suppression,* and *directed research malfeasance,* faculty members in each of the four disciplines represented in this study espouse similar levels of disdain. However, academic historians (mean = 4.65) tend to espouse a higher level of disdain for behaviors associated with the norm of

Table 6.2   Analysis of variance of the five inviolable norms by institutional type—universities of high and very high levels of research activity

Norm	F-ratio	Mean high RU	Mean very high RU
Disrespect toward student efforts	4.12	4.29	4.22
Misappropriation of student work	0.68	4.46	4.44
Harassment of students	0.15	4.56	4.52
Whistle-blowing suppression	0.03	4.46	4.45
Directed research malfeasance	0.03	4.98	4.98

Note: F-ratio for institutional type is independent of F-ratio for academic discipline.

misappropriation of student work than do academic chemists (mean = 4.34), biologists (mean = 4.39), and psychologists (mean = 4.42). The results of the analyses of variance conducted and displayed in table 6.3 provide empirical backing for these observations.

Research Question 4: Does faculty espousal of the empirically identified inviolable norms vary by gender and administrative experience?

As stated above, independent sample *t*-tests were conducted to address this research question. Table 6.4 exhibits the results of the *t*-tests conducted by gender, whereas table 6.5 displays the results of the *t*-tests conducted by administrative experience.

Female and male faculty members differ little in their level of contempt for behaviors indicative of the normative orientations of *disrespect toward student efforts, whistle-blowing suppression,* and *directed research malfeasance.* However, women academics (mean = 4.62) tend to express a higher degree of scorn for behaviors reflective of the norms of *harassment of students* than their male counterparts (mean = 4.49). Female faculty members (mean = 4.52) also tend to disparage behaviors subsumed under the inviolable norm of *misappropriation of student work* to a greater extent than male academics (mean = 4.43). The findings reported in table 6.4 support these observations.

Moreover, faculty members with administrative experience (mean = 4.36) voice a higher level of disdain for behaviors that manifest the norm of *disrespect toward student efforts* than their academic counterparts without administrative experience in the form of a deanship or department chairpersonship (mean = 4.23). Likewise, academics with administrative experience (mean = 4.57) disparage to a greater degree those behaviors reflective of the

Table 6.3 Analysis of variance of the five inviolable norms by academic discipline

Norm	F-ratio	Mean biology	Mean chemistry	Mean history	Mean psychology
Disrespect toward student efforts	3.67*	4.22	4.22	4.36	4.23
Misappropriation of student work	25.42**	4.39	4.34	4.65[†]	4.42
Harassment of students	0.70	4.53	4.52	4.56	4.55
Whistle-blowing suppression	1.72	4.49	4.43	4.51	4.39
Directed research malfeasance	1.17	4.99	4.97	4.98	4.99

Note: F-ratio for academic discipline is independent of the F-ratio for institutional type.

* p < .025
** p < .01
[†] Mean for history is greater than biology, chemistry, and psychology at the .025 level of statistical significance.

Table 6.4 Results of *t*-tests of mean differences by gender for the five inviolable norms

Norm	Mean female	Mean male	t-value
Disrespect toward student efforts	4.31	4.24	2.05
Misappropriation of student work	4.52	4.43	2.72**
Harassment of students	4.62	4.49	4.17**
Whistle-blowing suppression	4.48	4.44	0.75
Directed research malfeasance	4.98	4.98	0.23

** p < .01

norm of *misappropriation of student work* than academics without administrative experience (mean = 4.42). These observations find empirical support in the results exhibited in table 6.5.

Limitations

A set of four principal limitations temper the conclusions and recommendations derived from the patterns of findings from this research. The first limitation recognizes that the 124 behaviors included in GTMBI are not exhaustive of possible behaviors that might meet normative criteria. For example, those

Table 6.5   Results of *t*-tests of mean differences by administrative
experience for the five inviolable norms

Norm	Mean admin. exp.	Mean no admin. exp.	*t*-value
Disrespect toward student efforts	4.36	4.23	2.78*
Misappropriation of student work	4.57	4.42	4.46**
Harassment of students	4.57	4.53	1.06
Whistle-blowing suppression	4.52	4.44	1.56
Directed research malfeasance	4.99	4.98	2.22

* p < .05
** p < .01

aspects of graduate training and mentoring that center on preparation for college teaching are not reflected in the GTMBI.

The second limitation concerns our relatively low response rate of 22.6 percent. This limitation is blunted to some extent given that comparisons on gender, administrative experience, institutional type, and academic discipline of the respondents to the initial and to the subsequent mailing waves suggest that the obtained sample is representative of the population of inference on four of the five inviolable normative patterns. Nevertheless, respondents to the initial mailing tend to voice a somewhat greater level of disdain for the normative pattern of *whistle-blowing suppression* than do later respondents.

The third limitation acknowledges that this research is confined to those disciplines classified by Biglan as pure life and pure nonlife that are of high and low paradigmatic development. Hence, the normative preferences of faculty members in applied academic disciplines are not included.

Finally, this research included two of the three levels of the Doctorate-granting Universities category of the 2006 Carnegie Classification of Institutions: Research Universities–Very High and Research Universities–High. Thus, the normative preferences of faculty members in the Research/Doctoral university level are not included. This level is the lowest level on measures of university research activity.

Conclusion

We offer two conclusions that emanate from the pattern of findings of this study. First, the five empirically derived inviolable norms provide moral boundaries for graduate teaching and mentoring. The importance of such boundaries stems from the highly decentralized and privatized nature of graduate teaching and mentoring (Fox 2000). Such moral boundaries provide guides to faculty role performance that assure adherence to the ideal of service to graduate students as clients.

Second, institutional type and academic discipline constitute two structural dimensions of the academic profession. These two structural dimensions function to differentiate and fragment the academic profession (Ruscio 1987). However, the norms of *student harassment, whistle-blowing suppression,* and *directed research malfeasance* constitute core norms as the level of faculty espousal of these norms is invariant across institutional type and academic discipline. As a consequence, these three normative orientations function as compensatory integrating mechanisms for fragmentation in the structure of the academic profession.

Faculty malfeasance in graduate teaching and mentoring occurs when a graduate faculty member violates one or more of the five proscriptive normative patterns empirically identified in our research. In contrast to faculty misconduct in undergraduate college teaching, the stakes are substantially higher for graduate teaching and mentoring.

Faculty misconduct in undergraduate education generally has only transient negative effects on students. Because most graduate students will enter teaching, research, and collaborative endeavors similar to their graduate teachers and mentors, such mentors and teachers provide models for the professorial role that may be integrated in the professional careers of the next generation of the professoriate.

Moreover, Golde (2006) views doctoral education as preparation for stewardship of the academic disciplines. As previously stated, one aspect of stewardship involves service as a moral compass for the academic disciplines. As stated in our first conclusion, the five empirically identified inviolable norms provide moral boundaries for faculty engaged in graduate teaching and mentoring. As such, norms also function as a moral compass for graduate teaching and mentoring in the academic disciplines.

However, an imperfect correlation exists between norms and behavior (Merton 1976; Zuckerman 1988). Merton terms this disjuncture "a painful contrast between normative expectations and actual behavior" (1976, 40). As a consequence, faculty violations of these five inviolable norms do occur. Although the rate of these forms of faculty transgressions in graduate teaching and mentoring is unknown, imperfect graduate school socialization to the role of steward of an academic discipline results from such incidents of wrongdoing. Graduate students who personally observe or learn of incidents of norm violations may fail to internalize the moral compass needed for stewardship for one's academic discipline.

It seems obvious that violation of these norms will have direct impacts on the students involved, perhaps delaying, or even preventing, the completion of their graduate degrees. Students themselves desire mentors that respect the norms described here (Bell-Ellison and Dedrick 2008). But they are also likely to affect students' understanding of those norms, whether they are a victim of or witness to such behavior. Depending on the consequences of violating these norms, students may come to believe that a behavior is condoned or at least carries no repercussions.

Moreover, since norms are properties of a group, we need to consider the behavior of all faculty the student is exposed to, not simply that of the mentor or advisor. Most relevant research focuses on the mentor-mentee relationship. Less work has been done on the relationship a student has with all of his or her faculty. Graduate students not only take courses with other faculty members, but they may have them on thesis committees, work for them in laboratory rotations or during the summer, or seek them out for particular types of advice and mentoring. In their study of graduate and professional students, Bucher and Stelling found that students tend not to see themselves as having a single role model: "We were bent on pinning them down to one or two people who were role models, but they resisted our efforts" (1977, 149). Most role models were "partial" models—students wished to emulate some traits exhibited but not all. The authors also found that students used faculty as "negative" models (ibid.). That is, students described behaviors of specific faculty members as things they wished to avoid doing themselves.

The presence of negative modeling provides hope that norm violations may not unilaterally weaken students' internalization of professional norms. If norm violations receive sanctions, student respect for these norms may actually increase. In other cases, a lack of negative sanctions may make a student cynical about the profession while failing to change an underlying belief that the behavior is wrong. Sexual harassment, for example, is widely considered inappropriate in any workplace, and a graduate student who experiences it is likely to continue to believe it is inappropriate. Nevertheless, norm violations may inadvertently teach students that proscribed behavior is in fact acceptable, leading eventually to a breakdown of those norms. Conversely, a lack of norm violations may fail to register with graduate students. Unless appropriate professional values are discussed, students may not realize the strength of those norms and fail to follow them in their later careers. In other words, there is a value to discussion of norms and professional ethics; modeling them may be insufficient.

Without further research, anticipating the role faculty norm violations play in the graduate student socialization process is speculative. However, learning the appropriate norms in graduate school is preferable to learning about them as faculty members; the stakes are much lower. If current norms are not transmitted to the next generation of scholars, they are unlikely to model them.

Recommendations for Research and Practice

In addition to extending this research to applied academic disciplines and to research or doctoral-granting universities categorized as having the lowest level of research activity, the most important recommendation for research pertains to the measurement of the extent to which graduate faculty members violate the proscriptions of the five inviolable normative patterns empirically identified in this chapter. Given Merton's (1976) and Zuckerman's (1988) supposition that norms and behaviors are never perfectly correlated, we might expect some norm violations. However, the rate of such violations remains unknown. Graduate students should serve as the subjects for such research because they are the most likely observers of such incidents of wrongdoing. If they do not have direct personal knowledge, they may have heard of such occurrences from other graduate students. These estimates of wrongdoing in graduate teaching and mentoring would indicate the prevalence of faulty socialization of graduate students.

The extension of this research to graduate student populations provides another approach to gauging whether problematic socialization of graduate students transpires. Such research should ask the question, do graduate students and faculty members espouse similar levels of disdain for those behaviors reflective of the five inviolable normative patterns empirically delineated in this study?

Recommendations for practice also spring forth from the pattern of findings of this study. These recommendations are as follows:

1. Graduate-degree-granting departments and programs should develop codes of conduct for graduate teaching and mentoring. The five empirically derived proscribed normative patterns of *disrespect toward student efforts, misappropriation of student work, harassment of students, whistle-blowing suppression,* and *directed research malfeasance* could provide the basis for formation of the tenets of such a code of conduct.

2. Universities should create academic integrity committees, if they do not already exist. These committees might more explicitly be charged with considering reported incidents of faculty misconduct in graduate teaching and mentoring. Such committees loom important because of the reluctance of graduate students who observe such incidents of wrongdoing to bring such matters to the attention of department chairpersons and other individual faculty members. The deliberations of such committees should follow the procedures used by research integrity committees that already exist in many research-oriented universities. In particular, the committee must protect the accusing individual, especially graduate students, from retaliation that might damage their career prospects.

3. Sanctions for faculty graduate teaching and mentoring malfeasance should be formulated. The development of a range of sanctions for norm violations contributes to the effectiveness of graduate teaching and mentoring integrity committees. Sanctions serve as deterrents to graduate teaching and mentoring misconduct if known and well communicated (Ben-Yehuda 1985; Tittle 1980).

As concluded above, the five empirically derived inviolable norms provide moral boundaries for graduate teaching and mentoring. Thus, these norms provide guides to the professional choices graduate faculty make in teaching and mentoring graduate students. Put differently, this proscriptive normative structure promotes adherence to the ideal of service to graduate students as clients. Accordingly, the five inviolable norms function as a moral compass for stewardship of the academic disciplines.

The delineation of a normative structure constitutes an essential condition for the moral compass aspect of stewardship. However, such stewardship remains incomplete without a system of social control. Faculty violations of the five normative patterns of graduate teaching and mentoring constitute misconduct. Such deviance requires mechanisms of social control that deter, detect, and sanction wrongdoing (Zuckerman 1988). Taken together, the recommendations for research and practice delineated above provide a foundation for social control.

REFERENCES

Austin, Ann E., and Donald H. Wulff. 2004. The challenges to prepare the next generation of faculty. In *Paths to the professoriate: Strategies for enriching the preparation of future faculty*, ed. Donald H. Wulff and Ann E. Austin, 3–16. San Francisco, CA: Jossey-Bass.

Bayer, Alan E., and Helen S. Astin. 1975. Sex differentials in the academic reward system. *Science* 188 (May 23): 796–802.

Bell-Ellison, Bethany A., and Robert F. Dedrick. 2008. What do doctoral students value in their ideal mentor? *Research in Higher Education* 49:555–67.

Ben-Yehuda, Nachman. 1985. *Deviance and moral boundaries: Witchcraft, the occult, science fiction, deviant sciences and scientists*. Chicago: University of Chicago Press.

Biglan, Anthony. 1973. The characteristics of subject matter in different academic areas. *Journal of Applied Psychology* 57:195–203.

Blackburn, Robert T., and Janet H. Lawrence. 1995. *Faculty at work: Motivation, expectation, satisfaction*. Baltimore: Johns Hopkins University Press.

Braxton, John M., and Alan E. Bayer. 1999. *Faculty misconduct in collegiate teaching*. Baltimore: Johns Hopkins University Press.

Braxton, John M., and Lowell L. Hargens. 1996. Variations among academic disciplines: Analytical frameworks and research. In *Higher education: Handbook of theory and research*, vol. 11, ed. J. C. Smart, 1–46. New York: Agathon Press.

Bucher, Rue, and Joan G. Stelling. 1977. *Becoming professional*. Beverly Hills: Sage Publications.

Demsetz, Harold. 1967. Toward a theory of property rights. *American Economic Review* 57:347–59.

Durkheim, Emile. [1912] 1995. *The elementary forms of religious life*. Trans. K. E. Fields. New York: Free Press.

Finkelstein, Martin J. 1984. *The American academic profession*. Columbus: Ohio State University Press.

Fox, Mary F. 2000. Organizational environments and doctoral degrees awarded to women in science and engineering departments. *Womens Studies Quarterly* 28:47–61.

Gibbs, Jack P. 1981. *Norms, deviance and social control: Conceptual matters.* New York: Elsevier.

Golde, Chris M. 2006. Preparing stewards of the discipline. In *Envisioning the future of the doctoral education: Preparing stewards of the discipline, Carnegie essays on the doctorate,* ed. Chris M. Golde, George E. Walker, and Associates. San Francisco: Jossey-Bass.

Goode, William J. 1969. The theoretical limits of professionalization. In *The semi-professions and their organization,* ed. Amitai Etzioni, 266–313. New York: Free Press.

Goodwin, Laura D., and Ellen A. Stevens. 1993. The influence of gender on university faculty members' perceptions of "good teaching." *Journal of Higher Education* 64:166–85.

Horne, Christine. 2001. Sociological perspectives on the emergence of social norms. In *Social norms,* ed. Michael Hechter and Karl-Dieter Opp, 3–34. New York: Russell Sage.

Kish, Leslie. 1957. Confidence intervals for clustered samples. *American Sociological Review* 22:154–65.

Leslie, David W. 1973. The status of the department chairpersonship in university organization. *AAUP Bulletin* 59:419–26.

Merton, Robert K. 1976. The sociology of social problems. In *Contemporary social problems,* ed. Robert K. Merton and Robert Nisbet, 3–43. New York: Harcourt Brace Jovanovich.

Merton, Robert K., George C. Reader, and Patricia L. Kendall. 1957. *The student-physician.* 2nd ed. Washington, DC: National Academy Press.

Opp, Karl-Dieter. 1982. The evolutionary emergence of norms. *British Journal of Social Psychology* 21:139–49.

Rossi, Peter H., and Richard A. Berk. 1985. Varieties of normative consensus. *American Sociological Review* 50:333–47.

Ruscio, Kenneth P. 1987. Many sectors, many professions. In *The academic profession,* ed. Burton R. Clark, 331–68. Los Angeles: University of California Press.

Tierney, William G., and Robert A. Rhoads. 1993. *Enhancing promotion, tenure and beyond: Faculty socialization as a cultural process.* ASHE-ERIC Report, no. 6. Washington, DC: George Washington University.

Tittle, Charles R. 1980. *Sanctions and social deviance: The question of deterrence.* New York: Praeger.

Tucker, Allan. 1981. *Chairing the academic department.* Washington, DC: American Council on Education.

Zuckerman, Harriet E. 1988. The sociology of science. In *Handbook of sociology,* ed. Neil J. Smelser, 511–74. Newbury Park, CA: Sage.

PART III

Experience of the Academic Career

CHAPTER SEVEN

Scholarly Learning and the Academic Profession in a Time of Change

Anna Neumann

I n order to consider the condition and future of the academic profession, we must understand how professors' scholarly learning changes as their work and their "work worlds" (their campuses, fields of study, the academic profession) change, and as they too change as a consequence of their learning. In this chapter I argue that extant conceptions of the *academic profession* are incomplete because they give inadequate attention to individual professors' scholarly learning, as well as scholars' personal motivations to enact such learning. For the academic profession to survive and thrive, we must do more than ask, What keeps these collectivities alive? We also must ask, What keeps the people who are core to the work of these collectivities intellectually alive—vital in their thinking and learning? For higher education, those people are the faculty that carry out the central work of the academic profession: their work is to think and learn about subjects they have come to know deeply while also bringing their students and colleagues to deepened understanding of those subjects. I suggest that the future of the professoriate, including the future of what it means to be a professor, is tied to professors' scholarly learning in a world that is rapidly transforming what and how they learn.

Why scholarly learning? It may be said that just as our "mental faculties" define who we are as individuals and what we do in the world, so do faculty members define the university and its actions in society, its contributions to the life of our times. The faculty are at the core of colleges' and universities' reasons for being, their existence as social organizations that the public looks to for new and credible knowledge (see Schuster and Finkelstein 2006). This may be especially true for the major research university given its knowledge production (and relatedly, knowledge dissemination and application) mission in society and its broader aspirations to advance the "higher learning" of humanity. I define scholarly learning, in part, as individual professors' *substantive* (subject matter based) contributions to the knowledge production, dissemination, and application missions of the university, their fields, and academe broadly. To contribute in this way is to activate expertise, intellectual commitment, and motivation to learn. I have stated elsewhere that

> because universities strive to lead scholarly endeavor in society and because
> tenured faculty are those universities' scholarly leaders, these individuals'
> career-long learning must be viewed as a prized resource. Increasing demands
> for scientific knowledge, for policies and practices that advance the social and
> political-economic good, and for understandings that contribute to the flour-
> ishing of humanity all hinge on the learning that thoughtful learners can help
> to advance . . . scholarly learning is a concern for *all* faculty regardless of ap-
> pointment status and institutional type. (Neumann 2009, 8)

In this view, professors' scholarly learning occurs through individual professors' enactments of higher education's larger mission to produce, disseminate, and apply knowledge. If this mission constitutes the macro vision of higher education in society, then scholarly learning is that mission's person-level operationalization. A person committed to scholarly learning engages that learning within the professorial role, for example, as she carries out the role activities of teaching, research, and service.

I suggest that the professorial role within which a scholar enacts her or his expert learning is now threatened as a result of how deeply social changes have penetrated the "academic core" of the college and university organization in recent years. Among such changes I count pressing demands for substantive accountability, heightened attention to "transition to work" programs for students, and calls for educational productivity and efficiency. While we have felt the press for such change before, colleges in the past often responded to it in large-scale programmatic terms (for example, by creating new offices or public functions that shielded the faculty having to respond; Birnbaum 1988). Today colleges respond differently, often channeling change directly toward the faculty role. Change has come to the "academic core" of higher education organization (see Altbach 1999; Spillane and Burch 2006). Change at this primary level of the academic organization comes as close as anything structural can to touching the human beings who enact higher education's knowledge production, dissemination, and application mission.

The movement from a permanent tenured faculty to a contingent academic workforce—especially the disassembling of the full-time professorial role into its component role parts (teaching research, and service) that are then enacted by persons in much reduced roles (short-term, part-time)—changes altogether what it means to be a faculty member, especially with regard to scholarly learning. Faculty in contingent roles are subject, typically, to others' job expectations, and those may not coincide with their own interests and ideas. Typically contingent faculty are less able than their full-time tenure-track colleagues to form their work around their own sense of "what matters" and "what's interesting" intellectually. Peer review of some faculty work may be replaced by administrative oversight. Under such circumstances professional autonomy shrinks, as does academic freedom. Contingent faculty may feel bound increasingly to an organizational agenda for certain kinds of professional work including particular forms of organizationally directed learning, as opposed to following personal preferences that may be hard to justify under an organizational logic that values market demands and efficiencies of production. In the new culture that arises, an ethos of equity—of equal access to opportunities to learn about subjects of personal meaning—also may be questioned as faculties "split" between those on tenure lines, who may have more options to follow their interests, and those "on contract," whose learning may be far more regulated. In this view, the devolution of the American faculty into a contingent workforce is an example of broad social change getting as close as it can to the person in the faculty role, in fact, by taking apart that very role. In doing so, it threatens to extinguish also the more independent scholarly learning that professors' "lives in the role" have allowed.

It is challenging to consider the implications of change such as this for professors' scholarly learning without first articulating what that learning is—and thus, what we stand to lose in the face of changes like those I refer to above and that others in this volume take up in detail. But articulating the meaning of scholarly learning is not so straightforward since a language to "speak it" publicly is fairly nonexistent. Thus, scholarly learning is more private than public; it is altogether absent from public policy discourses. Its absence from policy makers' and leaders' open talk and thought puts it at risk. Why stand up for something that isn't clearly known to exist, much less matter?

My aim in this chapter is to provide a frame to facilitate talk about professors' scholarly learning. To pursue this aim, I describe the findings of my recently completed study of professors' scholarly learning and development in the early post-tenure career. Through this study professors spoke directly from their experiences of their own firsthand engagement in scholarly learning—what it is, what it feels like, and what they derive from it toward work that we all value. Although viewing scholarly learning as an issue for the full length of the professorial career, I studied it only in the context of newly tenured professors' remembered experiences of it. Assuming that newly tenured professors feel freer to pursue their scholarly passions than they have felt at any other time in their professional lives and that advanced-career professors may take on extensive organizational duties, I felt that the early post-tenure career would let me see and hear about professors' scholarly learning more clearly than I would at any other career stage.

Defining Scholarly Learning

To define scholarly learning, I restate selected findings of the *Four Universities Project*, a study of university professors' experiences of work and learning in the early post-tenure career. Starting in the late 1990s and through the early 2000s, I followed the development of forty professors' engagements with their subjects of study—in teaching, research, service, and outreach—over three years, interviewing these faculty members annually and analyzing their tenure narratives, curriculum vitae, publications, syllabi, and related materials. The professors participating in this study were tenured within three years of the year 1 interview and by study year 3 were three to five years post-tenure. The forty included between nine and eleven professors in each of the following disciplinary sectors: the arts and humanities, social sciences, sciences, and applied and professional domains. The forty professors worked at one of four major American research universities. Spread across three states, these institutions included two public and two private campuses, two small and two large, two urban and two suburban. At each site, I recruited between nine and eleven newly tenured professors, interviewing the full sample of forty in study year 1 and thirty-nine in study year 3 (for full discussion of study design and method, see Neumann 2006, 2009).

The phrase *scholarly learning* must be viewed initially through the idea at its center: learning. Although commonly referred to—in academe, other work settings, and personal and community life—learning is a complex but not well-defined endeavor. Its core assumptions are easily overlooked: that a learner and object of learning exist. Specifying the kinds of learners at issue and the kinds of knowledge being learned lends necessary precision to *learning* as a concept that is variable in meaning with regard to both its "subject" and "object."

Thus, as I use it, *to learn* is to create or assemble meaning (successfully or not, knowingly or not, intentionally or not) about *something (or some set of things) in particular* (the object of learning). That "something" assumes the existence of a structure of knowledge unique to the field or other category of knowledge of which it is a part. Learning in this view also assumes the existence of at least one *learner* (someone who learns). These assumptions matter for the meaning of learning because diverse learners (the people who learn) and the diverse objects of their learning (the different things they learn) presume distinctive ways of entering into the learning at issue. For example, as I (a certain learner, with particular proclivities and interests differing from those of others) enter into in-depth study of creative literature, I engage with a structure of knowledge that varies from the knowledge structure I would encounter were I studying history: the ideas that anchor my explorations and analyses in one field of study (e.g., in literature, attention to symbolism constructed by the author) are likely to differ from those that anchor explorations and analyses in others (e.g., in history, attention to continuity and discontinuity of a theme or idea over time, including their interplay). Such diversity in knowledge, knowing, and knowers can yield varied images of what goes on when learning happens. A deep understanding of learning requires appreciation of such "syntactical" differences in knowledge and thus in knowing and learning (Schwab 1978; Shulman 1987, 2004).

Further, learning, as I use it, should not be viewed as absolute and complete at any point in time. Rather, to learn is to glimpse, realize, or otherwise come to know something new or different in one's experience; to strive to expand one's partial knowledge about something; to question or doubt with reason something that one has known and believed for some time; or to revise, or work at revising, something that one knows or how one knows it. To learn does not necessarily assume that the learner has come to know something definitively. Rather, it means that the learner has expended some effort to know that thing, or that her experience of it has been altered, slightly or dramatically. As indicated already, this view requires that there be *something* to be learned, something with a knowledge structure to be entered. It assumes a learner's mental engagement with that *something*, be it the politics of an academic department or the content of a book that a particular professor is teaching in an introductory freshman English class (Shulman 2004). Learning may occur in the moments of an event, in action, or on reflection (Schon 1983, 1987). The following five propositions, derived from research on human cognition and development, summarize the perspective on learning that both framed and evolved through my study:

1. *Professors' learning as part of professors' work:* Professors' work requires that they learn.

2. *Learning as someone learning something:* To say that someone learns implies that some*one* (a learner) is learning some*thing* (the object of knowledge that the learner strives to discern or understand). Thus, to understand a professor's learning requires knowing *who* the professor-as-learner is and *what* that individual learns, given the knowledge that constitutes that "what."

3. *Professors' scholarly learning:* To understand a professor's scholarly learning is to understand how that individual learns *what* that individual professes through the practices of research, teaching, and/or service—subject matter knowledge and ways of knowing unique to it.

4. *Professors' scholarly learning as personal and emotional experience:* For many professors, scholarly learning holds personal meaning. It may be intensely emotional.

5. *Contexts as, in part, the contents of learning:* Professors' learning happens in contexts that shape *what* they learn (content). However, professors can also learn new ways to think about and act on those contexts, thereby influencing what they learn in them.

To recap, when a professor learns, that individual learns *something (or some things) in particular* (Shulman 2004). Learning assumes that a learner (in this case, a professor) strives to know something different or something new to her or him (Bransford, Brown, and Cocking 1999). That sense of something new or different to be learned often derives from "context," be that a relationship, family system, community, culture, or other social or historical milieu presenting shifting resources for or constraints on thought (Greeno, Collins, and Resnick 1996). When a professor focuses her learning on the subject matters that she teaches, pursues through research, or shares with others through service, and when those subjects hold great personal meaning for the person in that professorial role (Hansen 2001), that person engages in what I call *scholarly learning*. Further, when that professor pursues such subjects in purposeful and strategic ways, striving to revise the contexts of her work so as to permit a focus on personally meaningful substance, she acts as an agent of her learning (see Clausen 1991; Lerner and Busch-Rossnagel 1981; Marshall 2000; Pallas 2007).

As proposition 4 above indicates, scholarly learning refers to a learner's engagement with a certain kind of subject matter: it refers to the learning of subjects that hold personal meaning for the particular learner at issue. Those meanings may reflect emotional content; often they are tinged with desire for more of the same experience. They appear to be created within experiences that are felt inasmuch as they are carefully thought through. They emerge then as acts of cognition and of aesthetic response, often rooted in personal memory. To amplify this point, I turn to the words of a newly tenured professor of astronomy, David Mora (pseudonym), who, at the time of my study, worked at Libra State University (pseudonym), a leading and internationally renowned public research university in the United States. Although Mora and I never used the phrase *scholarly learning* in interviews, how he described being in this kind of learning reflects the meaning of the term as I heard it in the voices of thirty-seven other newly tenured professors participating in my study:

AN: What is it about your work that you love?

DM: I like to observe. I love to observe.

AN: You love to observe?

DM: Yes.

AN: Can you say more about that?

DM: Well, okay . . . on a ground-based observatory [as opposed to satellite based] . . . you . . . have to do a lot of planning . . . you go there, and [in contrast to satellite-based observation,] you actually carry it out. . . . [In] ground-based observing on a typical night . . . you'll have a problem with the clouds. You'll have a problem with the winds and you'll have a problem with the humidity. The telescope will break, the detector won't know how to operate correctly. I kind of like that. This is nuts and bolts, really getting down . . . in the dirt here, and you're dealing with the real point of contact between the science and nature. . . . [This] can be . . . exhilarating . . . extremely memorable.

AN: It sounds like observing is really big for you . . . I'm trying to understand . . . what it is about observing that really gets to you.

DM: Well, it's that dynamic aspect of it. . . . The sun sets. It's not gonna wait.
You've got to be ready. It's a challenge to use the telescope effectively all the
time. It can be a challenge. We had a run in . . . June . . . where we wanted
to know what we were getting instantaneously. So we had to reduce the data
right there and see what we were getting. And that was extremely valuable . . . we were seeing the new information right in front of our eyes within
minutes of taking the data. So it's a very dynamic process. It could be very
immediately rewarding. It can be very frustrating. Let me just put it this way.
Whatever it is, it's usually at the edges of your emotional response. . . . You're
rarely in a position where you're just sort of, la, la, la, you know. You have a
strong impression of something going on . . . it can be very exhilarating, very
frustrating, whatever. But it's always very something.

Realizing that I wanted to know more about what Mora sensed at the "edge of
emotional response," or as he described it, between "exhilaration" and "frus-
tration," I probed further into his initial response:

AN: Sometimes it's really hard to talk about what's going on inside of us when
we have experiences like observing that you just talked about. . . . I'm won-
dering if you could . . . try to put even more into words what's going on inside of you [when you observe].

DM: No, I know very well, I mean . . . when things are going well and you
really feel intimate, you feel like you're just working very effectively and
you've got all cylinders going. And outside, distractions are not entering
into the process and disrupting this flow. It's nice. I mean, it's hard. And I
think this is why there's a certain analogy here with people who do things
that require very intense concentration. You can really sense that all of your
efforts are working very effectively, in harmony, to do this one thing. So,
yeah, occasionally I'll notice that as I'm observing and say, "Wow, we're
clicking here. Things are going well. Everything is working to the same
purpose, and we're getting good results." And you get feedback, too, from
what you're doing. So you can see the whole cycle. You're working hard to
get something to work well and you can see that it's actually working well.
The flip side of that [is that] it can feel terrible if you think you've made a
mistake. I mean, really terrible.

With these words, Mora pointed out the range and depth of emotions he feels in his scholarly work. Clearly when things went badly, as when he made a mistake amid a complicated observation, he could feel "terrible . . . really terrible." But at his best moments—"extremely memorable" he said—he feels "exhilaration," a kind of "intimacy" with "all cylinders going" and no "outside distractions . . . disrupting the flow." I wondered when such feelings had begun for Mora, how far back in his life they reached, when and where they took root. I wondered what memories of early subject matter engagement situate at least some of his scholarly learning today:

AN: Looking back at your life, do you have a sense as to where this fascination with observation may have come from, or when it started for you?

DM: Ah, well, I can remember a few things that happened. I remember once when I was twelve or . . . maybe ten, I went to Mount Rushmore with my parents. . . . I don't know if you've been there at night. . . . But they turn on the lights at night, and they have this show of . . . patriotic songs. And then they turn everything off, and everyone heads home. And it's out in the Black Hills. It's quite far away from any big cities. And, of course, once all the lights on the mountain are off, it's pretty dark. And we were there in July. . . . And there was the Milky Way. And the Milky Way is really one of the most beautiful things you can see from Earth. People don't get a chance to see it very often, but when you do, and I remember—that made a very good, very strong impression. . . . I did then and I still do now appreciate it. It's just a beautiful thing.

AN: What's a beautiful thing?

DM: What you can see through these telescopes. It's really spectacular . . . it's true, the visual, and nowadays the nonvisual, images that we get are the thing that really turn people on in astronomy. It is the thing that gives you primal feedback . . . and sometimes you'll really think about it. There will be nights [at the observational site] I can see the Milky Way. Or a night, for example, that I wasn't actually on the telescopes, so I could let my eyes get adapted to the night. I'd look up and you really, suddenly feel that, "Wow, we're in this galaxy, big, big galaxy, and we're out here on the edge, and there's the galaxy. I see it." And . . . you can say, "Wow, it looks just like these other galaxies that I just took a picture of the other day in this system that's separate from all the others." Suddenly you can start to feel the whole picture of it. And it's a combination of both what you see, an instinctive or primal thing, and also your knowledge of what you put together. That's encouraging, too. . . . You really do get a feel that, "Wow, we're just here sitting floating on the edge of this galaxy." I mean, you really should do it. . . . It's spectacular, and you really see your location in the galaxy. So, yeah, that's one example. But there's other times where you just appreciate—this is a very beautiful thing to look at. Through a small telescope, even there, [there] are some objects that are just . . . they're different . . . they can be really pretty, very colorful, intricate in detail.

Through this interview segment, the astronomer explains that his present-day research is, in part, a response to the aesthetic pull of his past experiences drawn from his childhood memory of witnessed beauty. Asked about the sources of this "pull," David Mora describes his first sighting of the Milky Way, at age 10 or 12, during a summer night in South Dakota on a family trip he never forgot. His words suggest that his experiences on that first night, in his childhood, are with him still in adulthood, in his research. Although from his past, those memories attach to his work today, lending it continuity, folding it into the narrative he knows as his life. Although continuous, these memories evince a bounded immediacy; they speak to experiences that start and stop, caught in time. Whether as experience or memory, Mora's imagery portrays an aesthetic realization, an encounter with beauty that frames his research and, more broadly, his learning as a scholar, as a scientist.

To grasp the feeling of the experience that Mora describes, I turn to the philosopher Elaine Scarry (1999) for insights on the convergences of beauty and understanding, of desire, curiosity, and pursuit in scientific inquiry as in art. First, Mora's narrative suggests that research, even in a highly technical science, may grow from vivid images and sensations that a scholar experiences in bounded moments of time (here, in childhood) and then recalls, through memory, over the years. In *On Beauty and Being Just*, Scarry explains that pursuits of beauty and immersion in it may incite desire, intensely felt, to know that beauty in fullness, to understand it. A scholar may respond to such beckoning from an object of beauty through expressions of awe and curiosity: a desire to submerge one's self in the beauty at hand, a desire also to know and believe it, and a passion then to inquire, explore, ponder, come to know. In his interview, Mora describes how he saw the brilliance of the galaxy—how he took it in—for the first time in the blackness of the night on Mount Rushmore.

His experience that first night, of the Milky Way, was stamped in his memory, and it remains with him nearly thirty years later as he explores the sky, although now with the tools and concepts of modern astronomy. Technically skilled and conceptually trained, David Mora still returns to his childhood memories of beauty. He attaches them narratively to his professional efforts, now in adulthood, as a scientist—a practitioner of the scientific method, a constructor of the expert knowledge that constitutes his field. In memory, he is pulled back to desires for more.

Second, as Scarry also explains, beauty is an abstraction, requiring materials for its expression. Scholars whose visions of beauty beckon them to strive for meaning choose their materials—their subjects of study, such as literature, history, and astronomy—in light of images in which they had previously glimpsed them. In a scholar's life, the choice of such materials—of one's subjects of study and teaching, and of "fields" within which these materials may be found—can occur in moments of witnessed beauty. Such choice may occur long before college advisement sessions and orientations. It may occur on a summer vacation, or in a child's backyard—as she or he stares up at the sky, pores through a book, or looks deeply into a pond (see also Neumann 2006).

David Mora's interview substantiates this line of thought. He says that he witnesses beauty through the "materials" or subjects of astronomy. These subjects seem to awaken in him a capacity to see and engage with beauty, as well as its meanings, in ways that the other "materials" of his life do not. He is able to see something within the stuff of astronomy that he cannot access as deeply or fully in other matter. The beauty he sees in the night's brilliance beckons him to strive for meanings expressed in the terms of astronomy as a scientific tradition of thought. Mora thereby pairs, in Scarry's view, the search for beauty with a search for truth. He engages in this dual venture as an extension of the vision he encountered fortuitously on a summer night in his boyhood.

Finally, as David Mora's words also convey, a striving for beauty and meaning can be deeply emotional for a scholar, moving him from extreme to extreme in feeling. Mora expresses awe for the beauty that a telescope reveals; he describes the exhilaration of a good observation. His draw, then, to beauty—to the stars of the night sky, in memory and immediacy—is one of desire, of passion expressed through disciplined thought within a long-cultivated subject of study.[1]

For David Mora, scholarly learning reflects both the excitement of insight ("exhilarating . . . extremely memorable") and the struggle to achieve it ("a very dynamic process . . . very frustrating . . . hard"), including the disappointment of misconstrual and error ("it can feel terrible if you think you've made a mistake . . . really terrible"). It includes both the expert disciplinary knowledge of modern-day astronomy—expertise that Mora cultivated as an adult—and the infatuation of the 10-year-old on Mount Rushmore, looking up at the Milky Way, entranced by its beauty. Mora's learning reflects disciplinary knowing and emotional feeling, thinking scientifically and appreciating aesthetically, contemplating in the present and recollecting from the past, calculating and sensing. Post-tenure, David Mora pursues his subject of study at the juncture of these diverse streams of experience. Mora's experience is simultaneously intellectual (requiring expert disciplinary thought), professional (based in career and job, anchored in scholarly norms and institutional expectations), emotional (reflecting intense feelings, high and low points), aesthetic (seeking beauty), and personal (growing from life experience well outside academe).

Such efforts to know stir scholars' emotions, often calling forth their best efforts to learn and know. To engage in scholarly learning is to activate the intellectual or artistic interests—in particular subjects of study and in ways of knowing them—that drew a scholar to academic study in the first place, sometimes in childhood, and that hold that scholar to her study over many years, even as, with time and through learning, those subjects change.

It is necessary to qualify the definition of scholarly learning. As commonly used, the term *learning* conjures up images of individuals (learners) gaining knowledge in definitive ways: either a learner learns something or she does not. To assess such learning, one may test or somehow take stock of what the learner presumes to know, having learned it. My view of scholarly learning is broader since research-based learning, on the edges of what we know, cannot be tested in ways akin to school-based learning. Thus, the kinds of scholarly learning in which professors engage cannot be construed as involving definitive knowledge acquisition. Rather, scholarly learning involves wrestling with knowledge—a scholar struggling between her own long-held conceptions of a topic and new or different conceptions that counter her views. I counted as learning professors' awakening to an interest or to a turn of mind, raising questions or trying to raise them, experimenting with thoughts or images, becoming aware of misconceptions and responding to them, watching and waiting for insights, speculating, going wrong and trying again, and so on. In this view, scholarly learning refers to any or all of these facets of experience with disciplinary knowledge.

Given the many demands on university professors and the many activities in which professors engage on the job, where and when do they engage in scholarly learning while at work? More pointedly, in what domains of academic work—research, teaching, service—do they learn? It will come as no surprise that most of the professors in my study situated their scholarly learning in their research: 66 percent of the study sample portrayed themselves as learning in their research. But what is surprising is that over 90 percent of the sample associated their scholarly learning with their teaching, of both undergraduate and graduate students. Further, more than a third of the sample identified their service (institutional, disciplinary or professional, and public) as a site of their scholarly learning. The study suggests that professors' scholarly learning—their construction of subjects they love—can occur in teaching and service inasmuch as in research. Contrary to prevailing belief, tenured professors cannot be viewed as engaging their scholarly learning only in research. Nor can their teaching and service be cast as, necessarily, obstacles to it. Some engage their learning, simultaneously, across two or three of these activities at once. Well chosen, professors' teaching and service can advance their scholarly learning.

What Else Professors Learn: Beyond Scholarly Learning

Academic myth suggests that with tenure in hand, professors can do as they wish: they can throw themselves more fully than ever before into their scholarly learning, or they can relax, distancing themselves from the topics, questions, or ideas at the core of their intellectual endeavor, whether in the form of research, teaching, or service. Who they become professionally through the actions they take—or fail to take—is of their own making. Their futures are in their own hands.

My data highlight the inaccuracies of this too frequently voiced belief. With tenure in hand, university professors can, and those in my study did, continue to pursue their scholarly learning. Participating professors did not purposefully seek to distance themselves from the intellectual and artistic pursuits that drew many of them to deep academic study in the first place. Encountering barriers to their scholarly learning, the majority struggled to surmount them. Reaching occasional needs to pause, they soon exerted effort to put their scholarly learning back in motion.

Table 7.1   Range of learning in which newly tenured professors engaged

What professors learned	Prevalence (%)
Academic subject matters of one's scholarly learning	90+
Academic practices: teaching, research, service, outreach	90+
Academic contexts: campus, discipline/field, academic culture	75+
Patterns of academic constraint/opportunity: limits, possibilities	75+
Self-identity: as a professor, scholar, person	75+
Academic subject matters unrelated to scholarly learning	50+
Professional restraint: when and how to delay/withhold response	25+
Disengagement from scholarly learning or professional practice	< 15

Note: Adapted from Anna Neumann, *Professing to Learn: Creating Tenured Lives and Careers in the American Research University* (Baltimore: Johns Hopkins University Press, 2009).

What got in their way? Virtually all the professors participating in my study said that in addition to pursuing the scholarly learning that many of them said they loved, they also engaged in other learning, more instrumental in nature, that had little direct bearing on their intellectual and creative interests. Often that other learning got in the way of the scholarly, or it took up time that they would have preferred to devote to their scholarship. What then was the full range of learning in which the newly tenured professors engaged? Table 7.1 addresses this question.

Table 7.1 shows that upward of 90 percent of the professors participating in the study experienced themselves as engaged in the kind of scholarly learning that David Mora describes. Certainly the content of these professors' scholarly learning, in diverse disciplines and fields, varied from person to person, as did the quality of their feelings of being in the moments of scholarly learning (see Neumann 2006). As the table also shows, just as many professors claimed to expand their knowledge of the core academic practices of teaching, research, service, and outreach. A strong proportion of the sample (75% or more) indicated that they were learning the academic cultures of their campus or their discipline or field of study, including patterns of constraint and opportunity (how far they could push and when to stop), as well as their own identities as professors, scholars, or persons. Over half said they were learning academic subject matters unrelated to their scholarly learning—study that some deemed important but not at the center of their interests and passions. Over a quarter of the sample said they learned when and how to restrain themselves from action as opposed to responding to pressure or demands quickly or immediately. Less than 15 percent portrayed themselves as disengaging purposefully from their learning, usually in the context of their research or service.

In addition to pointing out the inaccuracy of the academic myth of professors' post-tenure decline (my data suggest that they are learning a great deal about the full range of academic work), these findings indicate the following: First, the early post-tenure years are flush with things to learn. Second, professors do not learn everything they need to know pre-tenure, in their scholarship and beyond it. When new post-tenure responsibilities come their way, they have to learn them; they also have to learn how to navigate the cultural and political worlds in which they carry out those new responsibilities. This means "learning the ropes" in their universities, fields of study, and other communities: how far they can go and when to stop, when to respond quickly and when to exercise restraint. Professors may learn a great deal too about themselves—as scholars, professional workers, and human beings, including what their talents and powers are, what they value and need, and what they need to improve. They gain all this professional knowledge even as they persist in their core scholarly learning.

But given the load of new learning that professors may encounter through the early post-tenure career as presented in table 7.1, how can they respond? How may they position themselves to advance their most meaningful learning, the scholarly, amid pulls on them to learn many other things—to devote their limited attention to the breadth of new challenges coming their way as they assume expanded campus responsibility? No human being can take in all that goes on in that person's environment (see Birnbaum 1988; Cohen and March 1986). Given demands on time, how do newly tenured professors remain anchored in their scholarly learning? What and who helps them do so?

My research suggests that help can come from two sources: from professors' own selves, including how they organize and direct their attention at work, and from their employing institution. Through this career period, professors may draw on a sense of personal agency to advance their scholarly learning (Lerner and Busch-Rossnagel 1981; Marshall 2000; Pallas 2007). Since their work and learning are closely linked, they can do so by using one or more of the following work strategies: (1) They may strive to *create space for their scholarly learning*, for example, by recreating the programs and institutes in which they engage it, or by negotiating to move their work to new organizational units that will be more conducive to it. (2) They may strive to *contain their attention to focused interests*, for example, by intentionally limiting the content of their scholarly learning, or by concentrating their service and teaching assignments deliberately onto topics of clear interest to them. In doing so, they may have to learn to say "no" to invitations to engage in work outside the boundaries of their committed interests, even if those interests appeal to them. (3) They may think of ways to use their scholarly learning to *connect* key scholarly concepts in one area of their work (for example, in their research) to concepts in other work domains (teaching, outreach, service); they also may select service and outreach, or teaching, that support their pursuits of their key substantive interests (for complete discussion, see Neumann and Pereira 2009; Neumann, Terosky, and Schell 2006). In my study, approximately 80 percent of the forty participating professors referred to using one or more of these work strategies to advance their scholarly learning: About 75 percent spoke of *creating space for their scholarly learning*. About 66 percent referred to themselves as *containing their attention to focused interests*. Approximately 80 percent indicated use of a strategy of *connecting* key features of their work by way of their scholarly learning.

Although professors can exert agency on their own behalves to advance their scholarly learning, the university can provide assistance in specific ways. In assessing professors' descriptions of where and when they engaged in scholarly learning, I identified three key features of campus life—I refer to them as campus contexts—that sometimes helped but occasionally slowed down or obstructed professors' scholarly learning: their local colleagueship; opportunities for cross-disciplinary learning; and opportunities for subject matter–related work outside the university, for example, by way of university outreach or public service. These are contexts that administrators, policy makers, and faculty colleagues can build up, shape, or reframe to benefit professors' scholarly learning.

The web of peer relationships that professors develop on campus—their *local colleagueship*—can both support and obstruct their scholarly learning. One's peers may be in or outside one's discipline or field, program, and department. Academic peers may engage with one another openly and frequently, or distantly and rarely. Viewed as a chain of peer relations, local colleagueship can support, obstruct, or be inconsequential; it may be bold or bland. Thirty-two of the thirty-nine professors I interviewed in year 3 of the study (80%) portrayed their scholarly learning as occurring amid their local colleagueship. Of the thirty-two participants, ten (a quarter of the original study sample) described their colleagueship as ineffectual or as getting in the way of their scholarly learning. Of these ten, eight were women. What this means is that just under half of the women in the study (n = 20) experienced colleague problems bearing on their scholarly learning. Women in the humanities were more concerned about the effects of colleagueship on their scholarly learning than were men. Of the five humanists reporting negative colleague relations, four were women. Women in the sciences also portrayed their colleagueship as inhospitable to their scholarly learning, but their concerns pointed at challenges exceeding peer relations: taking on nonsubstantive work that outwardly may appear more important than it really is (usually in the form of institutional service or research management) and that separates the women from substantive scientific endeavor; taking on unstrategized work that becomes further undirected, thereby pointless or seemingly unending; and assuming values-directed work (for example, action aimed at "righting gender-based wrongs" on campus) but at cost to themselves and their work (for a full report see Terosky, Phifer, and Neumann 2008).

In most cases, *opportunities for cross-disciplinary learning*—freedom, encouragement, and support to look, think, and talk with scholars outside one's field—enhanced professors' pursuits of their most meaningful subjects of study. Of the thirty-nine professors participating in year 3 interviews, sixteen (approximately 40%) related their scholarly learning to cross-disciplinary interaction in research, teaching, institutional service, or outreach. This is not to say that professors experienced cross-disciplinary endeavors uniformly as a "good thing." Some voiced concerns about colleagues who treated university-supported cross-disciplinary initiatives as opportunities for knowledge "poaching" (as indeed one called it)—a scholar taking concepts and methods from others' fields but without being willing to share much in return. At least one study participant worried that he had been exposed to cross-disciplinary research too early in his career, before he had established himself in a disciplinary community he could call his own.

Thoughtfully framed, *professors' work outside the university*—for example, in public service or campus outreach, or simply with friends and family, or in daily life—could usefully inform their scholarly learning. Twenty of the thirty-nine professors participating in year 3 interviews said their scholarly learning occurred within such endeavors, supported openly by the university (for example, as public outreach) or carried out by a professor alone.

The findings of the *Four Universities Project* indicate that conceptualizations of the academic career need to do more than highlight faculty work and workplaces. Especially during times of societal change—when faculty work may be pressed to change—policy makers, faculty, and higher education researchers need to attend to both changes in what faculty do in the name of work and also what they learn (or fail to learn) as they do that work. Policy makers, faculty leaders, and researchers are advised to consider demands for change in faculty work and workplaces relative to how the proposed changes will influence professors' scholarly learning.

Research on change is anything but new in the study of American higher education. Historically the field has attended to how academic organizations (colleges, universities) can adapt to external pressures for change, as well as how institutional leaders may proactively manage or redirect such change to institutional advantage (Birnbaum 1988, 1992; Chaffee 1984; Jedamus and Peterson 1980; Peterson, Dill, and Mets 1997). Recent extensions of this historic wave of writing assess the impact of organization-environment interactions on the academic profession: researchers today consider what will happen to the academic profession when institutions that support traditional faculty roles (by way of budgeting, jobs, and tenuring practices) literally change underfoot in response to new and turbulent environmental forces (Schuster and Finkelstein 2006; see also Gappa, Austin, and Trice 2007). Although such assessment is sorely needed, I suggest that a third consideration is warranted, one that takes as its point of departure the academic-role-inhabiting *persons* whose lives and careers situate the substantive learning that the academic organization and academic profession strive to advance and legitimate in an era when organization and profession are being closely scrutinized and, in some cases, reformed (see Altbach 1999). In the next section I discuss professors' scholarly learning in this context of change with implications for the future of the academic profession and for academe broadly.

Toward Complexity: Implications for the Future of the Academic Profession

I began this chapter by noting that knowledge production, alongside knowledge dissemination and knowledge application, represents the university's reason for existence in contemporary society. In common usage, this mission speaks to a macroscopic, open-systems view (Katz and Kahn 1978; Scott 1987) of higher education organization in society. In this view, knowledge production, in particular, is associated with research, including creative endeavor and other forms of scholarship; the "knowledge" produced, for the larger society's use, is an "output" of the organizational system. But as my discussion of professors' learning in their teaching and service shows, both these role activities also can yield knowledge (much as research can). Moved to the level of institutional mission, research, teaching, and service all reflect concern with knowledge creation.

In shifting this discourse from the plane of "institutional mission" (knowledge production linked to dissemination and application) to the plane of "faculty activity and experience" (faculty members' work in the form of research, teaching, and service and their scholarly learning within these activities), we move from a macro to a micro view. While these two planes may not be fully aligned with one another, I argue that for the most part they meld, or it is assumed they should. It is in this spirit—in effect, the micro instantiating the macro—that I discuss scholarly learning in this chapter's conclusion: I view the faculty as central to the university's large-scale function of knowledge creation, which is operationalized, commonly, through individual professors' scholarly learning occurring primarily within their research but also within their teaching, service, or outreach. This interrelationship—of knowledge creation (macro organizational) and scholarly learning (micro individually anchored)—captures how and why scholarly learning matters: scholarly learning can be viewed as the person-level instantiation of the larger university's knowledge creation function and, more broadly, of the mission of higher learning to which colleges and universities aspire.

Of course, one might counter with the argument that the university's mission of knowledge creation can also be instantiated by professors' learning of subjects that are distant from those they most favor. I suggest that although this version of my claim may strengthen university agendas in the short run, in the long run it may weaken them. Dissipation of individual professors' personal investments in their own favored learning could contribute to the erosion of the intellectual spirit of the profession on which higher education organizations draw to engage in high-quality knowledge production.

As the preceding discussion of the *Four Universities Project* indicates, scholarly learning must be understood as more than "of the institution" (i.e., it is more than an operationalization of the university's knowledge production goal) and also as more than "of the profession" (i.e., it is more than a sign of membership in the academic community and in disciplines and fields therein). Because scholarly learning is rooted in professors' personal lives, it must be construed also as "of the person" and of the personal life. As a personal activity, scholarly learning reflects how and why many individuals choose to enter scholarly careers within the American research university; it also may speak to why a fair number of these individuals persist in those careers. Asked to describe their professional paths, the majority of university professors I interviewed spoke at length and often emotionally about how they found and developed their particular subjects of study as opposed to how they found or selected their professorial careers. The academic career that they pursued, along with the academic profession they joined in so doing, was, for many, a vehicle for pursuing their more personal scholarly learning. Their membership in the academic profession, the career they constructed within that profession, and the particular professorial job (or jobs) they have held by virtue of their professional status all together allow them to pursue their scholarly learning in a socially legitimated and valued way—as a university professor, and in this case as one recently tenured. Thus, in addition to being "of the institution" and "of the profession," as well as "of the job," scholarly learning also is "of the person" drawn to a faculty career. David Mora and others I interviewed for the *Four Universities Project* (Neumann 2006, 2009) spoke to this multilevel view.

The interrelationship of professors' scholarly learning and the university's larger knowledge production function—their interweaving across institutional, professional, and personal contexts—is rarely addressed in higher education research, policy making, or leadership efforts (see, for example, Boler 1999; O'Meara, Terosky, and Neumann 2008). Views of scholarly learning in individual professors' lives are scarce; they rarely (if ever) inform public or institutional discourses such as what the university should invest in or how the university should hold its faculty accountable for their work. While this may not matter much during times of stability and growth when silent but meaningful features of the enterprise (like scholarly learning) rarely are called to a public accounting, during tumultuous times such accounting does come into play—especially if the larger system (the university) that supports scholarly learning is threatened. Recent changes in the large-scale composition, organization, and functioning of contemporary American higher education—including changes in ideas about what knowledge production is and how it happens, who controls its content, and who is allowed to engage in it (see Schuster and Finkelstein 2006)—render vulnerable the personal aspects of professors' scholarly learning. Because we have established no vocabulary for talking about scholarly learning, defending it, much less making a case for its advancement, is difficult.

I do not believe that the university's knowledge production function (research), as analytically distinct from professors' scholarly learning, has been affected in quite the same way. If anything, knowledge production as an organizational (macro) phenomenon may be growing in strength, even as it becomes increasingly decoupled from the person-centered scholarly learning to which it has historically been linked. These days, knowledge production continues to expand, becoming increasingly collectivity-anchored (consider the growth of "big science"), systems-based (emphasizing roles in larger systems with minimal attention to the persons occupying the roles), technologically mediated (lessening human interrelationship), and accountability-directed (concerned with products rather than means of production that involve human beings at their center). And unlike professors' scholarly learning, which rarely is talked about in public settings (rendering it as less usable for policy consideration, as well as less "real"), the university's knowledge production *is* discussed in public settings and remains a primary target of higher education leaders' work. (For a complete discussion of such trends and how they will likely affect the future professoriate, see Schuster and Finkelstein 2006.) Because we have a vocabulary for knowledge production and because we are practiced in the public uses of that vocabulary, we write policy around it as though knowledge production exists in and of itself without the underlay of committed human beings engaged in scholarly learning that, I suggest, constitutes it at its best.

Finally, I have already explained how changes in the basic role structure of the professoriate, as the primary unit of academic organization and of the profession as well, are having an effect on what it means to be a faculty member: from being a member of an intellectually autonomous expert body (symbolized by permanent, full-time, and empowered status) to being a member of a temporary (contingent) work corps created and directed by others who lay claim to a governing expertise. Thus, we may be witnessing, in our time, the deprofessionalization of the academic profession. To reduce or disassemble the traditional faculty role—where scholarly learning has existed largely without public name—is to threaten it, to question its continuance as a site of deep learning. If *academic knowledge creation*, *academic professionalization*, and *scholarly learning* are indeed cut of the same cloth—as I suggest that, ideally, they are—then the weakening of any of them speaks to the weakening of them all, gradually if not instantaneously. I suggest that to boost policies and practices for advancing all three requires acknowledging that they all exist, and that they all matter for higher learning in America. From the standpoint of policy and practice, it becomes essential to advocate for all three together. The future of the academic profession in the United States will depend in good part on whether we can learn to speak and think of the value of this inextricably interdependent trio.

NOTES

The research reported in this chapter was made possible by a grant from the Spencer Foundation. The data presented, the statements made, and the views expressed are solely my responsibility as author. My sincere thanks to Katie Conway for contributed expertise on the sociology of the professions and for assistance in earlier work related to this effort.

Earlier versions of some text in this chapter were published as *Professing to Learn: Creating Tenured Lives and Careers in the American Research University* (Baltimore: Johns Hopkins University Press, 2009); "To Glimpse Beauty and Awaken Meaning: Scholarly Learning as Aesthetic Experience," *Journal of Aesthetic Education* 39, no. 4 (2005): 68–88 (copyright 2005 by the Board of Trustees of the University of Illinois; used with permission of the University of Illinois Press); and "Observations: Taking Seriously the Topic of Learning in Studies of Faculty Work and Careers," in *Advancing Faculty Learning through Interdisciplinary Collaboration*, edited by Elizabeth G. Creamer and Lisa Lattuca, 63–83 (San Francisco: Jossey-Bass, 2005).

1. For further discussion of my use of "passion," a concept I derived through analysis of psychologists' representations of the concept of "flow" (e.g., Csikszentmihalyi 1990, 1993, 1996) yet as rooted in a long history of literary and philosophical thought, and for a historical overview of the term's meanings dating back to the seventeenth century, see Neumann 2006. That article also speaks to variations in emotion associated with "passionate thought" as at the core of professors' scholarly learning. While passionate thought may represent its high point (often brief), scholarly learning is rife with other emotions even as it is driven by trained, purposeful thought. For representation of related experiences across the life span, see Behar 1993, 1996; McAdams 1993; Myerhoff 1978.

REFERENCES

Altbach, Philip G. 1999. Harsh realities: The professoriate faces a new century. In *American higher education in the twenty-first century*, ed. Philip G. Altbach, Robert O. Berdahl, and Patricia J. Gumport, 271–98. Baltimore: Johns Hopkins University Press.

Behar, Ruth. 1993. *Translated woman: Crossing the border with Esperanza's story.* Boston: Beacon.

———. 1996. *The vulnerable observer.* Boston: Beacon.

Birnbaum, Robert. 1988. *How colleges work: The cybernetics of academic organization and leadership.* San Francisco: Jossey-Bass.

———. 1992. *How academic leadership works: Understanding success and failure in the college presidency.* San Francisco: Jossey-Bass.

Boler, Megan. 1999. *Feeling power: Emotions and education.* New York: Routledge.

Bransford, John D., Ann L. Brown, and Rodney R. Cocking, eds. 1999. *How people learn: Brain, mind, experience, and school.* Washington, DC: National Academy Press.

Chaffee, Ellen Earle. 1984. Successful strategic management in small private colleges. *Journal of Higher Education* 55 (2): 212–41.

Clausen, John. 1991. Adolescent competence and the shaping of the life course. *American Journal of Sociology* 96 (4): 805–42.

Cohen, Michael D., and James G. March. 1986. *Leadership and ambiguity: The American college president.* Boston: Harvard Business School Press.

Csikszentmihalyi, Mihalyi. 1990. *Flow: The psychology of optimal experience.* New York: Harper & Row.

———. 1993. *The evolving self: A psychology for the third millennium.* New York: HarperCollins.

———. 1996. *Creativity: Flow and the psychology of discovery and invention.* New York: HarperCollins.

Gappa, Judith M., Ann E. Austin, and Andrea G. Trice. 2007. *Rethinking faculty work: Higher education's strategic imperative.* San Francisco: John Wiley and Sons.

Greeno, James G., Alan M. Collins, and Lauren B. Resnick. 1996. Cognition and learning. In *Handbook of educational psychology,* ed. David C. Berliner and Robert C. Calfee, 15–46. New York: Macmillan.

Hansen, David T. 2001. *Exploring the moral heart of teaching: Toward a teacher's creed.* New York: Teacher's College Press.

Jedamus, Paul, and Marvin W. Peterson, eds. 1980. *Improving academic management: A handbook of planning and institutional research.* San Francisco: Jossey-Bass.

Katz, Daniel, and Robert L. Kahn. 1978. *The social psychology of organizations.* 2nd ed. New York: Wiley.

Lerner, Richard M., and Nancy A. Busch-Rossnagel. 1981. Individuals as producers of their development: Conceptual and empirical bases. In *Individuals as producers of their development: A life-span perspective,* ed. Richard M. Lerner and Nancy A. Busch-Rossnagel, 1–36. New York: Cambridge University Press.

Marshall, Victor W. 2000. Agency, structure and the life course in the era of reflexive modernization. Research paper presented at the annual meeting of the American Sociological Association, August, in Washington, D.C.

McAdams, Dan P. 1993. *The stories we live by: Personal myths and the making of the self.* New York: Guilford Press.

Myerhoff, Barbara. 1978. *Number our days*. New York: Touchstone / Simon and Schuster.

Neumann, Anna. 2006. Professing passion: Emotion in the scholarship of professors in research universities. *American Educational Research Journal* 43 (3): 381–424.

———. 2009. *Professing to learn: Creating tenured lives and careers in the American research university*. Baltimore: Johns Hopkins University Press.

Neumann, Anna, and Kimberley B. Pereira. 2009. Becoming strategic: Recently tenured university professors as agents of scholarly learning. In *Professing to learn: Creating tenured lives and careers in the American research university*, by Anna Neumann, 137–71. Baltimore: Johns Hopkins University Press, 2009.

Neumann, Anna, Aimee LaPointe Terosky, and Julie Schell. 2006. Agents of learning: Strategies for assuming agency, for learning, in tenured faculty careers. In *The balancing act: Gendered perspectives in faculty roles and work lives*, ed. Susan J. Bracken, Jeanie K. Allen, and Diane R. Dean, 91–120. Sterling, VA: Stylus.

O'Meara, KerryAnn, Aimee LaPointe Terosky, and Anna Neumann. 2008. *Faculty careers and work lives: A professional growth perspective*. ASHE Higher Education Report, no. 34(3). San Francisco: Jossey-Bass.

Pallas, Aaron M. 2007. A subjective approach to schooling and the transition to adulthood. In *Constructing adulthood: Agency and subjectivity in adolescence and adulthood*, ed. Ross Macmillan, 173–98. Amsterdam: Elsevier, JAI.

Peterson, Marvin, David D. Dill, and Lisa Mets, eds. 1997. *Planning and management for a changing environment: A handbook on redesigning postsecondary institutions*. San Francisco: Jossey-Bass.

Scarry, Elaine. 1999. *On beauty and being just*. Princeton: Princeton University Press.

Schon, Donald A. 1983. *The reflective practitioner: How professionals think in action*. New York: Basic Books.

———. 1987. *Educating the reflective practitioner: Toward a new design for teaching and learning in the professions*. San Francisco: Jossey-Bass.

Schuster, Jack H., and Martin J. Finkelstein. 2006. *The American faculty: The restructuring of academic work and careers*. Baltimore: Johns Hopkins University Press.

Schwab, Joseph. 1978. Education and the structure of the disciplines. In *Science, curriculum, and liberal education*, ed. I. Westbury and N. J. Wilkof, 229–72. Chicago: University of Chicago Press.

Scott, Richard W. 1987. *Organizations: Rational, natural, and open*. 2nd ed. Englewood Cliffs, NJ: Prentice-Hall.

Shulman, Lee S. 1987. Knowledge and teaching: Foundation of the new reform. *Harvard Educational Review* 57 (1): 1–22.

———. 2004. *The wisdom of practice: Essays on teaching, learning, and learning to teach*. San Francisco: Jossey-Bass.

Spillane, James, and Patricia Burch. 2006. The institutional environment and instructional practice: Changing patterns of guidance and control in public education. In *The new institutionalism in education*, ed. Heinz-Dieter Meyer and Brian Rowan, 87–102. Albany: State University of New York.

Terosky, Aimee LaPointe, Tamsyn Phifer, and Anna Neumann. 2008. Shattering plexiglas: Continuing challenges for women professors in research universities. In *Unfinished agendas: New and continuing gender challenges in higher education*, ed. Judith Glazer-Raymo, 52–79. Baltimore: Johns Hopkins University Press.

CHAPTER EIGHT

Anomie in the American Academic Profession

Joseph C. Hermanowicz

A social system is always in a state of change. The rate of change can, of course, vary. "Structural lag" refers to the condition that arises when social structures fail to keep up with the rate of social change (Riley, Johnson, and Foner 1972). An imbalance is produced between individual needs and wants on the one hand and opportunities available in organizational and institutional structures to satisfy them on the other. While, then, the American higher education system is always evolving, the magnitude appears significantly more consequential in the contemporary era. Recent scholarly studies convey a gravity of change even in their titles, which evince alteration in the *structure* of the academic profession: *Managed Professionals: Unionized Faculty and Restructuring Academic Labor* (Rhoades 1998); *Reconstructing the University: Worldwide Shifts in Academia in the 20th Century* (Frank and Gabler 2006); *Teaching without Tenure: Policies and Practices for a New Era* (Baldwin and Chronister 2001); *The New Academic Generation: A Profession in Transformation* (Finkelstein, Seal, and Schuster 1998); *The American Faculty: The Restructuring of Academic Work and Careers* (Schuster and Finkelstein 2006); *Wannabe U: Inside the Corporate University* (Tuchman 2009); *Saving Alma Mater: A Rescue Plan for America's Public Universities* (Garland 2009); *What Ever Happened to the Faculty? Drift and Decision in Higher Education* (Burgan 2006).

The French sociologist Emile Durkheim contended that when social systems undergo major, transformational shifts in their structure, serious institutional and individual consequences arise. They do so because prevailing structures are no longer able to transmit effective norms to guide interaction, which now transpires according to changed states of understanding. The chief potential consequence of major structural shift, according to Durkheim, is *anomie.* Anomie refers to a collective breakdown of order instigated by a divide between the realities of everyday situations and the needs and wants for a future (Durkheim [1893] 1984). Institutionally, the concept indicates a breakdown of norms that govern expectations, most particularly expectations about the present and future. Individually, anomie is expressed in "normlessness" or a sense of self-fragmentation, lack of meaning, or lack of purpose.

Examining changes in the economic structure of society, Durkheim argued that people can only be happy when their wants are proportionate to their means. Unanticipated and poorly negotiated change, bringing *either* financial despair *or* prosperity, exerts destructive force. According to Durkheim, it was not great financial loss that caused anomie, since anomie was observed in those who experienced great financial gain. Rather, anomie stemmed from a crisis in the collective order brought about by either downward or upward change, wherein the realities of the present foretold a life-altering contrast with the future (Durkheim [1893] 1984). How could lives be led meaningfully when the realities of the present departed dramatically from an anticipated future? Discrepancies between present and future could be so wide and so consequential as to allow anomie to constitute one of the four major types of suicide in Durkheim's well-known theoretic formulations (Durkheim [1897] 1951).

In the case of the academic profession, anomie may be specified as the "general absence of opportunities to achieve recognition" (Hagstrom 1965, 228). Anomie is the result of a divide between achievement aspirations among members of a profession and the profession's capacity to recognize individuals for their contributions. Following Durkheim, it is conceivable that when the academic profession (and all professions) experiences a marked change in structure, anomie is probable and spells problematic consequences for the operation of higher education institutions and the individuals who compose them. When structures experience significant alteration, they may fail to provide meaningful maps by which to guide interaction and thus meaningful bases by which to establish understanding about roles, expectations, and aspirations in the profession.

Consistent with Durkheim's line of thought, it is conceivable that anomie may be found in episodes over time in which the academic profession has experienced marked change, such as shifts from one period to another in the "ten generations" of American higher education elaborated by Geiger (1999) or perhaps between each of the historical eras explained by Thelin (2004).

Prior episodes of change have occurred generally in a context of expansion, not only in the number of higher education institutions or the amount of funding to support them, but also an expansion of individual opportunity to realize professional goals. Contemporary change in the American academic profession, by contrast, involves greater competition among and limitation of institutions and individuals. The stress is on adaptation to *greater scarcity* rather than to plenitude.

This chapter has three goals. First, drawing upon sociological theory, I outline a conceptual framework in which to examine anomie in the American academic profession. Second, I explore the ways by which anomie may vary in the contemporary era by career stages of academics, by organizational types of higher education institutions, by scholarly field, and by historical time. Finally, I discuss the implications that anomie presents to the status of academe as a profession.

Conceptual Framework

According to a structural-functional line of sociological theory, academic careers may be seen to be predicated on quests for recognition. The significance of recognition to academic careers has been explored extensively in the sociology of science, in particular by Robert Merton (Cole and Cole 1973; Merton 1973c; Zuckerman 1988). Merton explained that recognition is important to science, and by extension to academe as a whole, because recognition from those competent to judge a contribution is the prime indicator that an academic has fulfilled the institutional goals of higher education: to extend certified knowledge (Merton 1973b). "Recognition for originality becomes socially validated testimony that one has successfully lived up to the most exacting requirement of one's role as [an academic]" (Merton 1973b, 293). Recognition and quests for it are thus institutionalized: it is both essential to the advancement of knowledge and therefore expected in trained individuals, if as socialized members of the academic profession they seek to satisfy its institutional goals. All forms of recognition—publication, citation of published work, awards, honors, and so forth—are indexes of the academic community's assessment of individuals' achievements as academics in their respective fields.

The centrality of recognition to academe may, moreover, be observed by the importance of reward systems and their operation in the profession, in colleges and universities, and in schools and departments. Academic communities at each of these levels operate by a principle (if not always by the practice) that rewards are to be distributed according to universalistic criteria, that is, on the basis of merit, irrespective of particularistic factors associated with contributors, such as their race, gender, class background, political party affiliation, religion, or sexual orientation. Particularistic criteria are said to be "functionally irrelevant" to the operation of reward systems because they take into account considerations other than the merit underlying the contribution (Merton 1973a).

Furthermore, a concern with order of authorship and priority in discovery lends additional testimony to the social significance that academics assign both to recognition and to how recognition is distributed, highlighting a community's normative values that recognition should be allocated when and to whom credit is due and in ways that are commensurate with a contribution (Merton 1973a, 1973b). Instances where reward systems fail—when recognition for contributions is delayed or withheld or when the amount of recognition allocated is perceived as too little or too much—constitute occasions when members of an academic community question, privately or publicly, the validity of rewards (Chism 2006; Hermanowicz 2009; Zuckerman 1977). Such phenomena underscore the socially assigned significance with which academics construct and understand academic careers.

The theory of cumulative advantage and disadvantage, now widely applied in many social domains but which was developed by sociologists of science working within this structural-functional line of thought, is predicated on the distribution of recognition through the operation of reward systems (for discussion on theory origins, see Zuckerman 1977, 1988; for discussion on subsequent applications, see DiPrete and Eirich 2006). The theory holds that "certain individuals and groups repeatedly receive resources and rewards that enrich recipients at an accelerated rate and conversely impoverish (relatively) the non-recipients" (Zuckerman 1977, 59–60). At root, the theory explains how inequalities recursively differentiate, in academe as in many other social domains, the "haves" from the "have nots" over time. Again, the significance of recognition may be observed, in this case by "removing" it from the equation. Were recognition less vital, the theory would have nothing on which to stand; it loses its explanatory power.

According to this structural-functional framework, the centrality of recognition to academe holds even as academe comprises multiple functions, such as instructional, service, and administrative functions. One might contend that most academics are not active in research (Gustin 1973), that for others research productivity declines after early career stages (Bayer and Dutton 1977; Clemente 1973; Cole 1979; Cole and Cole 1973), or that many higher education institutions are not research oriented. Such observations isolate micro-level *components* of a higher education system. As outlined here, the structural-functional framework elaborated by sociologists of science and higher education researchers takes a *social system* as a basis for conceptualizing its macro-level operation. That many academics are not productive in and many institutions not oriented to research does not negate what such a framework asserts as the core social functions of the academic profession. Research is seen as central, since in the operation of the social system, all other functions are contingent on it.

> The research role . . . is central, with others being functionally ancillary to it. For plainly, if there were no scientific [or other scholarly] investigation, there would be no new knowledge to be transmitted through the teaching role, no need to allocate resources for investigation, no research organization to administer, and no new flow of knowledge for gatekeepers to regulate. . . . The heroes of [academe] are acclaimed in their capacity as [scholarly] investigators, seldom as teachers, administrators, or referees and editors. (Merton and Zuckerman 1973, 520)

Putting the point aside, success in other academic roles is also predicated on evaluation and, ultimately, on the conferral or withholding of recognition by and through, if not one's peers, then other committees, panels, assemblies, and administrators from the academic community. One is not usually a celebrated teacher, administrator, or servant in the absence of review and sanction by some set of peers. By this framework, recognition underlies the functioning of all academic roles that are themselves differentiated and linked by their contingent functions.

If recognition is so central to the academic profession, and if quests for recognition are institutionally expected of academics, then a problem emerges when the profession cannot confer recognition to numbers of people who may warrant it. If conditions change wherein there is an "absence of opportunities to achieve recognition" (Hagstrom 1965, 228), then rewards of academic work may not be viewed as to justify costs associated with doing the work. A consequence is anomie. In the section that follows, I examine ways in which anomie is most likely to arise in contemporary academe.

Anomie in Academe

If anomie arises from a disjuncture between expectations for the present and future, then an absence of opportunity to achieve recognition originates from a discrepancy between individuals' desired recognition and present conditions. If the problem centers on recognition, then the research role is arguably most suspect as the source of the problem, since it is this role that is centrally directed to the achievement of recognition in the academic profession. As a means to cast light on anomie in the American academic profession, I draw upon materials generated from a national longitudinal study of scientists' careers. Data from the study are presented fully elsewhere (Hermanowicz 1998, 2009). For present purposes, I provide an overview of the study design and selected findings. I then turn to a discussion of how anomie varies among four dimensions: career stages, organizational types of higher education institutions, scholarly field, and historical time.

Empirical Background

In 1994–95, I interviewed sixty academics, physicists specifically, employed at universities across the United States about their careers and aspirations. In 2004–5, I completed another series of interviews with the same people. I researched continuities and changes in careers, including what had developed as satisfactions and dissatisfactions for academics, and how they viewed their progress, or lack of it, toward what had been their professional goals. Fifty-five subjects from the original sample were interviewed as part of the longitudinal study, a response rate of 93 percent. (The response rate for the foundational study was 70%.)

Individuals were originally sampled by departmental rank as measured by assessments of graduate programs conducted by the National Research Council (Goldberger, Maher, and Flattau 1995; Jones, Lindzey, and Coggeshall 1982). Top, middle, and tail-ranked departments were selected and built into the study design to permit a comparison of careers that are experienced under different structural and cultural conditions. A major goal of the study was to examine how people's careers are shaped by the academic organizations in which they work.

To aid comparison and contrast, the academics and their institutions were classified into three types. I call one type *elite*—those universities that place a high premium on research and whose departments ranked at or near the *top*

Table 8.1   Academics by cohort and organizational type, longitudinal study

Organization	Cohort (by year of PhD)			Total
	Pre-1970	1970–80	Post-1980	
Elite	9	6	8	23
Pluralist	5	4	6	15
Communitarian	5	5	7	17
Total	19	15	21	55

of the NRC assessment. Examples include Caltech, Harvard, and Princeton. I call a second type *pluralist*—those universities that emphasize research as well as mass teaching and service and whose departments ranked in the *middle* of the NRC assessment. Examples include the University of Maryland, Florida State University, and the University of Oregon. I call the third type *communitarian*—those universities that primarily emphasize teaching and service, although not necessarily at the exclusion of research, and whose departments ranked at or near the *tail* of the NRC assessment. Examples include the University of Tulsa, University of Toledo, and the University of North Carolina–Charlotte.

Respondents in this work were also sampled by cohort, in order to include academics at a variety of career stages—early, middle, and late, generally speaking, at the time of the first study. These three cohorts were established by the year in which academics received their PhDs, which is used as a proxy of their career stage. The eldest cohort consisted of academics who received their PhDs prior to 1970. By the time of the longitudinal study, they were passing from late to post career stages. A middle cohort consisted of academics who received their PhDs between 1970 and 1980. By the time of the longitudinal study, they were passing from middle to late career stages. The youngest cohort consisted of academics who received their PhDs after 1980. By the time of the longitudinal study, they were passing from early to middle stages of their careers. The research design of the study is presented in table 8.1.

Since I examined how members of a profession experience work and interpret the career, the interview constituted the primary method of data collection. Interview questions dealt with change and continuity in outlook (such as "What changes have you seen with regard to research?" and "What changes have you seen with regard to teaching?"). Interviews also consisted of questions about satisfaction and dissatisfaction (such as "What have developed as the three biggest joys about your job?" "What have developed as your three biggest complaints about your job?" "Would you seek an academic career again, if you were starting all over?" "If so, what would you do differently?" and "Have there been ways in which an academic career has been unrewarding?") Interviewees were also asked about their current aspirations and where they see themselves having come and headed professionally. In addition, academics who had retired were asked about the best and worst parts of retirement, about how they experienced the transition into retirement, and about what "retirement" means, in order to research how such meanings might vary from one organizational type to another.

Selected Findings

There is little mistaking that the research role in the American academic profession has witnessed significant change as institutions themselves have changed in their favor of research. An indication consists in the normative expectations that govern research role performance in American universities.

Drawing upon data from the study of academic physicists, table 8.2 presents publication productivity and promotion timing among scientists across the three types of academic organizations and across the cohorts. To obtain their first academic jobs, the eldest scientists, who would have entered the job market between the late 1950s and late 1960s, published an overall average of 4.0 articles. For the middle cohort of scientists, who entered the job market between 1970 and 1980, the number of articles was 11.1. By further contrast, the youngest cohort of scientists, who entered the job market after 1980, had published an overall average of 14.3 papers.

The number of papers published by the scientists at the time of tenure also varied significantly over time, further highlighting intensification of the research role. To obtain tenure, the eldest cohort of scientists had published an overall average of 11.2 papers, the middle cohort 23.0, and the youngest cohort 32.0. At the time of their promotion to full professor, the eldest cohort of scientists had published an overall average of 21.1 papers, the middle cohort 41.5, and the youngest cohort 44.0. Put differently, younger cohorts of scientists typically published at a rate such that their productivity corresponded to a more advanced career stage characteristic of older scientists. Presumably academics did not engage in such a marked change in productivity out of a more intense love of science. The press for productivity intensified across

Table 8.2   Average publication productivity and event timing,
by cohort and organizational type

	Elites	Pluralists	Commu-nitarians	Overall average
Pre-1970 cohort				
Papers at 1st job	4.5	5.0	2.1	4.0
Papers at tenure	11.0	14.3	8.3	11.2
Papers at full prof.	22.0	24.3	17.0	21.1
Years to tenure	5.0	4.0	5.3	4.8
Years to full prof.	5.0	5.3	5.6	5.3
1970–80 cohort				
Papers at 1st job	15.0	11.3	7.0	11.1
Papers at tenure	29.0	24.3	14.4	23.0
Papers at full prof.	52.4	46.0	26.0	41.5
Years to tenure	3.4	4.5	5.2	4.4
Years to full prof.	7.0	5.3	5.0	5.8
Post-1980 cohort				
Papers at 1st job	20.0	12.0	11.0	14.3
Papers at tenure	46.0	26.0	24.0	32.0
Papers at full prof.	54.0	39.3	38.0	44.0
Years to tenure	7.0	5.2	5.3	5.8
Years to full prof.	5.0	4.8	6.0	5.3

Source: Hermanowicz 2009, tables 20, 23, and 26.

institutions, as apparent in the subgroup differences in table 8.2. Individuals changed in their behavior.

What is more, these productivity changes occurred in only modest changes in the time to tenure and to promotion to full professor. It took the eldest cohort of scientists an overall average of 4.8 years to achieve tenure. It took the middle cohort 4.4 years, and the youngest cohort 5.8 years. Thus, comparing the cohorts on the outer ends, the younger scientists published an overall average of 20.8 more papers prior to tenure compared to their eldest counterparts, and did so in only a one year greater span of time. A similar pattern is observed in time to promotion to full professor. For the eldest cohort it took an overall average of 5.3 years, for the middle 5.8 years, and for the youngest 5.3 years. Thus, at this juncture, strikingly different productivity patterns were established within roughly similar intervals of time. (It should be noted that the postdoctoral stage of scientific careers became institutionalized after the eldest cohort obtained their first academic positions. This also partly accounts for why one observes large productivity differences across the co-horts. However, it should also not be forgotten that while benefits may be derived from the stage, the stage itself points further to an additional set of hurdles on which subsequent career success is contingent.)

In light of these general conditions, how do academics perceive their careers and the quality of professional life in academe? Specific generalizations can be drawn about careers that represent the major distinctions across cohorts of academics in the three main organizational contexts. Twenty dimensions of academic careers surfaced from data analysis and coding to ground these com-parisons (see Hermanowicz 2009). I focus on three such dimensions—overall modal career patterns, overall satisfaction, and work attitudes—because they are the most overarching.

Overall modal career patterns. In passing from early to mid-career, elites stabilized and rededicated themselves to academe—to fulfilling the institu-tional goals of higher education by continuing in their research productivity. An individual put it in the following representative terms:

> The dream is to discover some fantastic new effect that knocks the socks off my friends and colleagues, that knocks the socks off the community, so that when I walk down the corridor, the young students know me and say, "There goes [Silverman], he invented the [Silverman] effect." That's what I want; I want my effect. I want to be the first person to predict such and such an event. (Hermanowicz 2009, 86–89)

By contrast, pluralists experienced a reversal. They questioned their inter-est and commitment to the profession. They grew disillusioned with academic research, as illustrated by the following scientist:

> My attitudes about the job, about me, and about the university have undergone tremendous changes in the past ten years. . . . I'm not sure I want to even submit things to published journals anymore. . . . I'm disgusted by the whole thing. . . . I got tired of getting referee reports . . . that spend a page talking about the bibliography; they were entirely concerned with whether I cited their work or their friends' work, and they hadn't read the paper. . . . I'm in a setting where the last thing people want is honesty. . . . You guys play your game; it's fine. There are more important things in life than getting grants from the National Science Foundation, getting Nobel Prizes even or any of that stuff. That's all just a game. (Hermanowicz 2009, 105)

By mid-career, most communitarians ceased in research. For communitarians, cumulative disadvantages accrued to the point of shutting down interest and motivation to continue in scientific research. Their career pattern may best be described as succumbing to a stasis—there was no forward progress. An academic, just at mid-career, said:

> I certainly have had a lot of distractions around here, and I think I could have been much more successful. . . . I think there's a lack of support, actually obstacles. I think there's been an orchestration of people not wanting people to succeed, not wanting to succeed in the department because there are things they can't do. I see it happen to other people. (Hermanowicz 2009, 119)

In their mid- to late career transitions, elites remained consistent in their identification with science and in their scientific productivity. Their publication productivity continued to accelerate. Pluralists either attempted to regenerate themselves following earlier fallow periods or continued in the research that they had been doing. Communitarians entered into a demise; they decreasingly identified with research. In ways consistent with the last passage above, they became increasingly disaffected with their departments and universities, which they saw as having crippled their research aspirations.

In moving from late to post career phases, elites for the first time lessened their intensity and embrace of research. Pluralists characteristically withdrew from work. Communitarians separated themselves completely from it, usually severing all ties with work and their employing organizations.

Overall satisfaction. Patterns in modal careers are in turn associated with patterns in satisfaction and in attitudes about work. Among elites, satisfaction begins high and rises through the career. It then drops at the end. Among pluralists, satisfaction starts out on a high, drops, and levels off. Finally, it rises at the end, coinciding with a time at which they withdraw from work. Among communitarians, there is a low in satisfaction throughout their careers, until the end. At the end of their careers, for the first time, communitarians experience the greatest high. Coincidentally, it is a time at which they are separating themselves altogether from work.

Work attitudes. Elites possessed positive attitudes toward their work throughout most of their careers. Only in the end do their attitudes turn ambivalent—about what they have done, how much they have achieved, and where they stand professionally. Unlike any previous period in their careers, there is a sense of regret and resignation about their efforts and what they have achieved. One academic put it in the following terms:

> Maybe there is some self-delusion in feeling that you're being a significant contributor to science. It's just [pause] you have been trained, you know this field, when you're an expert in something, you tend to take pride in it, and you tend to continue doing it. But I don't think it's always very significant in the grand scheme of things. . . . I could have worked harder to become a better professional physicist. . . . At some stages of my career, I could have easily done better. It would have made a difference. It might well have been a significant difference. . . . If I had worked harder, it would have given me a little more status. I would have accomplished more in the field (Hermanowicz 2009, 192–93).

Pluralists are, by turn, positive. Asked about a particular period in their careers thought to be the most positive, the following illustration was given:

> Now. This is it. Yes, absolutely. There's no question about it. . . . I'm a little older, and I've had the opportunity to look back and see how great it has been over the years, to see the whole career collectively and appreciate how lucky I've been to do all the things I have done. That's a good feeling, and it's like, wow, this has been great. (Hermanowicz 2009, 200)

Communitarians feel detached from work and institution. Their attitudes are far from the negative ones that were most common among them at earlier points in their careers.

> There really wasn't much else to look forward to. [Right now, I'm] not working as hard. I'm not doing research anymore. I had two or three pretty good ideas during the course of my career, and I haven't had any since. I really don't keep up with the literature. . . . I think early on, even though I did some fairly decent work, both as a graduate student and in the beginning of my career, I never was satisfied. I always thought that I could have done better or sooner or more. In more recent years [near and in retirement], I have become content, not only with what I was doing, but also how much. I think this is a reflection of my coming to like myself more. (Hermanowicz 2009, 207)

Diachronic change across the three prototypical academic organizations evinces *reversals*: reversals of career orientation, outlook, and attitude. Elites may be most dedicated throughout their careers, but most devastated at the end. Communitarians may be less dedicated throughout their careers, but most satisfied and positive in their outlooks at the end. Pluralists exemplify the greatest variability in their careers but in the end find a satisfaction that overcomes previous ambivalence. How might we account for these patterns? I argue that the answer is rooted in the contexts of work and draws on Durkheim's concept of anomie.

Anomie by Career Stage

Anomie and variation in its occurrence are observable across academic career stages. Variation in anomie by career stage stems from the dynamics underlying present and future expectations for careers. The findings presented in the preceding section suggest the following dynamics. Exposed to comparative wealth of professional opportunity and to cumulative advantages that promote productivity, elites successively heighten expectations for themselves and their careers. Achievement helps to create expectations for more achievement. At the end of the career, when greater achievement proves elusive, if only because of lack of time, but also often because of limits of ability, elites experience a reversal: they develop an ambivalence about work, deem their careers not to have progressed as expected, and find fault with the reward system of work that so vigorously directed their efforts over the preceding decades. For elites, it is at the end of their careers when divides between present and future wants are most felt.

Pluralists and communitarians also experience anomie. But they do so typically in earlier career stages, when it is possible in these organizational contexts to realize that their career expectations cannot be satisfied. Over many years, beginning in early and extending into mid-career stages, such expectations are abandoned or significantly modified. By the end, communitarians are, in Durkheim's words, "serene" ([1887] 1951). They are at greater peace with themselves and their careers than at any previous time, having achieved the detached attitude from work discussed earlier. While communitarians see failings of reward systems, they have withdrawn as participants. By the end of their careers, communitarians even see their careers as having progressed "as expected." In Durkheim's terms, "poverty" of their academic context protects them. Working in a "fixed society," with limited opportunity for recognition and advancement, communitarians develop limited aspirations because they know early on how much they can achieve.

Thus, the evidence suggests that, in a context of structural change, employing organizations trigger anomie at different times in an academic career.

They do so because gaps between present and future wants present themselves at systematically varying times across the organizations. In elite organizations, "dreams" of great attainment are sustainable, in part because of the concentration of high achievers, including, very occasionally, those who significantly alter the state of knowledge. A gap in wants appears late, as time elapses when the career is near its end. Gaps arise earlier in pluralist and still sooner in communitarian organizations. There are fewer examples of people and fewer professional opportunities to sustain a "dream of great attainment." Moreover, processes of cumulative disadvantage dampen motivation toward achievement and/or channel it toward other pursuits.

Anomie by Organizational Type

That anomie is traceable across varieties of higher education organizations is suggestive of the stress that varieties of universities have placed on research. The widespread embrace of research across varying institutional types itself indicates structural change in the profession (Birnbaum 1983; Morphew 2009). But given historic differences in the missions and identities of the various universities, it is plausible that anomie is more likely to arise unevenly among universities. What might be the logic underlying this dynamic?

"Mission creep" encompasses the increasingly widespread pattern wherein higher education institutions of various types mimic the American research university (Finnegan and Gamson 1996; Morphew 2002; Neave 1979). Institutions often engage in this process in order to garner greater rewards through research activity: federal and nonfederal funding, advanced degree programs, deeper pools of students and faculty, prestige, and so on. The process also entails change in institutional expectations for careers, leveraging a greater stress on research productivity. A variety of outcomes are likely generated, including a measure of the presumed benefits listed above. A proportion of faculty, existing and newly recruited, likely identify with such change, owing in part to career norms to which they were socialized in graduate and professional training.

But while such change may evince a positive net change in research opportunity among institutions, there is not necessarily congruency between expectations of individual academics and those of their employing organizations. In the sequence of events, two predominant situations are created. In one, older cohorts of faculty find themselves in the midst of mission change. Where their commitments were staked primarily in teaching, service, and comparatively modest research roles, the institution increasingly emphasizes research.

In the other situation, younger cohorts of faculty also find themselves in the midst of mission change. But their commitments are staked primarily in research to begin with, the relatively recent or new products of the intensified research enterprise in the American higher education system. In this situation, mission change cannot occur fast enough. Individual expectations exceed what prevailing opportunity structures can deliver. In the findings above, this situation was illustrated by a communitarian scientist who was motivated by research but perceived the local environment as stymieing.

Both situations create conditions of normlessness because expectations for the present fall out of alignment with an anticipated future. In the first situation, newly confronted high expectations in the present clash with more modest expectations for the future. In the second situation, high expectations in the present clash with future expectations that are higher still. Both are conducive to crisis brought about by a breakdown in the meaning individuals are able to interactively generate about a suitable career.

Furthermore, recognition for contributions to knowledge is by definition a scarce reward. The number of individuals in pursuit of such recognition increases as greater numbers of organizations emphasize research. Competition for recognition thus increases as the number of academics increase in pursuit of such a goal. Structurally, a greater proportion of "losers" is a potential outcome of the competition. A means by which this is translated individually is through anomie. Increased institutional emphases on research will likely be accompanied by increased individual probabilities of anomie throughout the system of higher education because of structural incapacities for individuals to realize goals.

Anomie by Scholarly Field

Anomie is detectable in the physicists who compose the study summarized here. It is not the case, however, that anomie is as equally likely to arise in one scholarly field as another. This is because expectations of career success vary by field. A line of work on codification in science and education provides an avenue by which to examine the possible dynamics of anomie by field. Codification refers to "the consolidation of empirical knowledge into succinct and interdependent theoretical formulations" (Merton and Zuckerman 1973, 507). Mature fields, such as physics and chemistry, are associated with relatively high codification. Less mature fields, such as sociology and education, are associated with relatively low codification.

An aspect of codification consists of consensus, the extent to which practitioners of a field agree: on problem choice, suitable theory, methods of research, and, arguably, definitions of career success. Accordingly, one would expect members of relatively high consensus fields to possess fairly clear definitions of success in their fields. Moreover, one would expect members of relatively low consensus fields to possess fairly weak definitions of success in their fields. Physicists who claim, for example, that members of the field can be ranked by achievement are testimony to high consensus. Members of other fields who claim that it would be difficult or impossible to rank practitioners by achievement provide evidence of low consensus.

By these dynamics, it is conceivable that members of high-consensus fields offer the clearest and strictest judgments of their peers' work and careers. By contrast, it is conceivable that members of low-consensus fields offer the vaguest and permissive judgments of their peers' work and careers. Consequently, one can argue that it is easier to satisfy expectations and enjoy a feeling of success in relatively low consensus fields, since success is defined in multiple ways. Individuals simply tailor their self-definitions to how their achievements correspond to one of the going collective definitions. Correspondingly, one can argue that it is more difficult to satisfy expectations and enjoy a feeling of success in relatively high consensus fields, since success is defined in more restricted ways. Success is defined collectively according to a more absolute scale.

Where is anomie likeliest to occur? Anomie is most likely to occur where the gulf between present conditions and future wants remains wide, and this seems most probable in high-consensus fields. Success is defined so strictly that expectations for recognition are more difficult to satisfy at all points along a career, thus creating fertile ground for anomie. In relatively low consensus fields, success is defined more loosely such that expectations for recognition can be satisfied in more numerous ways, making satisfaction more probable.

One should caution that low-consensus fields do not necessarily provide "safe havens" from anomie. Variety in the definitions of success corresponds to a prevailing variety of expectation. The multiplicity and concomitant ambiguity of expectation are themselves potentially problematic. Such ambiguity is also likely associated with weak solidarity and low confidence among members in a field (Hagstrom 1964). It is further possible that ambiguity of success norms creates confusion in the minds of individuals who, laboring in such fields, are unable to find a coherent structure within which to work over a long term. If almost all output in a field can count for something, one can question how meaningful it is to work in that field. Norms governing interaction and expectation may be insufficiently robust to establish clear indications of valued work. It remains an empirical matter to see whether, on balance, low-consensus fields provide more ample opportunity for satisfaction through the multiple channels of success that define them, or whether such multiple channels themselves create another ground for anomie.

Anomie by Historical Time

Warren Hagstrom's earlier work on anomie specified it as a condition of the marginal academic (1964, 1965). He understood anomie as a symptom of academics who work in highly arcane areas, where researchers are comparatively independent of one another and thus, he argued, more susceptible to having their work go unnoticed. In addition, Hagstrom suggested that anomie may have been more prevalent in early rather than in modern science and higher education because norms governing recognition were weaker, owing to a more loosely organized academic community.

The present work, however, finds contrasting patterns. Anomie is observed throughout academe, in both relatively marginal and integrated members of the profession. That is, it is observable among individuals highly as well as weakly committed to the institutional goal of academe—to contribute to the furtherance of knowledge production. Indeed, anomie could play a part in weakening professional commitment and in producing marginality.

What is more, while the field of physics may be considered arcane, it is highly collaborative. There are few independent researchers in this field. This is an indication of the field's maturity: the production of work requires the expertise of many minds. Whereas Hagstrom, basing his observations on mathematicians, speculated anomie more readily to arise in isolation, here it arises among company. Solo versus collaborative practice, then, does not appear to account for the likelihood of anomie's occurrence.

Moreover, whereas Hagstrom, like Durkheim, asserted that anomie is more typically found in early eras as a result of a weakness of norms, the present work suggests that anomie is as likely to arise when, in modern times, organizational press for recognition is so strong that prevailing norms are not strong enough to deliver on the expectation. At both points in time, norms are weak in absolute terms. Even as a community develops, however, and as its norms strengthen, divisions between present and future expectations can outstrip a structure's capacity to endow individuals with meaning.

Anomie and Academe as a Profession

Anomie is a pathology of organizations and institutions and is transmitted and experienced as a pathology in individuals. As a pathology, anomie may also serve as an indication of social conditions, a testament of the times in which human beings find themselves. Following Durkheim, I have suggested that anomie is apt to arise in periods of major structural change, and I have outlined ways in which anomie may express itself across careers, organizations, fields, and time, as the American academic profession experiences transformational shifts in the contemporary age. Because anomie is a pathology, it stands to reason that the consequences that it entails for the status of academe as a profession should be considered.

The consequences do not appear favorable. A general sociological principle holds that dissatisfaction is produced by conditions wherein present wants exceed what social structures can confer. A quest for recognition has intensified in the academic profession. This is explainable by the development of the research role throughout academe. As research is more greatly stressed, career expectations rise in accord with attempting to satisfy organizational demands. As expectations rise, the likelihood of satisfying them decreases. These conditions favor dissatisfaction and disaffection for the academic career, much as was found in the evidence from academics in this study.

Deviance has typically constituted an adaptive strategy to dissatisfaction in general and to anomie in particular. Merton outlined strategies individuals use to overcome the obstacles posed by their situations when wants exceed the means to acquire them ([1957] 1968). In the case of academe, aside from conforming to professional goals, individuals may engage in *retreatism*, withdrawing from creative work by renouncing both the goals and means of performing academic work. Retreatists may embrace alternative forms of reward in academic systems, such as in teaching or administration. Individuals may engage in *ritualism*, continuing perfunctorily in research but not believing in its ends, a renunciation of the goals but not the means of performing academic work. Ritualists may continue in modest research to benefit salary growth, for example, aware of the annual quota necessary to satisfy an organizational threshold. Individuals may engage in *innovation*, remaining committed to the achievement of recognition but attempting to garner it through illicit ways, a renunciation of the means but not the goals of performing academic work. Innovators may plagiarize the work of others, attempting to gain credit for accomplishment where recognition is not due. Finally, individuals may engage in *rebellion*, continuing to work, but by standards different from their main scholarly community. Rebels may reject the standards by which their work is judged in their professional community and insist on their own criteria to assess the importance of their work (see also Hagstrom 1964, 1965).

Aside from the forms of deviance, the present conditions of academe appear to favor a decline in the attractiveness of the academic career. Who wants to perform work in an environment where many of their expectations cannot be satisfied? On many objective criteria, chances of success in academe across many fields are low and, where achieved, are hard-fought. Obtaining regular employment, obtaining tenure, obtaining promotion through standard ranks, publication, citation of work, competitive salary and competitive salary growth—all of these are arguably more difficult to obtain than in any other historical time in the profession.

In his book *The Cost of Talent*, Derek Bok (1994) raised related concerns. Bok argued that a decline in earnings by academics, relative to other professions such as medicine, law, and business, would discourage the most talented people from entering PhD programs and thus academe. In the interim, academic employment conditions have worsened; the probability of obtaining a tenure-track position is considerably lower. It is therefore not surprising that the share of PhDs granted to American citizens at U.S. universities keeps decreasing in many fields (National Opinion Research Center 2009–10).

At stake on the one hand are individual satisfaction and moral commitment. These are significant stakes. When compromised, the institutional goals of the profession fail to be served. On the other hand, the overall welfare and functioning of the profession are at stake. The present work prompts the question of what types of people, with what levels of talent, the academic profession will be able to attract.

One scenario is that the profession will attract less talented individuals. More talented individuals, seeing the conditions under which academic careers are experienced, may increasingly enter other professions. It is conceivable that less talented individuals would possess lower expectations for achievement, thus muting the effects of anomie and leaving them more contented with work and the profession "more stable" at a reduced performance threshold. But at such a reduced performance threshold, the net quality of academic work would decline. Public value assigned to the profession would erode further. This effect would also have to overcome the processes of induction, training, and socialization that are aimed at inculcating moral commitment and associated high levels of expectations, as well as organizational and professional norms that press for productivity.

A remedy is for change to bring about greater alignment between present and future expectations. Such a remedy eludes the present times. Increasingly, this institutional problem appears left to the minds of individuals to sort out, which may rarely constitute an effective coping strategy. Structural conditions appear to have developed to create an enduring social problem of anomie in the American academic profession.

REFERENCES

Baldwin, Roger G., and Jay L. Chronister. 2001. *Teaching without tenure: Policies and practices for a new era.* Baltimore: Johns Hopkins University Press.

Bayer, Alan E., and Jeffrey E. Dutton. 1977. Career age and research-professional activities of academic scientists. *Journal of Higher Education* 48:259–82.

Birnbaum, Robert. 1983. *Maintaining diversity in higher education.* San Francisco: Jossey-Bass.

Bok, Derek. 1994. *The cost of talent: How executives and professionals are paid and how it affects America.* New York: Free Press.

Burgan, Mary. 2006. *What ever happened to the faculty? Drift and decision in higher education.* Baltimore: Johns Hopkins University Press.

Chism, Nancy Van Note. 2006. Teaching awards: What do they award? *Journal of Higher Education* 77:589–617.

Clemente, Frank. 1973. Early career determinants of research productivity. *American Journal of Sociology* 79:409–19.

Cole, Jonathon R., and Stephen Cole. 1973. *Social stratification in science.* Chicago: University of Chicago Press.

Cole, Stephen. 1979. Age and scientific performance. *American Journal of Sociology* 84:958–77.

DiPrete, Thomas A., and Gregory M. Eirich. 2006. Cumulative advantage as a mechanism for inequality: A review of theoretical and empirical developments. *Annual Review of Sociology* 32:271–97.

Durkheim, Emile. [1893] 1984. *The division of labor in society.* Introduction by Lewis Coser. Trans. W. D. Halls. New York: Free Press.

———. [1897] 1951. *Suicide.* Trans. John A. Spalding and George Simpson. New York: Free Press.

Finkelstein, Martin J., Robert K. Seal, and Jack H. Schuster. 1998. *The new academic generation: A profession in transformation.* Baltimore: Johns Hopkins University Press.

Finnegan, D. E., and Z. F. Gamson. 1996. Disciplinary adaptations to research culture in comprehensive institutions. In *Faculty and faculty issues in colleges and universities,* 2nd ed., ed. D. E. Finnegan, D. E. Webster, and Z. F. Gamson, 476–98. ASHE Reader Series. Needham Heights, MA: Simon and Schuster Custom Publishing.

Frank, David John, and Jay Gabler. 2006. *Reconstructing the university: Worldwide shifts in academia in the 20th century.* Stanford: Stanford University Press.

Garland, James C. 2009. *Saving alma mater: A rescue plan for America's public universities.* Chicago: University of Chicago Press.

Geiger, Roger L. 1999. The ten generations of American higher education. In *Higher education in the twenty-first century,* ed. Robert O. Berdahl, Philip G. Altbach, and Patricia J. Gumport, 38–69. Baltimore: Johns Hopkins University Press.

Goldberger, Marvin L., Brendan A. Maher, and Pamela Ebert Flattau, eds. 1995. *Research-doctorate programs in the United States: Continuity and change.* Washington, DC: National Academy Press.

Gustin, Bernard H. 1973. Charisma, recognition, and the motivation of scientists. *American Journal of Sociology* 78:1119–34.

Hagstrom, Warren O. 1964. Anomy in scientific communities. *Social Problems* 12:186–95.

———. 1965. *The scientific community.* New York: Basic.

Hermanowicz, Joseph C. 1998. *The stars are not enough: Scientists—their passions and professions.* Chicago: University of Chicago Press.

———. 2009. *Lives in science: How institutions affect academic careers.* Chicago: University of Chicago Press.

Jones, Lyle V., Gardner Lindzey, and Porter E. Coggeshall, eds. 1982. *An assessment of research-doctorate programs in the United States: Mathematical and physical sciences.* Washington, DC: National Academy Press.

Merton, Robert K. [1957] 1968. Social structure and anomie. In *Social theory and social structure,* ed. Robert K. Merton, 185–214. New York. Free Press.

———. 1973a. The normative structure of science. In *The sociology of science: Theoretical and empirical investigations,* ed. Norman W. Storer, 267–78. Chicago: University of Chicago Press. Article first published in 1942.

———. 1973b. Priorities in scientific discovery. In *The sociology of science: Theoretical and empirical investigations,* ed. Norman W. Storer, 286–324. Chicago: University of Chicago Press. Article first published in 1957.

———. 1973c. *The sociology of science: Theoretical and empirical investigations.* Ed. Norman W. Storer. Chicago: University of Chicago Press.

Merton, Robert K., and Harriet Zuckerman. 1973. Age, aging, and age structure in science. In *The sociology of science: Theoretical and empirical investigations*, ed. Norman W. Storer, 497–559. Chicago: University of Chicago Press. Article first published in 1972.

Morphew, Christopher C. 2002. "A rose by any other name": Which colleges became universities. *Review of Higher Education* 25:207–23.

———. 2009. Conceptualizing change in the institutional diversity of U.S. colleges and universities. *Journal of Higher Education* 80:243–69.

National Opinion Research Center. 2009–10. *Survey of earned doctorates*. Chicago: National Opinion Research Center.

Neave, Guy. 1979. Academic drift: Some views from Europe. *Studies in Higher Education* 4:143–59.

Rhoades, Gary. 1998. *Managed professionals: Unionized faculty and restructuring academic labor*. Albany: State University of New York Press.

Riley, Matilda White, Marilyn Johnson, and Anne Foner. 1972. *Aging and society*. Vol. 3, *A sociology of age stratification*. New York: Russell Sage Foundation.

Schuster, Jack H., and Martin J. Finkelstein. 2006. *The American faculty: The restructuring of academic work and careers*. Baltimore: Johns Hopkins University Press.

Thelin, John R. 2004. *A history of American higher education*. Baltimore: Johns Hopkins University Press.

Tuchman, Gaye. 2009. *Wannabe U: Inside the corporate university*. Chicago: University of Chicago Press.

Zuckerman, Harriet. 1977. *Scientific elite: Nobel laureates in the United States*. New York: Free Press.

———. 1988. Sociology of science. In *Handbook of sociology*, ed. Neil J. Smelser, 511–74. Newbury Park, CA: Sage.

PART IV

Autonomy and Regulation

CHAPTER NINE

Academic Freedom, Professional Autonomy, and the State

Sheila Slaughter

In the United States, academic freedom is generally understood as professorial ability to follow research where it leads and to communicate the results, whether through publications, in research forums, in the classroom, or to the public. Academic freedom is the cornerstone of academic expertise, which is central to professional autonomy and authority. The tacit social contract between professors and society allows faculty to engage freely in research in return for the fruits of research that enhance the public good.

However, academic freedom is to some degree dependent on the political climate and various state agencies, ranging from the courts to public colleges and universities, as well as on the business community's concern with preserving pro-business ideas, such as managerial authority over professional workers (Feaga and Zirkel 2006; Furner 1975; Jorgensen and Helms 2008; Veblen 1918). This essay explores recent shifts in politics that have produced changes in the organization of the state in order to understand what they mean for academic freedom. The "state" is not uniform; it varies within and among agencies and across levels (federal, state, local) and jurisdictions (i.e., different federal court circuits). Some state agencies are decidedly neoliberal (i.e., the Federal Reserve Board), while others remain liberal (i.e., the Social Security Administration) and still others are socially conservative (i.e., faith-based welfare and education programs). The various state agencies take different forms (i.e., liberal, neoliberal, socially conservative) when their policies are changed, usually through political-legal actions that alter rules and practices (i.e., the shift within the Federal Reserve from liberal regulation to neoliberal deregulation, or the shift in public higher education from liberal low tuition to neoliberal high tuition). Although the general direction of change is from liberal to neoliberal, change is uneven and inconsistent, and agencies can reverse direction, as we are currently seeing with the Federal Reserve's response to the current economic crisis.

The political turn toward the free market and neoliberalism[1] has created opportunities for universities to engage in entrepreneurial activity through new state forms characterized by public-private interaction that blur boundaries among public, non-profit, and for-profit activity. University and faculty entrepreneurism presents challenges to professorial norms and values when it puts profit before discovery, chooses secrecy with regard to intellectual property over openness, and makes decisions without consulting with faculty via governance mechanisms. At the same time, social conservatives,[2] perhaps in response to the changes wrought by the materialism promoted by free markets and the possibilities for social change created by the knowledge economy, for example, by stem cell research, have pressured the state for legislative and administrative rules and regulations that promote socially conservative values such as the teaching of intelligent design or curtailment of research on a variety of forms of sexuality, posing challenges to professors' academic freedom. Of course, neoliberalism does not pervade all state agencies; some remain liberal. Among those are agencies such as the Federal Bureau of Investigation and the Central Intelligence Agency, which have expanded greatly in the wake of 9/11. In much the same way as they monitored citizens thought to be involved with Communism during the Cold War, these established agencies work with new agencies created in response to the War on Terror, such as Homeland Security, to monitor citizens suspected of involvement with the Evil Empire. As was the case with the Cold War, the War on Terror has created a number of challenges for academic freedom, ranging from the right of professors to admit qualified students to their research programs based on the students' place of origin to professors' ability to engage in critique of foreign policy. In sum, recent political movements have unevenly altered the state, changing policies and practices in different branches and at various levels, creating new challenges for academic freedom.

I explore three cases that illuminate the complex relationship between academic freedom, politics, and the state in the early twenty-first century: the *UC Berkley–Novartis* case (*Novartis*), the *Urofsky v. Gilmore* (*Urofsky*) decision emanating from several Virginia universities, and the *Ward Churchill* (*Churchill*) case at the University of Colorado. The *Novartis* case illuminates the issues raised for academic freedom by entrepreneurial neoliberal state formations taking root in research universities. The *Urofsky* decision brings to the fore questions about the ways in which social conservatism, embodied in state laws, prevents professors from researching topics that are morally sensitive, while simultaneously strengthening the power of institutions, as represented by the administration. The *Churchill* case speaks to the ways in which security concerns play out in universities and governing boards during times of war, regardless of state form, severely challenging academic freedom in the United States.

Background

Academic freedom was defined by the American Association of University Professors (AAUP) in its 1940 Statement of Principles as "the free search for truth and its free exposition," justified because disinterested knowledge is necessary to "the common good" (AAUP 1995a). Academic freedom in research and teaching is inextricably linked to tenure. According to the AAUP, tenure provides protection for the written word and speech as well as economic security, the necessary corollary of freedom. With these "rights" come responsibilities: professors should not introduce controversy in the classroom unrelated to their subjects, and when speaking as private citizens "they should at all times be accurate, should exercise appropriate restraint, should show respect for the opinion of others, and should make every effort to indicate that they are not speaking for their institution" (AAUP 1995a). Academic freedom gives faculty a degree of professional autonomy vis-à-vis their institutional employers, whether the state, in the case of public institutions, or nonprofit boards of trustees, in the case of private institutions.

Over time, the AAUP definition of academic freedom has become the standard formulation, shared by the National Education Association and the American Federation of Teachers as well as many learned societies and professional associations. Many colleges and universities have adopted policies and procedures promoted by the AAUP to protect academic freedom. These are seen most clearly in personnel policies—specifically hiring, promotion and tenure, evaluation and dismissal of professors—that embed the Principles in university policy by allowing senior faculty to decide who should be hired, who merits tenure, or, should the possibility of tenure revocation arise, who should be dismissed. These personnel policies, however, are advisory, and final authority rests with senior administrators and regents or boards of trustees.

A separate but related aspect of the AUUP's approach to academic freedom is encompassed by academic governance. As the AAUP notes, "a sound system of institutional governance is a necessary condition for the protection of faculty rights" (AAUP 1995b, 179–86). The AAUP states that the areas in which faculty should have "primary responsibility" are teaching and research. However, the AAUP also makes the case that faculty must have a strong voice in "decisions about the institution's long-range objectives, its physical and fiscal resources, the distribution of its funds among its various divisions, and the selection of its president," precisely because these have such a powerful impact on professional autonomy in the areas of teaching and research (AAUP 1995b, 187).

The AAUP was organized in 1915 to protect professional norms and values in the face of dismissals of faculty from universities at the behest of heads of large corporations, university donors, and state officials and legislators (Metzger 1969). The AAUP acts as an extralegal body that attempts to enforce the Statement of Principles through investigating violations and censuring universities that deviate from the Principles. The investigative reports it produces serve as a body of extralegal case law. The AAUP has no formal legal authority, and the success of its censorship activity is mixed. Generally, the AAUP attempts to ensure that due process is followed. Many colleges and universities have established academic senates or other deliberative bodies, but academic governance at best advises university administrations, at worst legitimates administrative decision making (Slaughter 1994). Despite initiation of an investigatory capacity with regard to academic governance, AAUP governance practices have not been as widely institutionalized as the Declaration of Principles. Perhaps that is because the Principles are confined to due process with regard to personnel policies, while governance has the potential to shape institutional decision making in many other areas, including future planning and investment.

Although the AAUP insists that the U.S. Supreme Court has recognized a constitutional right to academic freedom, it is perhaps more accurate to say that the Court has acknowledged academic freedom on some occasions, but academic freedom has not been well clarified and has never been dispositive.[3] As Byrne remarks about academic freedom, "lacking definition or guiding principle, the doctrine floats in the law, picking up decisions as a hull does barnacles" (1989). Or as a *Harvard Law Review* article on recent cases put it, "Although the Supreme Court has identified academic freedom as a 'special concern of the First Amendment,' it has yet to articulate a coherent analytic framework for protecting that concern" (2002).

The AAUP's definition and defense of academic freedom represent codified versions of professional norms and values with regard to teaching and research. At the same time, academic freedom and governance serve as a bulwark of professional autonomy in that they constrain institutional decision making by administrative fiat that might jeopardize professors' authority with regard to teaching and research. However, as the Fourth Circuit Court of Appeals has pointed out, the AAUP's definition of academic freedom represents a norm, not a law or a "right," and remains vulnerable to politico-legal shifts that are embodied in the administrative state, including public research universities (*Urofsky v. Gilmore* 2000).

Approach

The cases selected for examination are not representative of post-2000 cases considered by the AAUP (Slaughter 1981, 1988), nor are they representative of post-2000 legal cases that deal with academic freedom (Baez and Slaughter 2001; Feaga and Zirkel 2006). Rather, they were selected to represent challenges to academic freedom stemming from changing state formations.

The *Novartis* case at Berkeley was reported by an impartial team hired by the University of California to investigate the relationship between Berkeley and Novartis, a biotechnology company.[4] The *Churchill* case at the University of Colorado was reported by the Standing Committee on Research Misconduct at the University of Colorado–Boulder (Wesson et al. 2006). Interpretation of *Urofsky* is made from the legal documents related to the case (*Urofsky v. Gilmore* 2000). Perhaps because of the complexity of the issues and the professorial turn to litigation, the AAUP investigated none of the cases.

Although I may speak about a state agency—for example, the University of California—the levels and laws are often recursive, with federal laws and agencies feeding into state administrative law and agency policy. In the *Novartis* case, for example, national competitiveness laws (Slaughter and Rhoades 1996) and federal mission agency funding, informed and facilitated actions at the state level, and state administrative law operationalized federal laws and policies, as with university intellectual property policies that concretized Bayh-Dole. So too, the political tendencies and movements discussed, while distinct, are not always separate.

University of California–Berkeley and the *Novartis* Case

The *Novartis* case illustrates how free-market politics resulted in legislation that reshaped state agencies to emphasize neoliberal characteristics that allowed state actors, among them faculty, to respond to new incentive structures, some of which challenge the historic academic incentives of discovery, publication, and prestige, creating challenges to academic freedom.

In 1993, Berkeley administrators responsible for strategic planning in biotechnology decided they wanted to increase industry investment substantially. The chair of Plant and Microbial Biology (PMB) worked to realize this by creating an International Biotechnology Advisory Board, which included fourteen representatives from industry. These initial results did not bear fruit, and the chair of PMB put together a small group of administrators (himself, another professor, the head of cooperative extension, and the dean of the College of Natural Resources) and approached the Office of Technology Licensing for advice on how to obtain private funding. The group had "at least the tacit approval of the highest administrators within the UC Office of the President" (Busch et al. 2004, 23). Together they agreed to a process of "auctioning" the department to the highest private bidder and sent a letter "announcing the availability of PMB expertise . . . to sixteen selected companies" (Busch et al. 2004, 24). Five replied, and Novartis Agricultural Discovery Institute (NADI), a wholly owned entity of Novartis, won the bid.

Like other corporations in agricultural biotechnology, Novartis sought to identify and utilize genes that would contribute to plants' insect resistance and herbicide tolerance as well as create or enhance valuable traits in plants. Novartis was a latecomer to the field and sought to use NADI as "the Bell Labs of plant biotechnology" (Busch et al. 2004, 26), which PMB researchers found reassuring. Generally, the agreement called for Novartis to spend $5 million a year on PMB for five years.[5]

Negotiations occurred in a thirty-day time frame and were open neither to the public nor to the Berkeley community. Those outside the PMB faculty, including graduate students, were unable to view the emerging contract. The agreement was with PMB as a whole and granted Novartis

> right of first negotiation on an exclusive license to commercial research conducted by signers of the agreement; the agreement gave Novartis the option to exercise that right on a portion of the results equal to the percentage of exter-

nal research funding that it provided. The right of first negotiation applied to all research conducted by signatories of the agreement, regardless of whether Novartis funded that research or not, with the exception of DOE and funding from other private parties. In other words, if funds from Novartis constituted one-third of PMB external research funding, Novartis got the first right of negotiation to one-third of all PMB discoveries, including research funded by the National Institutes of Health (NIH), the National Science Foundation, and other public institutions. (Busch et al. 2004, 50)

Although the agreement with the department as a whole was unusual, it was not unprecedented.[6] The leverage Novartis exercised on other external funds in PMB was unprecedented, but otherwise the agreement fell within evolving norms of university-industry partnerships.[7]

The agreement was negotiated over the summer when few faculty members were around. In August, the dean of the College of Natural Resources, perhaps anticipating opposition, contacted the Academic Senate about the impending agreement, even though Berkeley policies do not require Senate approval of contracts with industry. As faculty and students returned in the fall, opposition emerged. Students for Responsible Research began to organize against the agreement, and the Senate outlined its concerns. In November 1998, the Senate took the position that it could not endorse the agreement and requested that it be treated as an experiment and that ongoing assessment of its impact be undertaken. Despite the Senate's reservations, on November 23, 1998, the agreement was formally signed, marred only by a member of Students for Responsible Research throwing a pie at the signatories.

About the time that the Novartis agreement was finalized, indirect ties between the dean of the College of Natural Resources and Novartis came to light. In 1988, Professor Gordon Rausser, dean when the Novartis agreement was made with PMB, founded the Law and Economics Consulting Group (LECG) with several other Berkeley faculty members. Congruent with Berkeley policy, Rausser stayed on as a principal in LECG while he was dean, including the period when the Novartis agreement was negotiated.

LECG had ties to the forerunners of Novartis. . . . In 1996, Rausser earned $1.3 million from LECG, significantly more than his salary as Dean. The company followed by an Initial Public Offering on December 19, 1997, at which Rausser planned to sell 16 percent of his shares for $2.2 million. . . . Finally, less than one year later LECG was acquired by the Metzler Group for $200 million. (Busch et al. 2004, 48)

Although a Committee of the California State Legislature, headed by Senator Tom Hayden, held a hearing on the Berkeley-Novartis agreement on May 15, 2000, nothing came of it. Berkeley commissioned an external study of the Berkeley-Novartis agreement, which did not get underway until early 2003 (Busch et al. 2004, 26). The PMB's agreement expired on November 23, 2003. It was not renewed because Novartis had been taken over by Syngenta, an agricultural chemical company based in Basel, Switzerland, that was not interested in basic plant bioscience.

The Novartis-Berkeley agreement did not produce the intellectual property expected. Of fifty-one disclosures made by PMB faculty during the period of the agreement, twenty were patented. Ten of these patents were derived at least partially from funding provided by the Novartis-Berkeley agreement. Novartis expressed interest in six, but no options for exclusive licenses were exercised (Busch et al. 2004, 13).

The agreement exacerbated tensions within the College of Natural Resources and generated issues related to academic freedom. The College of Natural Resources was divided between faculty who favored productivity—enhanced crop production based on pesticides, insecticides, herbicides, and increasingly on biotechnology—and faculty who favored preservation of the natural environment and sustainability. Departments other than PMB were not included in the negotiations, but the dean extended the agreement to the College as a whole in the final negotiations. Many faculty not in PMB objected, particularly those in Environmental Science, Policy and Management (ESPM), a department committed to the natural environment and sustainability.

Ignacio Chapela was an assistant professor who was chair of the College Executive Committee, a member of ESPM, and an outspoken critic of the Novartis agreement. In 2001, he and a coauthor published an article in *Nature* "alleging that native maize landraces in Oaxaca, Mexico, contained introgressed transgenic deoxyribonucleic acid (DNA) constructs" and that these transgenes were unstable, which might lead to the destruction of local varieties of maize that would reduce the gene pool for future generations (Busch et al. 2004, 41). The article became the center of controversy, in which corporations weighed in against environmentalists. Academics in PMB, site of the Novartis agreement, sided with the corporations. As the controversy continued, *Nature* distanced itself from the article, undermining its credibility (Busch et al. 2004, 41).

Chapela was up for tenure during this period and was supported through all the steps of the review up to the university level. The chair of Chapela's committee asked that there be no one who was party to the Novartis agreement on the committee because PMB professors had led the public critique of Chapela's work. However, one of the professors on the university-level committee was also a member of the Novartis Advisory Committee. A number of people, including the dean of the College of Natural Resources, objected on conflict-of-interest grounds. The chancellor argued there was no conflict and the PMB professor on the Advisory Board stayed. Chapela was denied tenure at the university level, and despite appeals, the chancellor concurred.[8] Chapela responded by moving his office onto the lawn outside California Hall, which housed the offices of the Budget Committee of the Academic Senate, responsible for the university-level decision in his case, and the office of Chancellor Robert Berdahl, who had the final say. Chapela held office hours and spoke about what had happened (Tonak 2004). When the decision against Chapela was finally delivered, hundreds of letters, many from academics, flooded the Chancellor's office. Chapela chronicled the case on his Web site and also initiated a lawsuit against Berkeley for damages and injunctive relief.

According to the brief, posted on Chapela's Web site,[9]

> Dr. Chapela personally opposed the Novartis agreement and became a public leader of organized opposition to it. He asserted that the agreement was improperly negotiated in secrecy, that it was detrimental to the university's traditions of academic freedom and disinterested inquiry, that it resulted in the misuse of university resources, that faculty members and administrators who performed work under the agreement were subject to conflicts of interest under University policy, and that the fruits of the agreement could cause harm to the environment, to native plants, and to people's health and welfare throughout the world.

On May 17, 2005, a new Berkeley chancellor had Chapela's case reconsidered by a specially reconstituted budget committee, the standing nine-member panel of the Academic Senate, which has the final vote on tenure cases, and he was granted tenure (UC Berkeley News 2005).

A related case occurred outside the College of Natural Resources. Tyrone Hayes, an associate professor of Integrative Biology in the College of Letters and Sciences, worked for Ecorisk Inc., studying how the herbicide atrazine affected amphibians. Syngenta, which took over Novartis, funded Ecorisk. Syngenta and Ecorisk had the right to approve or deny publication of the research they sponsored. When Hayes tried to publish results that showed that frogs were physiologically affected by low levels of the drug, Syngenta and Ecorisk tried to stall and prevent publication. After he stopped working for Syngenta and Ecorisk, Hayes began to self-fund and publish his findings (Busch et al. 2004, 43). Although he published in journals such as *Nature*, his work was attacked by "Syngenta, the Kansas Corn Growers Association, a Fox News commentator known for minimizing the potential threat of global warming, and the Center for Regulatory Effectiveness, an organization based in Washington that is challenging the use of academic studies in federal rule making" (Blumenstyk 2003, 2).

Although Berkeley did accept Hayes's initial contract with Sygenta and Ecorisk, despite the confidentiality clause, it has not penalized Hayes. The Hayes case attracted a great deal of media attention, and while there were many attacks on Hayes's work by figures associated with the herbicide industry, he also received a great deal of support, and the quality of his work was affirmed when he won heavily refereed NSF funding. Although the EPA approved atrizine, it called for further studies, drawing upon the work of Hayes and that of other scientists that showed that small doses affected male frogs' sexual development. The EPA is requiring Syngenta to conduct further studies on the effects of atrazine on amphibians.

The issues that the *Novartis* case raises for academic freedom are (1) creation of new circuits of knowledge that link the academy to the economy; (2) development of an administrative preference for science and technology able to generate external revenues, which undermines academic autonomy and credibility and threatens institutional potential for critique; and (3) weakening of faculty self-governance, which underpins the exercise of academic freedom on campus. These issues arose as a result of the University of California acting on opportunities provided by a neoliberal state to shift the boundaries between the public and private sector, creating new opportunities for external funding and enhanced prestige for some faculty and research programs and not others.

The agreement between PMB and Novartis was made possible by the rise of the competitiveness coalition, beginning in the 1980s, through which a vigorous legislative initiative opened federally funded research performed in universities to faculty; institutional and corporate exploitation through university provision of incentives to faculty for patentable discoveries; university ownership of patents; university exploitation of patents through licensing; and faculty and university administrators working together to create start-up companies (Slaughter and Rhoades 2004). The opportunities presented by this legislation and the growth of a knowledge economy drew a number of faculty in a wide variety of departments toward entrepreneurial research.[10] In the Novartis agreement, PMB faculty, not corporations, initiated the search for corporate funding; faculty, not corporations, came up with the idea of "auctioning" the department. A segment of the Berkeley faculty and the administration pursued marketization opportunities opened up by shifts toward neoliberal principles in law and state and institutional policies.[11]

Competitiveness legislation increased the porosity of boundaries between the public and private sector, altering circuits of knowledge. Rather than valuing discoveries as judged by professional and scientific associations, some faculty and university administrators began to prefer discoveries with market potential as judged by business leaders, policy makers, and politicians seeking a high technology path to economic development. Taking a company public, as did Dean Rausser with LECG, signifies the new circuits of knowledge in which professors are simultaneously business persons and professors. Generally, professors who occupy both roles simultaneously do so based on the strength of their university expertise. However, the profits they make under the changed rules of the neoliberal state are individual. Great personal gain derived by professors in public research universities undermines their credibility and authority as experts. For example, Len Richardson, editor of *California Farmer*, acknowledged that Berkeley policy allows faculty members up to 48 days per year of paid outside activity but asked in regard to LECG, "Can you build a $30 million business on 48 free days? Is the good name and reputation of UC becoming a faculty profit center?" (Busch et al. 2004, 48).

As segments of the professoriate align themselves with the market and make great personal gains from the synergy between their university work and their corporate endeavors, their claims about the need for buffers from external pressures ring less true, undermining their historic stance as disinterested scientists and experts, which is the foundation on which the claim of academic freedom rests.

Despite neoliberal rhetoric, faculty members are not free agents. To enter the Novartis agreement, they had to work closely with Berkeley administrators, from the PBM department head and College of Natural Resources dean up through the chancellor and the president. At all levels, administrators favored the Novartis agreement. They were able to bring it to fruition because the administrative capacity of universities has greatly expanded in the past twenty-five years, to the point where universities are capable of engaging in almost any form of market activity (Slaughter and Rhoades 2004). The participation of the Office of Technology Licensing was emblematic of new administrative structures developed to support public-private partnerships. When the dean and the faculty wanted to secure support from corporations, they turned to administrative personnel already in place. The head of Cooperative Extension worked with the group, demonstrating the shift of public service function of land grant universities from service-for-free to offering service-for-fees (Slaughter and Rhoades 1993, 287–312).

The Novartis agreement points to the increasing power that administrators have to decide the research agenda of universities. Administrative support is essential for new directions in research, given the expenditures required for infrastructure such as facilities and equipment. The Novartis agreement brought funds to PMB, including substantial indirect cost recovery. As the external evaluation noted, the Berkeley administration has shown a preference for research initiatives perceived as likely to enhance external revenue flows, exhibiting a neoliberal preference for commercial solutions to public problems.

The opposite side of the coin is Berkeley's reluctance to invest in or support those departments, centers, or institutes critical of university-industry partnerships around biotechnology. Berkeley administrators turned down requests by ESPM to develop sustainable urban agriculture projects that were unlikely to increase external revenue flows. Berkeley initially turned down the assistant professor who vocally criticized Novartis and field trials of genetically altered crops.

In interviews the PMB faculty said they looked for external corporate funding because they needed an infusion of resources to put their research program in the top tier. Increased funding for research was what they valued most about the Novartis agreement. Conventional wisdom suggests that faculty members are driven into the arms of industry by decreases in funding. However, funding for research at elite research universities *increased* steadily from the mid-1990s until the present.

Since 1990, inflation-adjusted Federal dollars for academic R&D have grown continuously, increasing by about 66 percent through 2002. Real support to all other sectors declined during the decade, rebounding from its 2002 low but still contracting by about 14 percent over the period. (National Science Board 2004, 3)

In other words, academic R&D was a *preferred* social investment because such investment was deemed central to building a knowledge-based economy. Similarly, institutional funds committed to research have risen, now accounting for 20 percent of all funds (NSF 2007). After a half century of increase, institutional funds are now the second largest source of funding for academic R&D, topped only by the federal government (NSF 2007). PMB at Berkeley shared in these increased streams of research funds (NSF 2004).

Berkeley's and PMB's conception of themselves as lacking research funding suggests that they have embraced a neoliberal conception of unrelenting competition, under which resources, no matter how abundant, are never sufficient. If this is the case, research universities and departments and faculty within them that are able to intersect public and private research markets are likely to expand their efforts to do so. The ability of some departments, centers, and institutes to generate large amounts of external resources while others cannot, or will not, exacerbates divisions within universities.

Berkeley policies facilitated the Novartis agreement. Faculty were allowed to hold positions on corporate boards of start-up companies based on their intellectual property, to serve as CEOs of such firms, or to serve on advisory boards to such firms.[12] These rules are frequently spelled out in intellectual property policies, which are usually crafted by professors and administrators involved in university-industry activity. Intellectual property policies in general follow a neoliberal trajectory, allowing professors and institutions, as well as the corporations with which they partner, to use public resources as the basis for individual and institutional economic gain. Theoretically, professors, institutions, and society are the winners, but few studies carefully trace the returns to the citizenry.

Faculty members have not been able to exercise much control over these developments. Berkeley is often held up as an example of an institution with a strong faculty voice in university affairs, a position allegedly strengthened by Berkeley's constitutional status. However, effective self-governance assumes some unity among faculty with regard to norms, values, and the directions the university should take. There have been few studies of faculty senate voting patterns, so the degree of division among faculty, likely to be heightened in times of change, is unknown, as is the number of cases when the administration overrides a divided faculty. In other words, a strong faction backed by the administration might be able to implement policies of which a large number of professors might not approve.

Regardless of the unity of the Berkeley faculty, the senate was irrelevant to most of the negotiations surrounding the Novartis agreement. Indeed, Berkeley policies and procedures were such that there was no need to consult the senate. When the dean of PBM ran the agreement past the senate, whether as a courtesy or because he feared opposition, the senate was unable to get more than an external review. The Novartis agreement was signed and executed, and the five years of funding concluded before the external review began.

Berkeley faculty members have received deserved credit for their opposition to the Novartis agreement, but it was Syngenta, not Berkeley faculty opposition, that ended the agreement. Novartis tried to fund a Bell-like lab that could do basic science in a field where investments in fundamental science frequently led to discoveries likely to produce new forms of intellectual property. Novartis hoped to leapfrog over its competitors. Syngenta, already holding a top market share, was not interested.

The treatment of Chapela by his colleagues in PMB and by administrators at UC Berkeley raised academic freedom issues. Their treatment of Chapela suggests suppression of critique by groups internal to the university seeking external research sponsors and by the research sponsors themselves. Chapela fought back and was able to prevail. What is unknown is how many faculty members decide not to engage in critique because they do not want to face the all-consuming struggle that engulfed Chapela.[13]

In the other case, Hayes was supported by Berkeley, eventually becoming a full professor, but not by Syngenta and Ecorisk, corporations with which universities are willing to do business, even if a confidentiality agreement were part of the research contract. If pharmaceutical companies are able to retain control over publication of research that they sponsor and universities participate in such studies, as they routinely do when they adopt neoliberal state forms characterized by privatization, deregulation, and commercialization, academic research is no longer disinterested. New circuits of knowledge allow corporate scientists and business to play a role in deciding what merits publication. Peer review and the expertise of the discipline(s) lose authority.[14]

The *Novartis* case illustrates the ways in which public universities have embraced neoliberal state policies and processes that promote individual and institutional entrepreneurship. The goals of entrepreneurial research are individual faculty profit and increased institutional revenue flows. The market, not professors and peer review, judges success. Entrepreneurial research stands in contrast to traditional academic norms and values, which stress discovery, publication, prestige maximization, and separation from the business world. Individual faculty and institutional preference for entrepreneurial research sometimes raises academic freedom issues by seeking to silence critique of entrepreneurial science or institutions' entrepreneurial activities.

Urofsky v. Gilmore: Virginia Public Universities

The *Urofsky* case illustrates how legislation enacted to enforce a socially conservative morality restricts academic freedom. *Urofsky* also demonstrates the unexpected consequences of legislation. Although the obvious focus of *Urofsky* was academic freedom with regard to sexually explicit material, the decision in *Urofsky* also shifted power within public universities from faculty to administrators, strengthening the neoliberal state's tendency to concentrate power in the executive branches of government.

In 1996, the General Assembly of Virginia enacted a law that restricted state employees from accessing sexually explicit content on publicly owned computers.[15] The section of the act that triggered litigation on the part of faculty states the following:

> Except to the extent required in conjunction with a bona fide, agency-approved research project or other agency-approved undertaking, no agency employee shall utilize agency-owned or agency-leased computer equipment to access, download, print or store any information infrastructure, files or services having sexually explicit content. Agency approvals shall be given in writing by agency heads, and any such approvals shall be available to the public under the provisions of the Virginia Freedom of Information Act (Virginia Code 2.2-2827).

The definition of sexually explicit content was wide-ranging, covering any description or visual representation that depicted lewd nudity, sexual bestiality, sexual excitement, sadomasochism, urophilia, coprophilia, fetishism, or sexual conduct, including actual or simulated depictions of masturbation, sexual intercourse, homosexuality, as well as sexual stimulation, clothed or unclothed, derived from genitals, pubic area, buttocks, or, if female, breasts.

In 1998, in response to the act, a professor of history at Virginia Commonwealth University, Melvin I. Urofsky, and six other professors located at various public colleges and universities in Virginia filed suit in the Alexandria division of the District Court for the Eastern District of Virginia. The professors alleged that the Virginia Act interfered with their right to academic freedom. For example, Urofsky felt unable to continue making assignments to students in which he asked them to evaluate the power of the Communications Decency Act by searching the World Wide Web for easy access to sexually explicit images because he would violate the Virginia Act when he viewed his students' assignments. (Ironically, students were not covered under the act and can view such material without legal consequences.) The other professors told similar stories, claiming that their First Amendment rights were violated and their academic research jeopardized.[16] For example, if the act were enforced strictly, "a history professor's research on Argentina's Dirty war or human rights abuses in Guatemala might be banned under the Act," not because of speech related to sex or gender but because images of torture under study depicted material that could be construed as sadomasochistic abuse (*Urofsky v. Allen* 1998, 11).

The district court decided in favor of the professors, but the Fourth Circuit Court of Appeals reversed the district court's decision (*Urofsky v. Gilmore* 2000). The Fourth Circuit Court was not swayed by the professors' arguments that their academic freedom was violated because the decision about what was researchable—the ability to follow research where it led—was put into the hands of state agents when faculty were required to seek permission from administrators prior to accessing sexually explicit research materials via the Internet. Rather, the court held that academic freedom was the prerogative of the institution, not the individual.

Throughout the Fourth Circuit's judgment, faculty at public universities in Virginia were treated primarily as state employees rather than as professionals with autonomy in their fields of expertise:

> The speech at issue here—access to certain materials using computers owned or leased by the state for purposes of carrying out employment duties—is

clearly made in the employee's role as employee. . . . It cannot be doubted that in order to pursue its legitimate goals effectively, the state must retain the ability to control the manner in which its employees discharge their duties and to direct its employees to undertake the responsibilities of their positions in a specified way. (*Urofsky v. Gilmore* 2000, 7)

The Court understood that the issue was academic freedom, noting that the professors claimed that "by requiring . . . [them] to obtain university approval before accessing sexually explicit materials on the Internet in connection with their research, the [Virginia] Act infringes this individual right of academic freedom." The Court rejected this position and concluded that "to the extent the Constitution recognizes any right of 'academic freedom' above and beyond the First Amendment rights to which every citizen is entitled, the right inheres in the University, not in individual professors, and is not violated by the terms of the Act" (*Urofsky v. Gilmore* 2000, 7).

According to the Court of Appeals, the AAUP had conceived of academic freedom as a professional norm, not a legal one,[17] and the U.S. Supreme Court had "never recognized that professors possess a First Amendment right of academic freedom to determine for themselves the content of their courses and scholarship, despite opportunities to do so" (*Urofsky v. Gilmore* 2000, 11). Rather, "to the extent it [the Supreme Court] has constitutionalized a right of academic freedom at all, [it] appears to have recognized only an institutional right of self-governance in academic affairs."

The Court saw the First Amendment as protecting professors in their capacity as private citizens speaking on matters of public concern, not their right to speak as experts employed at public universities. In other words, the "public employer's interest in what the employer has determined to be the appropriate operation of the workplace" (*Urofsky v. Gilmore* 2000, 5) overrides claims to individual academic freedom. The case was appealed to the U.S. Supreme Court, which refused to hear it.

In the many commentaries on the case, scholars have argued that the Court misread Pickering, which balances knowledgeable public employees' rights to speak as public employees against mere employee disputes, which are not protected (*Harvard Law Review* 2002; Williams 2002; Lynch 2003). Several scholars say, as does Lynch, that the Fourth Circuit's "categorical denial of constitutional academic freedom to professors in Urofsky v Gilmore" is "clearly [an] incorrect result" (Lynch 2003, 1). But attorneys and judges can and do have different interpretations of the law. The Fourth Circuit is relatively conservative, and a similar case tried in another circuit may have a different result. However, as Jorgenson and Helms conclude, after reviewing proliferating academic freedom legal cases that involve conflicting "stakeholders"—faculty, students, administrators, citizen, and religious groups—"when faced with competing claims, courts usually conflate academic freedom with the idea of judicial deference and then apply it in support of institutional or employer prerogatives to exercise authority . . . the [current] case law suggests that rights traditionally associated with academic freedom attach primarily to institutions and that institutions, not faculty, exercise primary control over those rights" (2008, 19).[18]

Urofsky illustrates how social conservatism shapes state legislation in ways that challenge the norms of the academic profession. Prior to *Urofsky*, the academic profession, as represented by organizations of professors qua professor such as the AAUP, the National Education Association, and the American Federation of Teachers, invoked U.S. Supreme Court First Amendment cases in which academic freedom was at issue to uphold professional norms that conferred autonomy derived from expertise on individual professors. Social conservatives challenged this position through the Virginia Act. The act illustrates socially conservative values in that it upholds a morality that constrains access to explicitly sexual images by employees in state agencies, which include public universities. The focus of the act on computers, the Internet, and the World Wide Web perhaps arose from the perceived danger of a new media through which images were immediately available for professorial use and distribution, creating the possibility of corruption of the student body.

The Virginia Act is not an isolated instance of social conservatism gaining ground within state agencies. Federal administrative law with regard to stem cell research also illustrates conservative social values, as does state legislation that provides equal time for creationism and evolution. These changes in the state, at its several levels, substitute political judgment for professional expertise within the public sector of education, constraining academic freedom.

The Virginia Act does not forbid professors from accessing sexually explicit material. Rather, it requires professors to secure permission from a state agent, such as a dean. Although the shift in locus of authority from individual professor to state agent was likely made to ensure that professors did not access sexually titillating computer material on state time and with state resources, the recognition of an institutional rather than an individual right of academic freedom inadvertently shifts the balance of power within academe, reinforcing neoliberal tendencies within public institutions. "New public management" (Amaral, Meek, and Larson 2003) emphasizes increasing efficiency and reducing cost within public entities through market-like behavior and relies heavily on strong administrators able to make rapid decisions.

The professors who engaged in litigation in *Urofsky* very likely did not anticipate a ruling that established an institutional rather than an individual right to academic freedom. However, the decision suggests that socially conservative legislation, enacted within a state increasingly dominated by neoliberalism, can have unanticipated consequences. Beginning with the Reagan administration's approach to deregulation, neoliberals have favored the "theory of the unitary executive," asserting the supremacy of the executive over the regulatory functions of government (Light 2008; Moraff 2008, 32–36). Reagan Executive Order 12211 gave the Office of Information and Regulatory Affairs the authority to review all federal regulations, using risk assessment and cost-benefit analysis; Executive Order 12498 called for regulatory review to ensure that new regulations reflected administrative policy objectives. Such efforts continued, with some modifications during the Clinton presidency, to the present, when George W. Bush issued Executive Order 13422, in which agencies that propose new regulations must specify the market failure they address. *Urofsky* led to indirect U.S. Supreme Court affirmation of institutional rather than an individual faculty right to academic freedom, a position in keeping with the strong executive authority preferred by a neoliberal state. Deans and administrators, supported by segments of the faculty, may use the concept of institutional academic freedom to pursue initiatives favored by a neoliberal state, such as the increase of public-private partnerships, which raise their own set of challenges to academic freedom, as illustrated by the *Novartis* case.

The *Ward Churchill* Case at the University of Colorado

After World War II, the liberal state initiated the Cold War, characterized by Keynesian welfare/warfare or guns and butter programs. The U.S.

Congress and various state legislatures initiated a number of academic freedom cases, most of which turned on the Cold War and national security. Among the most prominent were the *Oppenheimer* and *Lattimore* cases (Bird and Sherwin 2006; Lattimore, Cook, and Lattimore 2003). McCarthyism challenged academic freedom on many fronts (Lazarsfeld and Thielens 1958; Schrecker 1986). Professors were swept up in academic freedom cases as a result of their participation in political activities in their capacity as private citizens (Lewis 1988). For example, Oppenheimer was brought before the U.S. Senate Committee not because of his work as a physicist, but because he was suspected of being a member of the Communist Party.

The liberal state continued to focus on loyalty to the nation in the Vietnam War, but rather than being dismissed for membership in the Communist Party, professors were dismissed for critique of the Vietnam War and support of social unrest at home. Among the more notable cases were historian Staughton Lynd, who was denied employment at the University of Illinois because of a trip to Vietnam; Michael Parenti, a political scientist at the University of Vermont who was denied tenure because of professional conduct detrimental to the image of the university; and Morris Starsky, a philosophy professor fired from Arizona State University for dereliction of duty stemming from involvement in antiwar activities (Goldstein 1978; Slaughter 1980, 46–61). The *Angela Davis* case was also a famous Vietnam-era case, but unlike others, Davis had been a member of the Communist Party.

The *Churchill* case shows the state, in this case the University of Colorado, continuing the liberal tradition of punishing professors who strongly critique an ongoing war.[19] As in the cases mentioned above, free speech was allegedly not the issue. Rather than bringing charges against Churchill for what he said and wrote about the World Trade Center bombings, the University of Colorado instead focused its case against Churchill on research misconduct.

Shortly after the 9/11 attacks on the World Trade Center and the Pentagon, Ward Churchill, a tenured professor of Ethnic Studies at the University of Colorado–Boulder, wrote an essay, "Some People Push Back: On the Justice of Roosting Chickens," in which he argued that the World Trade Center bombing was the "blowback" from the United States' interventions in the Middle East. The section of the essay that triggered the most criticism was his argument that World Trade Center victims were not innocent, but rather "little Eichmann's" who benefited from U.S. foreign policy.[20]

Widespread reaction to the essay did not come until 2005, when Churchill was invited to speak at Hamilton College in a forum on the limits of dissent. Professors at Hamilton who were unhappy with the Churchill invitation circulated his essay on September 11. The text of Churchill's essay was picked up and quoted on *The O'Reilly Factor* on the Fox News Channel, and Bill O'Reilly made reference to Churchill's work in several other segments of his program. Shortly after the first O'Reilly mention, Governor of Colorado Bill Ritter called for Churchill's dismissal, and the Board of Regents of the University of Colorado adopted a resolution apologizing to America for Churchill's essay. In May, the president of the University of Colorado System, Hank Brown, recommended firing Churchill (*Wikipedia*, Ward Churchill 9/11 controversy).

The University of Colorado determined that the First Amendment protected Churchill's speech, and rather than dismissing him for his unpopular essay, the interim chancellor of the University of Colorado initiated a review of Churchill's work by the university's Standing Committee on Research Misconduct. The Standing Committee appointed an Investigative Committee that looked at complaints of plagiarism and falsification as well as fabrication of data. It found Churchill guilty of six charges of research misconduct but disagreed on the punishment, with only one committee member firmly recommending firing (Wesson et al. 2006). The five-person Standing Committee accepted the findings of the investigating committee (Jaschik 2007). On appeal, the Appeals Panel of the Privilege and Tenure Committee found only three of the charges valid, and again the vote was split. The Board of Regents fired Churchill in an eight-to-one vote in July 2007 (Jaschik 2007).

As the case progressed, University of Colorado students voted for Churchill to receive a teaching award sponsored by the Alumni Association, which withheld the award (Newsome 2005). There was serious division within the national scholarly community about the findings of Colorado's Investigative Committee, with some scholars accusing the committee of stacking the deck against Churchill by appointing only one non-Eurocentric member to represent the field of Native American Studies, while others vehemently disagreed and supported the committee (*Open Anthropology*, April 25, 2007; Perez 2005). A number of University of Colorado faculty made countercharges, accusing the Investigative Committee of bias, and threatened to file research misconduct charges against the committee (*Open Anthropology*, April 25, 2007). In 2009, a Denver jury found that CU unlawfully fired Churchill for exercising his right to free speech but awarded him only $1 in damages. After considering the jury's ruling, Chief Denver District Judge Larry Naves decided against awarding Churchill his job back at CU or any compensation (*Boulder Daily Camera* 2010). In February 2010, Churchill began an appeal based on the argument that the trial court was wrong to grant CU regents absolute immunity, and given that there was a proven First Amendment violation, the presumed equitable remedy is reinstatement (Myers and Silverstein 2010).

The *Churchill* case illustrates that aspects of the liberal state continue in a neoliberal era, or that warfare calls forth state mechanisms—regardless of the dominant state form—that exert control over First Amendment rights, whether in academe or other sectors of society (Dadge 2004). The *Churchill* case differs from cases of previous eras, however, in that the issue of research misconduct directs attention to the scholarship of professors engaged in critique. In the McCarthy era, professors were charged with supporting the wrong side in the Cold War through membership in the Communist Party. In the Vietnam era, professors were dismissed on various technicalities, ranging from conduct unbecoming to professors to missing classes in order to engage in social protest. In the *Churchill* case, the charges of research misconduct are directed not toward professors' activities outside the university, but scholars' academic inquiry. Research misconduct calls for heightened scrutiny of academic work, raising the bar beyond what is required by peer review in making decisions about the merit of academic scholarship. In other words, faculty who engage in critique could be subjected to a higher standard of review than other scholars.

Conclusion

The point I have tried to make in this essay is that changes in state forms pose challenges to academic freedom because the state plays a large part in framing what is possible: the legislative branch enacts laws that impinge on academic freedom, the executive branch structures state agencies and administrative laws that reshape academic freedom, and the judiciary interprets these in new and sometimes unexpected ways. The cases examined highlight the direction of change. Generally, the state agencies are moving from liberal to neoliberal policies and practices, although some agencies have turned in socially conservative directions while others continue on a liberal course.

Examination of the context of the *Novartis* case illustrates the complexity and degree of change that has occurred with regard to the promotion of market activity through privatization, deregulation, and commercialization of state agencies. As discussed earlier, national competitiveness legislation, signified by the Bayh-Dole Act of 1980, reshaped the importance of intellectual property for universities. State legislation played a similar role, again beginning approximately in the 1980s, with legislation such as the California Enterprise Zones and Economic Incentive Areas, as well as legislation enabling state university system-wide incentives, for example, the University of California Biotechnology Research and Education Program, which put tens of millions of dollars into biotechnology aimed at technology transfer (Peters and Fisher 2002). The executive branch of government was as important as the legislative. At the national level, mission agencies—the National Institutes of Health, National Science Foundation, Department of Defense, Department of Energy, and the National Aeronautics and Space Agency—all developed university-industry-business partnerships in which most research universities became involved (Slaughter and Rhoades 1996). The California pattern of fostering market activity was repeated in many states: economic development agencies and universities frequently worked together to develop biotechnology initiatives, research parks, and incubators, all of which encouraged closer relations between universities and corporations.

When external partnerships with corporations are embedded in the fabric of the university, so are market values. Historically, market values contrast sharply with professional norms (Brint 1994). Markets value risk, market discipline, and profit. Professional norms for faculty emphasize research, teaching, and service as well as discovery, critique, and a disinterested habit of mind. These very different sets of values are not easily melded together, as the Berkeley-Novartis agreement demonstrates. Professors and administrators who auction off departments are likely to use their authority within the university to quell critiques of the knowledge they produce, posing problems for the academic freedom of professors who challenge them. In other words, the neoliberal state has created an institutional climate in public research universities in which market values collide with academic freedom as well as other professional norms and values (Pestel and Radermacher 2000). The governance structures developed by faculty seem unequal to the task of defending academic freedom in an increasingly segmented academy.

The *Urofsky* decision suggests that social conservatism continues to be able to shape legislation in ways that challenge academic freedom. The Virginia Act embodied socially conservative values by preventing faculty from accessing the Internet to view sexually explicit materials without permission from a supervisor, restricting faculty ability to pursue research as individual scholarly actors. Historically, social conservatives have tried to legislate morality with regard to sexuality and were sometimes successful (Lane 2006). The *Urofsky* case indicates that this struggle continues.

Although social conservatives were probably not concerned with the power of administrators, the Fourth Circuit Court was, illustrating the way in which politico-legal initiatives can be reformulated by a judiciary located in an increasingly neoliberal state. The Court affirmed the power of state agencies to subject professors to approval from supervisors prior to using the Internet to conduct some kinds of research and also unexpectedly affirmed an institutional right to academic freedom rather than individual professors' rights. The judiciary may continue to recognize institutional autonomy and defer to colleges and universities, but that is very different from recognizing individual professors' right to academic freedom in their area of expertise.

When the Fourth Circuit's decision was appealed to the U.S. Supreme Court, the Supreme Court let *Urofsky* stand. This was in keeping with a number of decisions the Supreme Court made about public sector employment in the 1990s (*Jett v. Dallas* 1989; *Waters v. Churchill* 1994) that favored institutions over individual plaintiffs, suggesting that public employees should be treated more like corporate employees, realigning public work practices with those of private corporations, where employees, regardless of their professional status, do not have much voice. In 2006, the Court confirmed this approach to professional employees in *Garcetti v. Ceballos* when it held that the speech of an assistant district attorney speaking correctly to his superior with regard to the factual basis of his work was unprotected (*Garcetti v. Ceballos* 2006; Jorgensen and Helms 2008, 8). As commentators on academic freedom have noted, "this ruling appears to threaten the basic notion that academic freedom should protect faculty speech related to official duties of research and scholarship." In these rulings, the courts are taking a neoliberal position in preferring manager/administrators to professors and giving managers—as "agency heads"—more authority than professors. Modeling pubic institutional practices after private may constrain academic freedom in that administrator/managers may be able to more easily make decisions without the faculty consultation on which academic freedom depends (see Baez and Slaughter 2001).

The *Churchill* case illustrates the state's enduring preoccupation with security in time of war, which includes silencing critics of war. As was the case with the Cold War, the War on Terror has created a number of challenges for academic freedom, ranging from increased secrecy and classification with regard to government information to cases like Churchill's (Bird and Brandt 2002; Cole 2003; Jaeger et al. 2004). Although wartime concern with security and containment of critique may be a feature of all state forms, whether liberal, socially conservative, or neoliberal (Gruber 1975; Summerscales 1970), I have read the War on Terror as an extension of Cold War policies, largely because both depend on the idea of *permanent* ideological mobilization against an axis of evil that divides the world. Moreover, the War on Terror uses many of the same agencies and techniques as the Cold War. However, there are differences—Homeland Security broadens the ability of the state to monitor citizens' activities, as do technological advances. The *Churchill* case, with its focus on research misconduct, indicates that universities and faculty continue to be willing to participate in policing professors engaged in critique. And charges of research misconduct are a new mechanism of surveillance that raises the bar for those who engage in critique, making them subject to increased scrutiny.

It is unlikely that we will be able to easily or quickly return to the status quo ante of the liberal state, which provided the basis for academic freedom from the 1950s through the 1980s. To do so, we would have to repeal a great deal of legislation that shifted state agencies in a neoliberal direction—for example, the array of competitiveness laws—dismantle agencies or parts of agencies like state and university economic development offices, and reverse two decades of judicial decisions at the state, court of appeals, and federal levels. We would also have to confront socially conservative state agencies and rewrite legislation to protect faculty as civil servants who possess expertise necessary to the public good, even when such expertise is threatening to conventional morality. And we should remember that the status quo ante presented substantial problems for academic freedom, as the many cases from the Cold War era indicate.

However, the difficulty of protecting academic freedom under new state forms, such as neoliberalism, should not cause us to abandon it. Rather, we should work to develop new politics and new strategies to reinvigorate the disciplines and professions that were responsible for beginning the struggle for academic freedom at the turn of the twentieth century. The biggest challenge will very likely be to get members of professions and disciplines—the organizations that began the defense of academic freedom at the turn of the twentieth century—to agree on what they want from the state. Some segments of these professions and disciplines have pushed to expand the neoliberal state and its opportunity structures—for example, intellectual property rights, differentiated salaries, reduced teaching loads—while other segments have tried to contain the neoliberal state by mobilizing against it, as did Ignacio Chapela at Berkeley. While disciplines and professions and the professors within them that benefit from the neoliberal state may not intend to constrain academic freedom, embrace of market values may nonetheless have that effect unless we are able to reformulate academic freedom in ways that respond to changing state forms.

If faculty are to be part of an academic profession rather than "mere employees," they have to develop means of defending academic freedom and asserting professional autonomy. If faculty cannot protect their exercise of expertise, then their status as professionals is jeopardized. Employers, state agencies, and political actors, whether students or citizens, can substitute their judgment for that of professionals, so that politics and power trump expert knowledge. Although faculty are not innocent of maneuvering with regard to power and politics and the research questions they ask have high political stakes (for example, climate change research) and professors sometimes fail to see their own biases (as is the case with social scientists and "market fundamentalism"), they nonetheless have to try to craft policies and positions in universities, state agencies, and the legal system that allow the possibility for relatively disinterested knowledge proved in the peer review process to have authority.

NOTES

1. Liberalism, or embedded liberalism, was a reaction to classic liberalism and sought to constrain capitalism to avoid depression, poverty, and social unrest. To achieve these ends, social and political oversight and regulatory and planning func-

tions were embedded in the state. The common goals of embedded liberal states were full employment, economic growth, and the welfare of the citizenry. If necessary, the state would intervene in market processes to reach these goals. Keynesian monetary policies were characteristic of the embedded liberal state. See Blythe 2002 and Carnoy and Levin 1985. In contrast, neoliberalism is "a theory of political economic practices that proposes that human well-being can best be advanced by liberating individual entrepreneurial freedoms and skills within an institutional framework characterized by strong private property rights, free markets and free trade. The role of the state is to create and preserve an institutional framework appropriate to such practices." While neoliberalism is presented as the key to freedoms of conscience, speech, meeting, association, and employment, this form of liberalism, as pointed out by Karl Polanyi in 1944, also allows "the freedom to exploit one's fellows, or the freedom to make inordinate gains without commensurable service to the community, the freedom to keep technological inventions from being used for public benefit, or the freedom to profit from public calamities secretly engineered for private advantage," and generally confers freedom on those "whose income, leisure and security need no enhancing," leaving little for others. Although neoliberal theory minimizes the role of the state, in practice state subsidies and oversight are not minimized; rather, they shift to new areas. See Harvey 2005 (quotes at p. 2). In particular, and important with regard to higher education, subsidies shift from broad general appropriations for the public good (for example, low tuition) to user taxes and fees (for example, high tuition) that emphasize individual rather than social gains accrued as a result of higher education. Generally, a neoliberal state shifts higher education from a public good knowledge/learning regime to what we have called an academic capitalist knowledge/learning regime. See Slaughter and Rhoades 2004.

2. Social conservatism is a political or moral ideology that sees government as having a role in encouraging or enforcing traditional values or behaviors. The meaning of traditional morality often differs from group to group within social conservatism. See Formicola 2008 and Lane 2006.

3. See the Amicus brief in Urofsky for AAUP's position with regard to constitutional right for academic freedom. See also Williams 2002. For alternative views see Lynch 2003 and Whitmore 2008.

4. See Busch et al. 2004. This study was commissioned by the University of California–Berkeley as an external review as protest and questions were raised about Novartis's relationship to UC Berkeley. It is a comprehensive, in-depth, sensitive case study of the Novartis–UC Berkeley partnership. Busch makes many of the points I do with regard to academic freedom.

5. This was reduced to $23,944,000 over the five years because of inability to agree on a building and various other items.

6. For examples of funding that embrace departments or large segments of departments see Krimsky 2003.

7. Although most contracts between business and industry do not specifically arrange for a corporation to have access to professors' knowledge gained from work-

ing on concurrent federal research projects, this may happen inadvertently, despite disclosures and confidentiality, because knowledge is held in the person of the professor who uses it to develop a variety of new approaches. See Slaughter, Archerd, and Campbell 2004.

8. However, Chapela eventually did receive tenure. His case became a celebrated cause among environmentalists, and Chapela prepared to sue the UCB for $25 million. For details see Maitre (n.d.).

9. Chapela's Web site is www.pulseofscience.org/ and has links to www.pulseof science.org/chapelalawsuit and www.pulseofscience.org/chapelalawsuit.pdf (accessed February 19, 2006; site discontinued). For an updated site, but without access to the brief, see http://ecnr.berkeley.edu/facPage/dispFP.php?I=568.

10. For an account of legal cases in the 1990s that led to neoliberal rules for research universities' engagement with the economy, see Baez and Slaughter 2001.

11. See www.ucop.edu/ott/genresources/equi-pol.html, www.ucop.edu/ott/pat entpolicy/patentpo.html#pol, and http://patron.ucop.edu/ottmemos/docs/ott02-01 .html.

12. See n. 11.

13. See Lazarsfeld and Thielens 1958 for the chilling effect that McCarthyism had on American social science. Although McCarthyism drew on quite different social forces than university-industry partnerships, such partnerships may engender similar responses from universities in that universities may be willing to "police" faculty to keep external constituencies happy.

14. See Krimsky 2003. See also Clark 2006 for a chilling discussion of the "neo-feudal order of academic plutocrats" (474).

15. Virginia Code Ann. 2.2-2827. My account of the case prior to the en banc hearing by the 4th Circuit in 2000 relies heavily on Williams 2002 and Lynch 2003.

16. Some institutions devised novel approaches to dealing with the act. The University of Virginia granted some of its departments blanket approvals—for example, the Health Sciences Center and the Office of Information Technology (Urofsky v. Allen 1998).

17. Indeed, the AAUP, which first formulated principles of academic freedom in 1915, did so in part to distinguish themselves from free speech advocates such as the International Workers of the World, who engaged in free speech political actions that relied on the First Amendment when they publically attempted to educate the masses. See Silva and Slaughter 1984.

18. Jorgensen and Helms explain the Supreme Court's shift from acknowledgment of academic freedom in the 1950s and 1960s to conflating academic freedom with First Amendment law as a result of proliferation of litigation by a variety of stakeholders and by "path dependence," which means that legal and administrative decisions in policy arenas depend on precedents in the larger body of case law. That may be the case, but it does not explain the neoliberal direction of the shift,

which favors employers and economic stakeholders, regardless of First Amendment issues.

19. Of course, there is the obvious difference that the neoliberal state no longer supports the welfare aspect of the welfare-warfare state, at least in terms of social programs for the citizenry. Generally the neoliberal state has cut back social welfare programs or attempted to privatize them, sometimes unsuccessfully, as in the case of Social Security.

20. I was unable to locate the original essay, which may have been posted on Churchill's Web site, which no longer resides at the University of Colorado. For later versions, see Churchill 2003, 2005.

REFERENCES

Amaral, Alberto, V. Lynn Meek, and Ingvild Larsen, eds. 2003. *The higher education managerial revolution? Higher education dynamics,* vol. 3. Dordrecht: Kluwer.

American Association of University Professors. 1995a. 1940 statement of principles on academic freedom and tenure with 1970 interpretive comments. In *Policy documents and reports,* 3. Washington, DC: American Association of University Professors.

———. 1995b. On the relationship of faculty governance to academic freedom. In *Policy documents and reports,* 179–87. Washington DC: American Assocation of University Professors.

Baez, Ben, and Sheila Slaughter. 2001. Academic freedom and federal courts in the 1990s: The legitimation of the conservative entrepreneurial state. In *Handbook of theory and research in higher education,* ed. John Smart and William Tierney, 73–118. New York: Agathon Press.

Bird, Kia, and Martin J. Sherwin. 2006. *American Prometheus: The triumph and tragedy of J. Robert Oppenheimer.* New York: Random House.

Bird, R. Kenton, and Elizabeth Barker Brandt. 2002. Academic freedom and 9/11: How the War on Terrorism threatens free speech on campus. *Communication Law and Policy* 7 (4): 431–59.

Blumenstyk, Goldie. 2003. The story of Syngenta and Tyrone Hayes at UC Berkeley: The price of research. *Chronicle of Higher Education* 50 (10 Oct. 2003).

Blythe, Mark. 2002. *Great transformations: Economic ideas and institutional change in the twentieth century.* Cambridge: Cambridge University Press.

Boulder Daily Camera. 2010. Ward Churchill begins appeal of decision upholding firing from CU-Boulder. *Boulder Daily Camera,* February 19, 2010. www.dailycamera .com/news/ci_14436298.

Brint, Steven. 1994. *In an age of experts: The changing role of professionals in politics and public life.* Princeton: Princeton University Press.

Busch, Lawrence, et al. 2004. *External review of the collaborative research agreement between Novartis Agricultural Discovery Institute, Inc., and the regents of the University of California.* East Lansing, MI: Institute for Food and Agricultural Standards. http://cshe.berkeley.edu/publications/publications.php?id=220.

Byrne, J. Peter. 1989. Academic freedom: A special concern of the First Amendment. *Yale Law Journal* 99 (2): 251–55.

Carnoy, Martin, and Henry Levin. 1985. *Schooling and work in the democratic state.* Pala Alto, CA: Stanford.

Churchill, Ward. 2003. *On the justice of roosting chickens: Reflections on the consequences of U.S. imperial arrogance and criminality.* Oakland, CA: AK Press.

———. 2005. The ghosts of 9/11: Reflections on history, justice and roosting chickens. *Alternative Press Review* 9 (1): 45–46.

Clark, William. 2006. *Academic charisma and the origins of the research university.* Chicago: University of Chicago Press.

Cole, David. 2003. The new McCarthyism: Repeating history in the War on Terrorism. *Harvard Civil Rights–Civil Liberties Law Review* 38.

Dadge, David. *Casualty of war: The Bush administration's assault on a free press.* Amherst, NY: Prometheus Books.

Feaga, M. K., and P. A. Zirkel. 2006. Academic freedom faculty members: A follow-up of outcomes analysis. *West's Education Law Reporter* 209:597–607.

Formicola, Jo Renee. 2008. *The politics of values: Games political strategists play.* Lanham, MD: Rowman & Littlefield.

Furner, Mary O. 1975. *Advocacy and objectivity: A crisis in the professionalization of social science, 1865–1905.* Louisville: University of Kentucky Press.

Garcetti v. Ceballos. 2006. 126 S. Ct. 1951.

Goldstein, Robert Justin. 1978. *Political repression in modern America, 1870 to the present.* Cambridge, MA: Schenkman.

Gruber, Carol Singer. 1975. *Mars and Minerva: World War I and the uses of the higher learning in America.* Baton Rouge: Louisiana State University Press.

Harvard Law Review. 2002. Recent cases: Constitutional law. *Harvard Law Review* 1414.

Harvey, David. 2005. *A brief history of neoliberalism.* Oxford: Oxford University Press.

Jaeger, Paul T., Charles R. McClure, John Carlo Bertot, and John T. Snead. 2004. The USA Patriot Act, the Foreign Intelligence Surveillance Act and information policy research in libraries: Issues, impacts and questions for librarians and researchers. *Library Quarterly* 74 (2): 99–121.

Jaschik, Scott. 2007. Ward Churchill fired. *Inside Higher Education,* April 25, 2007. www.insidehighered.com/news/2007/07/25/churchill.

Jett v. Dallas Independent School District. 1989. 491 U.S. 701.

Jorgensen, James D., and Lelia B. Helms. 2008. Academic freedom, the First Amendment and competing stake holder: The dynamics of a changing balance. *Review of Higher Education* 32 (1): 1–24.

Krimsky, Sheldon. 2006. *Science and the private interest.* Lanham, MD: Rowman & Littlefield.

Lane, Frederick. 2006. *The decency wars: The campaign to cleanse American culture.* Amherst, NY: Prometheus Books.

Lattimore, Owen, Blanche Wiesen Cook, and David L. Lattimore. 2003. *Ordeal by slander: The first great book of the McCarthy era.* New York: Carroll and Graf.

Lazarsfeld, Paul L., and Wagner Thielens Jr. 1958. *The academic mind: Social scientists in times of crisis.* Glencoe: Free Press.

Lewis, Lionel. 1988. *Cold war on the campus: A study of the politics of organizational control.* New Brunswick, NJ: Transaction Books.

Light, Paul. 2008. *A government ill executed: The decline of the federal service and how to reverse it.* Cambridge, MA: Harvard University Press.

Lynch, Rebecca Gose. 2003. Comment: Pawns of the state or priests of democracy? Analyzing professors' academic freedom rights with the state's managerial realm. *California Law Review* 91:1061.

Maitre, Michelle. n.d. Embattled professor gets tenure. *Inside Bay Area.* www.inside-bayarea.com/ (acessed February 23, 2006).

Metzger, Walter P. 1969. *The development of academic freedom in the United States.* New York: Columbia University Press.

Moraff, Christopher. 2008. Feeding the beast. *In These Times,* September 2008, 32–36.

Myers, Rachel, and Mark Silverstein. 2010. ACLU files amicus brief asking Colorado Court of Appeals to reinstate Ward Churchill after a jury found that CU fired him for expressing his beliefs. *American Civil Liberties Union of Colorado,* February 18, 2010. http://aclu-co.org/news.

National Science Board. 2004. *Science and Engineering Indicators* 3.

National Science Foundation, Division of Science Resources Statistics. 2004. *Academic research and development expenditures: Fiscal year 2002.* NSF04-330. M. Marge Machen, project officer. Arlington, VA. Tables B-32, B-36, and B-38.

———. 2007. *Academic research and development expenditures: Fiscal year 2006.* NSF 08-300. Ronda Britt, project officer. Arlington, VA.

Newsome, Brian. 2005. CU alumni group withholds award. *Gazette,* May 27, 2005. www.gazette.com.

Perez, Emma. 2005. A neocon test case for academic purges: The attacks on Ward Churchill. *Counterpunch,* February 28, 2005. www.counterpunch.org/perez02282005.html.

Pestel, R., and F. J. Radermacher. 2000. Equity, wealth and growth: Why market fundamentalism makes countries poor. European Union: Terra. http://files.Global marshallplan.org/equity_wealth_and_growth.pdf.

Peters, Alan H., and Peter S. Fisher. 2002. *State enterprise zone programs: Have they worked?* Kalamazoo, MI: Upjohn, University of California Biotechnology Research and Education Program. http://biotechsystem.ucdavis.edu.

Polanyi, Karl. 1944. *The great transformation: The political and economic origins of our time.* Boston: Beacon Press by arrangement with Rinehart & Company, Inc.

Schrecker, Ellen W. 1986. *No ivory towers: McCarthyism and the universities.* New York: Oxford University Press.

Silva, Edward T., and Sheila Slaughter. 1984. *Serving power: The making of the American social science expert.* Westport, CT: Greenwood Press.

Slaughter, Sheila. 1980. The danger zone: Academic freedom and civil liberties. *Annals of the American Association of Political and Social Science* 448:46–61.

———. 1981. Political action, faculty autonomy and retrenchment: A decade of academic freedom, 1970–1980. In *Higher education in American society*, ed. Philip G. Altbach and Robert O. Berdahl, 73–100. Buffalo: Prometheus Books.

———. 1988. Academic freedom in the modern university. In *Higher education in American society*, rev. ed., ed. Philip G. Altbach and Robert O. Berdahl, 77–105. Buffalo: Prometheus Books.

———. 1994. "Dirty little cases": Problems of academic freedom, governance and professionalization. In *Academic freedom: An everyday concern*, ed. Ernest Benjamin and Donald Wagner. *New Directions for Higher Education* 23 (4): 59–75. San Francisco: Jossey-Bass.

Slaughter, Sheila, Cynthia Joan Archerd, and Teresa I. D. Campbell. 2004. Boundaries and quandaries: How professors negotiate market relations. *Review of Higher Education* 28 (1): 129–65.

Slaughter, Sheila, and Gary Rhoades. 1993. Changes in intellectual property statutes and policies at a public university: Revising the terms of professional labor. *Higher Education* 26:287–312.

———. 1996. The emergence of a competitiveness research and development policy coalition and the commercialization of academic science and technology. *Science, Technology and Human Value* 21 (3): 303–39.

———. 2004. *Academic capitalism and the new economy*. Baltimore: Johns Hopkins University Press.

Summerscales, William. 1970. *Affirmation and dissent: Columbia's response to the crisis of World War I*. New York: Columbia University Press.

Tonak, Ali. 2004. The case of Ignacio Chapela. *Counterpunch*, June 26, 2004. www.counterpunch.org/tonak06262004.html (accessed February 15, 2006).

UC Berkeley News. 2005. Ignacio Chapela tenure. www.berkeley.edu/news/berkeleyan/2005/09/01_chapela.shtml (accessed September 2007).

Urofsky v. Allen. 1998. No. 995F. Supp. 634; U.S. Dis. LEXIS 2139, 13.

Urofsky v. Gilmore. 2000. No. 401. 216 F/3rd 401, 401 4th Circuit.

Veblen, Thorstein. 1918. *The higher learning in America: A memorandum on the conduct of universities by businessmen*. New York: Viking.

Ward Churchill and the witch hunters: Faculty calls for Churchill report retraction, consider filing research misconduct charges. *Open Anthropology*, April 25, 2007.

Ward Churchill 9/11 essay controversy. *Wikipedia*. http://en.wikipedia.org/wiki/Ward_Churchill (accessed September 24, 2008).

Waters v. Churchill. 1994. 511 U.S.661.

Wesson, Marianne, Robert N. Clinton, Jose E. Limon, Majorie K. McIntosh, and Michael L. Radelet. 2006. Report of the Investigative Committee of the Standing Committee on Research Misconduct at the University of Colorado, Boulder, concerning allegations of academic misconduct against Professor Ward Churchill. May 9, 2006. www.colorado.edu/news/reports/churchill/churchillreport051606.html.

Whitmore, Nancy. 2008. First Amendment showdown: Intellectual diversity mandates and the academic marketplace. *Communication Law and Policy* 13 (Summer): 397.

Williams, Kate. 2002. Loss of academic freedom on the Internet: The Fourth Circuit's decision in Urofsky v Gilmore. *Review of Litigation*, University of Texas at Austin Law School, Spring 2002, 21 Rev. Litig. 493.

CHAPTER TEN

Codes of Commerce

The Uses of Business Rhetoric in the American Academy, 1960–2000

Daniel Lee Kleinman, Jacob Habinek,
and Steven P. Vallas

E vidence abounds of the increasing collision of industry and academe. Newspapers cover university industry partnerships such as the $500 million University of California at Berkeley's biofuels research relationship with BP, the mega-energy corporation (Blumenstyk, 2007), and the earlier, highly controversial $25 million UC Berkeley–Novartis research arrangement (Rudy et al. 2007). Some scholars worry about the dangers to academic norms of openness and cooperation in scientific research, the likelihood of emerging conflicts of interest, and the threat to autonomous research agenda setting posed by these kinds of formal university-industry relations (Krimsky 2003). Other academic researchers explore when and how such partnerships work, as well as why and how they fail (Colyvas and Powell 2006; Etzkowitz, Webster, and Healy 1998; Owen-Smith 2005; Owen-Smith and Powell 2003).

While there is now a vast literature on the commercial orientation to knowledge production found in some of the highest-status U.S. universities, there is much less research that explores the place of commercial practices in areas of academic life other than (scientific) research (see Bok 2003; Donoghue 2008; Gumport 1997; Kirp 2003; Strathern 2000). We know little about how the world of commerce has affected teaching and university administration, central roles in the academic profession. Furthermore, there is virtually no scholarship that considers universities and commerce beyond major research institutions, and very little work explores questions of change and continuity in commercial practices in academic settings over time.

In this chapter, we seek to fill some significant holes in the existing scholarship and in so doing to broaden our understanding of the commercialization of American academe. In contrast to approaches emphasizing dramatic violations of academic norms in research or those that focus on the operation of top-tier research universities, we look at the more mundane everyday practices in the life of the academic profession. Actually, we look at administrative *talk* about these practices, drawing on publications of national organizations for university administrators and trustees over a forty-year time frame. This approach, while not documenting actual practices, allows us to explore the influence of the world of commerce on the broad culture of academe over an extended period.

Our research shows that codes of commerce are not entirely absent in any period we investigate. In their discussions with professors, business leaders, and one another, academic leaders illustrate that the world of commerce has influenced how they think about universities—about research, teaching, and administration—throughout the second half of the twentieth century. However, the ways in which the language of the world of business is used in discussions of academic administration and the future of the university vary across the forty-year span we study. Thus, in the 1960s, when major research universities felt flush with federal and foundation support, commercial codes were used relatively infrequently. When discussed, the world of commerce was not clearly distinguished from federal and foundational threats to autonomy. It was treated as foreign to the academy, but not sharply delineated, and talk of commercial practices was often limited to standardizing practices and bureaucratic organization in academic administration. In the 1970s, by contrast, academic leaders at both major research institutions and smaller colleges described increasing financial pressures and either worried about or actively promoted the replacement of academic-style collegial models of governance by business-like contractual agreements. By the 1980s, although it is true that much discussion focused on academic-industry partnerships in biological science research, this was only one area in which codes of commerce could be found in discussions among university administrators. In particular, we see widespread use of market language to describe the benefits university students gain from their education, advocacy of business models for university administration, and entrepreneurial framing of non-market-oriented faculty practices. Everyday life in the academic profession seemed to be changing. Finally, in the 1990s, when the boundaries between academe and industry seemed to be blurring (Vallas and Kleinman 2008), discussion focused on the use of very specific business practices in the governance and administration of the university and evidence of their spread.

Our chapter is divided into four parts. First, we explore the relevant scholarly literature, pointing to where we hope our research can fill substantial silences. Second, we describe our data and approach. Third, we draw on our data to describe the changing talk by and to academic administrators and trustees about commercial influences in academic life. Finally, we explore some of the implications of our findings.

Existing Approaches

The interaction between academe and industry in the United States in recent years has generated an extensive body of analysis, all in some fashion focusing on structural transformations in the practices and character of American institutions of higher education. This is not the place to provide a comprehensive review of this literature. Instead, we want to describe some of the major claims made by authors writing about the contemporary university and its relationship to the world of commerce and suggest what might be missing from the stories told in this work.

Commercial pressures faced by American universities came to the attention of scholars, journalists, and policy analysts when, in the wake of the revolution in genetic engineering, the intellectual capital housed in institutions of higher learning led science-based firms to develop contractual research-related relations with academic scientists. Among the first to point to this development was Martin Kenney, who, in his 1985 book, documented a number of cases that raised questions about the ways in which university-industry research relationships (UIRRs) might distort traditional academic research practices. Similar findings have been related more recently by journalists such as David Shenk (1999) and Jennifer Washburn (2006) and by the academic analyst Sheldon Krimsky (2003). These writers suggested that formal university-industry research relationships were leading to corporate setting of academic research agendas, increases in secrecy between researchers, and a loss of disinterested scholars.

The work of these authors mourns the disappearance of an insulated ivory tower in which academic scientists autonomously set research agendas, information flowed freely, and the public had access to disinterested experts to aid in the resolution of complicated and controversial policy dilemmas. As we have shown elsewhere (Kleinman 2003; Kleinman and Vallas 2001), the way academic research agendas are set today may be different from in the past, but patrons and the circulation of disciplinary and broader cultural norms have always shaped research orientations. Scholars restrict the flow of information for a host of reasons that have nothing whatsoever to do with the demands of corporate sponsors (Campbell et al. 2002), and we must, at minimum, question the very idea of autonomous and disinterested experts (Jacoby 1987).

Writing in this vein has a difficult time capturing what is novel about the contemporary U.S. university and its relationship to industry because much of the work fails to track change over time (Shenk 1999). Other research at once recognizes a history prior to 1980 or so *and* generally ignores the past (Washburn 2006). Formal university-industry relations date to the mid-nineteenth century, however, and dot the twentieth-century landscape prior to 1980 (Kleinman 2003). In sum, from this research it is difficult to capture what is new in the commercialization of academe and the character of the problem.

A second body of work is more interested in placing the university within the broader context of the emerging knowledge economy. Thus, for example, the Triple Helix approach developed by Henry Etzkowitz and his colleagues suggests the emergence of a kind of institutional fusion between academe, industry, and government in the midst of the biotechnology revolution and governmental fiscal crises (Etzkowitz, Webster, and Healy 1998; Webster and Etzkowitz 1998). These authors do see a long history of interaction between business and academe, but they suggest that in prior periods academic consultancy for industry and industry patronage of institutions of higher education were not uncommon, whereas today university-industry relations focus on formal joint ventures and networks across academic, industrial, and government settings, which aim to produce mutually beneficial and commercially oriented knowledge. In short, Etzkowitz and his colleagues see a twofold change in American academic life: a blurring of institutional boundaries and a focus on commercially relevant knowledge centrally through contractual research relationships. This work is valuable for its attention to historical change and contextualization of the commercialization of academe, but its focus is restricted to the place of UIRRs in economic development.

A third broadly conceptual approach was developed by Sheila Slaughter and her colleagues. These scholars put forward the idea of "academic capitalism." Here the claim is that universities are increasingly engaging in "institutional and professional market or market-like efforts to secure external moneys" (Slaughter and Leslie 1997, 8; see also Slaughter and Rhodes 2004).

Driven by science-based industry's need for academic assistance in the development of knowledge-based products and by the financial requirements of individual researchers and academic institutions, academic capitalism bestows status and power on those research fields, departments, and faculty members that are closer to the market, are economically relevant, and generate market-like demand.

Although more attentive to the broad culture of higher education than the work of Etzkowitz and his colleagues, academic capitalism is centrally focused on the pursuit of profit by universities through intellectual property protection, spinoff companies, and public-private collaboration. Furthermore, like much of the work on formal university-industry relations, Slaughter and her colleagues pay only limited attention to change over time in the commercial character of academic settings.

A fourth body of work has been developed by Walter Powell and his colleagues. Interested centrally in the production of commercially relevant knowledge in academic settings, this "neo-institutional" scholarship focuses on the relationship between organizational characteristics of universities and knowledge production and innovation and is often attentive to changes over time. Thus, for example, an article by Colyvas and Powell (2006) tracks the growing legitimacy of Stanford University's technology transfer office between 1970 and 2000. Looking more broadly, Jason Owen-Smith (2005) uses data covering the period from 1981 to 1995 to trace the shifting relationship between public and private science. This work is considerably more systematic in its tracking of change over time than the Triple Helix scholarship, but like that work, its focus is on the role of universities in economic development and not on the broader culture of academe.

The literature on the commercialization of American academe is rich and wide, but it does have gaps and shortcomings. In sum, the work points to two spaces we hope to fill. First, much of this research is either ahistorical or inadequately historical. As a consequence, it is impossible to fully understand what is new about the commercialization of American academe. The work critical of the UIRs often assumes a fundamental change from an isolated ivory tower to a commercially embroiled, morally weakened university but fails to show a transformation between the two. The academic capitalism approach, despite its broader scope, reifies the divide between the traditional role of the university and its place in postindustrial societies. Second, most of this work is concerned with practices and norms related to the production of commercially relevant knowledge and the university-industry networks associated with such knowledge generation and development. This scholarship, especially the historically attentive work, is either uninterested in or only peripherally attentive to the broader cultural landscape of academe broadly speaking.

In the pages that follow, we make a first stab at filling the gaps left by the existing literature. We cover a wider swath of time, thus enabling us to more fully capture continuity and change in the character of American academe over time, and we focus not on formal university-industry research relations or the production of commercially relevant knowledge, the central concern of the literature, but on the broader culture of the U.S. university.

Methods and Data

Our data are drawn primarily from the journals of the Association of American Colleges and Universities (AAC&U) and the Association of Governing Boards of Universities and Colleges (AGB). We selected these two sources because the membership of these two associations represents the great diversity of American higher education institutions and because both continuously published periodicals over a broad time period. This continuity of publication is especially important, given our desire to characterize changes and continuities in discussions of commercial involvement in higher education. The AAC&U is one of the oldest and largest organizations for degree-granting institutions of higher education, founded in 1915 as an organization for college presidents, and currently includes more than 1,100 institutions. Its membership is extremely broad, including two- and four-year institutions as well as most major universities, but limited to accredited degree-granting institutions. The AAC&U's periodical, *Liberal Education* (*The Association of American Colleges Bulletin* until 1959), has been continuously published since 1915. The AGB was founded in 1921 and is the only national organization for academic governing boards. Its membership includes more than 1,200 institutions and comprises a wide range of colleges and universities, as well as public college and university foundation boards. Its primary periodical, *AGB Reports* (*Trusteeship* since 1993), has been published since 1958. Including data from organizations representing both university boards and presidents / chief officers gives us the broadest possible window into the highest ranks of university and college administration.

Additional materials were drawn from publications of the National Association of State Universities and Land Grant Colleges and the Association of American Universities (an organization including sixty-two major research universities in the United States and Canada). We include these two organizations because both devote more attention to research than *Liberal Education* and *AGB Reports* (not surprising, as both include a higher proportion of research universities among their membership); however, neither continuously produced a periodical over the entire period of interest, and as a result, their reliability must be seen as more tentative. However, both include articles that speak more directly to the issues raised in current discussions of university culture, and consequently, both are important to help orient our description of the data.

There is a certain arbitrariness to any period breakdown we might utilize. Some authors divide periods of the history of American universities in terms of higher education trends (e.g., increases in numbers of enrolled students) or by key pieces of legislation such as the 1980 Bayh-Dole Act (Cohen 1998; Geiger 1993; on the origins of Bayh-Dole see Berman 2008). In our case, we are looking at very gradual trends over time, and we do not see sharp breaks in the usage and nature of codes of commerce at very specific points in time. Consequently, we break down our discussion by decade: 1960s, 1970s, 1980s, and 1990s.

Codes of Commerce

The 1960s

The end of the Second World War marked the beginning of what historian Arthur M. Cohen has termed the era of Mass Higher Education. The GI Bill greatly expanded access to U.S. postsecondary schooling, leading to a doubling of enrollment over prewar levels (Cohen 1998, 182). Research also expanded considerably, prompting the period of the mid-1960s to be characterized by some as the "golden age" of the U.S. university (Gieger 1993, 174). But although federal funding for education and research flowed into U.S. universities and colleges, an examination of the talk of academic leaders suggests that even during the 1960s, a period widely viewed as a high point in the history of U.S. higher education, U.S. postsecondary institutions did not develop in isolation from the world of commerce.

During the 1960s, in the periodicals we reviewed, academic administrators, trustees, and those who were speaking to them struggled with ways to bridge the academic-commercial divide without jeopardizing external support. While potential supporters of institutions of higher education pushed for business-like approaches to accounting and standardization, academic administrators sought to balance the autonomy of their institutions with demands for account-ability from corporate, foundation, and government patrons.

At least some figures from the business world, according to a University of North Carolina trustee, "expect their college or university to function with the same efficiency as their industrial or professional enterprises" (Bryant 1964, 11). Indeed, in a presentation before the Association of Governing Boards of State Universities and Allied Institutions, Walter Cisler, the president of the Detroit Edison Company, suggested that "a uniform system of accounting and reporting could be helpful to educational institutions, so that governance boards and ad-ministrators could make better comparisons as to the cost of doing things one way or another" (1963, 134). Along similar lines, Manning Pattillo of the Dan-forth Foundation called on institutions of higher education to improve systems of evaluation and provide "better measurement and documentation of outcomes of collegiate education" (1965, 510–11). In short, universities were called on to adapt business management practices to academic administration.

Academic leaders responded to these calls. In 1963, for example, John Alfred Hannah warned readers that the newly won status of U.S. higher education would likely lead to appraisal by "outsiders" (1963, 76). Would this lead to a chal-lenge to the institutional distinctiveness of the university? In this context, a vice provost at Stanford worried in 1965 about "accounting demands" and "standardization" requirements in the interest of university accountability.

Our review of periodicals from the 1960s suggests that the culture of com-merce was slipping into discussions about organizational governance and aca-demic administration. This is important since these deliberations might be seen as a precursor to the broader and more diverse ways in which codes of commerce are found in discussions among academic leaders in the following decades. That said, it is important to note that adopting or resisting commer-cial administrative practices was not a dominant area of concern among the writers and readers of the periodicals we reviewed. Indeed, even in the area of threats to the autonomy of higher education, the focus was not on commercial pressures but on the demands of the federal government and foundations, and when administrators and trustees considered adopting commercial practices, they were not so much concerned with efficient management of economic resources as with the growing scale of operations and, of course, increasing the legitimacy of their institutions in the eyes of patrons.

The 1970s

By the 1970s, the golden age of higher education in the United States was over. Historians describe the decade as a period of fierce competition among institutions for resources and students. The 1972 Education Amendments allowed a broader range of postsecondary institutions to compete for degree-granting status. Enrollment growth had begun to wane, as had state financial support for public institutions, and liberal arts institutions found themselves incapable of competing with lower-cost public institutions (Cohen 1998, 191). By the mid-1970s the proportion of income derived from tuition had dropped to just above a quarter among private institutions, but had remained steady for public institutions at about 12 percent (Cohen 1998, 251). Corporate giving had risen from its immediate postwar levels, but not by much—from about 12 percent in 1949–50 to 16 percent in 1975–76 (Cohen 1998, 268).

The historical literature places little emphasis on corporate influence during this period (see Cohen 1998; Gieger 1993; Graham and Diamond 1997), and we found little evidence of explicit university-corporate ties in the talk of university leaders during this period. However, our analysis suggests that, compared to the 1960s, academic administrators increasingly drew on commercial codes and were concerned about commercial practices in the academic world. The commercial talk of academic administrators can be broken into three broad categories: business-like concerns with efficiency and related issues of university and college accountability, the possibility of bringing business-world practices into academic settings, and the related matters of contractual obligations to students and labor relations.

In the face of the perceived tightening of financial resources frequently mentioned by authors, we found increasing calls for accountability by institutions of higher education. These appeals were often translated into terms commonly used in the world of commerce. Demands for increases in efficiency, viewed in the narrowly economistic sense of an input-output ratio, were common. As Bruce Smith, at the time a professor of public policy at Columbia, wrote in 1976 in the *Proceedings of the AGS*, "Public universities face the call for cost-effectiveness" (1976, 18). Universities faced criticism for failures in "modes of management" (Pray 1972, 491). And indeed, writing in *AGB Reports* in 1971, the chairman of American Can Company suggested that donors to postsecondary institutions would very much support the development of programs "designed to improve the efficiency of college operations." In this context, he called for "more effective utilization of human resources" (May 1971, 20, 21). Such discourse would, in an earlier period, have seemed foreign to the academic ear.

More concretely, readers of academic administrators' and trustees' periodicals during the period would have learned of the importance of cost-benefit analysis as a means to "measure" the social returns of education (Shull 1971, 50), which was described as a "service industry" (Ihlanfeldt 1975, 137). In a piece by a vice chancellor from the University of Pittsburgh, they would have read about the value of "systematic planning of resource allocation systems," which one writer indicated had long been practiced in business and government (Freeman 1976, 35–39). And along similar lines, writing in *AGB Reports* in 1977, a college and university association leader recommended that academic institutions improve their processes for finding high-level administrators by adopting executive search practices used in the business community (Fouts 1977, 8).

In the face of increased competition and financial worries, faculty also adopted business-world practices. Although we see sparks of unionization in postsecondary institutions beginning in the 1960s, the trend took off in the 1970s (Cohen 1998, 218, 219), and that is when the issue is discussed in the periodicals read by academic leaders. While some writers pointed to the tension between a desire among faculty for shared governance and a belief that the conflict of interest between faculty and higher education administration warranted collective bargaining and unionization (Pray 1972, 489), others accepted that the trade union approach would become increasingly common in the academic world (McConnell 1971, 22, 23). One high-level university administrator, the vice president of Central Michigan University, described the situation this way: "Faculty are employees; they have their own employee interest. It's not wrong to use a decision-making system that's based on adversarialism when that's what tradition had indicated often exists" (Bucknew 1975, 26).

Interestingly, the issue of the place of the contract in academic life came up well beyond the labor-management relationship in higher education. Reports in the periodicals we reviewed describe lawsuits by students against the institutions at which they studied. The reason: they did not get what they paid for. One article tells of a former student who sued the University of Bridgeport for $350 "claiming that she learned nothing when she attended a class in the College of Education" (Bonham 1975, 5). Another article suggested that such consumer-oriented lawsuits were legitimate: "Students can sue. Catalogs produced by a college or university come under the FTC's definition of advertising. More important, perhaps, is the fact that the catalog is considered a contractual document by the courts. Several rulings have already affirmed this concept" (Bender 1976, 27).

These suits are of a piece with a consumer orientation to higher education, which some of those writing in our periodicals during the 1970s saw as an emerging trend. Thus, for example, an article in *Liberal Education* from 1975 talked about the increasing discussion in "education circles about consumerism," and, indeed, this writer uncritically viewed students as "consumers" (Bonham 1975, 8). That students would sue for breach of contract suggests that not only were administrators and members of the business community blurring the institutional boundary between academe and business but so were students.

The 1980s

For students of formal university-industry research relations, as we described above, the 1980s are the crucial period. Central in the story told by many analysts is the passage of Bayh-Dole in 1980. This law substantially increased the ease with which universities could obtain intellectual property rights to inventions resulting from federally funded research and, as such, according to Slaughter and Leslie, "signaled the inclusion of universities into profit making" (1997, 45). Other legislation passed around the same time, as well as a series of court decisions, is commonly cited as prompting the trend to university-industry partnerships by reducing the barriers to technology transfer and facilitating intellectual property protection by universities (see, e.g., Slaughter and Leslie 1997). But as discussed above, university-industry relations have a long history that predates the 1980s, and while they may have expanded during this period, they do not come to dominate the academic landscape in the 1980s. Indeed, while in some fields industry support of academic research may have risen to as much as 25 percent from the 1980s forward, the jump in industry funding for university research between the early

1970s and the late 1990s was only from around 3 to 8 percent (Kleinman 2003, 44).

More importantly, the periodicals we reviewed suggest that the 1980s constituted *a period of consolidation*, when administrators became more unambiguously viewed as managers in the business mold, faculty as labor, and students as consumers. Areas from academic administration to research to teaching took on a commercial tinge. Trends we witnessed in the 1960s and 1970s, such as priority given to commercial notions of efficiency and contractually understood relations, appear to have become more widespread. During this decade, our periodicals reveal a great deal of talk among academic leaders and those who write to and for them about the importance of using business models in academic settings, measuring performance in all areas of academic life, and marketing the products of higher education.

Advocacy for business approaches to academic life was widespread in our periodicals from the 1980s. "Colleges and universities must," according to Louis Bender of Florida State, be viewed as business enterprises." Bender contended that "the historical view of the collegial organization is no longer appropriate" (1985, 36). A professor of management at Iona College went further, suggesting that "a profit motive can increase the incentive to achieve goals such as efficiency and customer (student) satisfaction" (Grunewald 1987, 33).

The chair of public administration at Baruch College at New York's City University described the state of affairs in a way consistent with many other writers in the periodicals of academic administrators and trustees when he pointed to concrete business practices that warrant adoption: "Increasing productivity means management improvement. By management, I don't mean simply what goes on in a college's business office. I mean the fundamental process of organizing and maintaining human and fiscal resources to accomplish an academic organization's goals. . . . We can borrow management approaches from business . . . but they often have to be adapted" (Lane 1981, 5). Although acknowledging that a simple transfer of practices from business to academe might not work, in a manner consistent with the aims of corporate managers, he nevertheless called for "measurement of outcomes" and employment management consultants for the purposes of marketing university programs (Lane 1981, 7). Use of legal and insurance audits (Perlman 1987, 21) was among other specific business practices advocated in the pages of our periodicals. Facility audits, said one university vice president, were a promising tool in justifying funding requests (Kaiser 1987, 37), and another university president suggested the value of hiring time management consultants to improve the efficiency of academic administrators (Dyson 1989, 8).

Part of the ongoing trend toward viewing students as consumers was the increased emphasis on marketing as reflected in the periodicals we analyzed. Indeed, a study described in *AGB Reports* found that institutions of higher education "have intensified marketing activities of all kinds" (Kauffman 1983, 17–21). In 1982, the vice president at Susquehanna University advocated the adoption of a marketing model by humanists. He suggested that "humanists need not be ashamed to learn from business a better way to conduct the business of the humanities" (Kamber 1982, 233).

In the context of this consumer view of higher education, we found echoes of the reports we saw during the 1970s about students suing academic institutions for breach of contract. In an article entitled "They'll Be Suing You," Kent Weeks told his readers that while in the current environment of "student consumerism" there have been relatively few cases in which "claims of negligence or misrepresentation have been sustained," the legal framework has been built (1980, 36, 41). From our perspective, it is much less important whether students were successful in their lawsuits than that students viewed their role vis-à-vis their college or university in such a manner that they would have thought it appropriate to sue in the same manner they might have challenged a car manufacturer believing they had purchased a "lemon" or have sued a store for failing to recognize a warranty on a television set.

The 1990s

If the presidency of Ronald Reagan (1981–89) marked a self-conscious move of the United States away from government provision of services and toward increasing emphasis on the role of the private sector in social provision, it was a Democrat, Bill Clinton, who declared in his 1996 State of the Union address that "the era of big government is over." This is the larger context—federal moves toward deregulation, fiscal crises of the fifty states, and increasing emphasis on the virtues of the private sector—in which U.S. universities found themselves in the 1990s.

As states faced increasingly tight budgets, in the early 1990s, tuition in public sector universities increased significantly and in many cases state contributions to public universities declined. In an era where the virtues of the private sector were widely accepted, issues of faculty productivity and their measurement became especially prominent. As industry sought to reduce the proportion of full-time staff with broad benefits and rights, universities acted similarly.

Historians see a broad mirroring of the universities and the private sector during the 1990s (Cohen 1998, 385). This is certainly the case, but our data suggest a more complicated process at work. If the 1980s constituted a period in which codes of commerce become firmly established—consolidated—the 1990s take this process a step further. Our data suggest a period of *institutionalization* underway (DiMaggio and Powell 1983; Meyer and Rowan 1977). That is, codes of commerce seem increasingly taken for granted among academic administrators in the 1990s. Our measure of institutionalization is somewhat informal, and our data are only suggestive. The kinds of justifications and linguistic modifiers we saw in previous periods seem less prevalent in the 1990s. Since writers seem to agree that the corporate approach is one reasonable way of being a university, they need not explain or justify the approach, but simply use language drawn from the world of commerce without having to first explain its relevance. All this being said, our data suggest that the institutionalization of codes of commerce in the 1990s was not smooth, a teleological unfolding. Instead, we see evidence of pushback against business language and associated practices.

If institutionalization is captured by the apparent lack of need to justify the use of business-like practices in academic settings, the writers of the articles we use as data are also pointing to an increasing spread of business practices and are moving beyond vague references to the virtues of business to very specific practices. With regard to the spread of business practices, Wayne Anderson, the president of the Associated Colleges of the South, noted in a 1991 article that while in the past some "considered outcomes assessment to be a fad," this is no longer the case. Indeed, Anderson points to the increasing use of business-like outcomes assessment in university settings. According to Anderson, "forty-one states have managed some form of assessment, and 75 percent of public and 56 percent of private higher education institutions have initiated assessment activities of one kind or another" (1991, 26).

Writing in the same year, Ellen Earle Chaffee, a vice president at the University of North Dakota, and Daniel Seymour, a planning and quality management consultant, spoke effusively about the State Board of Higher Education of North Dakota's employment of a specific business practice in university settings: total quality management (TQM). According to Chaffee and Seymour, North Dakota made TQM "the cornerstone of its first seven-year plan, committing itself and the university system to a new form of management and quality improvement." The authors go on to note that TQM "is a time-tested approach to managing described by the late Japanese scholar Kaoru Ishikawa as 'a thought revolution in management'" (1991, 14).

With assessment and TQM on the rise in the 1990s according to accounts by university administrators and their business colleagues, writers were also talking about deploying business consultants in higher education settings and reforming systems of financing. With regard to the former, Virginia Lester gave advice to administrators and trustees about how to hire consultants: "Colleges and Universities rarely used search consultants or 'headhunters' 15 years ago. But with increased involvement of diverse constituencies in the process and the desire to search widely and affirmatively, the process is now more complex. Using executive search firms is not a new concept for corporate trustees, but unless your college has conducted a recent presidential search, it may be a new idea for many engaged in your process" (1993, 25). With regard to university financing, in a 1994 article a University of Chicago trustee described the importance of rethinking. Robert Malott noted that the University of Chicago historically used a financing approach drawn on primarily by nonprofit institutions. This approach stressed the distinction between restricted and unrestricted sources of income. While Malott acknowledged the importance of the difference between these two sources, he suggested agreement among university trustees that "the time was right to overhaul the university's financial-reporting system." The revision of the system should, Malott argued, place the balance of revenues and expenses as the central piece of the picture. As Malott suggested, this gives the university a "clear bottom-line" (1994, 18). Beyond these examples, our data point to the value of human resource management and business-like reengineering in university settings.

Institutionalization is rarely an all-or-nothing process (Schneiberg and Clemens 2006). While many of the discussions of business practices in *AGB Reports* and *Trusteeship* during the 1990s seem to assume the value and virtues of these practices, even here talk was not univocal. In one piece in the late 1990s, a business professor at Pace University, who was also a trustee at Siena College, spoke of the importance of seeking a good fit between business practices and the distinct missions of institutions of higher education (Pastore 1997).

Challenges to business-like approaches to higher education were more forcefully put in *Liberal Education*. Commentators there were especially concerned about the "public good" mission of higher education, which a headlong business orientation might jeopardize. Elizabeth Coleman, the president of Bennington College, captures the sentiment succinctly: "What education is appropriate to a democracy? More specifically: What role does the common good play in shaping our educational practices, in contrast to a focus on individual fulfillment and needs? Would that there were as much said about the student-as-citizen as we hear of students-as-customers" (1997, 8). Even in *Liberal Education* voices of resistance were not uniformly from liberal arts institutions. The chancellor of the University of Georgia system decried legislators' simultaneous demands for accountability measures and significant budget cuts. He noted, further, some discomfort with "career education, especially if it doesn't fit our value system" (Portch 1997, 8).

Conclusion

The history of the relationship between academe and the world of commerce in the United States is neither simple nor straightforward. It does not begin with the advent of biotechnology and the development of formal university-industry relationships for the purpose of producing economically relevant knowledge, and it is not restricted to formal contractual relationships between universities and firms. Indeed, away from the research function of universities, our data suggest that the culture of academe in the United States has long been infused with codes of commerce. While this language did not appear prominently in the discussions of academic leaders in the periodicals we studied for the 1960s, its importance appears to have grown in the 1970s, and the 1980s seem to have witnessed a *consolidation* of commercial codes in academic administrative discussions and perhaps practices. The 1990s may mark a deepening of the *institutionalization* of the use of codes of commerce among academic administrators and trustees. At the same time, codes of commerce are not uniformly and fully institutionalized. We find statements of equivocation and even some resistance among the writers for our periodicals.

Our research indicates that the blurring of the codes and practices of academic professional life and industry is not new to the high-tech era. The data suggest that academic administrators have long adopted and adapted business practices (or at least the discourses associated with these practices), often apparently doing so in the interest of legitimacy in the eyes of external institutions: states and businesses. Faculty have sometimes adopted contractual market practices (unionization) and associated orientations (confrontational as against collegial), and students too have drawn from the business-world playbook, calling for the use of consumer law standards to be used to assess the quality of their educations. Perhaps the university was always a hybrid institution, but one where the relative place and dominance of academic and industrial codes change across time.

We view our findings as suggestive, not definitive. To some extent, the contours of the story we recount reflect the writers, topics, and positions selected by the editors of the periodicals we analyzed. One must assume that these editors tried to capture developments in the academic profession in the period we studied, but, of course, these editors certainly shaped the history as well. Furthermore, our analysis draws on a limited range of sources, and our evidence is of talk, not practice. Still, we believe that our work fills significant lacunae in the existing literature, providing a more fully historical approach to the commercialization of American academe and making clear that the influence of business on higher education extends well beyond research into academic culture. Systematic research that might trace changes in the administrative and more broadly organizational *practices* of U.S. universities over time would be most welcome and could help substantiate, add nuance to, or contradict our findings. Additional research that could more fully ascertain whether and how business-like practices are adopted in university settings would further help refine the analysis we provide.

From a normative and policy perspective, our research identifies a need to move beyond the virtues and drawbacks of academic-industry research partnership to the extent and value of the commercialization of the academic profession and academic culture. Perhaps some use of commercial practices can allow us to achieve more strictly academic goals, and surely there is a difference between wholesale adoption of commercial practices in academic settings and adaptation of these practices toward established academic ends. However, treating our students as consumers, measuring every possible "output," and more broadly adopting business management practices in higher education are likely having costs. We should consider these costs carefully before we move further to adopt business practices in higher education settings.

NOTES

An earlier version of this paper was presented at the INSITE conference in Madison, Wisconsin, in June 2008. This version was prepared for presentation at the annual meetings of the Society for the Social Studies of Science, Rotterdam, the Netherlands, August 2008. We thank the participants at the INSITE conference, and especially Jeannette Colyvas, for their comments. A version of this paper was also presented at the 2008 meetings of the Society for the Social Studies of Science and at the 2009 meetings of the American Sociological Association. Finally, the paper was presented in 2010 at a joint session of SCANCOR and STS at Stanford. We thank the participants in that session for their comments, especially Gili Drori. Support for this project came, in part, from the Buttel-Sewell Professorship held by Daniel Lee Kleinman, 2008–9.

REFERENCES

Anderson, Wayne. 1991. The bottom line assessment. *AGB Reports* (July/August): 26–29.

Bender, Louis W. 1976. Will your catalog stand FTS scrutiny? *AGB Reports* (March/April): 27–31.

———. 1985. Education in deregulation. *AGB Reports* (July/August): 34–36.

Berman, Elizabeth Popp. 2008. Why did universities start patenting? Institution-building and the road to the Bayh-Dole Act. *Social Studies of Science* 38:835–71.

Blumenstyk, Goldie. 2007. Berkeley professors seek voice in research-institute deal with energy company. *The Chronicle of Higher Education*, April 13, A33.

Bok, Derek. 2003. *Universities and the marketplace: The commercialization of higher education*. Princeton: Princeton University Press.

Bonham, George. 1975. The thirty-five billion dollar misunderstanding. *Liberal Education* 61 (1): 5–14.

Bryant, Victor S. 1964. The role of the regent. *Proceedings of the 42nd Annual Meeting and Annual Records, Association of Governing Boards of Universities and Colleges*, 9–18.

Bucknew, Neil. 1975. Collective bargaining: three campus models. *AGB Reports* (January/February): 24–27.

Campbell, Eric G., Brian R. Clarridge, Manjusha Gokhale, Lauren Birenbaum, Stephen Hilgartner, Neil Holtzman, and David Blumenthal. 2002. Data withholding in academic genetics: Evidence from a national survey. *Journal of the American Medical Association* 287, 4 (January 23/30): 473–80.

Chaffee, Ellen Earle, and Daniel Seymour. 1991. Quality improvement with trustee commitment. *AGB Reports* (November/December): 14–18.

Cisler, Walter. 1963. Parallels in the management of educational and business institutions. *Proceedings, Association of Governing Boards of State Universities and Allied Institutions*, 40th Annual Meeting, 129–34.

Cohen, Arthur M. 1998. *The shaping of higher education: Emergence and growth of the contemporary system.* San Francisco: Jossey-Bass.

Coleman, Elizabeth. 1997. Leadership in the change process. *Liberal Education* 83 (1): 4–11.

Colyvas, Jeannette A., and Walter W. Powell. 2006. Roads to institutionalization: The remaking of boundaries between public and private science. *Research in Organizational Behavior* 27:305–53.

DiMaggio, Paul, and Walter Powell. 1983. The iron cage revisited: Institutional isomorphism and collective rationality in organizational fields. *American Sociological Review* 48:147–60.

Donoghue, Frank. 2008. *The last professors: The corporate university and the fate of the humanities.* Bronx: Fordham University Press.

Dyson, Dave. 1989. Managing time wisely builds better presidential leadership. *AGB Reports* (March/April): 8–11.

Etzkowitz, Henry, Andrew Webster, and Peter Healy, eds. 1998. *Capitalizing knowledge.* Albany: State University of New York Press.

Fouts, Donald E. 1977. Picking a president the business way. *AGB Reports* (January/February): 6–10.

Freeman, Jack E. 1976. Trustees, money, and planning. *AGB Reports* (October/December): 35–39.

Geiger, Roger L. 1993. *Research and relevant knowledge: American research universities since World War II.* New York: Oxford University Press.

Graham, Hugh Davis, and Nancy Diamond. 1997. *The rise of American research universities: Elites and challengers in the postwar era.* Baltimore: Johns Hopkins University Press.

Grunewald, Donald. 1987. Privatization of colleges. *AGB Reports* (November/December): 32–33.

Gumport, Patricia. 1997. Public universities as academic workplaces. *Daedalus* 126 (4): 113–36.

Hannah, John Alfred. 1963. When does a public university cease to be a low cost institution? Transactions and Proceedings of the National Association of State Universities and Land Grant Universities. 61:76–78.

Ihlanfeldt, William. 1975. A management approach to the buyer's market. *Liberal Education* 61 (2): 133–48.

Jacoby, Russell. 1987. *The last intellectuals: American culture in the age of academe.* New York: Basic Books.

Kaiser, Harvey H. 1987. How to audit facilities. *AGB Reports* (May/June): 37–38.

Kamber, Richard. 1982. Marketing the humanities. *Liberal Education* 68 (3): 233–47.

Kauffman, Joseph F. 1983. Strengthening chair, CEO relationships. *AGB Reports* (March/April): 17–21.

Kenney, Martin. 1985. *Biotechnology: The university-industrial complex.* New Haven: Yale University Press.

Kirp, David L. 2003. *Shakespeare, Einstein, and the bottom line.* Cambridge, MA: Harvard University Press.

Kleinman, Daniel Lee. 2003. *Impure cultures: University biology and the world of commerce.* Madison: University of Wisconsin Press.

Kleinman, Daniel Lee, and Stephen P. Vallas. 2001. Science, capitalism, and the rise of the "knowledge worker": The changing structure of knowledge production in the United States. *Theory and Society* 30:451–92.

Krimsky, Sheldon. 2003. *Science in the private interest: Has the lure of profits corrupted biomedical research?* Lanham, MD: Rowman & Littlefield.

Lane, Frederic S. 1981. Making professors more productive. *AGB Reports* (March/April): 4–7.

Lester, Virginia. 1993. How to hire a search consultant. *Trusteeship* (November/December): 25–29.

Malott, Robert. 1994. In search of the bottom line. *Trusteeship* (January/February): 14–18.

May, William F. 1971. Donor expectations. *AGB Reports* (September/October): 20–22.

McConnell, T. R. 1971. Campus governance-faculty participation. *AGB Reports* (September/October): 19–26.

Meyer, John, and Brian Rowan. 1977. Institutional organizations: Formal structures as myth and ceremony. *American Journal of Sociology* 83:340–63.

Owen-Smith, Jason. 2005. Trends and transitions in the institutional environment for public and private science. *Higher Education* 49:91–117.

Owen-Smith, Jason, and Walter W. Powell. 2003. The expanding role of university patenting in the life sciences: Assessing the importance of experience and connectivity. *Research Policy* 32 (9): 1695–1711.

Pastore, Joseph. 1997. A trustee's core obligation: Ensuring economic performance and educational integrity. *Trusteeship* (September/October): 17–19.

Pattillo, Manning. 1965. Foundations and the private college. *Liberal Education* 51 (December): 504–11.

Perlman, Daniel H. 1987. The legal audit: Preventing problems. *AGB Reports* (January/February): 18–21.

Portch, Stephen. 1997. Looking in the mirror: Issues of integrity in the academy. *Liberal Education* 83 (2): 4–9.

Pray, Francis C. 1972. Trustees: Accountable or discountable. *Liberal Education* 58 (4): 488–91.

Rudy, Alan P., Dawn Coppin, Jason Konefal, Bradley T. Shaw, Toby Ten Eyck, Craig Harris, and Lawrence Busch. 2007. *Universities in the age of corporate science: The UC Berkley–Novartis controversy.* Philadelphia: Temple University Press.

Schneiberg, Marc, and Elizabeth Clemens. 2006. The typical tools for the job: Research strategies in institutional analysis. *Sociological Theory* 24 (3): 195–227.

Shenk, David. 1999. Money + science = ethics problems on campus. *The Nation,* March 22, 11–18.

Shull, Harrison. 1971. Panel discussion: The moratorium on research. Dean Harrison Shull. *Journal of Proceedings and Addresses of the Twenty-Third Annual Conference of the Association of the Graduate Schools in the Association of American Universities*, 44–50.

Slaughter, Sheila, and Larry Leslie. 1997. *Academic capitalism: Politics, policies and the entrepreneurial university*. Baltimore: Johns Hopkins University Press.

Slaughter, Sheila, and Gary Rhoades. 2004. *Academic capitalism and the new economy: Markets, state, and higher education*. Baltimore: Johns Hopkins University Press.

Smith, Bruce. 1976. Policies committee panel: Change in graduate education. *Journal of the Proceedings of the AGS in the AAU*, 9–33.

Strathern, Marilyn, ed. 2000. *Audit cultures: Anthropological studies in accountability, ethics and the academy*. London: Routledge.

Vallas, Steven P., and Daniel Lee Kleinman. 2008. Contradiction, convergence, and the knowledge economy: The co-evolution of academic and commercial biotechnology. *Socio-Economic Review* 6 (2): 283–311.

Washburn, Jennifer. 2006. *University, Inc.: The corporate corruption of higher education*. New York: Basic Books.

Webster, Andrew, and Henry Etzkowitz. 1998. Toward a theoretical analysis of academic industrial collaboration. In *Capitalizing knowledge*, ed. Henry Etzkowitz, Andrew Webster, and Peter Healy, 47–72. Albany: State University of New York Press.

Weeks, Kent. 1980. They'll be suing you. *AGB Reports* (January/February): 36–41.

CHAPTER ELEVEN

The Meaning of Regulation in a Changing Academic Profession

Erin Leahey and Kathleen Montgomery

H igher education and the academic profession have undergone profound change in recent years. This is true of both components of academic work—the teaching component that other chapters in this volume address, and the research component, which is our focus. Since the 1970s, one of the most pronounced changes in the practice of academic research has been the move toward increased regulation of research activity. For example, before the 1970s, university institutional review boards (IRBs) did not exist. Before 1989, the Office of Scientific Integrity (formally reconstituted as the Office of Research Integrity or ORI in 1992)—the federal agency charged with overseeing research conduct of federally funded researchers and handling misconduct allegations—did not exist.

The goal of this chapter is to review the extent and nature of this rapid change and assess its implications for constitutive elements of the academic profession: autonomy and control. We draw from institutional theory to delineate the organizational field of academic research and the relevant professional and organizational actors within the field who participate, through various roles, in regulation of academic research. Using this framework, we review historical changes in the nature of professional autonomy and research regulation, including shifts from a strong dependence on self-regulation, to a heavy reliance on (external) regulation, to the current hybrid model. The defining features of these different eras can be understood through a relational map of actors in the organizational field, which we employ to illustrate changes in the nature of regulation.

This relational map also helps identify important theoretical and empirical questions about the changing nature of academe. That is, while our focus is on the changing nature of research regulation, we realize that change is intertwined with a host of other changes, including efforts to promote interdisciplinarity as well as translational research that extends beyond the ivory tower. We therefore touch on how these trends align and intersect and how the resultant change has begun to alter the nature of regulation in academic research environments.

The Growth of Academic Research Activity

Research has always been a large component of academic work, but evidence suggests that its role has been increasing in the last two decades. The sheer number of research universities in the United States is one indication: in 1994 there were 236, in 2000 there were 261, and by 2005 there were 283.[1] In addition, our analysis of NSF's Survey of Doctorate Recipients shows that even in a three-year span (2003 to 2006), the number of PhDs serving as "research faculty" increased from 14 percent to 16 percent. National data from a longer time span also suggest the growing priority of research: total R&D budget allocations (in constant dollars) doubled in thirty years, from $68 billion in 1976 to over $144 billion in 2009 (American Association for the Advancement of Science 2008). The share of R&D budgeted for the National Science Foundation, which primarily funds academic research, more than doubled (from $2 billion to $5 billion) in that same time period (AAAS 2008). Increased research activity and research funding demand more research administration—not only to select and fund worthwhile projects, but also to oversee the way in which research is conducted. This reality has inevitable effects on academic researchers themselves, as we discuss below.

The Organizational Field of Academic Research

Scholars use institutional theory to help explain how and why individuals, organizations, and professions act as they do (Tolbert and Zucker 1996). A central premise in institutional theory is that the norms, beliefs, and rules in the relevant environment play a key role in shaping behaviors. The relevant environment is referred to as the "organizational field" (DiMaggio 1991) and defined as the "community of organizations that partake of a common meaning system and whose participants interact more frequently and fatefully with one another than with actors outside the field" (Scott et al. 2000, 13). Participants in the field can include individuals, informal groups, formal organizations and professional groups, and other actors involved in creating and enacting the common meaning system within a particular field.

For the purposes of this chapter, the organizational field is "academic research," and "the norms, guidelines, and regulations about the process of research" constitute the common meaning system of this organizational field. Actors in this organizational field include the individual researchers, research teams, universities, university committees (such as IRBs), public and private funding agencies, regulatory agencies, journal editors, and professional associations, as well as the general public as ultimate consumers of the research.

In figure 11.1 we delineate the range of actors involved in the organizational field of research. The figure places these actors within a set of concentric circles that depicts their relationships to the focal actor (the academic researcher) and to the focal activity (the research project), found at the center of the system. Those with a personal relationship are engaged in the actual performance of the research; those with a direct relationship are engaged in evaluation or oversight of a particular researcher and specific research project; those with an indirect relationship are engaged in setting standards and diffusing norms about research conduct more broadly within a discipline or institution; those with a distant relationship are engaged in general policy making, mass communication, and citizen advocacy about general issues pertaining to academic research, without reference to particular projects, individuals, or disciplines. Collaborators are shown on our model as having a direct relationship, rather than a personal one, with the recognition that each member of a research team has a unique personal relationship to a specific research project. This takes into account that not all collaborators approach the research process in an identical way even when working on the same project. We comment later in the paper on the complications that can arise with collaborators from different disciplines.

In the following sections we will use our model to illustrate how these actors are positioned to affect the work of academic researchers.

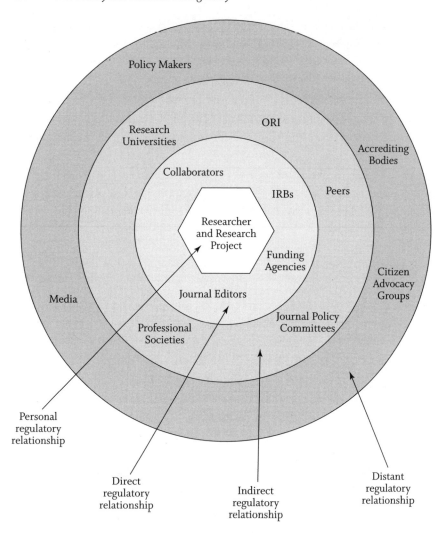

Figure 11.1. The organizational field of academic research

Shifts in the Organizational Field of Academic Research and Its Meaning System

The Tradition of Professional Autonomy and Self-Regulation

A long-standing sociological tradition aims to explain the high levels of autonomy granted to professions relative to other occupations. Early efforts focused on distinguishing characteristics, such as an elevated ethical sensibility and altruistic tendencies (e.g., Carr-Saunders and Wilson 1933; Parsons 1939; Scott 2008; Shapin 2008). By the 1970s, however, this functional perspective gave way to a more conflict-oriented one that theorized about how professions achieved and maintained their standing. Freidson argued that what distinguishes professions from other occupations is their ability to "exercise control over their work and its outcome" and to be the "arbiters of their own work performance, justified by the claim that they are the only ones who know enough to be able to evaluate it properly" (1973, 30). Freidson referred to control over work performance as the "basic prize" in work settings. With respect to academic professionals, autonomy has been similarly described by Bailyn as "the freedom to choose the problems on which to work, to pursue them independently of directives from anywhere except the precepts of a discipline, and to publish freely the results of research" (1984, 5).

While the concepts of autonomy and self-regulation persist as fundamental features of professional work, the nature of professional control has evolved in recent decades. In making this argument, some point to the shift in work setting: in the past, professionals were likely to be self-employed entrepreneurs, whereas now they typically work for an organization. Yet others counter that many professions, including the academic profession, have long performed their work within organizational settings. The fact that academics are employed by universities and colleges has not left them without significant freedoms. As Freidson argues, "Control over the terms and *conditions* [emphasis added] of work is certainly weakened by being an employee rather than an entrepreneur. . . . Nevertheless, control over the *content* [emphasis in original] of work is not at all necessarily so weakened" (1973, 38). Bailyn also contends that the value of professional autonomy for academics is actually "reinforced by the university, as educator and employer of scientists" (1984, 5). She notes that the central control mechanism of the university—the granting of tenure—evolved in order to protect freedom over the content of one's work.

Although academics' employment relationship may not substantially limit their autonomy and the nature of regulation, we contend that other recent changes in their institutional environment do. These changes include the growth of research as a component of academic work and the expansion of research funding (as documented above), along with a concomitant increase in the number, type, and duties of actors with an interest in how research is conducted, its reliability, and its validity. Such changes may have little to no effect on the *condition* of academics' work and only limited effect on the *content* of that work. But, if we consider an additional dimension of autonomy—control over the *process* of one's work—then, we argue, the effect of these changes could be substantial. In other words, an expansion of the organizational field of academic research has considerable consequences for academics' control over the research *process*, i.e., how they conduct their research. This shift also calls into question the traditional distinction between self-regulation and (external) regulation.

Shifts in Regulation of the Process of Academic Research

The meaning system in a relevant organizational field often emerges from the "collective sense-making and problem-solving behavior of actors who are confronting similar, problematic situations" (Scott 2008, 222). As the "problematic situations" confronting researchers have changed over time, so too have the meaning system and its concomitant set of actors and regulations. Below we discuss three distinct periods within the organizational field of academic research that reflect shifts in the common meaning system of regulation. These have been characterized by Montgomery and Oliver (2009) as "following 'normal' practice of science" (pre-1975), "preventing scientific misconduct" (1975–90), and "promoting research integrity" (1990–present).

Following "normal" practice of science. For many years, tacitly learned professional codes of behavior were developed by and used by academic researchers. Millions of dollars had been granted in support of faculty research, with the expectation that research would be conducted according to implicit norms, described by Merton (1973) as universalism, communalism, disinterestedness, and organized skepticism. These values were thought to be internalized by researchers through socialization into an implicit professional ethic and, hence, were not in need of institutional oversight, at either the local (university) or federal (government funding agency) level. "The prevailing attitude of the day was that formal policies were not needed because research, as a professional activity, was effectively self-regulating" (Steneck 1999, 169).

Underlying this attitude was a strong element of trust, defined as the willingness of a party (the Truster) to be vulnerable to the actions of another party (the Trusted) based on the expectations that the other will perform a particular action important to the Truster, irrespective of the ability to monitor or control that other party (Mayer, Davis, and Schoorman 1995). In the context of academic research, trust is the willingness of others (which can include any consumer of the research, from other researchers to funding agencies to the general public) to accept that the research has been proposed, conducted, and reported by a trustworthy researcher, even when each step of the research process is not monitored or controlled by the others.

Trust is fostered by *trustworthiness*, characterized by (a) competence, (b) benevolence, and (c) integrity-oriented action (Hardin 2002). Importantly, these three components of trustworthiness are the same characteristics on which the basis of self-regulation has long been defended. That is, *competence* represents appropriate application of research skills and knowledge, *benevolence* represents humane treatment of human and animal subjects, and *integrity* represents honesty, fairness, promise keeping, and responsible behavior toward colleagues.

Referring to figure 11.1, the organizational field during this early period was confined mainly to the central core of the model, the academic researcher and the research project. This personal regulatory relationship, as we call it, is closely aligned with strict interpretations of self-regulation and relatively unfettered professional autonomy. Most conceptualizations of self-regulation, however, also include what we call direct relationships and some indirect relationships that a researcher has with his or her community, typically a community of scholars and collaborators in the same discipline and/or institution. Yet, each of these relationships during this period could be characterized as consistent with the notion of self-regulation because there was little if any oversight of the *process* of research conduct. What external oversight existed was likely to be an evaluation of a research proposal for funding purposes and a review of the completed papers for publication purposes. And traditionally these funding and editorial review bodies were mainly composed of members of the researcher's own discipline.

Preventing scientific misconduct. By the 1970s, allegations of fraud and other questionable practices by federally funded researchers triggered widespread skepticism regarding researchers' trustworthiness and instigated a new era in academic professional regulation. The norms of trustworthiness that had previously constituted the foundation of self-regulation without monitoring were perceived to be inadequate, and Congress responded with mandates to add an explicit layer of institution-level oversight. These included requirements that universities establish local IRBs, to review research protocols that involved human subjects, and adopt formal policies for responding to allegations of professional misconduct, defined as "fabrication, falsification, or plagiarism in proposing, performing, or reviewing research, or in reporting research results" (Public Health Service 1986).

Although the oversight would be conducted by local institutions, rather than external parties, these actions nevertheless fostered an environment of administrative oversight that appeared to wrest much responsibility for self-regulation from the researchers themselves and hence carried with it an atmosphere of lack of trust. Oversight expanded dramatically during this period, and regulations were institutionalized through formal policies (Evans 2000; Lederer 2004; Moreno 2001).

The diffusion of such changes in the organizational field's common meaning system was facilitated by the emergence of "regulative professions" (Scott 2008) that generated and endorsed these changes. For example, a profession devoted to promoting and enforcing research regulation began to develop (e.g., University Research Compliance Officers; Bosk 1999; Jonsen 2003), along with the founding of related journals (e.g., *IRB: Ethics & Human Research*) and citizen advocacy groups (e.g., the Alliance for Human Research Protections).

Figure 11.1 depicts the growing set of actors as the circle of regulation widened during this period to include a set of distant actors such as policy makers, consumer advocates, and the media who declared an increasing interest as watchdogs in the conduct of research. In addition, several of the direct regulatory relationships became characterized by a combination of external actors (IRBs, journal editors, funding agencies) who were not personally involved in the actual research as collaborators, but whose oversight and evaluation were directly related to a particular researcher and/or research project. With the implementation of IRBs, in particular, far more careful evaluation and approval of research processes were required prior to beginning a research project.

Research on this era has shown that while external requirements establish formally "correct" ways to conduct research, they often failed to settle subsidiary debates and questions of interpretation among professional researchers themselves. This challenge has led researchers, universities, and funding agencies to acknowledge that regulation of the research process is more complex than individual or professional self-regulation at one extreme or explicit administrative regulation and monitoring at the other. Many researchers themselves were coming to understand external regulation as providing only a starting point for restraint in and reflection on the process of research and research practices and were looking within themselves and their research communities for additional guidance (e.g., Bosk 2001; Nathan 2005). Moreover, scholars such as Halpern have recognized that "for government regulation to be optimally effective, it must build on core features and strengths of scientists' informal morality. Where formal oversight stints or obstructs scientists' longstanding traditions, it is likely to generate regulatory failures" (2004, 132).

Promoting research integrity. The current environment therefore is a blend of renewed emphasis on the norms of unmonitored trustworthiness from the earlier era with the policies of oversight from the more recent past. The melding of these two models of research regulation, as well as the simultaneous operation of self-regulation and external regulation, complicates the picture greatly but is also more realistic and, we argue, critical to understanding how the academic profession and one of its primary foci—research—is changing. In this current era, the ORI has been leading a strategy to create and disseminate a new behavioral code for research performance ("responsible conduct of research" or RCR) and an expanded conceptualization of regulation that accommodates and fosters both individual self-regulation *and* institutional regulation and oversight.

To promote research integrity and allow regulation and self-regulation to peacefully coexist, the current era is witnessing another expansion of the organizational field of academic research and a shift in the roles of existing actors. As shown in figure 11.1, new actors such as ORI, journal policy committees, and new accrediting bodies (e.g., the Association for the Accreditation of Human Research Protection Programs) join with existing actors to shape the new common meaning system within this organizational field through a variety of regulatory relationships.

Sources of Behavioral Variation within the Organizational Field

Although the organizational field is a helpful heuristic, we recognize that there is significant variation within any organizational field. Within academic research, behavioral variation can be attributed to both an incomplete understanding of the regulatory system and recent trends in higher education, including emphases on interdisciplinarity and translational research.

Incomplete Understanding of the Regulatory System

We believe that much behavioral variation within the organizational field of academic research is attributable to an incomplete understanding of the regulatory system we have articulated in figure 11.1. There are several reasons for this. First, this is a dynamic model, depicting the set of key actors involved in regulation of academic research today and the typical relationship each actor has to the focal actor in the model—the academic researcher and the research project. As we have seen over the years, new actors emerge, and the roles may shift for existing actors. In addition, the boundaries (the "concentric rings" in the model) are porous, and actors' relationships to the researcher may shift under changing circumstances. For example, ORI is shown as having an indirect relationship with the researcher, because a main mission of the agency is to foster general research conduct norms. However, should there be a claim of research misconduct, ORI would become involved in a direct regulatory relationship to the researcher/project during the investigation of research conduct of a particular researcher and/or a specific project.

Second, many elements of research regulation are not explicitly recognized. Actors' roles, for example, remain unspecified, largely because actors are assumed to share an understanding of what constitutes regulation and self-regulation, when it should occur, and which types of actors are responsible for the various aspects of regulation. Yet, studies show that this assumption is unwarranted. For example, Leahey (2008) demonstrated that different regulatory actors (journal editors, IRB chairs, and funding agency directors) had very different views about the nature of oversight (at least with respect to a specific research practice—data editing) and about the division of regulatory labor, i.e., who was responsible for different stages and domains of research. Some actors trusted researchers to do the right thing, effectively following "normal" practice of science, whereas others saw the benefits of implementing guidelines, effectively imposing a form of standardization on researchers. This dilemma is not unlike that in other professions, such as medicine, where strong debates exist about the value and feasibility of clinical practice guidelines and standards (Timmermans 2005). These debates, whether in academic research or medicine, continue to occur in part because of an oversimplification of the relationship between professional self-regulation and external regulation, as well as an aversion felt by some professionals to any perceived encroachment on professional autonomy. This is one reason why we believe that it is critical to distinguish, as we do here, among different types of professional autonomy: control over work conditions, control over work content, and control over work processes.

Third, the various actors in the model have different degrees of power, and tensions can occur and be resolved in a multitude of ways. For example, competitive tensions can occur among actors of the same type: researchers competing for funding or journal space, or two IRBs claiming jurisdiction over the same study (Timmermans 1995). Tensions across different types of actors can occur over autonomy and control: researchers may resist certain IRB dictates, many of which affect the *process* of work (e.g., how sampling is conducted, how questions are asked, and how data are stored).[2] The theoretical concept of "loose coupling" (Edelman 1992; Weick 1976) helps to explain how some of these tensions are resolved, namely, by weak oversight within an institution or across an organizational field that permits much behavioral variation and allows noncompliance to go unrecognized and/or unchallenged. In some instances, noncompliance with relevant norms or policies may be intentional and may result in sanctions if revealed. But in other instances, behavioral variation may be a more complex phenomenon because (1) norms and policies were unclear or unspecified for certain aspects of the work, (2) responsibility for oversight was unclear, and/or (3) oversight was inadequate.

Recent Trends in Higher Education

Behavioral variation within the organizational field of academic research is also attributable to two recent trends in higher education: efforts to promote interdisciplinary research and efforts to move research beyond the ivory tower and foster what is called "translational research" and "technology transfer." Indeed, both of these trends engender a broadening of the number and types of actors involved in many stages of research: the evaluation and funding of research proposals, the conduct of research, and the interpretation and dissemination of research findings. Moreover, these new actors come from an increasingly diverse set of organizational fields, or what we might call organizational *subfields*, each with a potentially different institutional logic. This makes research regulation an increasingly complex and multifaceted endeavor.

Promoting interdisciplinary research (IDR). An interdisciplinary mode of research, which "integrates perspectives, information, data, techniques, tools, perspectives, concepts, and/or theories from two or more disciplines," is on the rise, largely because it is assumed to promote scientific innovation and breakthroughs (National Academies 2005, 188). At many universities, the sheer number of departments has been growing since the early 1900s; the number of departments at Columbia University, for example, has more than doubled since 1910 (National Academies 2005, 19). The National Science Foundation has also seen a large increase in the number of multiple-investigator awards— from 25 percent of all grants in 1982 to 66 percent of all awards in 2001—which served as a precursor to IDR efforts (National Academies 2005, 118). And our analysis of a systematic sample of social science journals suggests that journals classified as interdisciplinary by the Web of Science have a mean founding date of 1980, compared to a mean founding date of 1966 for disciplinary journals. Overall, there is ample evidence of a trend toward IDR in the academic profession.

Efforts to promote IDR in higher education are already altering the regulatory landscape and may affect the content and process of academic work. Collaboration between researchers from different disciplines may affect the speed with which research is conducted (e.g., an efficient division of labor may speed the process up, whereas attempts to learn new fields and their respective concepts and methods may slow things down) and broadens the direct regulatory relationship to include not only multiple individuals but multiple disciplines, each with a slightly different epistemological view on the significance, validity, and reliability of different approaches to research. The impact of IDR, however, is probably most apparent in the review and evaluation of research proposals and research papers. Whether researchers themselves affiliate with a single or multiple disciplines, top-down efforts to promote IDR mean that research funding announcements stress collaboration and integration of disciplines,[3] and review panels (which help select projects for funding) are composed of scholars from multiple disciplines. As many scholars have noted, there are unique challenges to evaluating interdisciplinary work (Lamont, Mallard, and Guetzkow 2006; Mansilla 2006). Multidisciplinary panels make consensus challenging, and while there is often deference to disciplinary experts, researchers from other fields influence the final evaluation, funding decision, and feedback provided to the investigator (Lamont 2009). Similar challenges are likely confronted by scholars who submit their work to interdisciplinary journals, as well as by scholars who must submit their research plans to an institution-wide IRB that may have jurisdiction over medical, social, and behavioral research. As IDR introduces new emphases and actors into the review process, it opens the door for influence from multiple organizational subfields—influence not over the conditions of work, but somewhat over the content (e.g., what questions are asked), and most certainly over the process (e.g., what theories are invoked and what methods are used). This, in turn, contributes to behavioral variation in the organizational field of academic research.

Promoting translational research and technology transfer. Efforts to push basic research (typically conducted in the academy) toward close interactions with applied settings like private industry and clinical medicine are well underway. Especially since the passage of the Bayh-Dole Act (1980), which allowed universities to collect royalties from federally funded projects, universities have established offices of technology transfer, which assist academics in disclosing their inventions and securing patents. Indeed, since 1980, the number of universities with technology transfer offices has more than quadrupled (Sampat 2006). Further, according to the Association of University Technology Managers, the number of new patents issued to U.S. universities has risen from 250 (in 1980) to 5,327 (in 2002), and the number of invention disclosures has almost tripled since 1991.[4] The National Institutes of Health and universities nationwide are also promoting translational research[5]—efforts to translate scientific discoveries in the academy into practical applications for clinical medicine, so that findings from "the bench" can be of assistance at the "bedside."

Such efforts to move research beyond the ivory tower introduce another set of actors into the regulatory system. The potential commercial application of some academic research gives industry actors (e.g., private firms such as pharmaceutical companies) a greater voice in the regulatory system. As financial sponsors of an increasing amount of academic research (National Science Foundation 2007), industry actors have a direct regulatory relationship with researchers, closely overseeing and monitoring the content but also the process of research. Although conflict-of-interest concerns aim to limit the influence that industry can have over research findings, industry actors readily impact the kinds of questions that are asked (content) and how the research is carried out (process), thereby altering and limiting researchers' autonomy and control.

Discussion

It is common these days for academics to lament what they perceive as their dwindling control over their research and an affront to their professional autonomy. In this chapter, we have documented the recent expansion of the regulatory system (shifting from a focus on self-regulation, to external regulation, to the current hybrid model) and discussed the increasing number and type of actors involved in research regulation. As researchers ourselves, we understand how greater research administration and external regulation can be frustrating for researchers. At the same time, historical and current instances of research misconduct (even in the social and behavioral sciences) suggest that efforts to uphold research integrity cannot be left to individuals alone.

Our conceptual contributions are multiple and allow us to see these recent shifts in the regulation of academic research in a new light. First, we add control over the work *process* to the traditional twofold emphasis on control over work conditions and content. Although academics (as professionals working for an organization) have never had as much control over the conditions of work as entrepreneurs, they generally maintain control over the content of their work (e.g., the questions they ask and the results they report). This is often neglected in discussions of academics' professional autonomy. What is being gradually relinquished is another kind of control: academics' control over the process of work, that is, how they conduct their research. Examples abound: journals require economists to archive their data and require sociologists to use specific levels of statistical significance tests; funding agencies favor interdisciplinary, collaborative research; and IRBs alter academics' research designs—including sampling decisions, interview protocols, questionnaire items, and modes of data collection.

Second, we highlight sources of misunderstanding in the regulatory system. We note that our model of relevant actors is dynamic and has changed over time as new actors come into play and jurisdictions change. We question the common assumption that all actors involved in regulation share an understanding of the meaning of regulation and self-regulation and note variation therein. We also acknowledge the differential power wielded by different actors.

Last, while subscribing to the utility of an "organizational field" framework, we suggest that organizational *subfields* exist and provide nuance to typical renditions of research regulation. Recent trends in higher education, specifically the promotion of both interdisciplinary and translational research, bring new and varied actors into the realm of research: actors from disciplines different from one's own, actors from industry, and actors in applied and clinical settings. These actors, who come from various organizational subfields with slightly different institutional logics, have some control over the content and process of research. Members of another discipline may help decide whether a project is funded, and members of industry and medical practitioners / clinicians can inform research questions and methods, thereby influencing both the content and process of research.

We conclude by observing that the segment of the academic profession devoted to research has indeed experienced substantial change in recent decades, when viewed through the lens of regulation of one's work. We hasten to point out that "pure" self-regulation for individual academic researchers has always been more a myth than reality, with strong professional norms in place that implicitly regulated one's work. Nevertheless, today's academic researchers operate within a far more complex regulatory environment, and we have reason to expect these complexities to grow for the academic researchers of tomorrow. We believe that prospects for a thriving academic profession of the future will be enhanced when new and existing members across professional disciplines recognize that these complexities have not arisen for sinister reasons designed to tie the hands of academic researchers. Toward this end, the model offered here can serve as a guiding template for academics to examine the changes that have taken place in their work environments within the context of research regulation and to better understand the shifting nature of professional autonomy and control resulting from these changes. And as the academy moves toward greater involvement in interdisciplinary and translational research, our model may also serve to make research regulation more efficient, effective, and acceptable to the broad swath of individuals involved in academic research and research regulation.

NOTES

Authors contributed equally to the paper and are listed alphabetically. We offer special thanks to Amanda Lubold and Will Hamilton for their excellent research assistance. In addition, we appreciate the careful feedback from Amalya Oliver as we prepared this paper. Both authors have received funding that helped to support the work: E. Leahey is grateful for time supported by the Radcliffe Institute for Advanced Study, and K. Montgomery acknowledges support from the University of California Academic Senate. An earlier version of the paper was presented at the Fifth Biennial Research Conference on Research Integrity, May 2009.

1. We consider this a rough estimate, as comparisons across time are complicated by changing classification schemes: in 1994, universities were categorized as Research

I, Research II, Doctoral I, or Doctoral II; in 2000, they were categorized as Extensive or Intensive; and in 2005, research universities were referred to as Very High Research Activity, High Research Activity, or Doctoral.

2. Examples of IRBs mandating a change in the research process abound, and we do not elaborate here. See www.institutionalreviewblog.com.

3. Examples include NIH's Roadmap initiative as well as NSF's Cross-cutting (e.g., Human and Social Dynamics) and Integrative Graduate Education and Research Traineeship (IGERT) programs.

4. See www.autm.net.

5. See http://nihroadmap.nih.gov/clinicalresearch/overview-translational.asp.

REFERENCES

American Association for the Advancement of Science. 2008. Historical Data on Federal R&D, FY 1976–2009. http://www.aaas.org/spp/rd/hist09p2.pdf (accessed September 15, 2009).

Bailyn, L. 1984. Autonomy in the industrial R&D lab. Sloan School of Management Working Paper 1592–84.

Bosk, C. 1999. Professional ethicist available: Logical, secular, friendly. *Daedalus* 128:47.

———. 2001. Irony, ethnography, and informed consent. In *Bioethics in social context*, ed. B. Hoffmaster. Philadelphia: Temple University Press.

Carr-Saunders, A., and P. Wilson. 1933. *The professions*. Oxford: Clarendon.

DiMaggio, P. 1991. Constructing an organizational field as a professional project. In *The new institutionalism in organizational analysis*, ed. W. Powell and P. DiMaggio, 267–92. Chicago: University of Chicago Press.

Edelman, L. 1992. Legal ambiguity and symbolic structures: Organizational mediation of civil rights law. *American Journal of Sociology* 97:1531–76.

Evans, J. 2000. A sociological account of the growth of principalism. *The Hastings Center Report* 30:31–38.

Freidson, E. 1973. Professions and the occupation principal. In *The professions and their prospects*, ed. E. Freidson, 19–38. Beverly Hills: Sage.

Halpern, S. A. 2004. *Lesser harms: The morality of risk in medical research*. Chicago: University of Chicago Press.

Hardin, R. 2002. *Trust and trustworthiness*. New York: Russell Sage Foundation.

Jonsen, A. 2003. *The birth of bioethics*. New York: Oxford University Press.

Lamont, M. 2009. *How professors think: Inside the curious world of academic judgment*. Cambridge, MA: Harvard University Press.

Lamont, M., G. Mallard, and J. Guetzkow. 2006. Beyond blind faith: Overcoming the obstacles to interdisciplinary evaluation. *Research Evaluation* 15 (1): 43–57.

Leahey, E. 2008. Overseeing research practice: The case of data editing. *Science, Technology, & Human Values* 33 (5): 605–30.

Lederer, S. 2004. Research without borders: The origins of the declaration of Helsinki. In *Twentieth century ethics of human subjects research: Historical perspectives on values, practices, and regulations*, ed. V. Roelcke and G. Maio. Stuttgart: Franz Steiner.

Mansilla, V. B. 2006. Assessing expert interdisciplinary work at the frontier: An empirical exploration. *Research Evaluation* 15:17–29.

Mayer, R., J. Davis, and F. Schoorman. 1995. An integrative model of organizational trust. *Academy of Management Review* 23:438–85.

Merton, R. 1973. *The sociology of science: Theoretical and empirical investigation*. Chicago: University of Chicago Press.

Montgomery, K., and A. L. Oliver. 2009. Shifts in guidelines for ethical research conduct: How public and private organizations create and change norms of research integrity. *Social Studies of Science* 39:139–55.

Moreno, J. 2001. Goodbye to all that: The end of moderate protectionism in human subjects research. *The Hastings Center Report* 31:9–17.

Nathan, R. 2005. An anthropologist goes undercover. *Chronicle of Higher Education* 51.

National Academies of Science, National Academy of Engineering, Institute of Medicine. 2005. *Facilitating interdisciplinary research*. Washington, DC: National Academies Press.

National Science Foundation. 2007. Survey of Research and Development Expenditures at Universities, Table 1.

Parsons, T. 1939. The professions and social structure. *Social Forces* 17:457–67.

Public Health Service. 1986. Policies and procedures for dealing with possible misconduct in science. Washington, DC: National Institute of Health.

Sampat, B. N. 2006. Patenting and US academic research in the 20th century: The world before and after Bayh-Dole. *Research Policy* 35 (6): 772–89.

Scott, W. 2008. Lords of the dance: Professionals as institutional agents. *Organization Studies* 29:219–38.

Scott, W., M. Reuff, P. Mendel, and C. Caronna. 2000. *Institutional change and healthcare organizations*. Chicago: University of Chicago Press.

Shapin, S. 2008. *The scientific life: A moral history of a late modern vocation*. Chicago: University of Chicago Press.

Steneck, N. 1999. Confronting misconduct in science in the 1980s and 1990s: What has and has not been accomplished? *Science and Engineering Ethics* 5:161–75.

Timmermans, S. 1995. Cui bono? Institutional review boards and ethnographic research. *Studies in symbolic interaction: A research annual*, vol. 19, ed. N. Denzin, 155–73.

———. 2005. From autonomy to accountability. *Perspectives in Biology and Medicine* 48:490–501.

Tolbert, P., and L. Zucker. 1996. The institutionalization of institutional theory. In *Handbook of organization studies*, ed. S. Clegg et al., 175–90. London: Sage Publications.

Weick, K. 1976. Educational organizations as loosely coupled systems. *Administrative Science Quarterly* 21:1–19.

PART V

Contemporary and Historical Views

CHAPTER TWELVE

Professional Control in the Complex University

Maintaining the Faculty Role

Teresa A. Sullivan

American institutions of higher education share a common interest in teaching, but they also espouse a variety of different missions, including research, patient care, civic and K–12 outreach, entertainment and cultural experiences, and economic development, among others. Their educational mission may also be differentiated to focus on particular student groups, a particular geographic area, distance education, remedial education, honors and advanced instruction, and/or continuing education. Various stakeholders watch all of these activities closely, including government agencies at various levels, the institution's own governing board, donors, alumni, parents, prospective students, and competitor institutions. What is critical to achieving each part of the mission and to satisfying each group of stakeholders is the faculty.

In my role as provost, it is clear to me that the most valuable resource at the university is the *time* of the faculty. Without the faculty, no part of the institution's mission can be met: the students will not earn their degrees, the patients will not receive state-of-the-art care, the research and scholarship will remain undone. And without question, the members of the faculty are, by and large, very generous with their time, with few of them working as little as forty hours a week.[1]

In addition to meeting the university's missions, most of these faculty are simultaneously supporting the professoriate more broadly through service to their discipline; peer review for journals or other universities; service on panels, councils, and review boards for the government and the private sector; and mentoring and counseling for colleagues and students. Burnout is a very real risk, and achieving a satisfying work-home balance is a major challenge.

Despite the obvious centrality of the faculty to the work of the university, however, a number of commentators have recently raised concern about the long-term vitality of the academic profession. Some of these concerns relate to the increased number of non-tenure-track and part-time faculty (Umbach 2007); some relate to the potential loss of the institution of tenure (Clawson 2009); still others raise issues of regulation or simply assaults on academic freedom (Hamilton 2009). Within each of these concerns is an implicit concern about the deprofessionalization of the faculty.

In this chapter I will examine the claim that academics are a profession. Academic freedom, peer review, and shared governance are three distinctive features of academic life that can be derived from applying the characteristics of a profession to academics. I then go on to delineate some of the dynamics that are potentially deprofessionalizing. My examples will focus on the most complex universities, the research universities, because they are most likely to have a multifaceted mission and therefore maximize the tensions within the professoriate.

Academics: A Profession?

In terms of the occupational coding used by federal agencies, postsecondary teaching in any field of specialty is regarded as a professional specialty (Federal Register 2009). In the more rigorous sense that sociologists use the term *profession*, college and university teaching may be considered a profession.[2]

A textbook definition of a profession reads: "A high-status knowledge-based occupation characterized by (1) abstract, specialized knowledge, (2) autonomy, (3) authority over clients and subordinate occupational groups, and (4) a certain degree of altruism" (Hodson and Sullivan 2008, 258). This is quite a general definition and could be used to describe a number of occupations. Within the professoriate, however, these characteristics interact in interesting ways that lead to two iconic characteristics of the academic profession: academic freedom and shared governance. It is the erosion of these two characteristics that has most bothered recent observers of the academy (Hamilton 2009).

The possession of a specialized body of knowledge is the underlying claim to qualification for any faculty member. Indeed, the dissertation required for PhD completion—the entry-level qualification for most faculty today—is expected to be an original contribution to knowledge. The dissertation therefore ensures that the newly minted PhD not only has mastered the body of knowledge in her field but also has added to it by becoming an expert in a sliver (however narrow) of that knowledge. Freidson (2001, 21) offers the opinion that the professoriate is the "host occupation" because it supports the teaching of all the professions.

Autonomy is the characteristic of a profession that permits professionals to rely on their own judgment in dealing with professional issues—in the case of academics, how to teach their courses or what issue to research. Peer review constitutes a limit on autonomy; peers can assess competence and presumably hold their colleagues accountable to a high standard of performance. Peer review also means that the most important professional rewards or sanctions are typically those invoked by peers.

The combination of their expertise and autonomy means, in most institutions, that the faculty within a program or field have very broad discretion within their fields over curriculum, the hiring of new colleagues, and the admission of graduate students who will train to become the future members of the profession. The faculty as a collective typically have even greater responsibility that reaches beyond the department or school to the entire institution. Within the university as a whole, the faculty may set policies that limit the teaching autonomy of their peers; for example, they might require that each course have a syllabus that contains certain elements and is distributed within a specified time period at the beginning of a term. The faculty as a group may also guide the curriculum, for example, by requiring that undergraduate degree candidates have completed certain general education requirements in mathematics or foreign language.

The twin characteristics of expertise and autonomy, while quite general among professions, within the university become the basis for academic freedom and for shared governance. Academic freedom protects the academic's right to teach and research, and shared governance provides the faculty's involvement in broader institutional issues that relate to the job security (such as tenure) and working conditions of the faculty (such as policies concerning the responsibilities of teachers and researchers).

These institutional arrangements are by no means as cut-and-dried as this discussion might imply. Within the academy, controversies such as intelligent design in biology or Holocaust denial in history potentially generate tensions between an individual's academic freedom and the collective faculty's governing rights. Outside the academy, both government agencies and interest groups seek to impose their views, often challenging the collective wisdom of the faculty. The recent Higher Education Act reauthorization, for example, undertook to dictate how individual faculty members and universities report textbook selections (Field 2008). Some states dictate required courses to be included in curricula.[3] One interest group "grades" the core curriculum of one hundred research universities based on its judgment of what constitutes a good core curriculum (ACTA 2009).

The Issue of Authority over Clients

The third characteristic of a profession, authority over clients and subordinate occupations, has been less frequently examined by the authors who are concerned about deprofessionalization, but it is a key issue for understanding the role of the faculty in the university. The principal clients of the faculty member are the students, and the faculty member typically has substantial leeway—again, within the parameters of institutional policy—to develop evaluations and grading techniques for a course. The faculty within a program have the authority to require completion of various courses, exams, and papers for a degree. Depending on the program and the institution's policy, the faculty may have the right to discipline a student, even to the point of suspending or expelling a student. These actions may be legally challenged, but assuming that the faculty have a process and have followed it, the courts appear to be reluctant to second-guess the grades that the faculty assign.

A more remote group of potential clients are those who use the research of faculty members. Unlike the students, who have applied to the institution and have presumably agreed to its demands, the users of research are impossible to identify in advance. Users constitute a broad group ranging from the casual reader of a research report to a patient whose use of a potentially dangerous drug was recommended in reliance on drug trial results. Providing due process to these unknown and disparate users is essentially impossible, and instead the professoriate relies on research rubrics that promote transparency and on peer review that provides at least a minimum level of confidence in the research. The altruism of the profession is reflected in the ethical norms that are enforced by peers to ensure that research is honestly reported.

Critics charge that researchers are too often affected by conflicts of interest with the sponsors of their research (especially corporate sponsors) or with other potential financial interests the faculty member might have. Sometimes the critics themselves may have conflicts of interest that lead them to seek to discredit research. The closer that a research area comes to an issue of public policy, the more likely it is that forces outside the university will react negatively. Researchers in areas ranging from endangered species to climate change to Islamic political movements have found their methods attacked and their motives impugned by critics outside the university (Lee 2006). Thus, the authoritative voice of the faculty is much more generally accepted inside the university, but subject to varying levels of respect outside the university.

The Issue of Authority over Subordinate Groups

Many professionals have authority over subordinate occupational groups. In hospitals, for example, physicians have authority over nurses, therapists, and pharmacists with respect to the treatment of a specific patient. Everett Hughes (1958) famously described this process as the delegation of dirty work to others—so that cleaning up bodily fluids of patients is delegated by the physician to a nurse, and thence perhaps to a nursing aide or orderly. Later, he qualified the delegation to make it clear that what is delegated is merely unwanted work: "Each profession seeks a monopoly; it does so in part by limiting its activities and the areas of its responsibilities and tasks, meanwhile delegating purposely or by default many related tasks and responsibilities to other occupations" (Hughes 1970, 151). The delegation may consist of more routine activities, with the nonroutine activities reserved for the more highly trained and compensated professional.

The development of subordinate occupational groups within the academy is striking. At the founding of most American universities, the employees consisted typically only of a group of faculty, one of whom might also be designated president. The faculty themselves took on the responsibilities of admitting, counseling, and certifying students; administering the library and any other collections; and overseeing the financial affairs of the university. Today, by contrast, there are specialized occupations of admissions officers, counselors, registrars, librarians and curators, coaches, cooks, drivers, and of course cadres of technicians, accountants, purchasing agents, administrative assistants, and student personnel workers of all types. And those were just the occupations emergent to serve the internal constituency of the university. Government relations officers, alumni association officers, public relations specialists, development officers, compliance officers, and a host of other occupations developed to handle universities' growing interactions with the constituencies outside the campus.

This differentiation is completely consistent with what has occurred in other spheres of professional activity. It is neither unusual nor blameworthy. The original faculty role set was simply too large; there were too many things to do, and the development of additional occupational groups to fulfill those tasks was accommodated as funds became available.

Nor has this proliferation yet stopped. The faculty role set was very large when American universities began, but at that time the missions of most universities were focused solely on education. The first set of additional workers was hired to perform administrative tasks and to work with students. Today, with the augmentation of university missions, the faculty role set has expanded, with implications for yet additional workers to help fulfill the new missions of the university.

I mentioned at the opening of this chapter that the many missions of the university compete with one another for the attention and time of the faculty. Research and patient care, to take two examples, are typically faculty-led, although both missions require a number of support staff. A single researcher may support twenty or more people on a research grant, including direct support for student assistants, postdoctoral fellows, laboratory technicians, IT specialists, and administrative or clerical staff and additional indirect support for compliance officers, research administrators, accountants, and others. A single faculty member with funded research has created, in effect, a small business. This is welcome news for the many local governments who view the university as an agency of local economic development. If these many small businesses within the university's research domain need to hire additional workers, so much the better for the university town. Reasoning of this sort—as well as the potential new products and techniques resulting from the research and stimulating the economy—led to the inclusion of extensive research funding within the 2009 American Recovery and Reinvestment Act (Grant 2009).

No one really expects a researcher to undertake complex research single-handedly. Without the help of additional workers, it is unlikely that the research would be successful. Using other occupational groups to extend faculty time also applies to other missions of the university. To take another example, the patient care function requires all the support personnel to be found in a busy hospital, with perhaps additional workers to handle responsibilities of translational research and clinical trials.

Why a researcher would need workers to help with research seems fairly clear, but many observers have been reluctant to admit that faculty members also require assistance in their teaching roles. In the balancing of both research and teaching roles, the faculty member often delegates to others the more routine parts of the work, maintaining supervision over them but also retaining the more intellectually challenging parts of the job. In teaching, one of the first jobs to be delegated is grading, which can be routine to the point of boredom. Student graders or assistants may be hired for this purpose; sometimes other staff may be asked to grade assignments. A pedagogy that requires frequent and repetitive drilling is often an attractive task for delegation. In foreign language instruction, for example, the basic teaching of grammar and vocabulary is often delegated to graduate student assistants or perhaps to non-tenure-track instructors or lecturers. Other common sites for delegation are lower-division recitation sections, English composition, and basic (often remedial) mathematics instruction.

The faculty typically retain authority over these delegated teaching activities, either as individuals or collectively as members of a program. But once these tasks are delegated, regular faculty are unlikely to wish to resume the grading, teaching sections, or drilling of basic information that they had once done. Thus, there will remain a fairly constant demand for teaching work that is not done by regular faculty. This delegation process—common to all professions—helps to explain why a stock of non-tenure-track faculty are being hired by universities.

Moreover, the amount of teaching that must be done every term is relatively constant and scales with the size of the student body. So if individual faculty shift the relative amounts of time they can devote to teaching—perhaps by securing a grant with released teaching time, or perhaps by going on sabbatical—then the university will need to take up the slack by engaging more teaching labor. Because this type of shift is not permanent, hiring additional workers on short-term contracts is attractive. This is precisely the dynamic that Cross and Goldenberg (2009) documented: not a conspiracy to reduce the wage bill, but rather a series of decentralized decisions that were made to cope with short-term staffing changes. This dynamic helps to explain why the numbers of non-tenure-track faculty at a specific institution fluctuate.[4]

Maintaining authority over subordinate occupational groups is no easy task. It is no surprise that faculty are often denounced as an elite class that disdains the staff who also work at the university. It is also no surprise that the permanent, tenured faculty are made uneasy by a large and perhaps growing number of temporary faculty, most of them qualified to be permanent faculty if the jobs were available. Concerns that the non-tenure-track faculty jeopardize tenure are reasonable, if only because of the dilution of faculty authority within the university.

While the process of delegating less essential work is a common one for a profession, the result in many research universities is that the tenure-track faculty are now outnumbered on the campus by all the other occupational groups. The tenure-track faculty remain critical to the multifaceted mission of the university, for only they contribute to each facet of the mission. But many of the other occupations' members can legitimately claim that they also help to meet at least one mission of the university. To the extent that a group of non-tenure-track faculty can claim to be the "real" teachers of the students, their assertions may find a sympathetic hearing among those outside constituents who believe that only the teaching mission is central to the university.

Meanwhile, within the university, it seems possible that there will be growing tension and perhaps even conflict between the tenure-track faculty and all the other employees of the university. In this conflict, the tenure-track faculty are likely to find themselves accused of not being loyal to the institution. The source of this charge lies in the tug that many faculty feel from their discipline, as opposed to their profession.

Profession versus Discipline

Professions commonly develop internal specializations, which tend to develop their own social structure and stratification. Among academics, these specializations are called disciplines. The disciplines develop a body of theory, methods, and findings specific to a subject area. The findings are presented to others in the disciplines through publication outlets, often journals, which are themselves controlled by a disciplinary organization. The peer review that leads to the publication within these journals is an important validation of a member of the discipline.

Besides publication in a peer-reviewed outlet, the discipline also controls a number of other symbolic awards that are highly valued by members of the discipline: election to office in their organizations, prestigious lectures and prizes, and citations by one's fellow disciplinarians. Members of the discipline serve as peer reviewers for grants and fellowships. The university needs the disciplines to generate peer reviewers for its own hiring and promotion processes, in keeping with the idea that only the members of the profession may judge one another (an implication of the specialized information and authority of the profession, as explained above).

But from another perspective, the discipline represents a set of activities that compete against the university for the valuable time of the faculty member. The clearest overlap is in research, which gains the faculty member status in both the discipline and the university. The least overlap is in teaching, which can be appreciated by one's local colleagues but is unlikely to be recognized by members of the discipline located at other schools. No administrator is likely to forbid a faculty member the right to edit an important journal, review grants, or sit on a prestigious advisory board—which bring at least some reflected glory to the university—but these opportunities also represent a diversion of effort away from the activities that matter more to the everyday upkeep of the university. Electronic communication makes it possible for a faculty member to be in constant touch with members of the discipline who are at other schools—perhaps to the neglect of faculty members in the same discipline who are in the office down the hall.

The conflict between discipline and profession was conceptualized by Alvin Gouldner (1957, 1958) as the local-cosmopolitan duality. "Locals" invested more of their time and energy within their own organization. For many professions, the local orientation predominates because professionals have local clienteles and offices and become closely integrated within their local communities. In addition, most professions require a license, and the licenses are granted state by state, with reciprocity sometimes difficult and time-consuming. For academics, however, there is a strong and competing pull from their field of specialty.

"Cosmopolitans" invest more of their time and energy within their discipline or specialty. Through this process, cosmopolitans tend to accrue prestige and other symbolic awards that can be translated into more tangible rewards (such as promotions and raises) within the university. The cosmopolitan also has a greater potential for manipulating the peer review process, either by becoming an important gatekeeper (such as an editor) or by influencing so many other members of the discipline as to obtain a high reputation. The successful cosmopolitan is often drawn more and more away from her university, giving lectures or accepting visiting appointments at other universities.[5] Perhaps the ultimate form of peer review is the outside offer, the offer of appointment at another institution that follows from a positive vote of its department. This offer leaves the administrator at the home university with the choice of either losing the faculty member or rewarding the faculty member with greater salary and perks in a retention effort. If the faculty member is retained in this fashion, there is an incentive to other faculty to do the same.

Electronic communication makes cosmopolitanism a much easier choice for nearly all faculty. E-mail makes possible the rapid dissemination of ideas, data, and gossip. Colleagues can collaborate from a distance, and it is very possible for a faculty member's closest friends in the discipline to be located hundreds or thousands of miles away. A virtual community is now a viable alternative to developing a community within the department or program. When travel and snail mail were the principal options for contact with others in the discipline, even the cosmopolitan had reasons to have close ties with local colleagues, if only for companionship.

Strong tensions often arise between the local and the cosmopolitan faculty members. The local faculty see themselves as the ones who maintain the university functions, because they often form the backbone of faculty governance and of many administrative committees. Such service, while recognized as important, is often not as well rewarded as the threat to leave for another university. Cosmopolitan faculty are likely to regard their local colleagues with a certain amount of condescension and not to value the type of service they perform.

Scientists and Humanists

Besides the tension between locals and cosmopolitans, many universities experience a strong tension between two distinct models of scholarship: the scientist and the humanist. I mean these two terms to serve as anchors for the two ends of a continuum, because many disciplines have members whose work contains elements of both approaches. Especially in the social sciences, both models may be represented and many colleagues may mix the models in their own work.

At first glance, the difference may appear to be one merely of quantitative versus qualitative methods and data, but in fact the two models have considerable differences. In the sciences, collaborative work is valued, and large teams are commonplace. The pace of the work and of publication is rapid, even frantic. Most graduate students in science and engineering are funded by the university, often through research assistantships that pay them for doing their research. Doctoral students in science and engineering typically finish their degrees more quickly[6] and enjoy daily interaction with their supervisor, in whose lab they are often working. In fact, the findings of the dissertation may be critical to the overall project of the supervisor. Young PhDs in the sciences commonly go on to postdoctoral positions, which provide them an opportunity to establish their own research careers and to establish their independence as scientists. The funded grant serves as a primary form of peer review for the sciences, and the typical form of publication is an article—although in some fields, such as computer science and physics, the preprint is sometimes the important form of publication. In many engineering specialties, conference proceedings are the most important form of dissemination, with the journals referred to as "archival journals" to indicate their function for the field.

By contrast, in the humanities the modal publication is still the singly authored monograph. Completion of the dissertation may take quite a long time—ten years or more—and the supervisor may have only sporadic communication with the graduate student during the writing phase. Graduate students in the humanities might have fellowships for support, but the more common form of support is a teaching assistantship. Teaching is valuable work experience, but the humanities doctoral candidate must combine teaching with research in a way that is similar to the life of the assistant professor. One advantage of this graduate school formation is that the humanist is typically able to demonstrate independent scholarship and therefore is less likely to need a postdoctoral position. The most important forms of peer review are the reviews of manuscripts by university presses and the review of journal articles.

The funding of these two academic enterprises is quite different. Typically the university will make a large investment to hire a young scientist because of the laboratory equipment that will be needed to begin a research career. A successful young scientist will begin to secure grants and begin to build a team of students and staff. This grant funding may also pay for reduced teaching loads and be seen by administrators as a return on investment. Although the young scientist may be in continuous contact with colleagues at other locations, the existence of the lab is a strong localizing influence in the sciences. It is difficult (but not impossible) to move to another university because the new university may not be interested in bearing the considerable costs of moving a laboratory and perhaps the lab's personnel to a new position.

By contrast, the investment made in a new humanist is relatively small; the start-up package is likely to consist principally of a computer and accoutrements, with perhaps some travel and research money included. If the humanist were able to secure a grant or fellowship to cover part of salary, that would be a bonus, but it is rarely expected. Instead, the flow of tuition is the principal means by which the humanities departments are funded. Released time from teaching is more rare and may come about through periodic sabbaticals or in exchange for administrative service. Luring away the humanist star is thus less expensive for another university. It is not clear that this difference in financial model actually leads more humanists to be cosmopolitans as a career strategy, but at least some universities have followed a strategy of hiring humanities stars as a means of raising the institution's visibility and prestige. The risk, of course, is that a third university may raise the ante still higher.

One conflict between humanists and scientists—or rather, between these two models—is the suspicion of each camp that it is subsidizing the work of the other. This tension became quite palpable at the University of California campuses when they instituted furloughs in 2009 (Wasserstrom 2009). Some scientists were exempted from the furloughs because their salaries were covered through a federal grant, but the humanists did not have such an alternative and therefore lost a percentage of their pay. There are also other conflicts that are more substantive and perhaps ideological. These conflicts are sometimes articulated when it is time to select a new administrator whose portfolio will include both groups. When both models are present within the same department, the tensions may be more pronounced in daily life and lead to the formation of camps or factions.

Implications for Occupational Control

Brint notes that "ties to a knowledge base, practical craft, and collective organization stand as protection against the overriding influence of markets and external hierarchies" (1994, 202). Professions are conceptualized as self-governing, at least in part because lay people are unable to judge the professional's expertise. The expression of the academics' occupational control has traditionally been academic freedom, peer review, and shared governance. To what extent are these methods of occupational control still protection against markets and external forces?

The community of faculty still tends to stand united in the face of threats to *academic freedom*. Groups outside the university, including some lay constituencies around the university (governing boards, legislators, perhaps parents), seem to be the most likely to challenge academic freedom. Even so, it seems to me that the *concept* of academic freedom is less likely to be under attack today than the *application of the concept* in a particular case. Academic freedom represents a situation in which the academic professionals seem to have won the war but will continuously engage in skirmishes.

Some of these skirmishes will be directed at what is not included in the curriculum, as opposed to what is, and they are most likely to be directed at social scientists and humanists. The claim may be that the professor's right to academic freedom has to be balanced against the student's right to academic freedom—for example, the student's right to learn about intelligent design or creationism in a biology course in addition to the standard exposition of Darwinian evolution.

Peer review, from my perspective, is robustly accepted within the university and is vigorously defended by various scholarly organizations and federal research agencies. Where it appears to be under attack is by critics who believe that the peer group is preselected for a certain point of view (theoretical or more likely ideological), and therefore the result is predetermined. In faculty hiring, it is alleged, this leads to the continued selection of faculty who are ideologically similar to the existing faculty—a charge often leveled by social conservatives (Lee 2006). With respect to the reviews of written work, the belief that the peer review has been skewed appears to carry more weight when the author is known to the peer reviewers—as opposed to the double-blind method of refereeing used in most sociology journals. A recent controversy concerning peer review in climate change research may lead to further questioning of the peer review system (*Wall Street Journal* 2009).

But it is in the area of *shared governance* that the issues of occupational control seem to me most troubled. Shared governance is nearly always defined as the necessity for faculty input into major decisions made by university administrators. The concept became popular when professors were numerically the predominant occupational group on the campus. As I have shown in the analysis above, however, today the university has many employees from other occupations. Even among the employees who do teaching and research, the tenure-track faculty may be a decreasing fraction. Relatively few campuses have extended the idea of shared governance to include adjuncts, lecturers, research staff, clinical faculty, and other groups not eligible for tenure. By the same token, the issues that face administrators today may be disproportionately nonacademic in nature, so that the fraction of the decision set requiring consultation is also shrinking.

A bigger threat to shared governance, however, may be the internal divisions within the faculty. Locals and cosmopolitans are likely to disagree about whether it is worthwhile to invest any time in shared governance. Scientists and humanists may find that their working conditions are actually quite different from each other's, and that they do not share common interests when a shared governance issue is being considered. Internal conflicts can obfuscate issues and make a sham of shared governance.[7]

Even if the tenure-track faculty were to remain completely self-governing, however, the broadening of the university's mission and constituencies may nevertheless move more issues away from their oversight. For example, distance learning develops a new constituency for the university; is this an area of teaching that the tenured faculty would prefer to delegate to a group of distance-learning specialists? Economic development has become an important part of the mission for many institutions, especially public ones. To what extent should the faculty be involved in the interactions with local development officials, business owners, and venture capitalists, and to what extent would they prefer to let these matters be handled by qualified staff members? Keeping in mind the many activities already competing for faculty time, it would not be surprising if many faculty decided that they would focus their attention on matters of more immediate import to their own careers.

Finally, the influence of finances is a critical issue. Many universities have tried to diversify their revenue streams to curb tuition growth and to make themselves less reliant on a single funding source, be it the state legislature or an endowment. As funding becomes tighter, and as the timeline for decision making grows shorter, decision making is likely to become more centralized, with fewer opportunities for input. Under these conditions, administrators are likely to become more reliant on specialists in finance. Faculty who are interested in shared governance could contribute in this situation by helping to articulate overall principles or policies, recognizing that dozens of everyday decisions will have to be made without formal consultation.

Summary

All professions today face potential deprofessionalization, if for no other reason than the great democratization of knowledge through the Internet threatens professional monopolies on knowledge (Hodson and Sullivan 2008, 273). External forces such as the general public, government regulators, and severe economic competition among organizational employers affect all professions. Academics are hardly immune from these pressures, as the cultural wars of recent years have demonstrated. Academic freedom always requires vigilance against those who would censor or control controversial content. On the other hand, the widespread acceptance within universities of peer review is still reflected in the evaluation of academic writing and in the hiring and promotion of tenure-track faculty.

Shared governance is the tenet of the academic profession that may be in the greatest jeopardy, principally because of the proliferation of other occupations within the university and because of tensions among the professors themselves. Maintaining professional solidarity in the face of intellectual diversity and shifting loyalties between discipline and university may prove to be the most difficult task for the faculty.

NOTES

1. Hermanowicz 2009 (2) notes that academics work 52.1 hours per week on average.

2. Primary and secondary teaching, by contrast, is sometimes classified as a semiprofession, principally because of a lack of autonomy in the control of work (Etzioni 1969).

3. For example, Texas state law requires that graduates of state universities and colleges have six semester hours of credit in U.S. history. University of North Texas, Department of History homepage, www.hist.unt.edu/.

4. The situation I am describing is in the research university context. The fact that there has been a large *national* increase in the number of non-tenure-track faculty has additional causes. One important cause is the growth of community colleges, which are overwhelmingly staffed by contingent faculty. The for-profit sector, another rapidly growing part of higher education, is also more likely to rely on contracts for specific periods rather than a tenure track (Schuster and Finkelstein 2008, 42–43). In addition, the financial crisis that began in 2008 has left some four-year institutions in a more precarious financial situation, which might encourage a short-

term substitution of temporary faculty for more permanent faculty. At least for now, that decision may be a result of financial exigency rather than a new policy.

5. A professor of chemistry once told me that the annual report form for faculty should include a place to indicate whether you had achieved platinum status in at least one frequent flyer program. If not, he argued, your work was not important enough to qualify for a merit increase because you weren't flying to enough other schools and conferences to read papers.

6. For new PhDs graduating in 2007, the median number of years to the PhD after entering graduate school was 6.8 years for physical sciences, 6.9 years for engineering, 7.1 years for life sciences, 9.3 years for humanities, and 12.0 years for education. NORC 2009, table 10, p. 12.

7. I have not discussed here the role of professionalism, or the internalized ethical professional identity of the faculty member. Hamilton 2006 has written persuasively about this issue. Not having any evidence about the comparative professionalism of academics and other professions, I am not inclined to speculate about the state of professionalism among professors. I do believe that a structural approach such as I have outlined is more fruitful than attributing problems to the personality or defective behavior of individual professors.

REFERENCES

ACTA (American Council of Trustees and Alumni). 2009. What will they learn? A report on general education requirements at 100 of the nation's leading colleges and universities. Washington, DC: ACTA.

Brint, Steven. 1994. *In an age of experts: The changing role of professionals in politics and public life*. Princeton: Princeton University Press.

Clawson, Dan. 2009. Tenure and the future of the university. *Science* 324 (May 29, 2009): 1147–48.

Cross, John G., and Edie N. Goldenberg. 2009. Off-track profs: Non-tenured teachers in higher education. Cambridge, MA: MIT Press.

Etzioni, Amitai, ed. 1969. *The semi-professions and their organization: Teachers, nurses, social workers*. New York: Free Press.

Federal Register. 2009. 2010 Standard Occupational Classification (SOC)—OMB's final decisions; notice. 74, 2 (January 21). Consulted at www.bls.gov/soc/soc2010final.pdf.

Field, Kelly. 2008. House passes sweeping bill to renew Higher Education Act. *Chronicle of Higher Education*, February 8. Consulted at http://chronicle.com/article/House-Passes-Sweeping-Bill-/483/.

Freidson, Eliot. 2001. *Professionalism: The third logic*. Chicago: University of Chicago Press.

Gouldner, Alvin W. 1957. Cosmopolitans and locals: Toward an analysis of latent social roles I. *Administrative Science Quarterly* 2:281–306.

———. 1958. Cosmopolitans and locals: Toward an analysis of latent social roles II. *Administrative Science Quarterly* 2:444–80.

Grant, Bob. 2009. Your guide to NIH stimulus funds. www.the-scientist.com/blog/display/55588/ (accessed April 2, 2009).

Hamilton, Neil W. 2006. Faculty professionalism: Failures of socialization and the road to loss of professional autonomy. *Liberal Education* 92 (4): 14–21. Consulted at General OneFile. http://find.galegroup.com (accessed November 27, 2009).

———. 2009. Proactively justifying the academic profession's social contract. In *The future of the professoriate: Academic freedom, peer review, and shared governance*, ed. Neil W. Hamilton and Jerry G. Gaff, 1–18. Washington, DC: Association of American Colleges and Universities.

Hermanowicz, Joseph C. 2009. *Lives in science: How institutions affect academic careers.* Chicago: University of Chicago Press.

Hodson, Randy, and Teresa A. Sullivan. 2008. *The social organization of work.* 4th ed. Belmont, CA: Thomson-Wadsworth.

Hughes, Everett C. 1958. *Men and their work.* Glencoe, IL: Free Press.

———. 1970. The humble and the proud: The comparative study of occupations. *Sociological Quarterly* 11, 2 (Spring): 147–56.

Lee, John. 2006. The "faculty bias" studies: Science or propaganda? Consulted at www.aft.org/newspubs.

NORC. 2009. Survey of earned doctorates: Doctorate recipients from United States universities, selected tables. Consulted at www.norc.org/NR/rdonlyres/2D5FD7C8-4AE0-4932-B777-0BC8EA7965EF/0/2007_selectedtabs.pdf.

Schuster, Jack H., and Martin J. Finkelstein. 2008. *The American faculty: The restructuring of academic work and careers.* Baltimore: Johns Hopkins University Press.

Umbach, Paul. D. 2007. How effective are they? Exploring the impact of contingent faculty on undergraduate education. *Review of Higher Education* 30 (2): 91–128.

Wall Street Journal. 2009. Rigging a climate "consensus": About those emails and "peer review" (November 27). Consulted at http://online.wsj.com/article/SB10001424052748703499404574559630382048494.html.

Wasserstrom, Jeffrey N. 2009. U. of California cuts: A faculty member's dispatch from the front lines. *Chronicle of Higher Education*, July 29. Consulted at http://chronicle.com/article/U-of-California-Cuts-a-Di/47491/.

CHAPTER THIRTEEN

All That Glittered Was Not Gold

*Rethinking American Higher Education's
Golden Age, 1945–1970*

John R. Thelin

A number of recent books have emphasized themes of deterioration
and crisis in the institutional conditions facing professors in the United
States. Notable among these works is Mary Burgan's perspectives as former
president of the Association of American University Professors, which lament
and dissect the shrinking influence of professors in governance—as detailed
in her book *What Ever Happened to the Faculty? Drift and Decision in Higher
Education* (2006). Illustrative of research on the problems of a changing professoriate and campus workplace is the systematic study by Jack Schuster and
Marty Finkelstein, *The American Faculty: The Restructuring of Academic Work
and Careers* (2008).

Although these two studies are current, their concerns are neither new nor
isolated. Some digging in the academic literature annals, along with op-ed
pieces in the *Chronicle of Higher Education*, shows that, to the contrary, these
are merely the latest variations on a familiar theme that has been central in
research findings about American higher education for over thirty-five years.
Consider a brief exhumation of titles since the early 1970s: *Academics in Retreat* (Deutsch and Fashings 1971); *The New Depression in Higher Education*
(Cheit 1971); *The American Professoriate: A National Resource Imperiled* (Bowen
and Schuster 1986); *The Academic Profession: The Professoriate in Crisis* (Finkelstein 1997); *The New Academic Generation: A Profession in Transformation*
(Finkelstein, Seal, and Schuster 1998); *Teaching Without Tenure: Policies and
Practices for a New Era* (Baldwin and Chronister 2002).

Certainly this is an extended tale of faculty woe. Its recurrent sound of
alarm over almost four decades backs us into a logical corner: if there is
decline, then it must represent a fall from grace or an erosion or slippage

from some high point. When and where was the high point? One plausible answer is that the quarter century from 1945 to 1970 has gained fairly wide acceptance as being called "Higher Education's Golden Age." It is, for example, central to Richard Freeland's title in his remarkable book about colleges and universities in the greater Boston area and Massachusetts (1992). It is a theme explored in detail in the documentary anthology *American Higher Education Transformed, 1940–2005* (Smith and Bender 2008). Whereas many of the scholars contributing to this volume are documenting and dissecting the downward spiral of the United States' present and future faculty, my emphasis is a bit different: I wish to rely on historical analysis to rethink and reconstruct how professors fared during the quarter century after World War II.

Reconstructing the Golden Era

To provide a snapshot of the affluence and optimism of the immediate post–World War II prospects for American higher education, one can do no better than peruse the October 25, 1948, issue of *Life* magazine. The issue featured a photographic essay of the University of California—ranging from a cover photo of Berkeley students cheering their championship football team to a succession of articles and full-colored illustrations that explored nooks and crannies and maps of the dynamic multicampus University of California system. Hard to believe today is that its leader was *not* Clark Kerr, who has been familiar to us for almost a half century as the enduring icon of the University of California and author of the influential 1963 classic *The Uses of the University*. To remedy the myopia of the present, it is important to recall the fame and longevity of Kerr's predecessor, Robert G. Sproul. He had been president of the University of California since 1930 and was the mastermind of its emphasis on high-powered physics and its expansion to include UCLA and a host of related research sites and institutes extending statewide. When Sproul was invited by Columbia University to serve as its president, University of California alumni and a host of state legislators and business leaders begged persuasively to have him stay put. His popularity extended into national politics, as he was keynote speaker at the Republican National Convention—despite never having sought elected office. Sproul was probably as famous in his own professional lifetime as Clark Kerr has been since 1960. Sproul's public celebrity status included his being featured on the cover of *Time* magazine, a popular presence overlooked if not forgotten since 1958 when he retired (*Time* 1947).

Sproul's University of California, then, was a showcase for a well-funded large-scale model of higher education after World War II. It symbolized the prosperity and optimism of an era characterized by one social and economic historian as the period in American life "when the going was good." (Hart 1982). Drawing from the University of California as a model and leader in showing how mass higher education could simultaneously be fused with excellence in scholarship, it is possible to reconstruct a summary of the major features of the period from 1945 to 1970 typically associated with making this a "Golden Age" for American higher education. First, the expansion of higher education enrollments created a concern about the possible shortage of PhDs— and signaled a robust market for graduate students who aspired to be professors (Machlup 1962). Second, the opportunities for faculty research were enhanced by a relatively new trend of generous federally sponsored research and development in selected fields. Third, as suggested by California's example, governors and legislators in many states endorsed increased tax support for higher education. Fourth, the Servicemen's Readjustment Act of 1944 (popularly known as the GI Bill) expanded college enrollments and contributed some diversification of the student body by providing portable financial aid. Fifth, the 1947 President's Commission on Postsecondary Education contributed a blueprint for sustained public commitment to accessible and affordable higher education (Geiger 1993).

In the 1960s one legacy of these immediate post–World War II initiatives was the substantial increase in the construction of new campuses. This included a relatively new institution, the "junior college," and its successor, the public "community college." Statewide coordination and planning included the formulation of state "master plans." Undergraduate expansion was accompanied by significant increase in the variety and number of PhD programs. And, for PhD students of the era, the academic job market continued to gain momentum during the years 1965–70. It was not unusual, for example, for one who had just completed a PhD at an established university to have multiple tenure-track faculty job offers (Finnegan 1993).

Quantitative growth was accompanied by qualitative gains for faculty in the United States. It included, according to sociologists Christopher Jencks and David Riesman in 1968, the ascendency of professors as respected experts in a variety of prestigious and valued fields. Psychologist Nevitt Sanford and economist Anthony Ostroff wrote in 1962 about rising salaries of faculty, as well as some gains in prestige alongside the learned professions of law and medicine.

To flesh out the statistical skeleton of growth, it is important to include an anecdotal item of this era of optimism and relative good feelings within academe. Here's a nostalgic view of campus life at the Johns Hopkins University in which "the Faculty Club" was central to the intellectual and social life of major colleges and universities:

> During the club's golden age in the '50s and '60s, some 16 chairs—every one of them filled—would be crowded around the big table. Departments would reserve tables in the main dining room, and come noontime, professors strolled for lunch with their colleagues. And, the best was yet to come: Those were the days when Milton Eisenhower, president of Johns Hopkins and brother of Ike, held court at the club, bantering with colleagues over meat loaf and mashed potatoes. Junior faculty members debated the issues du jour with senior professors, and scholars mingled across departmental lines. (Schneider 1997)

Creature comforts were symbolic perks of faculty prestige. Clark Kerr took time to note, "I find that the three major administrative problems on a campus are sex for the students, athletics for the alumni and parking for the faculty." (1963, 138). Presidential attention to making certain that faculty did have ample campus parking was a seemingly small gesture that accentuated this era of good feeling. Little wonder, then, that professors in the early twenty-first century would be inclined to say nostalgically, "Those were the days . . ."

Some Tarnished Spots in the Golden Era

Amidst this celebration were seeds of what would later be problematic to professors. Consider, for example, the aforementioned 1948 *Life* magazine issue showcasing the University of California. President Sproul (and his young chancellor of the Berkeley campus, economist Clark Kerr) advanced a deliberate, distinctive strategy for undergraduate education in the new, large university. It was an approach that *Life* and *Time* writers characterized as "Think or Swim." According to Sproul's academic plan, large lecture classes with enrollments sometimes as high as four hundred or more students was a model that allowed a university to hire at a competitive salary the best professors in their respective fields. The logic was that an undergraduate was better served by being part of a large class with a top professor than having a small class enrollment taught by a less distinguished scholar. The important point from this episode is that it shows that many American universities after World War II did not necessarily drift into a practice of large lectures. Often they did so by design, not accident—and with a clear pedagogical justification. What Sproul and others saw as a good solution to a problem in mass higher education would, in fact, become an Achilles' heel throughout the quarter century from 1945 to 1970. The practice was never embraced completely—and was especially resisted (and resented) by residential liberal arts colleges. It also would persist as a growing and consequential source of dissatisfaction from undergraduates in the 1960s whose credo was to deplore the "impersonality of the multiversity."

Nationwide prosperity following World War II had a side effect that higher education analysts today have usually overlooked: a high inflation rate. More consumers had more money at the same time that few goods were available because factories had not had time to retool from wartime production. The year 1948 was a good time to buy an army surplus armored tank—but not so good for a new Chevrolet, since so few were yet available to put on the market. And, for higher education, the late 1940s and early 1950s were unexpectedly shocking for private liberal arts colleges whose budget planning had not anticipated the inflation (*Life* 1949; Thelin 2006). For those private colleges with lean endowments, this went beyond being a nuisance as many had trouble meeting their payrolls or paying local vendors for repairs and furnishings. State universities, buoyed by admiring governors and legislators, were better able to lobby for increased appropriations than were the private colleges. Yet even some of the progressive states committed to supporting education, such as Wisconsin, were hard-pressed to provide their flagship universities with adequate subsidies to accommodate the influx of students who were sponsored by the federal GI Bill (Stransky 2006). Booming enrollments stretched campus facilities, from housing to laboratory space, as crowding edged from being an inconvenience to an impediment to sound education.

No doubt there was growth and increasing resources and prestige at colleges and universities as part of American life. To supplement and, hence, complicate this general (and accurate) depiction, it's useful to probe some significant cases to rediscover the fundamental tensions that surfaced. The first glimpse will be of the prestigious universities in the San Francisco Bay

Area—the University of California at Berkeley and Stanford University. Then, we shall look at trends on the East Coast—namely, Boston, a haven for higher education as home for Harvard, Massachusetts Institute of Technology, Boston University, Boston College, Tufts University, Northeastern, and dozens of other accredited colleges and universities.

One reason the immediate postwar years were not idyllic for professors was that essential tenets of academic freedom were at risk during the investigations of the so-called McCarthy era. Many campuses were probed and maligned by newspaper editors, governors, and legislators suspicious of Communist Party membership among faculty. The allegations were particularly intense at established state universities, including the University of California at Berkeley and the University of Washington and at Harvard and Columbia. For all the praise for the University of California as a high point of American higher education, the conflicts between university administrators and faculty over a campus-imposed loyalty oath led to widespread purges, firings, and angry departures of highly regarded professors. Most troubling about the episodes at state universities, especially at the University of Washington in Seattle, Berkeley, and UCLA, was that the campus presidents displayed more zeal than did the newspaper editors and state legislators in curtailing academic freedom (Schrecker 1986). The benefit of hindsight is that today we can assume that academic freedom was destined to survive these challenges. In fact, the outcome was hardly certain. Only the courageous public responses of a few university presidents in 1953, namely, Nathan Pusey of Harvard and Robert Maynard Hutchins of the University of Chicago, saved the day for faculty rights (*Time* 1954).

If the threats to academic freedom in the McCarthy era were the most dramatic trouble spots for professors immediately following World War II, there were other, more enduring and substantive changes wrought by the Cold War political environment. Today we take for granted the presence of high-stakes funding from such agencies as the National Institutes of Health, the National Science Foundation, and the Department of Defense. Yet as late as 1951 the Harvard faculty was still pondering and debating whether Harvard ought to seek federal research grants. Elsewhere, some university administrators showed little hesitancy in claiming federally sponsored research grants not only as a priority but also as an imperative. It was a decision that would have profound implications for the work and life of professors. An excellent example of this was the transformation of Stanford University due to the zeal of Provost Frederick Terman in making federal grants the currency of Stanford's realm. For enterprising professors in research specialties that were high priorities of federal agencies, this was welcomed news. A new generation of physicists and engineers who had worked on wartime problem solving for the Department of Defense, for example, were well poised to embrace and flourish under Terman's plan. Yet Terman, a distinguished professor of engineering, extended his mandate to *all* fields. The department chairs of history and of classics, for example, were chastised for not having brought in federal grants. Terman went so far as to hint that these two departments were expendable. Their reprieve from a departmental death sentence was their agreement to teach large undergraduate lecture courses that enrolled as many as three hundred students at this medium-sized university. As emphasized earlier, the utilization of the large lecture format at the University of California was a deliberate plan intended to be educationally effective and efficient. In contrast, Stanford's new practices signaled both drift and a punitive motive.

A frequent observation is that professors at universities nationwide were subject to the policy of "publish or perish" as a condition of being granted tenure. It was not altogether unreasonable for a dean or president to expect faculty in all fields at a PhD-granting university to write journal articles or books in their respective fields. Provost Terman's new ground rules at Stanford, however, when applied unilaterally, were markedly different in that they were coercive and patently unfair, not to mention unreasonable. Even within the sciences, Terman took distinguished professors to task. One eminent biologist whose research had earned him election to the National Academy of Sciences was chided by the provost for having been negligent in landing *federal* research grants. Some highly regarded geologists underwent a comparable scolding for devoting primary attention to state rather than national projects. On balance, by 1960 Stanford had, indeed, risen to the top tier of universities when evaluated by the criteria of successful competition for federal research and development. The price of this success, however, was to abdicate the institutional gyroscope to the external whims of vacillating federal funding priorities (Lowen 1997).

One legacy of the Stanford case is to conclude that it shows how over time research took priority over teaching in the American university (Cuban 1999). Equally important is to discern how it illustrated ways in which a university administration transcended its faculty in areas that were matters of academic policy. It showed the power of a provost or a president to impose an agenda on the faculty. And it provided an early, compelling model for using the banner of academic planning as a justification for a president or board to increase the resources and positions devoted to academic administration by proliferating the number of associate provosts, assistant deans, vice presidents, and their requisite office staffs, office space—and, of course, reserved campus parking spaces. The perplexing feature was not necessarily that research trumped teaching or that PhD programs were emphasized over undergraduate curricula. Rather, it was the way in which this transformation was implemented—not as an initiative by the collective faculty, but rather as a top-down directive, whether or not its design and deliberation included faculty and their representatives in shared governance.

Massachusetts shared with California a strong commitment to higher education. Both states could claim numerous nationally regarded private colleges and universities. Despite this similarity, the post–World War II situation for higher education in Massachusetts was markedly different than in California in part because investment in state universities in New England had neither the tradition nor appropriations for public higher education as found in the Pacific Coast and Midwest. In Boston, for example, there was no counterpart to a Berkeley or a UCLA. The University of Massachusetts was relatively small, had few PhD programs, and was located in the rural western part of the state far from the concentration of institutions, as well as from high school students who eventually would go to college. In contrast, the greater Boston metropolitan area was crowded with numerous private (or, independent) universities and colleges that typically were dependent on student tuition payments and private donations rather than state appropriations. The result was an intensely competitive environment after World War II as each institution attempted to define, clarify, and then stake out academic spheres of influence. Northeastern University, for example, lacked a large endowment and a residential campus. Hence, its resolution was to distinguish itself as an affordable commuter campus with a unique cooperative work curriculum. Elsewhere in the city, Boston College and Boston University, respectively, came up with plans to extend their traditional offerings and constituencies to include selected fields of graduate and professional study. And, of course, the powerful Cambridge institutions—Harvard University and the Massachusetts Institute of Technology—refined their strategies for increasing sponsored research funding as part of their larger scholarly missions.

The "Golden Era" from 1945 to 1970 in Massachusetts was energetic, intense, and fraught with risks. Competition for faculty, students, donors, and research funding was keen in what was a high-stakes, high-risk academic market (Freeland 1992). The local phenomenon evidently had a nationwide diffusion, as a landmark study of the academic marketplace in 1957 included an unflattering catalogue of devious strategies and even dirty tricks used by search committees in the hunt for faculty talent intended to raise departmental and institutional rankings (Caplow and McGee 1958). The combined effect of these pursuits by colleges and universities was to illustrate the phenomenon of what Clark Kerr wrote about in 1964 as "The Frantic Race to Remain Contemporary." The irony in the respective Boston area colleges and universities each pursuing a distinctive reputation was that over time each and all gravitated toward an increasingly similar hybrid American campus model in which sharp differences may not have disappeared but at least tapered.

Why is it important to resurrect the cases of universities in the San Francisco Bay Area and in Boston with their examples of competition and even coercion between 1945 and 1970? The primary reason is to set the historical record aright by noting that many of the real and imagined academic virtues attributed to the Golden Age were, in fact, changing or even disappearing at this time. It is important to temper nostalgia—or, at least, place it into the appropriate historical era—when lamenting the decline of traditional faculty roles and rights. Consider the thoughtful essay—a combination of manifesto and lament—written by a senior professor at the College of William & Mary as part of that historic institution's 1974 accreditation self-study, advancing the prototype of a "Miniversity" to counter the ascendency of Clark Kerr's "Multiversity":

> During the 1930's and on the eve of World War II the state university in this country was frequently a small, non-comprehensive university oriented toward undergraduates following a curriculum centered on the liberal arts. The total of many of these universities, undergraduates, graduate, and professional, ranged from about 2,500 to 7,500. (College of William & Mary 1974)

The concern was that the "miniversity" model of, e.g., 1940 was disappearing and, where it survived, was discouraged from trying to maintain its character. Its passing included the disappearance of professors as central to the institutional culture and educational values of the campus. The culprit was the hegemony of the "multiversity"—criticized for "its relative neglect of undergraduate teaching, its over-stressing of graduate education, and the frenzied publication activities of its professors. Misled by the popularity of the multiversity prototype elsewhere and therefore accepting the multiversity as the model of the university, they have tended, following the worst multiversity example, to associate graduate education with the neglect of undergraduate teaching. They have tended, thus, to define university status by some of the most unseemly qualities of the multiversities" (College of William & Mary 1974).

Leaders of this counterrevolutionary movement to reclaim traditional faculty roles via emphasis on the distinctive small university (the so-called "miniversity") viewed the 1950s and 1960s not as a "Golden Era," but rather as the period in which the rise of the multiversity was integral to American higher education losing its way—because it had displaced its educational and moral gyroscope. Central to their manifesto was the claim that the "miniversity" was waning in popularity and influence and, by 1972, was no less than an "educational model that has gone out of style." Whether or not one subscribed to this interpretation when it was drafted in 1972 or perhaps as analyst of the academic profession today, its articulate message suggests that, for many professors, the "Golden Age" of 1945–70 really was the period when the academic ethos started to go awry. This stance reinforces the perspective of sociologist Edward Shils, a highly regarded, highly visible professor at the University of Chicago. This distinction is important because it means that the values and views of the "miniversity" advocates also have a following by an internationally acclaimed scholar. For Shils, the faculty once were (e.g., in the 1930s from his experience and observations) comparable to an academic priesthood in ethos and bearing, and he deplored the erosion of that status (Shils 1982, 1984).

Finally, worth noting is that during the period 1945–70 all the prosperity and prestige gained by colleges and universities had yet to make higher education a good place, a welcomed place for many constituencies. The great federal student financial aid programs, such as Pell Grants and student loans, were still in the future as part of the reauthorization of the Higher Education Act in 1972. Representation of women in PhD programs and in prestigious professional schools of law, medicine, and business was miniscule—even though women were earning a large percentage of bachelor's degrees, including a disproportionate percentage of such academic honors as election to Phi Beta Kappa. Not only were African Americans underrepresented in undergraduate and graduate programs, but as late as 1960 the boards of trustees at some highly prestigious universities with *national* scholarly rankings still resisted racial desegregation (Kean 2008).

Sorting through the celebrations and criticisms of academic life from 1945 to 1970, what is a reasonable distillation? First, faculty at most institutions enjoyed some gains—whether or not they were at a multiversity or even aspired to its priorities (Morison 1967). Teaching loads tended to decrease, while institutional funds for faculty travel, sabbaticals, and library budgets increased. Few faculty, regardless of their philosophical stance about the university's mission, would want to return to the standard fare of teaching four courses per semester and essentially being landlocked at campus without scholarly conferences or journals. The diffusion of these gains to professors in all disciplines and at a growing range of institutions tended to mute the strident voice of the counterrevolutionaries who claimed to want a return to the campus of an earlier halcyon period. What was divisive was the crystallization of new factions and academic tribes within a campus. By 1963 Clark Kerr described matter-of-factly the differential in salaries, equipment, space, time, and resources enjoyed by departments and faculty in selected fields that were eligible for generous sponsored research grants. For those faculty, the post–World War II decades were literally and symbolically a "Golden Age." Even this, however, was a precarious achievement, as the pioneering 1962 systematic study of academe edited by psychologist Nevitt Sanford indicated that universities and colleges were hosts to serious problems in academic governance and student dissatisfaction that were likely to disrupt campuses sooner rather than later (Sanford 1962).

Why the End of the Golden Era?

What were events that signaled the end of this alleged Golden Era? First, the gradual yet growing spread of student unrest about the war in Vietnam and also a slate of complaints about dissatisfaction with the quality and lack of priority for undergraduate education ultimately succeeded in showing a crisis of confidence among many college and university presidents and deans. The year 1970 probably surfaces as a key date as a result of the May 1970 incidents of student protests and student deaths at Kent State University and Jackson State University. Second, the inability of presidents and their deans of students to maintain harmony and stability on their conferences ascended from a few "elite" campuses in the late 1960s to a nationwide expanse of all kinds of institutions by 1970. The price to pay by university trustees, presidents, and mid-level administrators was a loss of trust by Congress in the ability of college and university presidents to maintain order on campus. Third, Frank Newman's Report on Higher Education (1971) provided a blue ribbon task force endorsement and elaboration on the accuracy and correctness of the varied and sundry complaints that had been presented for several years by dissident student groups—which heretofore had been dismissed as the naïve protestations of petulant and privileged children. Fourth, a bit later, economist Earl Cheit of the University of California at Berkeley identified "Higher Education's New Depression" (1971).

What one finds in the 1970s is a combination of double-digit inflation and a net decline in the number of high school graduates. This meant that the number of students applying to college declined substantially and rather unexpectedly. The decline in the appeal of going to college among late adolescents was further accentuated by the end of the U.S. military draft—a policy that had for several years prompted high school graduates to enroll in college, especially public community colleges, as a strategy to delay or defer eligibility for military service in Vietnam. Changes in the market for college students had an impact on the demand for new hiring of faculty. Declining enrollments combined with the lack of turnover among professors hired during the preceding decade meant that the outlook for new PhDs after 1972 was dismal, marking the virtual collapse of the academic job market over several years (Smelser and Content 1980).

The result of this convergence of trends was declining confidence in higher education among both administrators and faculty. Numerous presidents and deans of student affairs either retired unhappily or were pressed out of office in the confrontations with outraged students—and, later, by impatient state legislators and outraged alumni. Task forces from the Carnegie Council on Higher Education and other groups foresaw a long, hard period. One of its reports looked over the landscape of the three thousand degree-granting institutions in the United States and warned that between one-quarter and one-third of colleges' and universities' survival was at risk (Carnegie Council on Policy Studies 1980). One best-selling book directed at college and university presidents reflected the mood of the era with its title, *Surviving the Eighties* (Mayhew 1980). Astute analysts such as George Keller provided campus officials with recommendations for creative, thoughtful academic planning (1983).

Given that in the 1970s both faculty and administrators were bruised and baffled by the reversal of fortunes, we are left with this puzzle: How is it that in the late twentieth and early twenty-first centuries the American professoriate sees itself as underappreciated and at risk while during the same period college and university administrators are seen by the faculty as having trumped them in power, prestige, perks, and pay?

The Great Crossover: How the Managerial Revolution Surpassed the Academic Revolution

Richard Freeland in the introduction to his study of universities in Massachusetts between 1945 and 1970 noted that during this period there were three revolutions in higher education: enrollment, financial, and faculty. To explain, then, how early in the twenty-first century there is an overgrowing gap in trust and in rewards between the administration and the faculty, consider the following historical resolution.

During the decades of growth, the academic and enrollment and managerial revolutions were parallel, with the greater visibility probably awarded to the professors as experts, including being interviewed on television and radio, guest commentators, book reviewers, or hosts of special media presentations. By 1970, however, and certainly even more so by 1980, adversity in higher education meant that the academic revolution subsided and simultaneously the managerial revolution ascended. The fact of institutional life was that in a time of crisis over finances and enrollments, the expansion of administration and creation of new kinds of administrative offices were perhaps seen as solutions worthy of investment. In essence, the managerial revolution came in part to be transformed into an entrepreneurial initiative (Thelin 2001). Fund-raising through a development office or vigilant pursuit of federal student financial aid monies via a director of financial aid and other expanded initiatives gave rise to a growing number of university vice presidencies, including such new or expanded offices as institutional research, planning and budget, enrollment management, community relations, research and development, and government relations. Each tended to provide high salaries and large staffs, also at relatively high salaries, not to mention prime office space and computer support equipment. Presidential salaries around the year 2008 typically ranged from $200,000 to $700,000 and included generous bonus incentives up to about 30 or 40 percent of the base salary. Illustrative of the faith and investment in high-level administrative personnel by boards of trustees was that by 2000 a university president often hired a "chief of staff" at a high salary. For example, at one state university with relatively modest faculty salaries, the president's chief of staff in 2007 had an annual salary of $145,000—substantially higher than the mean salary of a tenured full professor. At universities with NCAA Division I athletics programs, salaries for such positions as athletics director, head football coach, and head basketball coach usually were at least $500,000—and often substantially higher. Even assistant football coaches at the big-time institutions were earning over $200,000 annually—a compensation that did not include generous income from summer camps.

At the same time that this expansion took place within the campus, the 1970s emphasis on planning fostered creation of state coordinating councils stimulated in part by generous funding as so-called 1202 commissions established as part of the 1972 reauthorization of the Higher Education Act. Also, as multicampus systems developed for state universities, regional state colleges, and community colleges, each tended to establish and staff a distinct systemwide administrative headquarters quite apart from their member campuses. In sum, whether in lean or flush times the justification for new administrative offices and expertise increased—either as an urgently needed solution to a crisis or problem, or as an imperative for a college or university to seize an opportunity to move into a new, potentially lucrative venture such as commercial investment in building and leasing a research park or setting up a year-round government relations office in Washington, D.C.

The usual tendency is to document such changes at the most prestigious, high-powered universities—such as a Harvard, a Stanford, or a University of Michigan. In this case, it is interesting to consider the case of the California State University and Colleges System. This is not the University of California at Berkeley or UCLA, but rather the relatively young system of regional campuses that offer bachelor's and master's degrees and often have a fairly large percentage of students who are commuting. If one were to drive into Long Beach, California, and ask for directions to "Cal State," one most likely would receive two answers. First, the "Cal State Long Beach" campus, enrolling a little more than 35,000 head-count students, is on the east side of the city, adjacent to such suburbs as Lakewood, Bellflower, and Downey—all about ten miles from downtown Los Angeles. It is a fitting symbol of California's golden age, as it was founded shortly after World War II, leading to the imaginative sports mascot of "the 49ers"—referring to 1949, not the more traditional '49ers of the 1849 California gold rush. This campus employs about 1,020 full-time faculty members, 1,523 full-time staff, and 1,042 part-time faculty—who typically are not eligible for tenure, are paid on a course-by-course basis, and do not receive benefits. In sum, there are more full-time staff than full-time faculty, and there are more part-time faculty than full-time faculty. This provides a broad-stroke testimony to the success of higher education's managerial revolution.

The visit to Cal State in Long Beach, however, is not over. The second destination is the CSUC Chancellor's Headquarters, along the coast on Golden Shore Drive close to downtown Long Beach. This impressive complex of office buildings and conference rooms employs 589 full-time staff. It enrolls no students, has no faculty, offers no courses, and confers no academic degrees. When the entire CSUC system data are compiled, it shows twenty-three campuses with 12,063 full-time faculty, 21,000 full-time staff, and 12,030 part-time faculty for a student enrollment of a little over 415,000 head-count students. Six decades after the end of World War II, CSUC stands out as an eminent example of the American commitment to universal higher education—and its allocation and priorities of administrative and faculty service to students.

Conclusion

The conventional wisdom is that "history is a tale written by the winners." Given that the American professoriate is articulate and often focused on its own self-interest, one wonders if the succession of articles and books about the faculty's plight over more than a half century might be an instance in which "history is a tale written by the whiners." I have attempted to document in this essay the historical incidents and practices that show how and why the faculty's concerns are warranted. Customary faculty roles have, indeed, experienced some erosion and compression, the seeds of which were planted in the decades immediately following World War II and have gained momentum and force since 1970. In the opening paragraphs I referred to Mary Burgan's 2006 book, *What Ever Happened to the Faculty?* A partial answer is that along with the most serious patterns in campus presence and influence, at most colleges and universities the once-revered Faculty Club typically now has been closed—and renovated and upgraded as a club for administrators, alumni, and donors. As for those coveted parking spaces that Clark Kerr as president of the University of California took pains to ensure for faculty, the trend in recent years has been for university parking authorities to eliminate the special "faculty parking" decal and lots in favor of an omnibus "employee" parking permit. Presidents, provosts, vice presidents, and deans, however, at many campuses often have their respective "reserved" spaces. One surmises that, after all, rank has its privileges.

In the United States it is customary to invoke the importance of "shared governance" as a hallmark of how our colleges and universities work. Such invocations need to be tempered by the historical fact that since the founding of the colonial colleges in the seventeenth century, American colleges and universities have been characterized by placing ultimate power in the hands of the board of trustees and the president. Thanks to the bad example of sloth and abuses by entrenched faculty at Oxford and Cambridge Universities who had great statutory powers in controlling the colleges within the university structure, the founders in the colonies made certain when drafting charters and bylaws that such a mistake would not be transplanted to the New World. Despite this preventive measure, however, a significant change in the mid-twentieth century was increasing respect and acknowledgment of faculty commitment and expertise as central to the institutional missions. From time to time this was even translated into some deliberative rights and powers for professors. However, even though there has been since 1970 creation or resurrection of the faculty senate as a formal body at many institutions, this has often been a Pyrrhic victory for faculty rights. Robert Birnbaum, who has been both a university president and a professor who studies higher education, noted that faculty senates—ostensibly the voice and vote of a collective faculty—are easily ignored or evaded by university presidents and boards of trustees. To add insult to injury, Birnbaum discovered that faculty senates also often have the latent function of providing presidents and provosts with a way to identify and recruit future academic administrators—with preference being given to those active in the faculty senate who display loyalty to the administration, and avoidance of those troublesome professors who demonstrate signs of dissent (1989). Disparagement of faculty, including identifying them as "the problem" with American higher education, extends into the recently published memoirs and autobiographies of university presidents (Kennedy 1997). Whether such stereotypical and critical depictions of professors are considered valid by campus presidents, provosts, and board members in the twenty-first century will be crucial in policy deliberations over faculty tenure and other hiring policies as colleges and universities sort through their new status as a "mature industry" (Levine 1997).

REFERENCES

Baldwin, Roger G., and Jay L. Chronister. 2002. *Teaching without tenure: Policies and practices for a new era.* Baltimore: Johns Hopkins University Press.

Birnbaum, Robert. 1989. The latent organizational functions of the academic senate: Why senates do not work but will not go away. *Journal of Higher Education* 60 (4): 423–42.

Bowen, Howard R., and Jack H. Schuster. 1986. *The American professoriate: A national resource imperiled.* New York: Oxford University Press.

Burgan, Mary. 2006. *What ever happened to the faculty? Drift and decision in higher education.* Baltimore: Johns Hopkins University Press.

Caplow, Theodore, and Reese J. McGee. 1958. *The academic marketplace.* New York: Basic Books.

Carnegie Council on Policy Studies in Higher Education. 1980. *Three thousand futures: The next twenty years for higher education.* San Francisco: Jossey-Bass.

Cheit, Earl F. 1971. *The new depression in higher education: A study of financial conditions at 41 colleges and universities.* New York: McGraw-Hill.

College of William & Mary. 1974. Purpose and aims: William & Mary as the prototype of the miniversity. Report of the Self-Study, 1–21. Williamsburg, VA: College of William & Mary.

Cuban, Larry. 1999. *How scholars trumped teachers: Change without reform in university curriculum, teaching and research, 1890–1990.* New York: Teachers College Press.

Deutsch, Steven E., and Joseph Fashings. 1971. *Academics in retreat.* Albuquerque: University of New Mexico Press.

Finkelstein, Martin J. 1997. *The academic profession: The professoriate in crisis.* London: Routledge.

Finkelstein, Martin J., Robert K. Seal, and Jack H. Schuster 1998. *The new academic generation: A profession in transformation.* Baltimore: Johns Hopkins University Press.

Finnegan, Dorothy E. 1993. Segmentation in the academic labor market: Hiring cohorts in comprehensive universities. *Journal of Higher Education* 64:621–56.

Freeland, Richard M. 1992. *Academia's golden age: Universities in Massachusetts, 1945–1970.* New York: Oxford University Press.

Geiger, Roger L. 1993. *Research and relevant knowledge: American research universities since World War II.* New York: Oxford University Press.

Hart, Jeffrey. 1982. *When the going was good: American life in the fifties.* New York: Crown.

Jencks, Christopher, and David Riesman. 1968. *The academic revolution.* Garden City, NY: Doubleday.

Kean, Melissa. 2008. *Desegregating private higher education in the South: Duke, Emory, Rice, Tulane, and Vanderbilt.* Baton Rouge: Louisiana State University Press.

Keller, George. 1983. *Academic strategy: The management revolution in American higher education.* Baltimore: Johns Hopkins University Press.

Kennedy, Donald. 1997. *Academic duty.* Cambridge, MA: Harvard University.

Kerr, Clark. 1963. *The uses of the university.* Cambridge, MA: Harvard University Press.

———. 1964. The frantic race to remain contemporary. *Daedalus* 93:1051–70.

Levine, Arthur. 1997. Higher education's new status as a mature industry. *Chronicle of Higher Education* A48 (January 31).

Life. 1948. University of California: The biggest university in the world is a show place for mass education. October 25, 88–112.

———. 1949. Williams College: In an era of mass teaching it considers smallness a virtue. January 24, 53–62.

Lowen, Rebecca S. 1997. *Creating the cold war university: The transformation of Stanford.* Berkeley: University of California Press.

Machlup, Fritz. 1962. *The production and distribution of knowledge in the United States.* Princeton: Princeton University Press.

Mayhew, Lewis. 1980. *Surviving the eighties: Strategies and procedures for solving fiscal and enrollment problems.* San Francisco: Jossey-Bass.

Morison, Robert S., ed. 1967. *The contemporary university: U.S.A.* Boston: Beacon Press.

Newman, Frank, chair. 1971. Report on higher education. Washington, DC: Task Force of the U.S. Department of Health, Education and Welfare.

Ostroff, Anthony. 1962. Economic pressures and the professor. In *The American college: A psychological and social interpretation of the higher learning,* ed. Nevitt Sanford, 445–62. New York: John Wiley & Sons.

Sanford. Nevitt, ed. 1962. *The American college: A psychological and social interpretation of the higher learning.* New York: John Wiley & Sons.

Schneider, Alison. 1997. Empty tables at the Faculty Club worry some academics. *Chronicle of Higher Education* A12 (June 13).

Schrecker, Ellen W. 1986. *No ivory tower: McCarthyism and the universities.* New York: Oxford University Press.

Schuster, Jack H., and Martin J. Finkelstein. 2008. *The American faculty: The restructuring of academic work and careers.* Baltimore: Johns Hopkins University Press.

Shils, Edward. 1982. The university: A backward glance. *American Scholar* 51 (May): 155–69.

———. 1984. *The academic ethic.* Chicago: University of Chicago Press.

Smelser, Neil J., and Robin Content. 1980. *The changing academic marketplace: General trends and a Berkeley case study.* Berkeley: University of California Press.

Smith, Wilson, and Thomas Bender, ed. 2008. *American higher education transformed, 1940–2005: Documenting the national discourse.* Baltimore: Johns Hopkins University Press.

Stransky, Elizabeth. 2006. The impact of the GI Bill beyond students: Faculty challenges and university-state-federal relations at the University of Wisconsin, Madison. ASHE conference research paper.

Thelin, John R. 2001. Institutional history in our own time: Higher education's shift from managerial revolution to enterprising evolution. *CASE International Journal of Educational Advancement* 1 (1): 9–23.

——. 2006. Small by design: Resilience in an era of mass higher education. In *Meeting the challenge: America's independent colleges since 1956*, 3–36. Washington, DC: Council of Independent Colleges.

Time. 1947. Big man on eight campuses—California's Sproul: Is everyone entitled to a college education? October 6, 69–76.

——. 1954. Unconquered frontier: Nathan Pusey, president of Harvard. March 1, cover story.

Contributors

Ann E. Austin is Professor of Higher, Adult, and Lifelong Education and the Director of the Global Institute for Higher Education (GIHE) at Michigan State University. Her scholarly interests focus on faculty roles and professional development, work and workplaces in academe, organizational change in universities and colleges, doctoral education, teaching and learning, and higher education issues in developing countries. She was the 2001–2 President of the Association for the Study of Higher Education (ASHE) and a Fulbright Fellow in South Africa (1998). She is currently Co-Principal Investigator of the Center for the Integration of Research, Teaching, and Learning (CIRTL), a National Science Foundation Center. She has authored numerous articles, chapters, and books, including *Rethinking Faculty Work: Higher Education's Strategic Imperative* (with Judith Gappa and Andrea Trice) and *Educating Integrated Professionals: Theory and Practice on Preparation for the Professoriate* (coedited with Carol Colbeck and Kerry-Ann O'Meara).

Alan E. Bayer is Professor Emeritus of Sociology at Virginia Polytechnic Institute and State University and Director Emeritus and Founder of the Virginia Tech Center for Survey Research. Among other previous positions, he was Associate Director of the Office of Research at the American Council on Education, Research Associate with the Commission on Human Resources and Advanced Education of the National Academy of Sciences, Research Scientist with the Institute for Research in Education of the American Institutes for Research, and Director of the Center for the Study of Education in the Institute for Social Research at Florida State University. He has served on the Editorial Boards of the *Review of Higher Education* and *Sociology of Education*, as a Consulting Editor of the *Journal of Higher Education*, as a Contributing Editor of the *Review of Education*, and for the past twenty-five years as an Associate Editor of the annual *Higher Education: Handbook of Theory and Research*.

John M. Braxton is Professor of Education in the Higher Education Leadership and Policy Program at Peabody College, Vanderbilt University. His research interests focus on faculty teaching and scholarship role performance and the various social forces that influence such role performances. Braxton is particularly interested in the social control of faculty research and teaching misconduct. His publications on these topics include *Faculty Misconduct in Collegiate Teaching* (with Alan E. Bayer) and *Institutionalizing a Broader View of Scholarship through Boyer's Four Domains* (with William Luckey and Patricia Helland). He has also edited three books focused on faculty issues: *Analyzing Faculty Work and Rewards Using Boyer's Four Domains of Scholarship, Faculty Teaching and Research: Is There a Conflict?* and a coedited volume (with Alan E. Bayer) titled *Addressing Faculty and Student Classroom Improprieties*.

Steven Brint is Professor of Sociology at the University of California, Riverside and the Director of the Colleges & Universities 2000 study. He also serves as Associate Dean of the College of Humanities, Arts, and Social Sciences. Brint is the author of three books: *The Diverted Dream* (with Jerome Karabel), *In an Age of Experts*, and *Schools and Societies*. He is the editor of *The Future of the City of Intellect* and coeditor (with Jean Reith Schroedel) of the two-volume series *Evangelicals and Democracy in America*. His articles have appeared in the *American Journal of Sociology, Sociological Theory, Minerva, Work and Occupations, Sociology of Education, Journal of Higher Education*, and many other journals. He has won awards from the American Sociological Association and the American Educational Research Association for his scholarship. He was elected a Fellow of the American Association for the Advancement of Science in 2008. He is currently at work on a new book, *Creating the Future: Organizational and Cultural Change in American Colleges and Universities, 1980–2005*.

Roger L. Geiger has written widely on the history of American higher education, American research universities, and academic science policy. He is Distinguished Professor of Higher Education at Pennsylvania State University and former Head of the Higher Education Program. His most recent book, on universities and economic development, is *Tapping the Riches of Science: Universities and the Promise of*

Economic Growth (with Creso Sá). He is also the author of *Knowledge and Money: Research Universities and the Paradox of the Marketplace*; *To Advance Knowledge: the Development of American Research Universities, 1900–1940*; and *Research and Relevant Knowledge: American Research Universities since World War II*. He has edited *Perspectives on the History of Higher Education* since 1993 and is Senior Associate Editor of the *American Journal of Education*.

Neil Gross is Associate Professor of Sociology at the University of British Columbia. His recent publications include *Richard Rorty: The Making of an American Philosopher* and "A Pragmatist Theory of Social Mechanisms" in the *American Sociological Review*. He is the editor of *Sociological Theory*.

Jacob Habinek is a PhD student in sociology at the University of California, Berkeley. His research interests include organizations, culture, science, and social networks. His dissertation is a comparative study of discipline formation in the life sciences in France, Germany, the United Kingdom, and the United States.

Joseph C. Hermanowicz is Associate Professor of Sociology and a Fellow in the Institute of Higher Education at the University of Georgia. His research interests center on academic careers, the academic profession, and the structure and operation of reward systems in organizations. His publications include *The Stars Are Not Enough: Scientists—Their Passions and Professions*, which examined the structure and unfolding of academic careers in contemporary American universities as revealed through the lives of sixty physicists; *Lives in Science: How Institutions Affect Academic Careers*, a longitudinal study of academic careers based on the preceding work; *College Attrition at American Research Universities: Comparative Case Studies*; and articles appearing in sociology and higher education journals.

Daniel Lee Kleinman is Professor and Chair in the Department of Community and Environmental Sociology at the University of Wisconsin–Madison, where he is also the director of the Robert F. and Jean E. Holtz Center for Science and Technology Studies. Over the past decade, his research has focused on three central areas: the commercialization of the university, the politics of agricultural biotechnology policy, and the relationship between democracy and expertise. He is the author of three books: *Politics on the Endless Frontier: Postwar Research Policy in the United States, Impure Cultures: University Biology and the World of Commerce*, and *Science and Technology in Society: From Biotechnology to the Internet*. Among

Kleinman's edited volumes is *Controversies in Science and Technology (volume 2): From Climate to Chromosomes* (with Karen Cloud-Hansen, Christina Matta, and Jo Handelsman). He has recently initiated a collaborative project on the social organization of interdisciplinary science in large academic research institutes.

Erin Leahey is Associate Professor of Sociology at the University of Arizona. In her previous work, Leahey has taken research and research practices as a subject of inquiry. She has been particularly interested in the oversight of a research practice—data editing—and learned about that process from interviews with scientific gate-keepers (*Science, Technology, and Human Values* 2008). Another track of her research program focuses on specialization in scientific careers (*American Sociological Review* 2007); she is also expanding this work to include management science and the legal profession. Her current research projects include an investigation of whether and how scientists benefit from engaging in interdisciplinary research and a study of how highly cited scientists explain their influence.

Kathleen Montgomery is Professor of Organizations and Management at the Anderson Graduate School of Management, University of California, Riverside. She also is affiliated with the Centre for Values, Ethics, and the Law in Medicine at the University of Sydney and has been a visiting scholar at Stanford and UCLA. Her PhD in sociology is from New York University. She uses institutional theory to study professional-organizational relationships, incorporating the issues of trust and integrity in her recent work. Papers from these research streams appear in *Organization Studies, Work and Occupations, Social Studies of Science, Current Research in Occupations and Professions, Journal of Management Studies, Human Relations, Social Science and Medicine*, and elsewhere. Her work has been funded by the National Science Foundation, the Robert Wood Johnson Foundation, the American Foundation for AIDS Research, and the American College of Physician Executives.

Anna Neumann is Professor of Higher Education at Teachers College, Columbia University and Coordinator of the Program in Higher and Postsecondary Education. Her research explores teaching and learning in higher education, scholarly learning and development in professors' careers, and doctoral students' learning of research and development as researchers in education. She is the author of *Professing to Learn: Creating Tenured Lives and Careers in the American Research University*. Prior books include *Faculty Careers and Work Lives: A Professional Growth Perspective* (with KerryAnn O'Meara and Aimee LaPointe Terosky); *Learning from*

Our Lives: Women, Research, and Autobiography in Education (with Penelope L. Peterson); *Redesigning Collegiate Leadership: Teams and Teamwork in Higher Education* (with Estela M. Bensimon); and other volumes on academic leadership and qualitative inquiry. Her research also has appeared in numerous educational research journals.

Eve Proper is a doctoral candidate in Higher Education Leadership and Policy at Vanderbilt University. Her primary areas of interest include governance, fundraising, and institutional effectiveness at four-year institutions.

Gary Rhoades is currently General Secretary of the American Association of University Professors, on leave from the University of Arizona, where he served as Professor and Director of the Center for the Study of Higher Education from 1997 to 2009. His research focuses on the restructuring of higher education institutions and of professions in the academy. His two books are *Managed Professionals: Unionized Faculty and Restructuring Academic Labor* and *Academic Capitalism and the New Economy* (with Sheila Slaughter). As General Secretary he continues to write on higher education and faculty issues, including a column in *Academe*.

Jack H. Schuster, Professor Emeritus of Education and Public Policy at Claremont Graduate University, is author or coauthor of six books on various aspects of higher education and the American faculty, among them *American Professors* (with Howard R. Bowen), which received the Frederic Ness Award, and *The American Faculty* (with Martin J. Finkelstein). Prior to joining Claremont Graduate University's faculty in 1977, Schuster was Legislative Assistant, then Administrative Assistant, to Congressman John Brademas of Indiana. He next served as Assistant to the Chancellor at the University of California, Berkeley and as Lecturer in Political Science. He has been Visiting Professor or Guest Scholar at the Universities of Michigan, Oxford, Melbourne, and Haifa; Harvard University; and the Brookings Institution. Recipient of the Association for the Study of Higher Education's Distinguished Career Award (2007), Dr. Schuster has a BA (in history) from Tulane University, JD from Harvard Law School, MA in Political Science from Columbia University, and PhD in education from the University of California, Berkeley.

Sheila Slaughter is the Louise McBee Professor of Higher Education in the Institute of Higher Education at the University of Georgia. Her research areas are political economy of higher education, science and technology policy, academic freedom, and women in higher education. Her most recent book is *Academic Capitalism and the New Economy* (with Gary Rhoades). Her most recent articles include "Policies on Institutional Conflict of Interest at U.S. Research Universities" (with Maryann Feldman and Scott Thomas) in the *Journal of Empirical Research on Human Research Ethics* and "The State Sponsored Student Entrepreneur" (with Matthew Mars and Gary Rhoades) in the *Journal of Higher Education*. Slaughter received the Association for the Study of Higher Education Research Achievement Award in 1998 and the American Educational Research Association Career Research Achievement Award in 2000.

Teresa A. Sullivan is the President of the University of Virginia, where she is also the George M. Kaufman Presidential Professor and Professor of Sociology. She was previously Provost and Executive Vice President for Academic Affairs and Professor of Sociology at the University of Michigan in Ann Arbor. Her academic interests are economic marginality, especially debt and marginal employment, and the sociology of work. She received her PhD in sociology from the University of Chicago, and she served for twenty-seven years as a member of the sociology faculty at the University of Texas at Austin.

John R. Thelin is University Research Professor in Educational Policy Studies at the University of Kentucky. He also has been Chancellor Professor at the College of William & Mary in Virginia from 1981 to 1993, Professor of Higher Education & Philanthropy at Indiana University from 1993 to 1996, and Research Director for the Association of Independent California Colleges and Universities from 1978 to 1981. An alumnus of Brown University, he concentrated in history and was elected to Phi Beta Kappa. He received his MA and PhD from the University of California, Berkeley. He has served as President of the Association for the Study of Higher Education, and in 2007 he received the AERA award for outstanding research in higher education. He is author of *Games Colleges Play: Scandal and Reform in Intercollegiate Athletics* and *A History of American Higher Education*.

Steven P. Vallas is Professor and Chair of the Department of Sociology and Anthropology at Northeastern University. He writes and teaches on the sociology of work and on sociological theory. Vallas has studied a wide array of workplace settings, focusing on organizational change in deeply traditional manufacturing settings, institutions of higher education, and high-tech, science-intensive industries. His work has appeared in the *American Journal of Sociology*, *American Sociological Review*, *Social Problems*, and *Sociological Theory*, among many other venues. He is currently working on the theoretical paradigms that inform the study of work and economic institutions.

Index

280–81; 1970s relations with, 275, 282–84, 285; 1980s relations with, 275, 284–86; 1990s relations with, 275, 285, 286–89; and *Novartis* case, 246–55; partnerships with, xvi, 275, 276, 284; and research regulation, 307. *See also* business; corporations
institutional associations, 107, 108
institutional organizations, 99–103
institutional theory, xvi, 295, 296
intellectual property, 242, 253, 263, 266, 278, 284
interdisciplinarity, 26, 27–28, 32, 149–50, 151, 157, 296, 305–7. *See also* disciplines
Internet/Web, 54, 59, 329. *See also* technology

Jackson State University, 342
Jett v. Dallas, 264
John Templeton Foundation, 55
journals, 303, 305, 306, 322–23, 325

K–12 education, 55, 61, 77
K–12 National Assessment of Educational Progress, 66
Keating, Frank, 66
Kennedy, Edward M., 68
Kent State University, 342
Kerr, Clark, 7, 12, 47, 333, 335, 340, 342
Kilpatrick, William Heard, 50
knowledge: abstract, specialized, 316–17; abstract, theoretic, vii; application of, 192, 208; commercially relevant, 277, 278, 279; disinterested, 243, 266; dissemination of, 192, 208; diversity in, 195; and doctoral students, 157; and economy, 242, 250, 277, 289; and epistemic cultures, 115; expansion of, 149–50; expert, 266; and learning, 195; meaning of, 115; monopoly on, 111; and *Novartis* case, 263; objective, value-free, xiii, 113, 117–27; and politics, xii–xiii; and practical outcomes, 151; production of, xiv, 57–58, 192, 208–9; and recognition, 218, 230; and scholarly learning, 192, 202–3; sociology of, 114–15. *See also* expertise; objectivism/objectivity
knowledge-politics problem, xii–xiii, 111–39; defined, 115; and economics, 122–25; and

epistemic cultures, 118; and literature, 119–20; and science, 120–22; and sociology, 125–27; and teaching, 127–34. *See also* politics
Kuh, George D., 56

Lattimore, Owen, 260
Law and Economics Consulting Group (LECG), 247–48, 251
League for Innovation (LfI), xii, 93, 99, 100–102, 103, 107
learning, 113; achievement standards for, xii, 45–46, 75–76; active, 46, 49, 50, 56, 72–73, 74–75, 77; and administrators, 76; and American Association of University Professors, 97; and American Federation of Teachers, 98, 99; of analytical thinking and writing, 65; applied, 102; and Association of American Colleges and Universities, 102, 103, 107, 108, 109; centers for, 52–53; centrality of, 100; characteristics of, 194–96; and civic engagement, 46, 49, 50, 55, 74; and cognitive apprenticeships, 57; and cognitive skills, 55, 65, 75, 76, 82n8, 83n16; collaborative, 50, 55, 75; contexts of, 196; cooperative (small group), 74; and critical and analytical thinking, 71; of discipline-specific knowledge, 65; distinctive ways of, 195; effects on, 46; and essay writing, 75; evaluation standards for, 50; experiential, 50; and expressive skills, 55; and faculty organizations, 96–99; and full-time, non-tenure-track appointments, 34–35; and grades, 56–57; of higher-level general skills, 69; and in-class presentations and debates, 50; and independent study, 50; individual projects for, 50; integrative, 55, 102; and integrative research papers, 71; of intellectual and practical skills, 102; interdisciplinary, 206, 207; and internships, 50; and interstitial units, 104; and large lecture format, 335–36, 338; and League for Innovation, 100–101, 103, 107, 108–9; maximization of, xi, 22; and National Education Association, 98, 99; and oral presentations, 74; organizationally directed,